PSYCHOLOGY AND

PSYCHOLOGY, CRIME AND LAW SERIES
Series Editor: David Canter

Forthcoming titles in the Series

David Canter is Professor of Psychology at The University of Liverpool, where he directs The Centre for Investigative Psychology, which he established there in 1994. He is a Fellow of the British Psychology Society and the American Psychological Association and an Academician of the Academy of Social Sciences. He is a Chartered Forensic Psychologist and member of the Forensic Science Society, and a Fellow of The Royal Society of Medicine and the RSA. He has edited over 30 academic books, bringing together the work of others as well as publishing five major books that he authored directly. He has published at least 200 papers in academic and professional journals. He is the founding editor of the *Journal of Environmental Psychology*, and has recently established the new *Journal of Investigative Psychology and Offender Profiling*.

David is regularly invited to give keynote addresses at international conferences all over the world. His book, *Criminal Shadows* not only won the Golden Dagger award for True-Crime but also the US equivalent, an Anthony award. He frequently contributes to television and radio documentaries and news programmes, having written, presented and co-produced a six-part documentary series on 'Mapping Murder'. From time to time he also writes for various newspapers including *The Times* and *The News of the World*. David is internationally known for his cross-disciplinary research and consultancy as well as providing evidence in a number of high profile court cases and government enquiries.

Psychology and Law
Bridging the Gap

Edited by
DAVID CANTER
Centre for Investigative Psychology, University of Liverpool, UK

RITA ŽUKAUSKIENĖ
Mykolas Romeris University, Lithuania

ASHGATE

Published by
Ashgate Publishing Limited
Gower House
Croft Road
Aldershot
Hampshire GU11 3HR
England

Ashgate Publishing Company
Suite 420
101 Cherry Street
Burlington, VT 05401-4405
USA

Ashgate website: http://www.ashgate.com

British Library Cataloguing in Publication Data
Psychology and law : bridging the gap. - (Psychology, crime
    and law)
    1. Law - Psychological aspects 2. Forensic psychology
    I. Canter, David V. II. Žukauskienė, Rita
    340.1'9

Library of Congress Cataloging-in-Publication Data
Psychology and law : bridging the gap / edited by David Canter and Rita Žukauskienė.
        p. cm. -- (Psychology, crime and law)
    Includes bibliographical references and index.
    ISBN-13: 978-0-7546-2656-5
    ISBN-10: 0-7546-2656-3 (hbk.)
    ISBN-10: 0-7546-2660-1 (pbk.)
    1. Law--Psychological aspects. I. Canter, David V. II. Žukauskienė, Rita.

    K346.P798 2007
    340'19--dc22

                                                                    2007011096

ISBN 13: 978 0 7546 2656 5 (hardback)
ISBN 13: 978 0 7546 2660 2 (paperback)

Printed and bound in Great Britain by MPG Books Ltd, Bodmin, Cornwall.

Contents

Series Preface

Over recent years many aspects of law enforcement and related legal and judicial processes have been influenced by psychological theories and research. In turn concerns that derive from investigation, prosecution and defence of criminals are influencing the topics and methodologies of psychology and neighbouring social sciences. Everything, for example, from the detection of deception to the treatment of sex offenders, by way of offender profiling and prison management, has become part of the domain of a growing army of academic and other professional psychologists.

This is generating a growing discipline that crosses many boundaries and international frontiers. What was once the poor relation of applied psychology, populated by people whose pursuits were regarded as weak and arcane, is now becoming a major area of interest for many students and practitioners from high school through to postgraduate study and beyond.

The interest spreads far beyond the limits of conventional psychology to disciplines such as Criminology, Socio-Legal Studies and the Sociology of Crime as well as many aspects of the law itself including a growing number of courses for police officers, and those associated with the police such as crime analysts or forensic scientists.

There is therefore a need for wide-ranging publications that deal with all aspects of these interdisciplinary pursuits. Such publications must be cross-national and interdisciplinary if they are to reflect the many strands of this burgeoning field of teaching, research and professional practice. The *Psychology, Crime and Law* series has been established to meet this need for up to date accounts of the work within this area, presented in a way that will be accessible to the many different disciplines involved.

In editing this series I am alert to the fact that this is a lively new domain in which very little has been determined with any certainty. The books therefore capture the debates inherent in any intellectually animated pursuit. They reveal areas of agreement as well as approaches and topics on which experts currently differ. Throughout the series the many gaps in our knowledge and present-day understanding are revealed.

The series is thus of interest to anyone who wishes to gain an up-to-date understanding of the interplays between psychology, crime and the law.

Professor David Canter

Foreword

Psychology is spreading through many aspects of the legal process across the world. The enlargement of the EU is further increasing the speed with which the application of psychological expertise, currently prevalent in the US and Western Europe, is being taken up in forensic practice and the courts throughout the newly emergent democracies. The rather different social contexts in which this interaction between psychology and law is now taking place is set to influence our understanding of criminals and the influence of the law. It is therefore timely to produce a book that captures many of these developments.

The occasion of the fifteenth European Conference on Psychology and the Law in Vilnius in July 2005, organised by the European Association of Psychology and Law (http://www.law.kuleuven.be/eapl/) provided a suitable starting point for identifying leading contributors from both sides of this dialogue, across many different countries, in order to put together a book that would capture contemporary attempts to build bridges between these two very different disciplines. The book is thus unusual both in including lawyers as well psychologists, sociologists and criminologists as authors, as well as in the very diverse range of jurisdictions from which they come, including the USA, across Europe and Australia. It thus sets out to bridge the inherent gap between the practice of law and the profession of psychology at an international level.

The book shows that bridges are needed for the many different contexts in which the law interacts with psychology. Chapters have therefore been included to throw some light on how psychology connects with, *inter alia*, the courts, prisons, community care, clinics, long-stay hospitals, police investigations and legislative bodies. This allows coverage of well-established areas, such as the study of and challenges to, for example, eyewitness testimony, and the nature of Psychopathy. Much more recent areas of social science contribution to legal proceedings are also covered, such as the liability that arises from not preventing crimes happening or the systematic prediction of likely violence by an offender.

What emerges from all these accounts is that psychological involvement in legal processes has rapidly evolved over the past decade from limited clinical concerns with the diagnosis of defendants' mental states, and academic studies of the memory processes involved in providing testimony through to a full-blooded range of studies and professional contributions. These arise at every stage of the legal process, from the police officer attending the scene of a crime, through how evidence may be presented in court, on to the implications of aspects of prison life and then decisions about how offenders may be dealt with thereafter. Beyond these criminal proceedings there is also a growing contribution in civil cases, whether it be matters of liability or likely consequences of judicial decisions.

This evolution and broadening reach of the transactions between those involved in all aspects of the law and psychologists is not without its stresses. Therefore, an important aspect of the book is to explore the sources of the tensions and how their resolution can enrich both the law and psychology. This will include both recognition of the pressures on psychologists and their potential weaknesses as experts and the understanding of where jurists need a fuller understanding of the potential and limitations of psychology.

The book will therefore be of value not only to academics and professionals, in psychology, the law, and related disciplines, wishing to understand the broadening base of psychology within the legal process, but also to students trying to form an understanding of the emerging science and the associated career opportunities for this exciting field.

David Canter
Centre for Investigative Psychology, The University of Liverpool, UK

Rita Žukauskienė
Mykolas Romeris University, Lithuania

List of Contributors

Anna-Karin Andershed PhD, is assistant professor and Senior Lecturer in psychology at the Department of Behavioural, Social, and Legal Sciences at Örebro University, Sweden. Anna-Karin Andershed was supported by grants from the Swedish Research Council during the preparation of this chapter.

Henrik Andershed PhD, is associate professor and Senior Lecturer in psychology at the Department of Behavioural, Social, and Legal Sciences at Örebro University, Sweden. He is also currently director of research and development at the National Reception Unit of the Swedish Prison and Probation Service.

David Canter is Professor of Psychology at the University of Liverpool, where he set up the Centre for Investigative Psychology in 1994. He has advised the police on many investigations and given expert evidence to a variety of court cases. He has published over 30 books and 200 papers, as well as being the managing editor of a number of book series and the founding editor of the *Journal of Environmental Psychology* and the *Journal of Investigative Psychology and Offender Profiling. In addition, he has* presented plenary lectures at major conferences throughout the world. His book *Criminal Shadows* won the UK Golden Dagger award for crime non-fiction and the US Anthony Award for Crime Non-Fiction.

David J. Cooke is Head of Forensic Clinical Psychology in Glasgow, Scotland and Professor of Forensic Clinical Psychology at Glasgow Caledonian University. He has a longstanding interest in personality disorder and violence.

Michael R. Davis is a Lecturer in Clinical Forensic Psychology, Monash University and Psychologist, Victorian Institute of Forensic Mental Health (Forensicare).

Ian Freckelton is a barrister in full-time private practice in Melbourne, Australia. He is also an Honorary Professor of Law, Forensic Medicine and Forensic Psychology at Monash University, an Honorary Professor in Law at La Trobe and Deakin Universities and in Mental Health Policy at Auckland University. He is the Victorian President of the Australian and New Zealand Association of Psychiatry, Psychology and Law and has published very widely in the area of law and mental health.

Craig Haney is Professor of Psychology at the University of California, Santa Cruz. One of the researchers in the Stanford Prison Experiment, Haney has been studying the psychological effects of prison conditions for over 30 years, and is the author of the recently published book, *Reforming Punishment: Psychological Limits to the Pains of Imprisonment.*

Viktoras Justickis PhD is Professor of Legal Psychology and Criminology at Mykolas Romeris university in Vilnius, Lithuania. His research interests are in psychology, criminology, sociology and the philosophy of law.

Daniel B. Kennedy PhD, is professor of criminal justice and sociology at the University of Detroit Mercy. He is a consulting and testifying expert in civil litigation across the US and internationally. His areas of expertise include crime foreseeability, criminal behaviour, police, security and corrections standards of care, and criminological issues pertinent to legal proximate causation.

Ewout Meijer MSc, works in the Psychology Department of Maastricht University in The Netherlands. His primary area of expertise is the psychophysiological detection of deception in various settings.

Amina Memon is a Professor of Psychology at the University of Aberdeen. Her research interests lie in Social and Cognitive Psychology. She has co-authored a text on Psychology and Law. In addition, she and Andrew Roberts are currently writing a text on Identification Evidence.

John Monahan a psychologist, holds the John. S. Shannon Distinguished Professorship in Law at the University of Virginia, where he is also a Professor of Psychology and Psychiatric Medicine. He directs the Research Network on Mandated Community Treatment for the MacArthur Foundation.

James R. P. Ogloff is a Foundation Professor of Clinical Forensic Psychology and Director of the Centre for Forensic Behavioural Science, Monash University. Director of Psychological Services, Victorian Institute of Forensic Mental Health (Forensicare).

David Ormerod is Professor of Criminal Justice at Queen Mary, University of London and a Barrister in the Middle Temple. His research interests are in all aspects of criminal law, evidence and procedure.

Michael L. Perlin is professor of law, director of the online mental disability law program, and director of the International Mental Disability Law Reform program at New York Law School. He writes and publishes about all aspects of mental disability law, and lately has been concentrating on the relationship between international human rights law and mental disability law. He serves on the Board of Directors of the International Academy of Law and Mental Health, and on the Board of Advisors of Mental Disability Rights International.

Andrew Roberts is an Assistant Professor in the School of Law at the University of Warwick. His research interests lie in criminal procedure and the law of evidence. He has published widely on the subject of eyewitness identification.

Jason R. Sakis, J.D. is a partner in the law firm of Sakis & Sakis, located in Troy, Michigan, USA. His practice focuses on civil litigation with a special emphasis on premises liability cases involving negligent security and cases concerning victims of crime. He was recently named a *Super Lawyer*, a designation bestowed upon the top five percent of practicing Michigan lawyers. Mr Sakis is licensed to practice law in both Michigan and Georgia.

Peter J. van Koppen is a psychologist. He is senior chief researcher at the Netherlands Institute for the Study of Crime and Law Enforcement (NSCR) Leiden, professor of law and psychology in the Faculty of Law of Maastricht University and professor of law and psychology in the Faculty of Law of the Free University Amsterdam. Currently he is serving as president of the European Association for Psychology and Law.

Dr Donna Youngs currently works with Professor Canter directing a series of recently won research projects looking at a variety of crimes and criminals. These studies explore a range of Investigative topics from the Geographical Profiling of Burglary, to Street Robbery, Youth Crime and Antisocial behaviour, Fraudulent Crime Reporting, Insurance Fraud and the Social Networks of Prolific Offenders. A further study is exploring prostitution, in particular violence against prostitutes from an investigative perspective. Dr Youngs and Professor Canter lead a team of eight researchers interviewing offenders both in and out of prison, as well as working with police forces and other agencies to collect data on patterns of offending.

Chapter 1

In the Kingdom of the Blind

David Canter

Professional Humility

The 15th century philosopher Erasmus claimed that 'In the kingdom of the blind, the one-eyed man is king'. His argument was that if everyone around you were ignorant then even a little knowledge would make you significant in that community. But in a witty and perceptive short-story, the late-19th century novelist H.G. Wells shows how in a kingdom entirely peopled by the blind, that the one-eyed person is an aberration more likely to be regarded as mad than appropriate for high office.

This paradox is directly relevant to the interactions between psychology and law. It is productive to suggest that the Law is often a kingdom of people who are blind to many insights that psychologists have. Psychologists for their part often do not appreciate that they are only partially sighted and that there are other ways of exploring reality than theirs. Furthermore, if psychologists are not aware of these problems and do not take them into account when they interact with legal processes they will be regarded as less then capable. Their very insights will be what mark them off from lawyers, probation officers, detectives and all the other people who have daily commerce with crime and criminals.

Examples of the reciprocal distortions provided by this interplay of these two different perspectives are everywhere to be seen. The quest to predict how dangerous a person will be in the future; proposals of courses of treatment or methods of managing offenders; the preparation of 'profiles' for police investigations; systems for determining deception; explanations of criminality; questions about eyewitness testimony; or even the more recent exploration of whether the owner of a public venue may be liable for a crime that happens there – and many other areas of forensic psychology – all pose challenges for the effective dialogue between psychologists and those involved in legal processes.

The present volume is therefore a rare attempt to explore the mix of viewpoints that make up these overlapping areas of professional and scientific activity. Like H.G. Wells' one-eyed man, there is an inherent conflict between people who have different ways of interacting with the world. It is tempting for each sub-group to believe that their perspective has a unique hold on truth and a special contact with reality, but for the gaps to be bridged it is essential that all those involved have 'professional humility'. By this I mean that each profession recognises that it sees only part of the whole picture and that there are equally legitimate if rather different perspectives.

This humility is particularly difficult for many professions to embrace. The training of professionals, whether they be lawyers, psychologists, police officers, criminologists or any of the many other disciplines that crowd our universities, is such as to imbue students with a framework for understanding the world and the people within it. This framework implies, and often directly states, that the particular professional perspective being absorbed is the dominant road to the truth. Psychologists will dismiss anthropological studies as being 'merely anthropological'. Lawyers will see psychologists' experiments as being 'only of academic interest', and criminologists will regard judges as uninformed about the social processes that create criminality.

Many years ago, Bromley (1986) argued that psychologists had much to learn from the approach to evidence and decision making that was characteristic of the law. This was as subversive an argument then as it is today, and its implications have still not been thoroughly explored. But it does offer a counterbalance to a view, still strong within psychology, that knowledge can by furthered only through the conduct of highly controlled laboratory experiments. The challenge from the legal perspective on this is not just a question of whether research findings are reliable enough to draw on in court, but a much more profound questioning of what it means to be human, and the most appropriate way of modelling the mechanisms that give rise to human actions.

Therefore, to bridge the gap between psychology and law it is important to explore further the differences between the different perspectives and how they may complement, rather than challenge, each other. A step towards this exploration is to review the dominant traditions and world views that characterise psychology and law and how their differences may be productively combined.

Table 1.1   Summarising the differences between the nature of the law and of psychology

The Law	Psychology
Focus of Interest	
The Individual	Mostly Group Trends
Forms of Contribution to Knowledge	
Plausible Narratives	Processes
Preferred Methodologies	
Due Process	Scientific Method
Intended Outcomes	
Verdict	Contribution to Knowledge
Approach to Information	
Evidence	Data
Explanations of Human Actions	
Personal Agency	External Causation

Comparing the Law and Psychology

As summarised in Table 1.1, six broad issues can be identified that distinguish between, on the one hand, lawyers and those involved in the legal profession, and on the other psychologists and other social and behavioural scientists. These cover conceptual aspects of the ways in which each set of disciplines actually formulate the questions they consider it important to answer, as well as pragmatic issues that relate to the ways they go about answering these questions. At the heart of these differences are very diverse attitudes towards the nature of evidence, as well as differences in the central models of what the nature of human beings is.

Nomothetic versus Ideographic

Perhaps the most obvious difference between the two traditions being explored is that the law is focused on the case at hand and gives great emphasis to the particularities of the individuals involved in that case. The courts need definitive answers about the actual person they are dealing with. Yet despite more than a century of psychological therapies and other areas of professional practice in which services are set up to deal with unique people, psychology as a science and profession is still fundamentally nomothetic, focused on trends and patterns across sub-groups not on descriptions of actual persons. Those involved in the law see only the trees, like people with limited vision. Psychologists are aware of a wood, only able to recognise individual trees from knowledge of where they are in the wood. Indeed, part of Bromley's (1986) argument for psychologists to consider the value of legal processes was as a defence for the case study as a viable scientific methodology.

But the dominant framework for psychologists is still one in which differences between group averages are the basis of their claims to find results. ANOVA, 't' tests, and the measures of central tendency which populate published studies are all summaries of trends across groups. The significance of the standard deviation and other measures of variability is testimony to the fact that averages do not characterise more than a small proportion of individuals within any sample. Indeed, the much derided 'mode', may often be a practically more useful summary of the trends within a group than the arithmetic means on which significance tests are based.

This issue comes into high relief when considering the assessment of risk of future violence. Politicians and the public at large, through the mass media, are horrified by even one person who was deemed to pose little risk, who subsequently commits an act of violence. It is little consolation to the victim of that violence to point out the error terms in the statistical calculations on which the judgement that the person was low risk was based. In the present volume this issue is tackled directly by Davis and Ogloff in Chapter 11 and Monahan in Chapter 12. There the complexities of predicting violence, as of predicting any significant aspect of human behaviour, are carefully explored. The conclusions that these authorities come to have general significance because they show that a blind following of results of empirically established trends are not enough on which to base important decisions about individuals. However, as is made clear, these considerations should not lead to a simple advocacy of 'personal experience' and uninformed 'clinical judgements'. Instead, the challenge of taking account of the individual puts a great demand on the practitioner. That person is required to understand the processes and principles involved in creating the activities being predicted as well as an informed understanding of the empirical trends that characterise those processes.

One crucial aspect of this understanding, which is remarkably often omitted from forensic discussions, is explored in Chapter 7 by the Andersheds. This is the heterogeneity of those who are involved in crime and antisocial behaviour. They show in detail the many pathways into anti-social behaviour and the various risk factors that distinguish between anti-social individuals. They also point out that their perspective challenges some strongly held views about the fundamental similarities between criminals. But although there may well be some common psychological, or even genetically based, processes that underlie a great deal of criminal activity, it is only of little help to the courts, probation services, or others whose task is to work with criminals to focus on what criminals share. To be effective and just, the legal process needs to recognise what is significant about the person with whom they are currently dealing.

Narratives versus Processes

The pressures under which psychologists are placed to deal with the individuality of the case in hand, even though they are drawing on the general trends that emerge from research findings, is possibly most clearly revealed in the general approach that the law takes to any form of 'offender profiling'. Freckelton explores these issues thoroughly in Chapter 6, making the crucial point that most jurisdictions are very reluctant to accept the opinions of profilers as expert evidence. He further points out that in all the cases in the US in which profiling evidence was allowed, subsequent appeals disallowed that evidence and the case was overturned if the evidence had been deemed significant to the verdict.

The reasons why profiling evidence is unacceptable to most courts is instructive. It relates to a legal perspective on what the nature of expert evidence should be. The courts require of experts that their opinion is based on information or knowledge that is not available to the non-expert. Profilers are not seen as offering an opinion based on substantive knowledge or empirically derived facts. Or, if their expertise is recognised, it may be considered to offer the crucial judgement of innocence or guilt, which is the prerogative of the court, not of any given witness.

There is, of course, a great deal of sense in this legal approach to expert evidence from profilers. As a number of authors have made clear (e.g. Canter, 1994, Hicks and Sales, 2006) profilers are often offering a personal opinion that has little justification beyond their own arbitrary experience. Where their opinions draw on general trends derived from empirical research, the results of that research is rarely precise enough to be applicable with great confidence to the case with which the court is dealing.

However, there is a curious divide here between what the courts are seeking and what they derive from psychological expertise. The courts expect experts to derive their opinions from the study of general processes, revealing trends that can be applied to individuals. They look for those trends to be converted into a form that can be dealt with as a coherent package that makes a simple definitive statement. The strongest example of this is the readiness with which the courts will accept evidence of some sort of syndrome or disease as an explanation of human actions. Raitt and Zeedyk (2000) raise grave concerns about this from an overtly feminist perspective. They argue that the courts' acceptance of Rape Trauma Syndrome, Premenstrual Syndrome and other medicalised explanations of women's actions limit the possibilities for examining the appropriateness of women's actions and understanding them within a broader social context.

The gap here comes from scientists being seen as revealing underlying processes that can be distilled into distinct sets of facts, whilst the courts are actually trying to derive a plausible narrative that will show the role of the defendant in an unfolding story. Judges and juries will accept that there can be other protagonists that influence the pattern of events beyond the key people involved. These agents may be drugs, or physiological responses or disorders of the mind or body. But for an expert to be allowed to indicate the impact of these agents there must be some scientific basis for proving that they have an effect in a predictable manner. If ever a profiler could say that a particular genetic abnormality was known to play a role in acts of violence, then evidence for that abnormality in the defendant just might get past challenges of prejudice and be allowed into court. Certainly, the assessment of an individual's personality is an acceptable component in judgements about the sentencing of convicted people in many jurisdictions.

One consequence of the legal determination of the roles that experts can play is that much of what can be offered by behavioural scientists has to be subsumed within the arguments offered by lawyers in court rather than being directly presented by the experts themselves, and thus being open to the appropriate challenges. An interesting example of this, discussed by Freckelton in Chapter 6, is the conviction for murder of Eddie Gilfoyle, whose eight-and-a-half-month pregnant wife, Paula, was found hanging in their garage. The details of this case (Canter, 2005b) show just how much of the expertise that might have been produced by a psychologist was taken by the courts and appeal judges to be within their own area of expertise because it would be common knowledge to people at large.

The Gilfoyle case revolved around the fact that Paula had secretly left a series of explicit suicide notes but had not indicated to anyone with whom she had contact that she was at all concerned about her pregnancy or intended to take her own life. The jury, and later appeal court judges, accepted that the notes were not sufficient to outweigh the circumstantial evidence that could be interpreted to indicate that Eddie had persuaded Paula to put her head in the noose whilst he was standing

behind her so that he could lift her legs and thereby hang her. The expert brought in
to defend Eddie's case at the appeal (Canter, 2005b) attempted to develop a plausible
alternative narrative derived from the documentation available. He also tried to
draw attention to the possibility of situations in which a person intending to commit
suicide may keep this secret from everyone (cf. Canter *et al.*, 2004). However, the
courts chose to treat his opinion as a 'profile' of a deceased person or 'psychological
autopsy' and to look for distinct scientific experiments that would show how genuine
suicides could be distinguished from murders.

In other words, the appeal Judges regarded themselves as the arbiters of rational
opinions on the conditions under which a person might commit suicide. They
would not allow any professional opinion to hold sway unless it was limited to
the implications of very specific scientific results dealing with matters in the form
that the judges believed scientific opinion should be couched. This gave rise to the
somewhat unreal situation in the appeal court of a barrister discussing with judges the
acceptability of the expert's opinion whilst the expert sat mute behind the barrister
unable to explain to the judges, or the barrister, their misunderstanding of the expert
evidence they had in front of them.

Due Process versus Scientific Method

The search by judges for information that appears scientific but will inform their
views on the particular narrative that characterises the events at issue in a case is
often misunderstood by those who explore the links between psychology and the
law. It is often assumed that lawyers are looking for definitive scientific answers and
that they can evaluate the scientific merit of whatever is put before them. However,
as is made very clear by Roberts and Ormerod in Chapter 5 the courts evaluate any
evidence not on the basis of the scientific methods that might be applied to that
evidence but in relation to whether the processes set up within the law, the 'due
process' has been followed.

In the area of testimony the processes required by the law are often informed by
psychological research, but they still operate within the legal framework as jurists see
it. The most obvious area of this discrepancy, discussed both by lawyers in Chapter 5
by the psychologist Amina Memon in Chapter 4, is aspects of eyewitness testimony.
Understandably, the courts regard the accounts given by witnesses as at the heart of
legal proceedings and therefore very much a matter for evaluation by judges and
juries. Psychologists on the other hand usually regard testimony as a product of
human memory and therefore very directly open to assessment and consideration by
psychologists.

These different perspectives may almost be regarded as territorial battles over
who has ownership of the issue of testimony, but it is helpful to appreciate that it is
more fundamentally a clash between different procedures for determining objectivity
or truth. The law sets up the details of the legal process as the search for truth,
whereas scientists look to quite different procedures. In particular, the experimental

tradition, as mentioned earlier, seeks to find general differences between groups that are larger than differences within those groups. But this may show what are regarded as statistically significant differences which nonetheless are still so small as to be open to masking in relation to any particular case. Perhaps even more importantly it may only be possible to indicate statistical differences in studies that are so highly controlled, and essentially artificial, that their results cannot be applied or reproduced in the rough and tumble of the real world.

It is therefore possibly reasonable that the courts will often form their own judgement of the relevance of results and procedures presented as scientific, even when there is little clear evidence of the validity of these procedures. Possibly the most graphic example of this in practice was the initial acceptance by British appeal courts of the approach, known as Cusum, to the identification of the authorship of a document. This procedure looks to the uninitiated as if it is an objective scientific procedure. In essence, the number of short words per sentence is compared with the number of words in a sentence, adjusting both for the averages across the text. Two lines are produced on a chart, one for short words and one for total number of words per sentence. It is then claimed that these lines diverging is an indication of different authorship.

This Cusum procedure was accepted into court as evidence despite the fact that no obvious and appropriate experimental tests had been carried out. All that had been done was to show that the system gave the expected answers in a number of selected examples. It was only when Canter (1992) carried out direct tests with random samples and showed the results were totally random that the courts no longer accepted Cusum evidence.

It is interesting that Cusum, which has no scientific value or even scholarly presence, was accepted into court because it looks like what science should look like, but the reasoned argument put forward in the Gilfoyle case was not even acceptable for presentation because it did not look like expert knowledge, even though it was acknowledged as relevant by the Criminal Case Review Commission and paid for by legal aid, being presented to the court by probably the leading UK Defence barrister, Michael Mansfield. Psychologists that ignore the importance the courts assign to due process and the ways in which that does itself determine what the nature of expert evidence is will continue to find their evidence is dismissed.

Verdict versus Contribution to Knowledge

The central reason why the courts are so tied to their own view of what is acceptable and what not is that their central mission is to determine a verdict. This really does contrast with the research psychologist's objective of contributing to knowledge. This contrast is clear in the very different styles of Chapter 4 written by a psychologist and Chapter 5 written by lawyers. For although the authors of these different chapters do agree on the challenges to testimony that have emerged from both recognised miscarriages of justice and experimental studies of memory, they approach the development of their arguments and their implications in different ways. Memon organises her argument in terms of the processes that can influence memory, whereas the lawyers review the safeguards and procedures of which the court should be more aware.

This difference in emphasis can make the uptake of psychology particularly problematic when the processes involved (as in the Gilfoyle case) are rather subtle and potentially complex. This is revealed in the exploration of the use of psychophysiological indicators of deception, otherwise know as the 'polygraph test', which Meijer and van Koppen explore in Chapter 3. The legal questions that emerge around any attempt to detect lying are: does it work, and what are the safeguards that need to be introduced to ensure it is not abused. But this assumes that there are specific procedures that can be isolated from a range of other activities and that the outcome of the procedures is a clear yes or no answer. But the 'polygraph' can be one of a range of procedures that can be administered in many different ways, some of which depend very much on the nature and details of the crime. Furthermore, its application is inevitably part of an unfolding legal process that is very different from the austere conditions of experimental studies of the physiological correlates of deception.

Thus, the development of our understanding of the psychology and physiology of deceptive responses may be of great interest to biological scientists but a long way from being used directly in the legal process. The utilisation of the lie detector is further complicated by the value it often has, not in detecting lies but in encouraging people to confess. This is a case where public understanding of the processes involved, derived from research, could actually undermine the effectiveness of the procedure. There is the additional finding from a number of studies that it is often more accurate in supporting a person's claim to be telling the truth rather than detecting lying as such.

Thus, the understanding of the psychological mechanisms involved and their inherent complexity poses real challenges to those who would utilise the resulting procedures. It places a direct burden on the experts who understand these processes to find ways of enabling investigators and the courts to make effective use of the applications. This may look like special pleading to give the experts more power, but it is really a call for a closer co-operation between those who are seeking to contribute to knowledge and those who are trying to obtain a clear verdict.

Perhaps the most unchallenged aspect of the legal process – which really would benefit from a much greater understanding of the psychological implications – relates to the use of imprisonment as a form of punishment. This may seem a far cry from the consideration of lie detectors, but similar issues emerge about the application of a procedure, which is what imprisonment is, and an understanding of if, or how, it works. In general, the judiciary have little direct involvement in considering the psychology of imprisonment, even though they may have cause to visit prisons and, of course, regularly make decisions about the incarceration of convicted people.

In the important Chapter 9, Haney explores the psychological implications of imprisonment.

The picture that Haney paints is one that emphasises the negative consequences for individuals and society of imprisonment, but in unpacking the human costs of imprisonment he provides a much richer picture of what imprisonment comprises. This develops our understanding of the significance of confinement and the ways in which it can be detrimental or even beneficial. He shows that imprisonment has to be considered very much as part of a larger social context, thereby feeding back into broader strategic issues of how criminals are dealt with.

This richer understanding, as we have seen for example with polygraph testing and the review of witness testimony is often very difficult for the legal process to deal with if it is presented within the scientific framework of a general contribution to our understanding. However, if it can become part of the court proceedings through the consideration of the actions and experience of particular individuals then a richer understanding can influence the decisions of judges and from that the lives of many people.

An interesting example of this that contrasts markedly with the Gilfoyle case is the environmental psychology evidence given as part of the case for the appellant Mr Napier. There has so far been no published account of this evidence except for the judgement handed out. I will therefore step out of the professional, third person description and comment directly on my understanding of my role in this.

What especially interests me about my contribution in this case is that what I offered was a systematic summary of a complex process informed by a theory I called *The Psychology of Place* (Canter, 1977). In other words, what the judge was prepared to draw upon was a set of concepts and ways of thinking about the issues, contrasting very much with the appeal judges in the Gilfoyle case, where they ignored the framework offered and just looked at whether there were any facts that the lay person might not know.

The case was brought against the Scottish Ministers, as a judicial review by a Mr Napier. He claimed that the conditions of his confinement when in prison were inhuman and degrading and therefore illegal under Articles 3 and 8 of the European Convention on Human Rights. He had to share a small, poorly ventilated cell with another man, with only a portable potty as a toilet, when he was suffering from severe eczema.

It is instructive to quote directly what the judge, Lord Bonomy, said in his argument in April 2004, for why he found in favour of Mr Napier, quoting directly from my evidence:

1. Within the cell, the lack of opportunity to create appropriate 'places' for activities, most notably the lack of a distinct place of excretion and associated

washing facilities.
2. The sharing of the cell, causing the lack of possibility for creating a 'personal space' and distinct area or 'territory' for his own activities.
3. The pressure of overcrowding and lack of enough facilities, on the landing and in the block, on the opportunities there might otherwise have been for hygiene, recreation and 'psychological release'.
4. The arbitrariness yet excessive control of the regime over the minutiae of daily activities.
5. The impact of Mr Napier's eczema on his ability to make use of coping strategies that may have alleviated the brutalising quality of his incarceration.
6. The uncertainties associated with being on remand.
7. In my opinion, these conditions interact to create circumstances that in total are more debilitating and dehumanising than could reasonably be expected for imprisonment.

Lord Bonomy said 'that view is consistent with the impact that the conditions did in fact have upon the petitioner'. In other words, as any student of architectural psychology will recognise, the judge completely accepted the relevance and importance of a conceptual analysis that was derived directly from a quarter of a century or more of the study of how people use and experience their surroundings. The Judge thus accepted that the contribution of science is not a set of facts or a finding, but a way of thinking about processes. This may seem very abstract but as Kurt Lewin said 'there is nothing as applicable as a good theory'.

The case for Mr Napier was given strength by drawing on understanding of the processes by which people make sense of places and the influences that enable them to use those places in an effective and human way. This does seem to me to be a much richer and more scientifically appropriate way for the law to interact with psychology. It is worth noting that Lord Bonomy did not take my analysis of Mr Napier's experiences at face value and that of course many other experts offered opinions from many different perspectives. The judge was therefore very overtly involved in sifting the evidence and different perspectives and making sense of them in relation to his own understanding of the prison conditions, so that he was eventually able to say that he considered my analysis to be consistent with the facts; a clear judicial opinion rather than some naïve acceptance of an expert viewpoint. In many ways it is probably much easier for a judge to formulate this sort of independent opinion than a jury, who may be much more overawed by the apparent stature of an expert.

There are, though, many others involved in dealing with crimes and criminals, who even if they have their own expertise can benefit from a fuller understanding of the psychological processes that relate to their work. The Napier case draws attention to the whole experience of imprisonment, which until recently has been little explored by psychologists, but which is a prime candidate for the sort of fuller, theoretical understanding that Lord Bonomy was so prepared to draw upon. In

Chapter 9, Haney reviews the recent developments in the mapping out of the effects of imprisonment, showing how much the whole process of law could benefit from a clearer picture of what is being done to people when they are sentenced to spend time in goal.

Haney makes clear that it is not imprisonment in any general sense that is necessarily wholly negative in its consequences for individuals and society. He shows that it is the particular way in which imprisonment is managed and how the prison interacts with the society of which it is part that generates the negative consequences that have now been well documented. By creating a broader perspective on what imprisonment entails psychologically and a fuller account of its crucial constituents and how they interact, this contribution to our knowledge about prisons helps to show that verdict and consequent sentencing of the courts carries many more implications than may often be realised.

Evidence versus Data

The idea that the police and courts are only interested in exploring evidence whereas scientists seek data is drawn from the insight of Superintendent Vince McFadden when commenting on how I contributed to the investigation that led to the arrest and conviction of John Duffy for three murders and five rapes attributed to the 'Railway Murderer' (Canter, 1994). Yet I think it elegantly captures one of the most fundamental differences between psychology and the law and consequently one of the most important gaps to be bridged. Evidence is information that directly relates to the case for or against a verdict. It can, of course, be circumstantial and can relate to the character of the individuals involved, so it is not entirely a matter of fingerprints and DNA. In contrast data is any information that can help us to understand the phenomena we are exploring. So, for example, in one case in which I was involved the police had a shoe print from which they could identify the make of shoe. They therefore did house-to-house enquiries to determine if anyone knew someone who wore shoes of that make: this would have provided evidence. I was interested in the sorts of people who bought shoes of that kind as this would be data to help us to understand the characteristics of the perpetrator, but could never be used as evidence.

All evidence has some potential for offering data for research, but all data cannot be used as evidence. There is, nonetheless, a great value in trying to understand the interplay between these two perspectives on the information collected during an investigation. This benefit is most clearly seen in Chapter 2 in which Youngs explores the possibility of scientifically deriving characteristics of offenders from information about how they commit their crimes. This inference problem, or 'Canter profiling equation' as she characterises it, bridges the gap between the evidence the police need to identify an offender and the research basis which is fundamental to an Investigative Psychology.

However, by treating the evidence the police have about the actions of offenders as the basis for psychological research, Youngs shows that we can develop a much wealthier understanding of the processes that generate that evidence. She argues that, from a psychological perspective, it is possible to provide a detailed analysis of the mechanisms that can influence criminal actions. This leads to the exploration of which actions really are relevant to understanding a crime and what are the contingencies that might modify the control that the offender has over criminal activity. So, although Youngs presents these arguments within the framework of psychological contributions to police investigations, a wider applicability to other areas of the legal process can be perceived.

One of the strongest examples of treating police evidence as data is the information available on where a crime happens and how it relates to where the offender was living. This provides an example of what Youngs calls integrative modelling. She mentions general principles drawn from personality theory being the bedrock on which to build generic models of the relationship between crime and criminal, but environmental psychology principles that relate to an offender's cognitions of the geographical context of the crimes can also provide general principles that are applicable across a range of different forms of criminal activity. This has emerged as an area known as Geographical Profiling (Canter, 2005a).

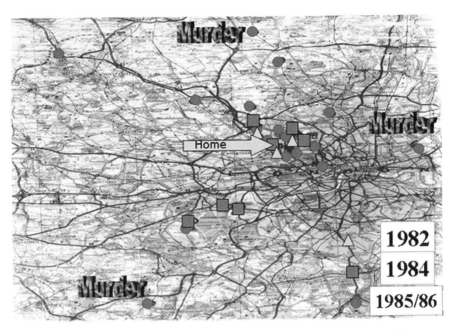

Figure 1.1   The series of rapes and murders carried out by John Duffy

The first application of this was in contributing to the investigation of the rapes and murders committed in London in the mid 1980s. The police had evidence of the location of the series but had not really considered them as data giving up a simple pattern that was of investigative relevance. My analysis of the locations of the crimes suggested that they centred on an area of North West London where it was likely, therefore the offender was living.

The police had a number of suspects but only one had been living in the area that the analysis indicated. It also turns out, as I discovered very fortuitously in this case, which led to the conviction of John Duffy, that many criminals have patterns of spatial behaviour that yield interesting results when interpreted from the point of view of the sort of mental maps they imply. I was able to explore this possibility in direct application to a number of investigations, as I describe in *Mapping Murder* (Canter, 2005a). We have now been able to take that even further and develop decision support systems, such as my software Dragnet, which can be used directly by police officers.

But the take-home message from the contribution to Duffy's conviction was that the police were only interested in the results of research once it could be of direct value to their investigation. Similarly, psychological contributions to legal processes only take on significance for lawyers once it can be shown that they influence a case in court. In other words, the results of data are only of value if they can have a direct bearing on the access to, or be converted into, evidence.

Personal Agency versus External Causation

The integration of psychological understanding into the legal process goes further than just being able to draw on it for evidence. It requires a bridge between two fundamentally different ways of thinking about people. The essence of the law is that people make choices, they act and make decisions. They are culpable because they intend their actions and have some awareness of the likely outcomes. In a word they are *agents*, indeed free agents, with free will. Psychologists and other biological and medical experts found their way into the law initially by being able to demonstrate that it was inappropriate to consider some people to be such free agents. Through mental illness, or some other disease, it was shown that it was unjust to regard them as having any real control over their actions.

This wresting of the agency of the individual away from that person is the essence of assigning a person to a medical syndrome roundly attacked by Raitt and Zeedyk (2000) from a feminist perspective. But it is not necessary to embrace a full-blown feminist ideology to recognise how much of psychology and related disciplines are devoted to taking the causal explanation away from the person and his or her intentional actions and putting the causality in some other process over which the person does not have any real control; their biology, physiology, personality, or social context.

The clearest indication of this difference of perspective is in the exploration of psychopathy that Cooke explores so fully in Chapter 10. The recognition that certain individuals relate to others in such an abnormal way, without overt signs of what might be regarded as classical mental illness, especially psychoses, that it is appropriate to characterise them as having a disordered personality and to place on them the label of psychopath, has now passed into popular culture so thoroughly that its abbreviated form of 'psycho' is an acceptable component in the titles of films and books. The study of people for whom such a label appears appropriate has become a major area of forensic psychology in its own right.

This intense study has opened up the prospect that the assignment of the label 'psychopath' to an individual removes the ownership of any challenges they may pose to society from the responsibilities of the legal system into the realms of clinicians. This process is already gathering momentum in English law with the suggestion that a person *diagnosed* with a personality disorder may be confined even though that person has not committed any crime. This is part of a general move to reduce risk by predicting the conditions under which it may happen. This seems to me to have more of the characteristics of the appeal judges in the Gilfoyle case who would not accept psychological evidence unless is was couched in the pseudo-causal terminology of medical syndromes and contrasts greatly with Lord Bonomy's understanding that an enriched perspective on the processes that were relevant to the case at hand does not need to detract from the legal decision being totally the responsibility of the courts.

A paradoxically similar process seems to be at work in the utilisation of behavioural science in negligence and liability cases that Kennedy and Sakis describe in Chapter 8. Instead of putting the causality of the crime within the personality distortions of the offender, the cause is now seen to be in the setting and those who manage and control it. Apparently, this is opening up a whole new area of professional consultancy from psychologists and criminologists in support of legal proceedings to claim negligence against the owners of facilities who did not take precautions to reduce the risk of crime against those who used their premises.

In these cases of negligence there is an interesting interplay between the knowledge that is emerging about crimogenic environments and the requirements on agents responsible for those environments to take account of that knowledge. This therefore illustrates the subtle transactions that now typically occur between social sciences and the law. The diagnosis of psychopath can lead the defendant out of the legal system into a sort of limbo between the courts and the health professionals, whereas the claim that a shopping mall is not protected against muggers can make the management of that location indirectly, but legally, responsible for the crimes that take place there. I wonder if it is fanciful to propose that soon parents and schools will be held responsible for the crimes of their children. Probably not as fanciful as many people may think. Some jurisdictions already allow parents to be punished if their children abscond from school.

These examples of the courts absorbing concepts and theoretical models from psychology and related social sciences, which remove the agency of the actions from the actual perpetrator, are powerful illustrations of how the understanding of people, which is inherent in the legal process, is being profoundly influenced. In some cases judges may regard a behavioural science perspective as fundamental to their understanding of the case before them, as seemed to be the approach of Lord Bonomy. In other cases the judges may regard their own understanding of human nature, and that of a jury, as requiring no input from psychologists unless the input revealed causal processes outside of the agency of the individual. This appeared to be the stand of the judges in the Gilfoyle case. In yet other circumstances, the facts of the case may be accepted as so direct that explorations of the agency of the culprit are not required.

These processes are not confined to the courts. The considerations of causality and the control of the offender over his or her own actions run throughout the whole process of dealing with and making sense of offending. Treatment programmes, as

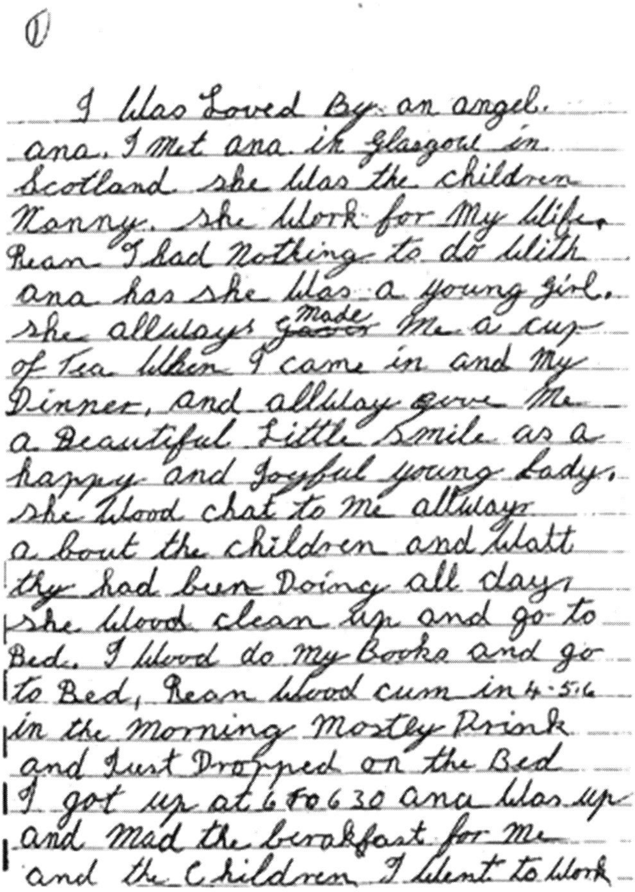

1

I Was Loved By an angel.
ana. I Met ana in Glasgow in
Scotland she Was the children
Nanny. she Work for My Wife.
Rean I had Nothing to do With
ana has she Was a young girl.
she allways ~~gave~~ made Me a cup
of Tea When I came in and My
Dinner, and allway gave Me
a Beautiful Little Smile as a
happy and Joyful young Lady.
she Wood chat to Me allways
a bout the children and Watt
thy had been Doing all days
she Wood clean up and go to
Bed. I Wood do My Books and go
to Bed, Rean Wood cum in 4·5·6
in the Morning Mostly Drink
and Just Dropped on the Bed
I got up at 6 to 630 ana Was up
and Mad the brakfast for Me
and the Children I Went to Work

Figure 1.2 Page 1 of Fred West's memoir

is clear from that generic title, see some distortions in the criminal's make up that can be 'treated' and thus in some sense repaired. Whereas if criminality is a way of being and very much part of a person's approach to dealing with world, quite different frameworks may be put in place to encourage them to deal with the world differently. These may well include broader matters of education, training and the development of effective life management skills.

One final example is worth briefly mentioning, to show the complexity and subtleties involved in trying to determine the causes of crime and using those as part of any process for dealing with criminals. This is the example of Fred West who killed at least a dozen – probably many more – young women over a 20-year period. It is tempting to try to explain the actions of this serial murderer as caused by an early brain injury that resulted in low impulse control, but such an argument does not really account for the steady abuse over many years that he inflicted on many young women whilst presenting to the various police officers and other agencies with whom he came into contact a face of a minor villain who had a happy family. The attempt to assign the cause of his actions to some process outside of his own control seems even less appropriate when considering the memoir that he wrote while in prison, awaiting trial, before he killed himself.

There are many aspects of this handwritten diary that raise important questions about why West killed and how he managed to avoid detection over many years, that are discussed in detail in *Mapping Murder* (Canter, 2005). But the one aspect that is particularly pertinent, which is revealed in the diary, is how West was able to create a personal narrative for himself in which the murders are never mentioned. Even though he borders on illiteracy and lacks fluency in his writing he nonetheless invents a world of a happy family in which he serenades his love on the steps of their caravan and she expresses eternal love and they share the joy of her pregnancy. He never hints at the fact that he killed and buried her before the child was born.

The memoir shows an ability of this killer to develop a storyline that covers his activities the way he wants to see them. He was doubtless able to present this to the authorities with whom he came into contact, so that for many years his personal narrative masked his vicious killings. But it seems likely that he was able to sustain this fiction for so long because, as his memoir reveals, he believed it himself and had interpreted the actions of others to fit in with his inner understanding.

The exploration of the personal narratives of offenders seems to me to bridge the legal requirement of determining intention and the role of the offender in the criminal acts, whilst still allowing us to develop a psychological understanding of the processes that underlie the unfolding patterns of criminal behaviour. This narrative perspective still recognises that the individual is responsible for his or her own actions, but facilitates the unpacking of how those responsibilities emerge. Personal narratives do not exclude influences on actions from the social context, nor do they rule out the value of such quasi-medical constructs as psychopathy. Narratives provide a broader framework for considering all the evidence that may be available about an offence and an offender in order to make sense of it within his or her conscious actions.

Conclusions

The different perspectives of psychology and law that have been touched on are relevant right across the spectrum of interactions between these different disciplines. It is fruitful to see this spectrum as starting with the investigation of the case, as Youngs does in Chapter 2, then to embrace the exploration of the nature of the evidence and its validity – matters that are dealt with in Chapters 3 and 4. There then emerge issues of how psychological findings and perspectives on evidence may be dealt with in the courts as Roberts and Omerod explore in Chapter 5. The broader interactions between psychology and legal proceedings, especially the way in which the behavioural sciences can offer direct evidence of relevance to a case, rather than comment on the acceptability of other evidence, are considered in Chapters 6 and 8, but central to these considerations are the important differences between people, which the Andersheds review in Chapter 7.

Beyond the courts there is the very important area of study and professional activity that looks at the experiences of prison, which Haney deals with in Chapter 9, leading on to the many explorations of the nature of offenders and how they may be assessed. The dominant theory of psychopathy is a crucial part of any assessment of offenders, as Cooke discusses in Chapter 10. But there is also a great need for procedures to assess the risks that offenders may pose if they are let back out into the community, as discussed in Chapters 11 and 12.

The whole area of the management and treatment of offenders is not covered in any detail in the following chapters, although it is touched on from time to time throughout the book. This is partly to keep the book a manageable size, partly because dealing with offenders outside of the legal system could be considered beyond the range of a book attempting to bridge the gaps between psychology and law, but it is also because there are many other books that explore these issues that are so central to forensic psychology, such a Needs and Towl (2004) or the earlier book by McGuire (1995).

Other omissions in the present volume are due to the lack of interaction between psychology and law in those areas. In Chapter 13, Justickis provides a robust review of the current limits in the range of interaction between the law and psychology. He phrases his central question as asking what psychology can do for the law. It is tempting, though, to ask the reciprocal, but more fundamental question, of what the law can do for psychology. In reviewing the interactions between psychology and the law it is apparent that the trend has been for the law to embrace causal explanations of behaviour that have roots in essentially reductionist views of human nature. Referring back to Bromley's (1986) arguments, it may be productive to consider how the legal emphasis on the intentionality of an offender may find its way more fully into legal psychology.

This is an intricate interaction that is at the heart of Perlin's thoughtful, yet polemic final chapter. He argues that the courts embrace medical and quasi-medical approaches in so far as they contribute to the social control functions of law. This puts pressures on experts to seek explanations within the more reductionist ends of their disciplines, forcing them into a corner defined by the legal professions rather than a real engagement with the central issues of the law. Just like those in H.G. Wells' kingdom of the blind, the one-eyed man is forced to act to accommodate to their blindness rather than helping them to see the world more clearly.

In conclusion then, it is clear that there are tensions created by the differing visions of the crime and criminals. For lawyers, police officers, prison governors and others, these tensions may be dealt with either by dismissing psychology because it cannot see what is the focus of psychologists' attention, or by squeezing definitive statements out of psychologists that are not supported by their science. Psychologists for their part can have the clarity of their vision reduced by seeking to respond to these demands when they do no have the capacity to do so. Their one-eyed viewpoint also often gives them a two-dimensional image of the topics they are considering.

To increase our success in communicating with people who see the world in different ways, it is necessary to find the common ground that both groups share in their perceptions. One aspect of this is a much clearer focus and understanding of individual differences and the effective categorisations of variations between offenders. A second, realised by a growing number of people, is to see this common ground being in the sharing of narratives. Psychologists can offer alternative 'storylines' to those that are derived from legal processes. These narratives need to be grounded in the appropriate research, but that research needs to be translated from the computer print-outs and academic reports into the Braille that the legal profession can read.

Epilogue

This volume and the present chapter emerged from considerations at a conference held under the auspices of the European Association of Psychology and Law held in Vilnius in 2005. As an ending to my keynote presentation I was granted the opportunity to have my first String Quartet played brilliantly by *Musica Camerata*.

I therefore took the opportunity to develop this Quartet as another way of exploring the integrative relationship between psychology and law. To do this I took two related musical themes. Theme 1 has a steady beat that swells gently, although its harmonies are not always conventional and give a questioning quality to the theme.

Theme 1:

Theme 2 was altogether more vibrant and quirky, although the harmonies are more conventional and give the theme more stability and a greater feeling of excitement. However, whenever this theme appears the counterpoint is stronger, creating a mild feeling of inner tension that nonetheless moves the music on.

Theme 2:

In fact the two themes relate quite closely to each other so that from some perspectives they could be seen just as variations of one another. They have the same overall shape, moving forward in similar ways. This means that after the themes have been introduced it is possible to explore musically the various ways in which they can be combined.

Themes Combined

The combination gives a richer, yet more satisfying, musical form. It also allows a much more flexible movement around the different instruments. When the combination emerges it seems as if that is what the music has been moving towards and out of which a wide range of new musical possibilities can take shape.

Musical structures have an inevitable dynamic quality because they only emerge over time. They therefore capture, at least metaphorically, the changing interactions between different processes and agents. The complexities of the interplay between psychology and law, the gaps in the contacts between them, and the way that all changes over time, is exceptionally difficult to capture and discuss in words except by taking the various components of it as I have done in this chapter. Music, however, allows at least a suggestion of what the possibilities might be for the transactions between these two disciplines and the illustration that no matter how poignant the themes of legal and psychological considerations, or different the variations on how they see the world, there is still the possibility of satisfying harmony when they are each treated as equals within one human composition.

References

Bromley, D.B. (1986) *The Case-Study Method in Psychology and Related Disciplines* (Chichester: Wiley).

Canter, D. (1977) *The Psychology of Place* (London: Architectural Press).

Canter, D.V. (1992) An evaluation of the 'Cusum' stylistic analysis of confessions. *Expert Evidence*, 1, 93–99.

Canter, D. (1994) *Criminal Shadows* (London: HarperCollins).

Canter, D. (2005a) *Mapping Murder* (London: Virgin Books).

Canter, D. (2005b) Suicide or murder: implicit narratives in the Eddie Gilfoyle case, in: L. Alison (ed.) *The Forensic Psychologist's Casebook*, pp. 315–332 (Devon: Willan).

Canter, D., Giles, S. and Nicol, C. (2004) Suicide without explicit precursors: a state of secret despair? *Journal of Investigative Psychology and Offender Profiling*, 1(3), 227–248.

Hicks, S.J. and Sales, B.D. (2006) *Criminal Profiling: Developing an Effective Science and Practice* (Washington: American Psychological Association).

McGuire, J. (1995) *Wahar Works: Reducing Re-offending: Guidelines from Research and Practice* (Chichester: Wiley).

Needs, A. and Towl, G. (Eds) (2004) *Applying Psychology to Forensic Practice* (Oxford: BPS Blackwell).

Raitt, F.E. and Zeedyk, M.S. (2000) *The Implicit Relation of Psychology and Law: Women and Syndrome Evidence* (London: Routledge).

Chapter 2

Contemporary Challenges in Investigative Psychology: Revisiting the Canter Offender Profiling Equations

Donna Youngs

A quarter of a century ago the FBI drew attention to what investigators have long known: Deductions about the likely perpetrator can be drawn from a consideration, in detail, of the crime itself (Douglas *et al.*, 1986). Although thrown into high relief much earlier in the writings of Arthur Conan Doyle, the FBI drew particular attention to this process and gave it the label 'Offender Profiling'. Coming from a scientifically grounded psychological perspective, David Canter saw that the process being alluded to was a rather more profound one and, as a first step in unpacking this, tried to specify the central question that was being implied by the profiling process. This led him to the assertion that the relationship between actions and characteristics was one that, in mathematical terms, should be represented as a canonical form (Canter, 1993).

In doing this, two things quickly became clear. The first was that if the relationships between the offending and the offender could be mapped out mathematically, these 'Profiling Equations' (Canter, 1989; 1993) could be used to systematically inform many of the tasks that comprise the whole police investigation and judicial process beyond the simple painting of suspect profiles. Moreover, the substantive remit would extend far beyond the serial murder and serial sex offences assumed to delimit offender profiling, potentially to all types and forms of criminality. The second thing that became clear in specifying the potential relationships between the offending and the offender in these formal terms was that there were many reasons why 'offender profiling' just wasn't going to be possible (see Canter and Youngs, 2008).

However, the empirical literature now boasts a growing number of studies that show that these links between offending style and offender characteristics do exist and can be established (e.g. Canter and Fritzon, 1998; Lobato, 2004; Santtila *et al.*, 2005; Youngs, 2004). Clearly such findings must point to the general feasibility of the inferential process, but rather than seeing them as simple proof of profiling, we need to recognise that they have emerged despite the complexities inherent in the process.

Criminal Pertinence

Establishing solutions to these equations requires, in the first instance, an understanding of how offenders differ in their criminal styles. But there is a range of conceptual challenges in the modelling of criminal variation that we need to find a way through if we are to pull out any differences as fully as we might. The first of these is the issue of Criminal Pertinence. This is the question of what, in the general case, should be looked at in considering a crime. The following pattern of criminal action might comprise a burglary offence:

> One Monday afternoon in November, a suburban house in Manchester is burgled. The offender disabled the alarm, and then entered by smashing a downstairs window. He stole cash and jewellery without making any mess but leaving fingerprints. The larger electronic goods in the house were not stolen. Just as he was about to leave the offender encountered the occupant and reacted violently punching her in the face several times before running off.
>
> (Crime Description A)

The issue of criminal pertinence is about establishing which of these component parts is relevant, indicating anything about the offenders' criminal style, and which we should ignore. The behaviours that comprise the above burglary will not all be equally revealing of the individual who carried out this offence. But deciding which are relevant is not straightforward. Does the damage done to property by the offender tell us something about him or her but not the way in which the offence was initiated or what time of day it happened? Is the offender's readiness to be violent a key consideration for Investigative Psychologists but his choice of a flat rather than a house unimportant? In part then Criminal Pertinence will relate to the nature of the behaviours.

But determining the pertinence of the behaviours also requires an overall understanding of the incident within which the individual behaviours occurred. Some behaviours may only occur in direct response to situational stimuli, so that what they tell us about the offender may be limited. So, for example, is the entry method important or was this method adopted just because the window was open? Are apparently incongruous behaviours, which run contrary to the general script, particularly significant? For instance, should the fact that an offender who was experienced enough to disable an alarm in advance but who then also, incongruously, left fingerprints be regarded as crucial or incidental? Should we focus just on the behaviours that did happen or are there things that the offender didn't do that are relevant? For example, is it significant that the offender didn't carry any tools with him? Identifying appropriately those behaviours that have Criminal Pertinence must be an essential first step in the inference activity.

In establishing the criminally pertinent offending actions, theory is crucial because the question is not simply one of which behaviours are indicative but one of which behaviours indicate something about criminals that we actually want to know. Different behaviours are going to be indicative of different aspects of the individual. So, for example, degree of preparedness may indicate something of an offender's intelligence but very little of his or her interpersonal style, which may, rather, be revealed in the level of aggression displayed. The criminally pertinent subset of behaviours that investigative psychologists need to be considering should be constantly growing, expanding and being refined in response to developments in the identification of individual differences that are investigation-relevant and legal-process relevant. This will be a process that truly captures the investigatory rather than applied approach to science (c.f. Canter, 2005).

Contingency Destabilisation

A second conceptual complexity in the profiling process can be most readily understood through consideration of an example:

> At 2 a.m. one Saturday morning, a suburban house in Manchester is burgled. The offender disabled the alarm, then entered by smashing a downstairs window. He stole cash and jewellery without making any mess but leaving fingerprints. The larger electronic goods in the house were not stolen. Just as he was about to leave the offender encountered the occupant and reacted violently punching her in the face several times before running off.
>
> (Crime Description B)

This offence differs from the previous one (A) on a single action – when the offender chose to carry out the offence. Yet this change in one behavioural detail in an entire event casts a whole new light on many of the other components of the offence. For example, the smashing of the window is rather different in the middle of the night than in the middle of the day. Similarly, the offender's violent reaction to encountering the occupant is less readily construed as a panic-based reaction given that he must have expected someone to be in at that time. So, single modifications can change our view on which of the components of the offence are pertinent to the establishment of criminal style, as well as on what they actually mean.

This effect of Contingency Destabilisation is something that investigative psychologists, are highly vulnerable to because we work with real-world data, which are what Canter has referred to as 'patchy' (i.e. incomplete but unreliably so). Yet clearly it needs to be considered in our assessments of criminal style.

Criminal Salience

Related to the issue of Criminal Pertinence is the issue of Criminal Salience. Criminal Salience is not simply about what indicates criminal style in the general case but what allows you to define criminal style in a way that distinguishes it from other criminal styles. One complexity in establishing salience is that some of the behaviours any individual carries out will be common to all or many other offenders and so will not allow us to differentiate. Others will be carried out by a fairly large proportion of offenders. Others will be relatively rare. What is required therefore is a way of modelling differences in criminal style that can take into account these variations in the prevalence as opposed to rareness of the behaviours.

One conceptual template, which a number of investigative psychology researchers are starting to draw on that allows this and so draws attention to the salient aspects of criminal action that define distinct styles is the Radex (Canter, 2000). Canter advances a conceptual model of criminal differentiation within which the variations in offenders' styles are the product of differences in two aspects of criminal behaviour. The first, described by the 'thematic facet', are differences in qualitative aspects of the behaviour. The second, described by the 'specificity facet', are qualitative differences in the specificity as opposed to generality of the behaviours within the given area of criminal activity. Canter argues that these two processes interact such that the qualitative variations in style emerge in relation to the more 'specific' behaviours, while the more 'general' behaviours remain undifferentiated, forming a subset of behaviours that tend to be common to all offences.

The Radex has facilitated tremendous progress in modelling criminal variation. Radex structures have been revealed in, for example, studies of behavioural variation in crimes ranging from homicide (Santtila *et al.*, 2001), rape (Canter and Heritage, 1990; Canter *et al.*, 2003) and paedophilia (Canter *et al.*, 1998) to burglary (Merry and Harsent, 2000).

Along the same lines, recent work on differentiation at the level of the type of offence, has shown a Radex structure of criminal differentiation within which variations in the salience of the behaviours relate to the particularity of the target (Canter and Youngs, 2008). The model of criminal differentiation revealed in this work suggests that offenders show specialised styles in relation to targets that are significant or selected but not targets that are unknown or non-particular. Where the targets are significant or selected, distinct styles emerge that may be conceptualised in terms of the means through which the abuse of the other is perpetrated. Three means were identified: Stealing, Physical Assault and Damage.

This model informs the long-standing criminological debate on criminal specialisation or versatility (e.g. Farrington *et al.*, 1988) by showing that criminality is not either a generalised phenomenon underpinned by a single factor or a number of distinct, specialised propensities, but both. So what the Radex draws attention to is not just the idea that some offenders will be more specialised than others in the range of criminal activities that they get involved in but, that, quite independently of this, the behaviours themselves will tend to vary in terms of how common or rare they are. By developing theoretical definitions of the specificity facet in the context of different forms of criminality and types of crime we move towards a richer understanding of criminal salience (Canter and Youngs, 2008).

Integrative Modelling and Inferential Fluency

The next stage in the development of investigative psychology is to relate all of these distinctions to an overall, formal psychological theory for general behavioural differentiation. This means seeking to understand different criminal styles of action, not simply in terms of ideas specific to that type of activity (although I am not for one moment suggesting this has not been tremendously useful) but rather in terms of more generic frameworks such as Bandura's fundamental human incentives (Bandura, 1986), interpersonal behavioural style models such as Schutz's FIRO (Schutz, 1992), Shye's Action Systems (Shye, 1985) or Narrative Action Systems (Canter and Youngs, 2008). This overall approach is at the heart of addressing the other conceptual challenges of Integrative Modelling and Inferential Fluency.

General frameworks would allow us to understand crime style differences in terms that are related to a recognised formal psychological process facilitating the Inferential Fluency between the ideas we use to distinguish styles and the theories we then rely on to move from those styles to infer the characteristics of the offender in the profiling process.

Drawing upon general frameworks will also allow us to understand crime style differences in terms that facilitate the direct comparability of models of criminal variation from across different cultural contexts and within different crime types. This translation of the stylistic differences within different crime types and from different cultures into a common psychological language is the challenge at the heart of Integrative Modelling.

The Canonical Form of the Offending Actions – Offender Characteristics Relationship

The general feasibility of modelling criminal variation that all the work so far points to, does of course open up the possibility of establishing solutions to the A(ction)-C(haracteristics) equations. Indeed, there is now quite a weight of studies showing some differential patterns of correspondence between particular styles of offending and particular sets of characteristics (e.g. Canter and Fritzon, 1998; Hakkanen *et al.*, 2004; Lobato, 2004; Salfati and Canter, 1999; Santtila *et al.*, 2005; Youngs, 2004).

This is all tremendously encouraging, indicating that offender action to offender characteristics inferences are possible. The substantive findings also start to point us towards the types of psychological and social processes that underpin the relationships between these two domains. As an exploratory phase in the defining of a discipline, it has been incredibly fruitful.

However, do these get us near to the point where we can look at any given crime and make inferences about the likely perpetrator on the basis of the style of offending exhibited? There are a number of issues about the way in which offending actions relate to offender characteristics that mean that we need to be cautious in assuming these results can be used, whether by investigators or researchers, in this way.

The central challenge relates to the canonical nature of the relationship. Particular actions do not map on to particular characteristics in any simple or direct way. The same action can, on a consistent basis, indicate more than one characteristic, and equally, the same characteristic can be inferred from different actions. So for example, extreme violence may be threatened in a robbery carried out by an inexperienced or a highly experienced offender. And, conversely, both rapists and robbers will tend to have criminal histories that include burglary convictions.

The actions–characteristics relationship is further complex in that the same action can indicate different characteristics in different contexts or at different points in an offender's criminal progression. So, for example, the carrying of a gun by a lone offender may indicate a rather different individual than of the carrying of a gun as part of a group at an offending event. Equally, the use of an accelerant may indicate an above average intellect in a young arsonist but less so in one that was more experienced (Canter, 1993; Youngs, 2004).

What this means is that the A-C mapping does not take the form of multiple one-to-one relationships that accumulate to provide the description of an offender. Rather, the mapping between the two domains takes the form of a given combination of interacting action variables that map on to a given combination of interacting characteristic variables. Technically, this type of relationship can only be fully represented as a canonical correlation (Canter, 1993)

$$F_1 A_1 + ... + F_n A_n = F_1 C_1 + ... + F_m C_m \qquad \text{(Canter's Profiling Equations)}$$

On one side of this equation are variables derived from information about the offence that would be available to investigators. On the other side, are the characteristics of the offender that are most useful in facilitating the police enquiry. So, if $A_{1...n}$ represents n actions of the offender (including, for example, time, place and victim selection) and $C_{1...m}$ represents I characteristics of the offender, then the empirical question is to establish the values of weightings ($F_{1...n}$ and $F_{1...m}$) in an equation of the above form. Solving canonical equations (c.f. Tabachnick and Fidell, 1983) requires establishing 'the relationships between two sets of variables' (*op cit.*, p. 146). These can be understood as multiple regression equations that have a number of criterion variables as well as a number of predictor variables.

The important point for investigative psychologists is that changes in any one predictor variable (the actions) can destabilise the relationship of any other predictor variable with any criterion variable or set of criterion variables (the characteristics). This means that inferences can become invalid. So, for example, it could be established that in rape a high level of control, a rapid aggressive initial approach, a moderate use of demeaning language and a high level of forensic awareness, predicts an offender age of 26. However, within this, for specific combinations of other characteristics, the most likely age of the offender carrying out an offence in this way may be lower. This may be the case where, for example, the offender has a particularly extensive criminal history.

Where the relationships between the two domains (offending actions and offender characteristics) have this complex form, there are two possible approaches to moving forward to build the scientific body of knowledge that will allow the specific inferences. The first is to build a catalogue, empirically, of what C variables any given action relates to, for every combination of other action variables. This would be an enormous task requiring specification of every single pertinent factor, including aspects of the broader context, the cultural context and even the epoch. The other option is to focus on the development of theory that will allow an understanding of the underlying processes so that particular inferences can be drawn on this basis.

Conclusion

Within the present chapter I have attempted to give a flavour of the conceptual complexities inherent in the 'profiling' process. Issues of (a) Criminal Pertinence, (b) Contingency Destabilisation, (c) Criminal Salience, (d) Integrative Modelling, (e) Inferential Fluency, and (f) the Canonical Form of the A-C relationship were touched upon. These issues all highlight the need for investigative psychologists to focus on formal specifications of the problem and, in particular, on the theoretical and conceptual developments that will allow full solutions to the original Canter Profiling Equations mapped out at the birth of Investigative Psychology.

References

Bandura, A. (1986) *Social Foundations of Thought and Action* (Englewood Cliffs, NJ: Prentice Hall).

Canter, D. (1989) Offender profiles, *The Psychologist*, 2(1), pp. 12–16.

Canter, D. (1993) Psychology of offender profiling, in: Bull, R. and Carson, D. (Eds) *Handbook of Psychology in Legal Contests* (Chichester: Wiley).

Canter, D. (1995) Psychology of offender profiling, in: Bull, R. and Carson, D. (Eds) *Handbook of Psychology in Legal Contests*, chapter 4.5, pp. 343–335 (Chichester: Wiley).

Canter, D. (2000) Offender profiling and criminal differentiation, *Legal and Criminological Psychology*, 5, pp. 23–46.

Canter, D. (2005) *In the Kingdom of the Blind.* Keynote presentation to 15th Conference of the European Association of Psychology and Law, Vilnius, Lithuania.

Canter, D. Hughes, D. and Kirby, S. (1998) Paedophilia: pathology, criminality, or both? The development of a multivariate model of offence behaviour in child sexual abuse, *The Journal of Forensic Psychiatry*, 9(3), pp. 532–555.

Canter, D., Bennell, C., Alison, L. and Reddy, S. (2003) Differentiating sex offences: a behaviourally based thematic classification of stranger rapes, *Behavioural Sciences and the Law*, 21, pp. 157–174.

Canter, D. and Fritzon, K. (1998) Differentiating arsonists: a model of firesetting actions and characteristics, *Legal and Criminal Psychology*, 3, pp. 73–96.

Canter, D. and Youngs, D. (2003) Beyond 'offender profiling': the need for an investigative psychology, in: D. Carson and R. Bull (Eds) *Handbook of Psychology in Legal Contexts*, 2nd edn, pp 171–205 (Chichester: Wiley).

Canter, D. and Youngs, D. (2008) *Investigative Psychology: Analysing Criminal Action* (Chichester: Wiley).

Douglas, J., Ressler, R., Burgess, A. and Hartman, C. (1986) Criminal profiling from crime analysis, *Behavioral Science and the Law*, 4(4), pp. 401–421.

Farrington, D.P., Snyder, H.N. and Finnegan, T.A. (1988) Specialization in juvenile court careers, *Criminology*, 26(3), pp. 461–485.

Hakkanen, H., Puolakka, P. and Santtila, P. (2004) Crime scene actions and offender characteristics in arson, *Legal and Criminological Psychology*, 9(2), pp. 197–214.

Lobato, A. (2004) The criminal activity and lifestyle of robbers and burglars: a model for identifying criminal behaviour. PhD Thesis, Liverpool University.

Merry, S. and Harsent, L. (2000) Intruders, pilferers, raiders and invaders: the interpersonal dimension of burglary, in: D. Canter and L. Alison (Eds) *Offender Profiling Series: IV. Profiling Property Crimes*, pp. 31–56 (Aldershot: Ashgate).

Santtila, P., Canter, D., Elfgren, T. and Häkkänen, H. (2001) The structure of crime-scene actions in Finnish homicides, *Homicide Studies*, 4, pp. 363–387.

Santtila P., Junkkila J. and Sandnabba N.K. (2005) Behavioural linking of stranger rapes, *Journal of Investigative Psychology and Offender Profiling*, 2, pp. 87–103.

Salfati, G. and Canter, D. (1999) Differentiating stranger murders: profiling offender characteristics from behavioural styles, *Behavioural Sciences and the Law*, 17, pp. 391–406.

Schutz, W. (1992) Beyond Firo-B – 3 new theory derived measures – Element B: Behaviour, Element F: Feelings, Element S: Self, *Psychological Reports*, 70, pp. 915–937.

Shye, S. (1985) Nonmetric mulitvariate models for behavioural action systems, in: Canter, D. (Ed.) *Facet Theory: Approaches to Social Research* (New York: Springer-Verlag).

Tabachnick, B.G and Fidell, L.S. (1983) *Using Multivariate Statistics* (London: Harper and Row).

Youngs, D. (2004) Personality correlates of offence style, *Journal of Investigative Psychology and Offender Profiling*, 1, pp. 99–119.

Chapter 3

Lie Detectors and the Law: The Use of the Polygraph in Europe

Ewout H. Meijer and Peter J. van Koppen

In the 1990s, the Belgian Police found themselves confronted with a number of major criminal investigations they had been unable to solve. In order to force a breakthrough, they decided to submit suspects to lie detection tests using the polygraph. Experienced polygraphers were flown in; from South Africa to test Flemish suspects, from Canada for suspects from Wallonia. The introduction of the polygraph in Belgium turned out to be successful. Not necessarily because the cases were solved by the polygraph per se, but because a number of suspects confessed during or after the test.[1] Following these successes, the Belgian Federal Police in Brussels had their own people trained. Currently, three dedicated polygraphers test over 300 suspects per year.

> Belgium is not the only example of recent developments in the use of polygraph testing in Europe. In the United Kingdom and the Netherlands, the polygraph is used for periodical testing of sex offenders. The test is used to assess the veracity of sex offenders' self reports about both treatment compliance and sexual history. Again, practitioners are content with the results (Grubin, 2002).

These examples illustrate that polygraph testing is not exclusively an American affair. Several European countries have adopted the use of polygraph testing to some extent, but others have not. Meanwhile, the use of the polygraph tests is heavily debated. Arguments for this debate not only include scientific properties of the test, such as accuracy, but also legal and ethical issues, for example, whether it is alien to the right to remain silent. Legal systems in different European countries weigh these arguments differently, resulting in different legal restraints on polygraph test outcomes.

In this chapter, we will discuss the use of the polygraph in Europe, and how legal systems in various countries deal with the issues surrounding it. We do not pretend to give an exhaustive review. This is impossible, since polygraph testing is partially in the hands of the secret services and military, and thus confidential. Even information

---

1   This effect is also referred to as the bogus pipeline effect. See Roese and Jamieson (1993).

that is not confidential is rarely published and often inaccessible. Therefore, only applications of the polygraph on which information is publicly available will be discussed.

For a better understanding of the issues affecting legal status, we will first discuss the basic principles of polygraph testing. After that, we will discuss how far polygraph testing has penetrated into the legal arena of several European countries.

Polygraph Testing

The Polygraph

The words 'lie detector' and 'polygraph' are often used synonymously. The term 'polygraph' refers to the recording device that is used for registering different physiological parameters. Polygraphs designed for lie detection tests used to be briefcase-sized machines, measuring physical signals from the subject and recording them with multiple pens on a lengthy roll of paper. Nowadays, they consist of a small amplifier/digitizer and a laptop recording the signals. The sensors attached to the subject are generally (1) two expendable bands positioned around the thorax measuring respiration, (2) two electrodes attached to the inside of the hand measuring palm sweating and (3) an inflatable cuff positioned around the upper arm registering blood pressure. An example of a recording is given in Figure 3.1.

The physiological parameters registered with a polygraph co-vary with a number of psychological processes, including emotions such as fear and stress. Although it is widely accepted that there is no unique physiological pattern associated with lying (Lykken, 1998), the tracings can still be used to infer guilt or innocence, as will be discussed below.

The Questions

Various forms of polygraph testing exist. The two main forms are the control question test (CQT, see Reid, 1947) and the Guilty Knowledge Test (Lykken, 1960). The method of choice in most applications is the CQT.[2] During a CQT, the suspect is asked three different types of questions, relevant questions, control questions, and irrelevant questions. The relevant questions deal directly with the incident under investigation, for example 'on the 25th of March, did you shoot Gordon Shumway?' The physiological reactions to each relevant question are compared with those accompanying the control question directly preceding or following it. These control questions have a more generic nature, but also deal with undesirable behaviour, for example 'In the first 25 years of your life, have you ever done anything illegal?' The irrelevant questions are neutral, and take the form of, for instance, 'Is today Wednesday?' They are used as fillers.

---

2   We will discuss the GKT later in the chapter.

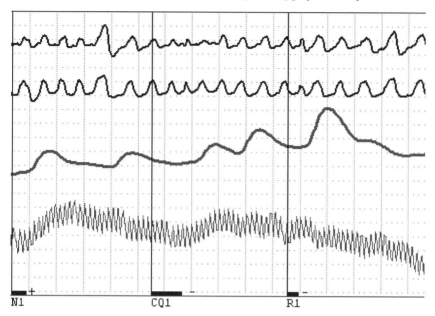

Figure 3.1   Computerized recording of physiological signals during a control question polygraph test

Note: From top to bottom, tracings represent thoracic respiration, abdominal respiration, skin conductance and blood pressure. Vertical lines represent the start of an irrelevant question (N1), a control question (CQ1) and a relevant question (R1).

Manipulation

A typical CQT starts with a lengthy pre-test interview. During this interview, the suspect is led to believe that lying is accompanied by involuntary changes in physiological activity, and that the polygraph registers these changes, and can thus determine whether he is lying or not. Most importantly however, the suspect is told that for the test outcome to be 'innocent' he needs to answer all questions truthfully.

Meanwhile, the polygrapher emphasizes the importance of answering both the relevant and the control questions with 'No'. This is achieved by giving the suspect the impression that disclosure of previous illegal behaviour will negatively influence the polygrapher's opinion of the suspect ('You don't look like somebody who would engage in illegal activities, do you?'). Assuming that somewhere in their youth everybody has overstepped the mark, the suspect will feel forced to give a deceptive answer to each control question. Supposedly, this results in a situation where for an innocent suspect the control questions become most stressful, since he is led to believe that his deceptiveness to this question will be picked up by the polygraph, and will cause him to fail the test. A guilty suspect is thought to be less worried about the control questions. For him, his deceptive answer to the relevant questions poses the greatest threat of failing the test. This assumption underlying the CQT has also been referred to as the inference rule: 'each examinee will focus his or her concern on the questions that present the greatest threat of failing the test' (Elaad, 2003, p. 38).

Inference

The use of the CQT is continuously subjected to a long ongoing discussion. In particular, the validity of the inference rule has been debated since the 1970s (Ben-Shakhar and Furedy, 1990; Furedy and Heslegrave, 1991; Iacono and Lykken, 1997, 1999; Podlesny and Raskin, 1977; Raskin, 1989; Raskin et al., 1997, 1999; Raskin and Podlesny, 1979; Saxe, 1991). The notion that guilty suspects show the greatest concern to the relevant questions while innocent show the greatest concern to the control questions has little foundation in psychological theory nor is it very compelling. Why would an innocent suspect be so much concerned with the control question, while being the subject of a murder investigation? Could the relevant question not be perceived as more threatening and thus elicit larger responses?

The control questions in the main interview are based on the discussion between polygrapher and suspect during the pre-test interview. According to proponents of the CQT, a skilled polygrapher is capable of both formulating control questions and creating an atmosphere in which an innocent examinee is most worried about these, whereas a guilty examinee is most worried about the relevant questions. Consequently, the quality of a test heavily depends on the intuition of the polygrapher in each and every case.

As a result, large differences in the quality of tests exist. This can be illustrated with a case one of the authors (EM) was confronted with. He was asked to give his opinion on the quality of a CQT in a sexual abuse case, and the weight that should be given to its outcome. The accused underwent a polygraph test with a private commercial polygrapher from London. The only documentation of the test consisted of a video tape directed at the ex-wife of the accused, on which the polygrapher stated 'There's no way that the accused is having any form of sexual contact with your children or with anybody else's children. He is not attracted to children. He is however very, very much in love with you.' When trying to get hold of more documentation, it turned out that there was no audio or video recording of any portion of the test, because this, according to the polygrapher, would distract the examinee (strikingly, during the test the examinee was seated next to a running washing machine). Furthermore, the polygrapher had disposed of the graphs because he maintained a paperless office. It should be plain to the reader that we needed little time to come up with a verdict on the quality of this specific test.

Accuracy

Estimations of the error margin of the CQT vary. This variation is in part due to difficulties that characterize research on the method's accuracy. In a typical laboratory study, subjects are instructed to commit a mock crime and are subsequently tested with a CQT. Their results are compared to tested subjects who did not commit the mock crime. The main problem of such laboratory studies is that the CQT is based on detecting the fear of being exposed. This fear is largely absent in laboratory studies. One may therefore expect huge differences between a murderer who is subjected to the CQT and may face life imprisonment, and an undergraduate psychology student who – serving as subject to gain study credits – is ordered to 'steal' something by the experimenter.

Field studies have more ecological validity, but face other problems. Most importantly, they lack an objective measure of guilt (i.e. ground truth). Whether the suspect was convicted afterwards is a suboptimal measure, since a conviction is, directly or indirectly, influenced by the results of the CQT. In particular, admissions or confessions made by suspects under the influence of a polygraph test result in a sampling bias overestimating the validity of the CQT (Iacono, 1991).

Keeping these limitations in mind, field studies typically show that guilty suspects are correctly classified as guilty by the CQT in 83–89% of the cases (and 10–17% as innocent, with 2–10% inconclusive), while innocent suspects are deemed innocent in 53–72% of the cases (and 12–47% as guilty, with 5–29% as inconclusive, see Ben-Shakhar Furedy, 1990; Carroll, 1991; Honts and Perry, 1992; Iacono and Patrick 1997; Lykken, 1998; Raskin and Honts, 2002). Besides highlighting the differences in accuracy rates between studies, these data also show that the probability for an innocent suspect to be classified as guilty is relatively high.[3]

Recently, the authoritative National Research Council (2003) reviewed the literature on the accuracy of the CQT. Strikingly, not a single study was found that met the criteria for good scientific research. The 37 laboratory studies and seven field studies that passed the minimum standards for review showed an accuracy index of 0.85 and 0.89 respectively, corresponding to an accuracy rate of around 80%. It led the National Research Council to conclude that specific-incident polygraph tests can discriminate lying from truth telling at rates well above chance, though well below perfection.

The National Research Council did make the reservation that these studies primarily included examinees that were untrained in countermeasures. Countermeasures refer to anything that a subject might do in an effort to defeat or distort a polygraph examination (Honts and Amato, 2002). They can be divided into

---

3   This means that the probability of a false positive result is much higher than the probability of a false negative result. This is alien to legal doctrine that prescribes that it should be the other way around, abbreviated in the so-called Blackstone Maxim: 'Better that ten guilty persons escape than that one innocent suffer.' See Blackstone (1882, Book 4, Ch 27). See also Volokh (1997).

two families, the *general state* countermeasures and *specific point* countermeasures. General state countermeasures are aimed at disturbing the subject's psychological and physiological state during the entire test, for example by taking drugs. Specific point countermeasures are aimed at augmenting or reducing the responses to different questions, for example through biting ones tongue or by mental imagery. In a laboratory setting, Honts and colleagues (Honts *et al.*, 1996, 1985) showed that a non-neglectable proportion of participants can successfully be instructed to defeat a polygraph test by using such countermeasures.

Sex Offenders

In the previous section, we focused on the use of the CQT in crime investigations. The CQT, however, is also used in post conviction management of sexual offenders. Although this application is only partially related to the legal issues, it may serve as a good example of how polygraph testing is used. The reported successes may result in grown confidence, and can in turn affect the legal status of polygraph test outcomes.

Successful treatment of sex offenders often poses special problems. The recidivism rates among this type of offenders are high (Hanson *et al.*, 2003; Prentky *et al.*, 1997) and cause public indignation and discussion. The frequent failure of the treatment is partly due to the fact that sex offenders, more than other offenders, have a long history of concealing their behaviour and lying about it. Having them tell everything, essential to many forms of therapy, is equally as important as it is difficult.

According to practitioners, using the polygraph aids breaking through this pattern of lying and deceit. According to English and colleagues it is akin to urine testing drug offenders: a method of validating offenders' self-reports of treatment compliance and monitoring very specific behaviours (English *et al.*, 2003). More precisely, the use of the polygraph in sex offender management serves three functions: (1) to verify the accuracy and completeness of the sexual history information an offender provides during treatment; (2) to verify the details of the conviction offence; and (3) to verify whether a probationer or parolee is complying with the conditions of community supervision and cooperating with treatment expectations (English *et al.*, 2003). The usefulness of the polygraph in sex offender management seems undisputed among practitioners who use it. Several studies show that it aids in having offenders disclose information about the number of previous offences, victims, and behaviours that increase the probability of recidivism (Ahlmeyer *et al.*, 2000; Emerick and Dutton, 1993; English *et al.,* 2003; Grubin *et al.*, 2004).

The use of the polygraph in sex offender management, however, has not remained free from criticism (Blasingame, 1998; Branaman and Gallagher, 2005; Cross and Saxe, 1992, 2001; Faller, 1997). It is argued that many sex offenders suffer from personality disorders that prevent them from experiencing anxiety when lying. This would make their physical responses during a CQT test meaningless. Additionally, these kinds of offenders routinely engage in cognitive distortions. These distortions include perceiving children as wanting sex with adults, seeing sexual contact with children as socially acceptable and rationalization of their behaviour towards their victims ('This is not abuse, but in the interest of the child', see Ward *et al.* 1997). These cognitive distortions are likely to reduce feelings of guilt and anxiety, resulting in reduced detection during a CQT. Finally, many sex offenders are engaged in patterns of lying to conceal their pattern of abuse, often spanning many years. They are habituated to presenting lies, which again makes their lies less detectable during a CQT.

The biggest concern with the use of the CQT in sex offender management is the wording of the relevant questions. In criminal investigations, relevant questions deal with a known offence and are univocally worded (e.g. 'On the night of March 25th, did you shoot John Doe?'). In sex offender management, on the other hand, the relevant questions deal with unknown offences or behaviour. Consequently, the relevant questions are generic, for example 'Did you have any sexual contacts with children other than Kevin?' As a result of this, the relevant questions become more similar to the control questions.

This can be illustrated by the following example. To what extent does a relevant question like: 'Have you had unsupervised contact with children over the last 3 months?' differ from the adjacent control question: 'Have you done anything over the last 3 months that would concern your probation officer?' (Grubin *et al.*, 2004, p. 213). Comparing these questions is stressing the inference rule to its limits, because now both the control and the relevant questions focus on general, non-specific misconducts.

Notwithstanding the critique, the use of the polygraph in sex offender management is widespread in the United States. Over 70% of community-based sex offender treatment programs use the polygraph for adults and over 45% for juveniles (McGrath *et al.*, 2003). As mentioned earlier, the United Kingdom and the Netherlands are following suit. The reason for this popularity does not lie in the method's accuracy, but in the method's capability to elicit confessions. Abrams and Abrams (1993), for example, acknowledge that part of the disclosure of offences and behaviour is made before the actual testing takes place. Offenders disclose information upon learning that a polygraph test is going to be administered in the future and during the pre-test interview, well before the polygraph is actually attached. Data from the British pilot study by Grubin and his colleagues (Grubin *et al.*, 2004) corroborate this. They found that sex offenders admitted more sexual deviant behaviour as a result of polygraph testing, but a substantial proportion of these admissions were made during the pre-test interview.

Ambiguous Questions

The problem of ambiguous questions is not confined to sex offenders. To demonstrate this, we will use an example drawn from a Belgian murder case.[4]

---

4   One of the authors (PvK) served as expert witness in this case.

In the early morning of 2 June 1998, the Dutchman Ran Biemans, 58 years old, is found dead in his apartment in the Belgian town of Meerle. He is found lying next to his bed with his throat cut. He has evidently been tortured before he was killed. From the beginning, the Belgian police suspect his Dutch wife Els L. She claims having been in bed at the time the murder took place, but did not notice anything. She testifies she woke up with a very bad taste in her mouth and that her hands and feet were taped together. Consequently, she claims having been drugged by the killers. This claim is supported by shoe prints found on the bed and signs of a struggle. The police discover that Ran Biemans led a double or even triple life. He spent much time in the Amsterdam red light district and was involved in illegal trade of various kinds. It should also be noted that Els L. was not faithful to Ran either: she had a lover named Wilco. In police interrogation she evidently lied stating that she had no relation with Wilco at the time of the murder.

Els L. denies any involvement in the crime, and is subjected to a CQT by the Belgian Federal Police. The police hypothesis is that she benefited from the death of Ran Biemans, because of his wealth. Thus, according to the police, she either killed him herself, or was involved in some other way.

By the time Els L. had to undergo the polygraph test, she was convinced that Wilco committed the crime. The testing of Els L. consisted of two sessions. The first probed whether she killed Ran Biemans (see Box 3.1 for the questions asked). She came out truthful. In the second session however – completed the same afternoon – the questions were much more ambiguous. For example 'Concerning the facts committed on Ran on the night of 1st to 2nd June 1998, do you know with certainty who did commit these?' The outcome of this test was 'not truthful'.

Box 3.1

An example of non-ambiguous (first session) and ambiguous (second session) relevant questions in one single case (our translation from Dutch).

First session with Els L.

Relevant 1: In the night of 1st to 2nd June 1998, did you slice open the throat of Ran?

Relevant 2: In the night of 1st to 2nd June 1998, are you the one who sliced open the throat of Ran?

Relevant 3: In the night of 1st to 2nd June 1998, are you the person who sliced open the throat of Ran?

Control 1: Apart from this case, do you remember ever telling an important lie?

Control 2: Apart from this case, do you remember ever hurting anybody?

Control 3: Apart from this case, do you remember ever doing something illegal for which you have not been caught?

Second session with Els L.

Relevant 1: Concerning the facts committed on Ran on the night of 1st to 2nd June 1998, do you know with certainty who did commit these?

Relevant 2: Concerning the facts committed on Ran on the night of 1st to 2nd June 1998, did you help in committing these?

Relevant 3: Concerning the facts committed on Ran on the night of 1st to 2nd June 1998, did you organize these?

Control 1: During the first 40 years of your life, you remember if you ever told an important lie?

Control 2: During the first 40 years of your life, do you remember you ever hurt anybody?

Control 3: During the first 40 years of your life, do you remember if you did something illegal for which you have not been caught?

The ambiguity of the relevant questions in the second session introduces two problems. First, as in sex offender testing, the more generic wording makes the comparison with the control questions cumbersome. Second, even in case that the 'not truthful' outcome is correct, the generic wording makes interpretation difficult. In this case, the prosecution inferred that Els L. must have hired someone else to commit the killing. This inference is neither warranted nor logical, as there is reason to believe that she responded to the relevant questions only because at the time of the polygraph test she believed she knew who committed the murder: Wilco. This however does not mean that she knew it at the time of the killing or that she was in any way involved in organizing it.

Guilty Knowledge

There is a second polygraph technique, first described by Münsterberg (1908) and later named the Guilty Knowledge Test (GKT) by Lykken (1960). During a GKT, the physiological measures recorded are the same as those in a CQT, but the questions differ. All questions concern details of the crime, presumably only known to the police and the perpetrator. These questions are presented with multiple answer alternatives. These answer alternatives include the correct answer, but also several plausible incorrect answers (e.g. 'Was the victim killed with a … (a) gun, (b) knife, (c) rope, (d) bat, (e) ice pick?'). The suspect answers all alternatives with a 'No'. For an innocent suspect, all alternatives are equally plausible. Therefore, over the whole test, responses to the correct alternatives will not significantly deviate from those to the incorrect alternatives. A guilty suspect, however, will recognize the correct alternatives and show enhanced physiological responses to them. Thus, consistent stronger physiological responding to the correct alternatives is indicative of knowledge of intimate details of the crime and involvement can be inferred.

The most important advantage of the GKT is that it protects the innocent (Elaad, 1999). The probability that an innocent suspect will fail the test depends on the number of questions and the number of alternatives. Using the aforementioned example, the probability that an innocent suspect shows the strongest reaction to 'rope', while this is the true murder weapon, is 20%. If several of these questions are asked, this probability drops dramatically. The probability of an innocent suspect consistently showing the strongest reaction to the correct answer on five questions with five alternatives each is 0.03%.

The disadvantage of the GKT lies in the formulation of the questions. These questions need to fulfil two requirements: (a) the details asked need to be known to the culprit and the investigating authorities, and (b) the details asked must not be known to an innocent suspect. Thus, questions should concern aspects of the crime that are obvious enough for the perpetrator to have noticed, and also the culprit should not have been under the influence of alcohol or drugs impairing his/ her memory. Furthermore, this means that once a suspect has gained knowledge through other means than being the perpetrator – for instance by extensive police interviews or by reading his case file – he or she can no longer be discerned from a guilty suspect. Therefore, the GKT can only be applied in the first stage of a police investigation, and construction of enough questions may be difficult is many cases (Podlesny, 1993; 2003).

The GKT is only used on a large scale in Japan (Hira and Furumitsu, 2002; Nakayama, 2002). Approximately 5000 tests are performed annually. They are performed by specially trained experts, who are not involved in the case. These experts are not police investigators but are employed as researchers by a forensic laboratory. If requested, they visit the crime scene in order to formulate questions. Provided the GKT meets certain requirements, it is admissible as evidence in Japanese courts (Ben-Shakhar *et al.*, 2002; Nakayama, 2002).

In sum, the term 'polygraph testing' covers a number of techniques. For practical rather then theoretical reasons, the CQT is the most widely used technique. Different tests serve different goals. These goals range from veracity assessment of a statement to the elicitation of a confession. Besides the accuracy of the different techniques, a number of ethical issues characterize the legal discussion on the use of polygraph testing. These include the manipulation during the pre-test interview of a CQT (is one allowed to lie to a suspect during interrogation?), the voluntariness of the test (given that the physiological signals are largely involuntary) and the fact that the outcome of a test is often used to pressure an interrogee into confessing. How legal systems in various countries deal with these issues is the topic of the following section.

The Polygraph in Europe

Legal Systems

The application of the polygraph in different European countries varies considerably. It ranges from a significant role in the judicial system in Belgium to, for instance, Spain where the use of polygraph testing has apparently never been suggested.

Before we give a concise description of the application of the polygraph in a number of European countries, we should shortly venture into the manner in which courts treat evidence in many European countries.

In most common law countries – such as the United Kingdom and most of the states in the United States – the legal system is based on a jury trial. In a jury trial, the judge serves as the gatekeeper with respect to evidence: he or she decides which pieces of evidence are put before the jury. This has resulted in an extensive body of rules on the admissibility of evidence (e.g. Heydon, 2004; Strong, 1999). In most European countries however, the criminal trial is modelled after a bench trial. Here, the judge – or court – is both gatekeeper and finder of fact.

The latter system has resulted in a tradition where all potential evidence is presented to the fact finder. In these systems, rules on admissibility of evidence serve little purpose. The emphasis lies not so much on the admissibility of evidence,[5] but on rules governing the use of evidence by the court in decision making. Since these rules tend to be scarce in many countries, this has resulted in a 'free evidence' system (Damaška, 1986).

The lack of admissibility rules is usually compensated by the rules that courts – in contrast to juries – have to argue their decisions. Two different versions of this exist in Europe. In the one system the final evaluation of evidence is governed by the *conviction intime*: the court convicts when it is convinced the suspect is guilty. In the other type – with *conviction raisonée* – the court must argue its verdict in a manner that conforms to certain statutory standards, although also these standards tend to be rather lenient. Typically, in these systems, an appeal to the Supreme Courts can only concern matters of law, not the manner in which evidence was weighed by the lower court. This may explain why in some European countries, in spite of a policy or precedents that forbid the use of polygraph tests as evidence, it is used nevertheless.

---

5 Exceptions are rules on the admissibility of evidence obtained by the police unlawfully.

The Polygraph in Europe[6]

In Belgium, over 300 CQTs are performed annually. Cases include murder, rape, theft and arson. The introduction of polygraph testing in Belgium raised some legal concern. When questioned in Parliament, the minister of Justice indicated that the results should only be used in police investigations, and would not be offered as evidence in court (see also Bockstaele, 2001; Verhaegen, 2000).[7] Practice turned out to be different. Although refused as evidence by bench courts (Traest, 2001), the results of polygraph tests have been offered as evidence before the Court of Assisen, the Belgian jury, among which was the aforementioned case of Els L. Since juries do not have to explain their use of evidence, polygraph tests are *de facto* accepted as evidence in Belgium.

In the Netherlands, the outcome of a polygraph test is neither used as evidence in court, nor in police investigations. In the 1990s, it appeared to go the other way. The Werkgroep Leugendetectie (Taskforce Lie Detection, 1993), consisting primarily of police officials and policy advisors, concluded that 'the polygraph could have a certain value for the Dutch criminal law system'. According to the taskforce, lie detection could give an indication of the veracity of a statement and, as such, aid to defining the direction and priorities in criminal investigations. The taskforce, however, did acknowledge the technique's error margin and expressed reservations about using the outcome of a CQT as evidence in court. In 1996 this report was succeeded by two reports on the request of the Dutch minister of Justice by four professors of psychology (Boelhouwer *et al.*, 1996; van Koppen *et al.*, 1996). Their recommendations were generally similar to those made by the taskforce. They concluded that, provided certain conditions are met, application of the polygraph in criminal investigation could be meaningful. Still, the minister of Justice rejected the introduction of polygraph testing, primarily because it is alien to the right to remain silent,[8] an argument that returns in other countries across Europe as well. More

---

6   Our gratitude goes to Anna Baldry, Vivi Bang Pallesen, Wolfgang Bilsky, Vicente Garrido Genoves, Pär Anders Granhag, Helinä Häkkänen, Andreas Kapardis, Martin Killias, Annika Melinder, Pekka Santtila, Sven Svebak, Peter Tak and Rita Žukauskienė, who served as informants for this section.

7   The minister of Justice wrote: 'but it should be emphasized that not so much the results of the test with the lie detector would enable the court to solve a criminal or other case, but the confession to which the test may lead, as far as the confession is believable and supported with other data in the investigation. The lie detector thus is a tool among others; as it has proved useful in certain cases – sometimes incriminating, more often exculpatory – investigating judges will continue to use it in the future.' Our translation from questions and answers Kamer (2000–2001), 22 May 2001, 12 (question number 4689 by Schoofs).

8   In that she followed Article 6 of the European Convention of Human Rights. This article reads as follows: (1) In the determination of his civil rights and obligations or of any criminal charge against him, everyone is entitled to a fair and public hearing within a reasonable time by an independent and impartial tribunal established by law. Judgement shall be pronounced publicly by the press and public may be excluded from all or part of the trial

recently, a request for a polygraph test was rejected by the The Hague Appellate Court. This decision was upheld by the Dutch Supreme Court (Hoge Raad) because 'it is widely known that the use of polygraphs in criminal investigation is disputed because of its unreliability.'[9] In contrast to criminal law, polygraph testing has been introduced in the Netherlands in sex offender management.

In the United Kingdom, polygraph testing is not used in criminal law either. The British government did announce the intention to initiate pilot studies on its effectiveness in the 1990s, but after a report by the Working Group of the British Psychological Society (British Psychological Society, 1996), the plans were abandoned. The British Psychological Society recently published a new report (BPS Working Party, 2004),[10] concluding that 'the use of the polygraph has inherent weaknesses, and that the error rates can be high. [...] Polygraphic deception detection procedure should not be ascribed a special Status.' Meanwhile, the United Kingdom is serving as a pioneer in the use of the polygraph in sex offender management.

In Germany, the Supreme Court (Bundesgerichtshof) abandoned the CQT from penal procedures in 1998. This decision was based on a report written by three professors of psychology. There was however, less agreement among these experts then in the aforementioned countries. According to Professor Klaus Fiedler (1999), the CQT does not meet the standard criteria of scientific validity. Professor Max Steller (Steller and Dahle, 1999) was a little more lenient; acknowledging that polygraph testing should not be completely excluded from forensic application. Psychology professor and practicing polygrapher Udo Undeutsch was most lenient (Undeutsch and Klein, 1999). Nonetheless, based on these reviews, the German Supreme Court forbade the CQT from penal procedures (see also Burgsmüller, 2000; Fiedler 1999; Fiedler *et al.*, 2002; Offe, 2001; Steller and Dahle, 1999; Undeutsch

---

in the interest of morals, public order or national security in a democratic society, where the interests of juveniles or the protection of the private life of the parties so require, or the extent strictly necessary in the opinion of the court in special circumstances where publicity would prejudice the interests of justice. (2) Everyone charged with a criminal offence shall be presumed innocent until proved guilty according to law. (3) Everyone charged with a criminal offence has the following minimum rights: (a) to be informed promptly, in a language which he understands and in detail, of the nature and cause of the accusation against him; (b) to have adequate time and the facilities for the preparation of his defence; (c) to defend himself in person or through legal assistance of his own choosing or, if he has not sufficient means to pay for legal assistance, to be given it free when the interests of justice so require; (d) to examine or have examined witnesses against him and to obtain the attendance and examination of witnesses on his behalf under the same conditions as witnesses against him; (e) to have the free assistance of an interpreter if he cannot understand or speak the language used in court.

   9   See Supreme Court (Hoge Raad der Nederlanden), 18 June 2004, *LJN* AU 5496 to be found on www.rechtspraak.nl. See also the The Hague Appellate Court Hof Den Haag), 14 March 2006, *LJN* AP 2846.

   10 The Working Party consisted of Ray Bull, Helen Baron, Gisli Gudjonsson, Sarah Hampson, Gina Rippon and Aldert Vrij.

and Klein, 1999).[11] Still, the most widespread use of the polygraph in Germany used to be in civil cases, mainly child custody disputes with allegations of sexual abuse of the children. In a recent ruling however, the Bundesgerichtshof put the outcomes of a polygraph test in these cases on par with those in criminal cases.[12]

In the Nordic countries, only Finland has used the polygraph on a relatively large scale. The Finnish National Bureau of Investigation (NBI) has used it in around 300 cases since 1995, mostly homicides and sexual crimes. The NBI is the only institution within the Finnish police using the polygraph, primarily to give direction to the investigation. In addition, the GKT has been used in about five cases to detect the location of a hidden body in a homicide case. The use of the polygraph at the NBI is managed by two detectives.[13] Even though the outcome of a test is not supposed to serve as evidence in court, evidence in Finland is also governed by the 'free evidence' system of presenting evidence in the courts we discussed above. This has resulted in occasional cases where the outcome of a polygraph test has been presented as evidence. At the time of writing, one case is under review by the Finnish Supreme Court (Korkein Oikeus). This procedure will likely set a precedent for future cases.

Norway and Sweden are only modest users of the polygraph. In Norway, it has been used in the pre-trial phase in at least three cases during the last 10 years. The admission to use polygraphs as an evidence gathering method for the trial itself was questioned however, and the Norwegian Supreme Court (Høysterett) rejected the use of polygraphs in 1996.[14] More recent cases have been met with the same scepticism and reference to this verdict. In one of the three cases, the defence made considerable efforts to convince the Appellate Court (Lagmannsrett) to accept polygraph testing as evidence. They failed, and the Court decided on traditional evidence and witness testimony only. However, the Norwegian evidence rules are also characterized by the 'free evidence' system. As such, the precedent set by the Høysterett does not prevent use in court because of evidential reasons, but because it violates the civil rights of the suspect. It could, the court argued, be an imperative for others (e.g. other suspected, victims, etc) as well and, as such, threatens civil rights and reflects an unhealthy pressure. In addition to criminal cases in Norway, the polygraph is also used in civil cases.[15]

In Sweden, the polygraph is not used on a regular basis either. It was used two or three times during the 1990s in cases where men were accused of molesting children. The results were offered as evidence by the defence, to prove that the suspect was innocent. In one of these cases, the court held a small hearing with one expert pro

---

11 Bundesgerichtshof, 10 February 1999 (3 *StR* 460/98; *NStZ-RR* 2000, 35).

12 See Bundesgerichtshof, 24 June 2003 (VI ZR 327/02).

13 The equipment was originally developed at the University of Jyväskylä by professor Karl Hagfors.

14 Høysterett (Supreme Court). Kjennelse (verdict). Rt-1990114 (343–96).

15 Sven Svebak, a university professor, reports that he, as far as he knows, is the only one conducting polygraph examinations in Norway. He conducted some 100 polygraph tests, almost exclusively in civil cases.

and one expert con the polygraph. The court decided to give very little weight to polygraph evidence, which had a precedential effect. Therefore, even though there is no formal ban and free examination of evidence, the use of the polygraph is still limited. In Denmark, the polygraph is not used at all. It has, however, also not been forbidden on statutory grounds or through precedents set in legal decisions of courts.

In Switzerland finally, the use of the polygraph is considered an unlawful means of investigation. In this, the Swiss follow Article 6 of the European Convention on Human Rights (see above). The courts interpret this in an manner that nobody can be forced – directly or indirectly – to accuse themselves, even if the suspect complies (Piquerez, 1987; Schmid, 1993).[16]

The Future

The search for a more accurate lie detection procedure continues. Many think that with the advancement of technology, polygraph tests will become more accurate. The review by the National Research Council, however, contradicts this idea. In their review, they plotted the accuracy of the selected polygraph studies against the year of publication (National Research Council, 2003, p. 346). If technological advancement would lead to an increased accuracy, a positive trend should be apparent. This was not the case. As we have seen earlier in the chapter, erroneous outcomes of a CQT can be the result of an unsuccessful pre-test interview, a problem that is not solved by technologically more sophisticated measuring devices. In other words, even the most sophisticated machine will not pick up an emotional state that is absent. In all, it led The National Research Council to conclude that 'Almost a century of research in scientific psychology and physiology provides little basis for the expectation that a polygraph test could have extremely high accuracy'.

Also relatively new are measures of brain activity, such as functional magnetic resonance imaging (fMRI) and electro encephalography (EEG). The idea is that these measures more directly tap into the process of deception. EEG, however, has not yet been shown to outperform the simple and cheaper skin conductance measure, while fMRI has not yet been shown even to be reliably able to detect deception in individual cases. Nonetheless, at the time of writing, at least two commercial companies offer fMRI-based lie detection tests, and one offers an EEG-based lie detection test. Even when these new technologies turn out to be highly accurate, they will be subjected to the same ethical and legal restraints as current polygraph tests.

---

16 Schweizerisches Bundesgericht, 26 April 1994, *BGE* 118 Ia, that can be found on http://www.oefre.unibe.ch/law/dfr/a1120031.html.

Conclusion

Lie detection by means of the polygraph is a form of applied psychology that should be handled with care. The different techniques each have their strengths, but also inherent weaknesses and dangers. In general, courts around Europe seem to be aware of that. Although many courts have rejected the results of a polygraph tests as evidence, due to the 'free evidence' system that governs evidence in most countries, this has almost never been a general ban. Moreover, besides serving as evidence, polygraph test outcomes are also used to direct police investigations, without ever reaching the courtroom. A general ban on polygraph testing might result in tossing the baby out with the bathwater. If supervised by research psychologists, polygraph testing, particularly the GKT, can serve as a valuable addition to the police's and courtroom's toolkit.

References

Abrams, S. and Abrams, J.B. (1993) *Polygraph Testing of the Paedophile* (Portland: Ryan Gwinner).

Ahlmeyer, S., Heil, P., McKee, B. and English, K. (2000) Impact of polygraph on admissions of victims and offences in adult sexual offenders. *Sexual Abuse: A Journal of Research and Treatment*, 12, pp. 123–138.

Ben-Shakhar, G. and Furedy, J.J. (1990) *Theories and Applications in the Detection Of Deception: A Psychophysiological and International Perspective* (New York: Springer).

Ben-Shakhar, G., Bar-Hillel, M. and Kremnitzer, M. (2002) Trial by polygraph: reconsidering the use of the guilty knowledge technique in court, *Law and Human Behavior*, 26, pp. 527–541.

Blackstone, W. (1882) *Commentaries on the Laws of England*, 3rd edn (London: Murray).

Blasingame, G.D. (1998) Suggested clinical uses of polygraphy in community-based sexual offender treatment programs, *Sexual Abuse: A Journal of Research and Treatment*, 10, pp. 37–45.

Bockstaele, M. (Ed.) (2001) *De Polygraaf* (Brussel: Politeia).

Boelhouwer, A.J.W., Merckelbach, H., van Koppen, P.J. and Verbaten, M.N. (1996) *Leugendetectie in Nederland* (Rapport aangeboden aan de minister van Justitie).

BPS Working Party (2004) *A Review of the Current Scientific Status and Fields of Application of Polygraph Deception Detection.* s.l. (British Psychological Society).

Branaman, T.F. and Gallagher, S.N. (2005) Polygraph testing in sex offender treatment: a review of limitations, *American Journal of Forensic Psychology*, 23, pp. 45–64.

British Psychological Society (1996) Report of the Working Group on the use of the polygraph in criminal investigation and personnel screening, *Bulletin of the British Psychological Society*, 39, pp. 81–94.

Burgsmüller, C. (2000) Das BGH-Urteil zu den Glaubhaftigkeitsgutachten: Eine späte Folge der sog. Wormser Strafverfahren vor dem Landgericht Mainz? *Praxis der Rechtspsychologie*, 10, pp. 48–59.

Carroll, J.D. (1991) Lie detection: lies and truths, in: R. Cochrane and D. Carroll (Eds) *Psychology and Social Issues: A Tutorial Test*, pp. 160–170 (London: Falmer).

Cross, T.P. and Saxe, L. (1992) A critique of the validity of polygraph testing in child abuse cases, *Journal of Child Sexual Abuse*, 1, pp. 19–33.

Cross, T.P. and Saxe, L. (2001) Polygraph testing and sexual abuse: the lure of the magic lasso, *Child Maltreatment*, 6, pp. 195–206.

Damaška, M.R. (1986) *The Faces of Justice and State Authority: A Comparative Approach to the Legal Process* (New Haven: Yale University Press).

Elaad, E. (1999) A comparative study of polygraph tests and other forensic methods, in D.V. Canter and L.J. Alison (Eds) *Interviewing and Deception*, pp. 211–231 (Aldershot: Ashgate).

Elaad, E. (2003) Is the inference rule of the 'control question polygraph technique' plausible? *Psychology, Crime, and Law*, 9, pp. 37–47.

Emerick, R.L. and Dutton, W.A. (1993) The effect of polygraphy on the self report of adolescent sex offender: Implications for risk assessment, *Annals of Sex Research*, 6, pp. 83–103.

English, K., Jones, L., Patrick, D. and Pasini-Hill, D. (2003) Sexual offender containment: use of the postconviction polygraph, *Annals of the New York Academy of Sciences*, 989, pp. 411–427.

Faller, K.C. (1997) The polygraph, its use in cases of alleged sexual abuse: an exploratory study, *Child Abuse and Neglect*, 21, pp. 993–1008.

Fiedler, K. (1999) Gutachterliche Stellungnahme zur wissenschaftlichen Grundlage der Lügen-detektion mithilfe sogenannter Polygraphentests, *Praxis der Rechtspsychologie*, 9, pp. 5–44.

Fiedler, K., Schmid, J. and Stahl, T. (2002) What is the current truth about polygraph lie detection, *Basic and Applied Social Psychology*, 24, pp. 313–324.

Furedy, J.J. and Heslegrave, R.J. (1991) The forensic use of the polygraph: a psychophysiological analysis of current trends and future prospects, in: J.R. Jennings, P.K. Ackles and M.G.H. Coles (Eds) *Advances in Psychophysiology*, Vol. 4, pp. 233–245 (London: Kingsley).

Grubin, D. (2002) The potential use of polygraphy in forensic psychiatry, *Criminal Behaviour and Mental Health*, 12, pp. S45–S53.

Grubin, D., Madsen, L., Parsons, S., Sosnowski, D. and Warberg, B. (2004) A prospective study of the impact of polygraphy on high-risk behaviors in adult sex offenders, *Sexual Abuse: A Journal of Research and Treatment*, 16, pp. 209–222.

Hanson, R.K., Morton, K.E. and Harris, A.J. (2003) Sexual offender recidivism risk: what we know and what we need to know, *Annals of the New York Academy of Sciences*, 989, pp. 154–166; discussion 236–146.

Heydon, J.D. (2004) *Cross on Evidence*, 8th edn (London: Butterworths).

Hira, S. and Furumitsu, I. (2002) Polygraphic examinations in Japan: application of the guilty knowledge test in forensic investigations, *International Journal of Police Science and Management*, 4, pp. 16–27.

Honts, C.R. and Amato, S.L. (2002) Countermeasures, in: M. Kleiner (Ed.) *Handbook of Polygraph Testing*, Vol. 251–264 (San Diego, CA: Academic).

Honts, C.R. and Perry, M.V. (1992) Polygraph admissibility: changes and challenges, *Law and Human Behavior*, 16, pp. 357–379.

Honts, C.R., Hodes, R.L. and Raskin, D.C. (1985) Effects of physical countermeasures on the physiological detection of deception, *Journal of Applied Psychology*, 70, pp. 177–187.

Honts, C.R., Devitt, M.K., Winbush, M. and Kircher, J.C. (1996) Mental and physical countermeasures reduce the accuracy of the concealed knowledge test, *Psychophysiology*, 33, pp. 84–92.

Iacono, W.G. (1991) Can we determine the accuracy of polygraph tests? in: J.R. Jennings, P.K. Ackles and M.G.H. Coles (Eds) *Advances in Psychophysiology*, Vol. 4, pp. 201–207 (London: Jessica Kingsley).

Iacono, W.G. and Lykken, D.T. (1997) The validity of the lie detector: two surveys of scientific opinion, *Journal of Applied Psychology*, 82, pp. 426–433.

Iacono, W.G. and Lykken, D.T. (1999) Update: the scientific status of research on polygraph techniques: the case against polygraph tests, in: D.L. Faigman, D.H. Kaye, M.J. Saks and J. Sanders (Eds) *Modern Scientific Evidence: The Law and Science of Expert Testimony*, Vol. 1, Pocket Part, pp. 174–184 (St. Paul, MI: West).

Iacono, W.G. and Patrick, C.J. (1997) Polygraphy and integrity testing, in: R. Rogers (Ed.) *Clinical Assessment of Malingering and Deception*, pp. 252–281 (New York: Guilford).

Lykken, D.T. (1960) The validity of the guilty knowledge technique: the effects of faking, *Journal of Applied Psychology*, 44, pp. 258–262.

Lykken, D.T. (1998) *A Tremor in the Blood: Uses and Abuses of the Lie Detector*, 2nd edn (New York: Plenum).

McGrath, G.J., Cumming, G. and Burchard, B.L. (2003) *Current Practices and Trends in Sexual Abuser Management: The Safer Society 2002 Nationwide Survey* (Brandon, VT: Safer Society Press).

Münsterberg, H. (1908) *On the Witness Stand: Essays on Psychology and Crime* (New York: Doubleday, Page).

Nakayama, M. (2002) Practical use of the concealed information test for criminal investigation in Japan, in: M. Kleiner (Ed.) *Handbook of Polygraph Testing*, pp. 49–86 (San Diego, CA: Academic).

National Research Council (2003) *The Polygraph and Lie Detection* (Washington, DC: National Academy Press. Committee to Review the Scientific Evidence on the Polygraph. Division of Behavioral and Social Sciences and Education).

Offe, H. (2001) Fallbericht: Polygraphentest im Familienverfahren, *Praxis der Rechtspsychologie*, 11, pp. 55–57.

Piquerez, G. (1987) *Précis de procédure pénale Suisse* (Lausanne: Payot).

Podlesny, J.A. (1993) Is the guilty knowledge polygraph technique applicable in criminal investigation? A review of FBI case records, *Crime Laboratory Digest*, 20, pp. 57–61.

Podlesny, J.A. (2003) A paucity of operable case facts restricts applicability of the guilty knowledge technique in FBI criminal polygraph examinations, *Forensic Science Communications*, 5.

Podlesny, J.A. and Raskin, D.C. (1977) Physiological measures and the detection of deception, *Psychological Bulletin*, 84, pp. 782–799.

Prentky, R.A., Lee, A.F.S., Knight, R.A. and Cerce, D. (1997) Recidivism rates among child molesters and rapists: a methodological analysis, *Law and Human Behavior*, 21, pp. 635–659.

Raskin, D.C. (1989) Polygraph techniques for the detection of deception, in: D.C. Raskin (Ed.) *Psychological Methods in Criminal Investigation and Evidence*, pp. 247–296 (New York: Springer).

Raskin, D.C. and Honts, C.R. (2002) The comparison question test, in: M. Kleiner (Ed.) *Handbook of Polygraph Testing*, pp. 96–110 (San Diego, CA: Academic).

Raskin, D.C. and Podlesny, J.A. (1979) Truth and deception: a reply to Lykken, *Psychological Bulletin*, 86, pp. 54–58.

Raskin, D.C., Honts, C.R. and Kircher, J.C. (1997) Polygraph tests: B. Scientific status, in: D.L. Faigman, D.H. Kaye, M.J. Saks and J. Sanders (Eds) *Modern Scientific Evidence: The Law and Science of Expert Testimony*, pp. 565–582 (St. Paul, MI: West).

Raskin, D.C., Honts, C.R., Amato, S.L. and Kircher, J.C. (1999) Update: the scientific status of research on polygraph techniques: the case for the admissibility of the results of polygraph examinations, in: D.L. Faigman, D.H. Kaye, M.J. Saks and J. Sanders (Eds) *Modern Scientific Evidence: The Law and Science of Expert Testimony*, Vol. 1, Pocket Part, pp. 160–174 (St. Paul, MI: West).

Reid, J.E. (1947) A revised questioning technique in lie detection tests, *Journal of Criminal Law and Criminology*, 37, pp. 542–563.

Roese, N.J. and Jamieson, D.W. (1993) Twenty years of bogus pipeline research: a critical review and analysis, *Psychological Bulletin*, 114, pp. 363–375.

Saxe, L. (1991) Lying: thoughts of an applied social psychologist, *American Psychologist*, 46, pp. 409–415.

Schmid, N. (1993) *Strafprozessrecht: Eine Einführung auf der Grundlage des Strafprozessrechtes des Kantons Zürich und des Bundes* (Zürich: Schulthess).

Steller, M. and Dahle, K.-P. (1999) Wissenschaftliches Gutachten: Grundlagen, Methoden und Anwendungs-probleme psychophysiologischer Aussage-

bzw. Täterschaftsbeurteilung ('Polygraphie', 'Lügendetektion') *Praxis der Rechtspsychologie*, 9, pp. 127–204.

Steller, M. and Volbregt, R. (1999) *Wissenschaftliches Gutachten: Forensisch-aussagepsychologische Begutachtung (Glaubwürdigkeitsbegutachtung)*.

Strong, J.W. (Ed.) (1999) *McCormick on Evidence* (St. Paul, MI: West).

Traest, P. (2001) Recente tendensen in het bewijsrecht in strafzaken, in: Vlaamse Conferentie der Balie van Gent (Ed.), *Straf recht?: Strafrecht* (Antwerpen: Maklu).

Undeutsch, U. and Klein, G. (1999) Wissenschaftliches Gutachten zum Beweiswert physiopsychologischer Untersuchungen, *Praxis der Rechtspsychologie*, 9, pp. 45–126.

van Koppen, P.J., Boelhouwer, A.J.W., Merckelbach, H. and Verbaten, M.N. (1996) *Leugendetectie in actie: Het gebruik van de polygraaf in de praktijk* (Leiden: Nederlands Studiecentrum Criminaliteit en Rechtshandhaving (NSCR). Rapport aangeboden aan de minister van Justitie).

Verhaegen, P. (2000) *De polygraaf en zijn potentiële plaats in het Belgisch strafrechtelijk bewijssysteem: Advies voor de heer Minister van Justitie en het College van Procureurs-generaal inzake het gebruik van de polygraaf in de Belgische strafrechtsprocedure* (Brussel: Ministerie van Justitie, Dienst voor Strafrechtelijk Beleid).

Volokh, A. (1997) *n* Guilty men. *University of Pennsylvania Law Review*, 146, pp. 173–211.

Ward, T., Hudson, S.M., Johnston, L. and Marshall, W.L. (1997) Cognitive distortions in sex offenders: an integrative review, *Clinical Psychology Review*, 17, pp. 479–507.

Werkgroep Leugendetectie (1993) *De leugendetector: Een verkennend onderzoek naar de mogelijkheden van de polygraaf* (Den Haag: Ministerie van Justitie).

Chapter 4

Eyewitness Research: Theory and Practice

Amina Memon

Evidence in criminal trials is often based upon eyewitness testimonies. However, the reconstructive nature of our memories means that an eyewitness's evidence cannot always be relied upon. In England, as many as one in five witnesses mistakenly identifies a volunteer at identity parades, despite warnings that the culprit may not be present (Wright and McDaid, 1996; Valentine *et al.*, 2003). The shooting of Jean Charles de Menezes at Stockwell Tube Station following the July 2005 London bombings provides a poignant example of how eyewitnesses can get it wrong. On the day Jean Charles was killed, he was described by eyewitnesses as suspicious, as having jumped over the ticket barrier and as wearing a bulky jacket ostensibly concealing a device. According to information gathered by the Independent Police Complaints Commission, Jean Charles was wearing a light shirt or jacket, walked though the barriers and only ran when he saw his train approaching (BBC News, 24 August 2005).

The introduction of DNA testing procedures have shed further light on this the problems associated with evidence based on eyewitness memory (www. innocenceproject.org). DNA analysis has been conducted on people who were convicted prior to the introduction of forensic DNA analysis in the 1990s. These tests have resulted in the exoneration of people who were actually innocent of the crime for which they were convicted in the USA. Scheck *et al.* (2000) describe 62 exoneration cases (eight of those convicted were sentenced to death). In 52 of these 62 cases the conviction was directly a result of evidence from an eyewitness who was mistaken. In the most recent case, Thomas Doswell was released in August 2005 after serving 19 years in prison for a crime of which he was innocent. In March 1986, a white woman was the victim of a rape by an African American male as she entered the hospital where she worked. The victim was shown a line-up of photographs the day after the attack. Doswell's was the only photo in the line-up that was marked with an 'R' and the police explained at trial that this was to represent that he had been previously charged with rape. The analysis of serum samples from a rape kit was inconclusive, so the jury who convicted Doswell relied heavily on the eyewitness identification from a faulty line-up. Also in August 2005, Luis Diaz was exonerated after serving 25 years for the 'Bird Road' rapes. Over 25 women were attacked in Florida and Diaz was arrested after a highly publicised investigation. Multiple victims described their attacker as weighing approximately 200 pounds and as between 6'0 and 6'2 inches in height. At the time, Diaz weighed 134 pounds and was 5'3 inches tall. He worked as a fry cook and so smelled heavily of onions, a detail no witnesses had mentioned. Five of the 14 victims identified Diaz from line-ups of photographs. A short time later, the victims were shown video line-ups from which several more identifications of Diaz were made with eight charges brought by the prosecution. The charges were consolidated in a single jury trial. There was no forensic evidence so the prosecution focused on the identifications. Diaz was found guilty of seven charges. DNA testing proved Diaz's innocence 26 years later.

Courts in most common law jurisdictions have acknowledged that there is a significant risk that identification evidence is unreliable, proposing that the circumstances under which eyewitnesses viewed the offender and made their identification should come under close scrutiny. For example, English law requires the judge to issue a caution to jury members to question the circumstances under which an eyewitness made their identification (R v Turnbull, 1976; see the chapter in this volume by Roberts and Ormerod). However, research shows that jurors do not heed such warnings (Kassin and Sommers, 1997) and there has been a great reluctance on the part of the courts to allow expert witnesses to testify about factors germane to the reliability of the eyewitnesses' identification of the accused (see Roberts and Ormerod's chapter). The chances are high that the courts will rule the expert evidence as inadmissible on the basis either that admitting such evidence offends against the common knowledge rule, that is, that eyewitness identification is a matter of common-sense and judges and jurors are not assisted by expert opinion. Warnings or instructions to jurors also undermine the validity of the claim that eyewitness identification is a matter of common-sense. Thus, there is a strong argument for experts to testify about factors affecting the reliability of eyewitness identification so that the trier of fact, be it a judge or a jury, can better assess the reliability of any identification evidence.

The current chapter examines whether research on the factors that influence the quality of evidence from eyewitnesses can inform police investigators and the courts about the reliability of witness evidence under different conditions.

Variables that Influence Eyewitness Accuracy

There are many reasons why errors in eyewitness evidence can occur. For example, a witness who has seen a crime take place from a considerable distance and late at night is less likely make an accurate identification of the perpetrator than a witness who has had more favourable viewing conditions. On the other hand, the witness may have made a wrong identification because the police conducted a line-up that was biased in some way.

In order to test eyewitness performance under various conditions, researchers have employed staged events, post-event manipulations and various types of identification procedures (see below). Experimental studies have been supplemented by a number of archival studies. A host of variables have been associated with an increase in mistaken identification. Wells and Loftus (2002) have suggested that a useful way of organising the research findings is to categorise the variables into those relating to witness characteristics (e.g. age, race), those relating to the witnessed event (e.g. length of exposure, presence of weapons), post-event factors (e.g. exposure to mugshot photographs, discussion with other witnesses), the nature of the identification task (e.g. the type of identification parade) and any information or feedback that a witness encounters post-identification (see Loftus, 2005, for a review). While the legal system has no control over witness characteristics and conditions at the time the event is witnessed, post-event influences can be controlled to some extent. Moreover, knowledge about the most effective procedure for eliciting an accurate identification decision from eyewitnesses can also be applied.

Witness Characteristics

One witness characteristic that could influence accuracy of identification is the race of the witness and the race of the person that they are trying to recognise. A witness is more likely to accurately recognise a person of their own race than a person from a different racial group (see Meissner and Brigham, 2001, for a meta-analysis of studies). Ninety percent of the experts we surveyed said the so-called cross-race identification effect (or own-race bias) was robust enough to present in court (Kassin *et al.*, 2001) and mock juror research suggests the layperson is insensitive to the effect (Abshire and Bornstein, 2003). The cross-race effect has been supported by archival research. Behrman and Davey (2001) in their analysis of 271 police cases in California found higher suspect identifications for own-race faces. Wright *et al.* (2003) conducted a field study of the cross-race effect in South Africa and England. In each country, they had a black or white male confederate approach either a black or white member of the public in a shopping centre to enquire if they had seen some jewellery that they had lost. A few minutes later, another confederate asked questions about the stranger and asked if they could identify him from a line-up. An own-race bias was found in response to questions about the target as well as the ability to identify accurately the target from the line-up. One hypothesis as to why the own-race bias occurs is a lack of contact and hence familiarity with other race facial features (Meissner and Brigham, 2001). More recently Meissner *et al.* (2005) have accumulated evidence to suggest that the cross-race effect occurs as a result of superior encoding-based processing of own-race faces. In other words, people encode more qualitative information about own-race faces, information that can be used when making subsequent identification attempts.

Another factor that can influence visual identification evidence is the age of the witness. The typical finding in laboratory studies of unfamiliar face recognition (the recognition of faces seen only once before) is that older adults (60–80 years) are more likely to make false alarms (Bartlett *et al.*, 1991). In order to examine the recognition performance in eyewitness identification situations, a series of studies comparing young (18–32 year-old) and older (60–80 year old) adults was conducted in Aberdeen and Dallas. Searcy *et al.* (1999) presented mock witnesses with a crime video followed by a line-up of photographs and asked them if the culprit (target) was present. While there were no differences in correct identification rates, older witnesses made more erroneous foil choices regardless of whether the target was present or absent in the line-up. The age-related increase in false identifications was replicated in subsequent studies (see Bartlett and Memon, 2006 for a review). One factor that may be responsible for the age-related increase in false alarms to faces that have not been seen before is that older adults rely on 'familiarity' as a basis for responding. Ageing is typically associated with a reduction in cognitive resources (Craik and Byrd, 1982) and an increased reliance on 'automatic' familiarity processes as opposed to a 'conscious' effortful recollection process (Jacoby, 1999). Accurate recollection of source information is critical in an eyewitness setting as illustrated in the section on post-event influences. Thus, older adults may rely more on non-analytic strategies such as 'availability' and 'fluency' when making identification (Bartlett *et al.*, 1991). Searcy *et al.* (2000) manipulated availability by presenting participants with a crime-relevant or irrelevant narrative shortly after young and older witnesses viewed a simulated crime and prior to a target-absent line-up (i.e. the perpetrator was not present in the line-up). As expected, false identification rates for older adults increased when they were presented with the crime-relevant narrative. Contrary to what one might expect, older adults who recalled more details about the culprit were actually *more* likely to make false identifications than younger adults.

Characteristics of the Event

A good illustration of the impact of situational variables on eyewitness memory comes from an appeal case that came before the high courts in Australia: *Dominican v. Queen* (1992). The accused was charged with attempted murder. The appeal case was based on appellant claims that the trial judge misdirected the jury on the issue of the identification of the gunman by failing to give specific warnings concerning various features of the evidence of an eyewitness to the shooting. There were a number of weaknesses in the identification evidence. At the time of the shooting, the witness claimed she did not know the appellant. Nearly nine months elapsed before she formally identified him from photographs that had been altered to show the appellant wearing a wig and a false moustache. By that time the appellant was a definite suspect, the witness had seen him on television on a number of occasions and allegedly in the vicinity of her home.

The conditions of witnessing were as follows for the witness in the *Dominican v. Queen* case. When she saw the gunman, he was some distance away. She was hiding behind another vehicle. He was leaning across the passenger's seat and he was disguised. Her opportunity to observe him was fleeting. Moreover, her first observation of the gunman took place after about 30 shots had been fired in her direction, after she had seen her husband shot through the hand, and after her husband had physically pushed her head down. As a result of the shooting, she suffered shock. The direction the judge gave to the jury was as follows:

> His Honour told the jury that '(s)udden and unexpected acts of violence such as Mrs F described in this case, can affect people caught up in the events in different ways. The terror of the occasion can serve to impress indelibly on the minds of some people the features of anyone they see involved in it. With other people the effect may be to obscure their judgment and their later recollection.'

The judge's directions were deemed inadequate in *Dominican v. Queen* the appeal was allowed, the conviction quashed and a new trial ordered.

If an expert on eyewitness testimony had been permitted to give evidence in this case, what factors could they have drawn the jury's attention to? A review of studies that have examined the effect of stress on eyewitness memory leads to the conclusion that heightened stress has a detrimental effect on the ability to recognise a perpetrator as well as to recall details of the crime (Deffenbacher *et al.*, 2004).

A good illustration of the effect of emotional arousal at the time of witnessing is the research on the so-called weapon-focus effect. A crime is typically classed as emotionally arousing on the basis of the presence of emotional stimuli at the crime scene (e.g. a gun). Research on 'weapon focus' has found that memory for some details (e.g. the face) is impaired but memory for other details (e.g. a weapon) is enhanced (see Steblay, 1992, for a meta-analysis of studies). There are two explanations for the weapon focus effect: (i) that it increases level of arousal in the witness and (ii) it focuses attention on the weapon such that other more central details are not attended to (see also Christianson, 1992). The effects were convincingly shown by Maass and Köhnken (1989). Participants were approached by an experimenter who was either holding at hip level either a syringe or a pen. Later on, the participants were asked to identify the experimenter in a target-absent line-up and to recall details about the experimenter's face and hand. Twice as many participants in the syringe-present condition (64%) than in the pen-present condition (33%) made a false identification in the line-up task. Moreover, the more fear that participants had self-reported about injections prior to the study, the more hand cues and the fewer facial cues they accurately recalled.

More recently, researchers have critiqued the method used to manipulate emotional arousal (Laney *et al.*, 2003; 2004). Laney *et al.* argue that prior studies have manipulated emotion by using a salient visual stimulus that could serve as an attention magnet (e.g. showing people blood, injuries, a weapon and so on). They argue a more naturalistic manipulation of arousal is to examine witness involvement and empathy with an unfolding event. Laney *et al.* have examined how participants recall events that involve arousal that is induced thematically (e.g. by using a script that accompanies the stimulus that increases empathy with the victim). These data show that emotional arousal measured this way improves memory for all aspects of the emotional event.

How do the laboratory studies compare with actual cases? An archival study a single shooting incident in Canada involving 21 witnesses (of which 13 were corroborated) noted that eyewitnesses gave detailed and accurate information about actions and objects. However, there were numerous errors in person descriptions. The estimates of the height, weight and age of the offender had only a 50–50 chance of being correct. At the initial interview, three out of the 13 witnesses either were unable to describe or wrongly described hair colour. Four out of the 13 were unable to describe or wrongly described hairstyle. In an analysis of capital cases of rape and robbery in Germany, Sporer (1992a) examined the data from 100 witnesses. Again, the quality of person descriptions were poor and only 30% of witnesses described the face of the perpetrator. Interestingly, the quality and pattern of descriptions found in this archival study resembled those of a staged event study in which a confederate interrupted a lecture to remove a slide projector (Sporer, 1992b). These findings suggest that the stress associated with being a victim or witness of a rape/ robbery does not increase errors in person descriptions any more than witnessing an innocuous staged event. Person descriptions tend to be rather poor in both cases (see also Meissner *et al.* in press).

Finally, a recent archival study reports null effects of stress on the accuracy and completeness of person descriptions (Wagstaff *et al.*, 2003) questioning the generalisability of some laboratory studies.

Post-event Influences

A commonly-used procedure to test the visual identification ability of an eyewitness early in the investigative process is to show the witness a mugshot of a suspect or to ask the witness to review a book of photographs. This can range from a dozen or so photographs (see Memon *et al.*, 2002) to hundreds of photographs (Dysart *et al.*, 2001). One of the problems of exposing witnesses to mugshots is that they may later be asked to identify the suspect at a formal identification parade. There are two types of biases that could ensue. The first is a source monitoring error – a face appears familiar because of a prior encounter. The familiarity from seeing the face in a mugshot photo is incorrectly attributed to the crime context. Alternatively, if a face is selected from a mugshot album and the same face selected again in the formal identification parade, what might be occurring is what Dysart *et al.* (2001) refer to as the commitment effect (a social bias to choose the same face as chosen before). Memon *et al.* (2002) found that any choice made from mugshots shown earlier (even if it wasn't the suspect that was chosen) increased the tendency for witnesses to make a choice from a subsequent identification parade. This could have been a problem in the case of Luis Diaz discussed at the start of this chapter, where several witnesses viewed photographs followed by multiple identification parades. Another real-world example of the potential dangers of mugshot-induced biases comes from the case of Gary Graham, a convicted murderer whose case relied primarily on eyewitness evidence. Gary was identified from a live parade a day after the witness had been exposed to his face in a mugshot album. Now the witness may have been accurate, but we will never know for certain because Gary was executed in Texas in 2000 (see Doyle, 2005, for further details).

Identification Procedures

A show-up is when a single photograph of a suspect is presented to the witness for identification with the option to identify the person as the perpetrator or not. This form of identification has been described as 'suggestive' (Malpass and Devine, 1984) and 'biased' (Behrman and Davey, 2001). The witness is be placed under added pressure to make an identification because they believe the police have evidence that the person in the photo is the culprit; or because they believe the show-up is the only opportunity they will have to identify the perpetrator. These suggestive mechanisms hold equally for the similar practice of a visual identification of the perpetrator – standing in the dock of a courtroom (Bromby and Memon, 2005, Roberts and Ormerod's chapter in this book). A recent field study of 271 actual cases using files from the Sacramento Police Department reported higher rates of suspect identification from show-ups than photographic line-ups (Behrman and Davey, 2001). One of the consequences of using a show-up therefore is that it increases a bias to choose a suspect from an identity parade or line-up.

An analysis of multiple studies (Steblay *et al.*, 2003) comparing identification accuracy in show-ups and line-ups reports no differences in rates of correct identifications (when the real perpetrator is present in a line-up). In a situation where the perpetrator is not in the line-up or is not the person in the show-up (i.e. in the eventuality that the police have arrested an innocent person) show-ups can increase false identifications. In other words, show-ups are inferior to photo-lineups when it comes to protecting the innocent. Several studies have reported an increase in false identifications when show-ups are used (Dekle *et al.* 1996; Lindsay *et al.* 1997; Yarmey *et al.*, 1996). Moreover, there are some conditions (e.g. alcohol intoxication) under which witnesses are even more likely to make false identifications from show-ups (Dysart *et al.*, 2002).

In Scotland, in-court identifications (also referred to as dock identifications) are seen as a necessary element to establishing evidence of eyewitness identifications. A recent case, *Holland v. HMA*, identifies the intrinsic problems associated with pre-trial identification and subsequent dock identifications at the trial. The accused, in this case, was charged with two counts of armed robbery and assault at a private dwelling and at a newsagent. Eyewitness testimony was the sole form of identification evidence led at the trial. There were several witnesses. One witness (Mr L) was blind in one eye and could not see well out of the other. Two of the other witnesses (Miss G and Mr S) had identified the accused from police photographs but selected two foils from the live parade. Miss G's son had identified the accused from the live parade but there was some dispute as to whether this was an identification or a statement that the accused resembled the robber. During the trial, the Crown led no evidence about the identification parades but relied solely upon Miss G and her son who identified the accused in the dock. No identification evidence from Mr L was led. An air pistol found in the accused's flat at the time of the arrest was identified by all of the above eyewitnesses as 'similar in appearance' to that used in the robbery. In 2005, the Judicial Committee of the Privy council considered the *Holland* case and accepted that identification parades offer safeguards that are not available when a witness is asked to identify the accused in court. They conviction was overturned but the principle of dock identification was upheld.

In the *Holland* case, dock identifications of the accused were corroborated by the description of the weapon used and the two crimes associated, using the *Moorov* Principle (see Duff, 2002). Essentially, the principle permits single sources of evidence, such as one eyewitness or one fingerprint to be corroborated by evidence from other sources such as a second eyewitness. However, corroborating evidence from two witnesses is of little value unless it has been obtained independently and the procedures are not flawed (see Walker, 1999 for examples).

Identifications in the Real World

A typical identification parade consists of one suspect and known non-suspects (foils). The witness's task is to decide if one of the people in the line-up is the culprit.

Slater (1994) recorded the outcome of identification attempts by 843 witnesses in England who inspected 302 live line-ups. Suspects were identified by 36% of witnesses, foils were identified by 22%, and 42% of witnesses made no positive identification. Also in England, Wright and McDaid (1996) examined the outcome of 616 live line-ups involving 1561 witnesses, the suspect was identified by 39%, a foil by 20 with 41% making no identification. Valentine *et al.* (2003) analysed data from 640 attempts to identify the perpetrator from 314 line-ups conducted by the Metropolitan Police (London), recording characteristics of the victim, suspect, witness's viewing condition and type of crime. Consistent with some of the laboratory findings, data analysis revealed a suspect is more likely to be identified by younger witnesses (under 30 years), that white European suspects (as opposed to Afro-Caribbean) are more often recognised and that witnesses who gave a detailed description had viewed the suspect for more than one minute. The witnesses who gave a detailed description also made their choice more speedily from the line-up and made more identifications of the suspect. These findings are not consistent with the results of laboratory studies, which typically find no relationship between person description quality and identification performance (see Meissner *et al.* in press, for a review).

As pointed out by Valentine *et al.* the identity of the suspect and culprit are not necessarily the same in these field studies, as investigators cannot be certain how many line-ups contain the culprit. More recently, Behrman and Richards (2005) examined suspect and foil identifications (a total of 461 identification attempts from six-person line-ups) from the Behrman and Davey archival study to see if any criteria could be used to discriminate the two types of identifications. Confidence was the most effective discriminator. In those cases that were corroborated by extrinsic evidence, 43% of the suspect identifications were made with high confidence while only 10% of the foil identifications were made with high confidence.

Summary

Mistaken identification continues to be a significant source of wrongful convictions. Laboratory and archival studies have demonstrated the inaccuracy of eyewitness memory and the dangers of relying on eyewitness identification evidence. Importantly, the studies have highlighted the conditions under which eyewitness evidence is most likely to be unreliable and procedures that can be implemented to reduce eyewitness error. The time has now come for the courts to draw upon this research base when evaluating evidence from eyewitnesses.

References

Abshire, J. and Bornstein, B. (2003) Juror sensitivity to the cross-race effect, *Law and Human Behaviour*, 27, pp. 471–480.

Alexander v The Queen (1981) CLR 395.

Bartlett, J.C. and Memon, A. (2006) Eyewitness memory in young and older adults, in R. Lindsay, R. Ross, D. Read and M. Toglia (Eds) *Handbook of Eyewitness Psychology: Memory for People*, Vol. 2, pp. 309–338 (Mahwah, NJ: Lawrence Erlbaum and Associates).

Bartlett, J.C., Strater, L. and Fulton, A. (1991) False recency and false fame of faces in young adulthood and old age, *Memory & Cognition*, 19, pp. 177–188.

Behrman, B. and Davey, S. (2001) Eyewitness identification in actual criminal cases: an archival analysis, *Law and Human Behaviour*, 25, pp. 475–491.

Behrman, B. and Richards R. (2005) Suspect/foil identifications in actual crimes and in the laboratory: a reality monitoring analysis, *Law and Human Behavior*, 29, pp. 279–301.

Brigham, J.C. and Bothwell, R. (1983) The ability of prospective jurors to estimate the accuracy of eyewitness identifications, *Law and Human Behaviour*, 7, pp. 19–30.

Bromby, M. and Memon, A. (2005) Scots Law and the issue of dock identification. Manuscript submitted for publication.

Christianson, S.-A. (1992) Emotional stress and eyewitness memory: a critical review, *Psychological Bulletin*, 112, 284–309.

Clark, S. and Tunnicliff, J. (2001) Selecting foils in eyewitness identification experiments: experimental control and real world simulation, *Law and Human Behaviour*, 25, pp. 199–216.

Craig v The King (1933) 49 CLR 429.

Craik, F.I.M. and Byrd, M. (1982). Aging and cognitive deficits: the role of attentional resources, in: F.I.M. Craik and S. Trehub (Eds) *Aging and Cognitive Processes*, pp. 191–211 (New York: Plenum).

Davies v The King (1937) 57 CLR 170.

Dekle, D.J., Beale, C., Elliot, R. and Huneycutt, D. (1996) Children as witnesses: a comparison of lineups vs. showup methods, *Applied Cognitive Psychology*, 10, pp. 1–12.

Deffenbacher, K.A., Bornstein, B.H, Penrod, S.D. and McGorty E.K. (2004) A meta-analytic review of the effects of high stress on eyewitness memory, *Law and Human Behaviour*, 28, pp. 687–706.

Devenport, J., Penrod, S. and Cutler, B. (1997) Eyewitness identification evidence: evaluating commonsense evaluations, *Psychology, Public Policy and Law*, 3, pp. 338–361.

Dominican v The Queen (1992) 173 CLR 555 f.c. 92/011.

Doyle, J. (2005) *True Witness: Cops, Courts, Science and the Battle Against Misidentification* (Palgrave Macmillan).

Duff, P. (2002) Towards a unified theory of 'similar facts evidence' in Scots Law: relevance, fairness and the reinterpretation of Moorov, *Juridical Review*, pp. 143–181.

Dysart, J.E., Lindsay, R.C.L., MacDonald, T.K. and Wicke, C. (2002) The intoxicated witness: effects of alcohol on identification accuracy, *Journal of Applied Psychology*, 87, pp. 170–175.

Dysart, J., Lindsay, R.C.L., Hammond, R. and Dupuis, P. (2001) Mug shot exposure prior to lineup identification: interference, transference and commitment effects, *Journal of Applied Psychology*, 86(6), pp. 1280–1284.

Ellison, K.W. and Buckhout, R. (1981) *Psychology and Criminal Justice* (New York: Harper and Row).

Fox, S. and Walters, H. (1986) The impact of general versus specific eyewitness testimony and eyewitness confidence upon mock juror judgement, *Law and Human Behaviour*, 10, pp. 215–228.

Garrioch, L. and Brimacombe, E. (2001) Lineup administrators' expectations: their impact on eyewitness confidence, *Law and Human Behaviour*, 25, pp. 299–315.

Garry, M. and Loftus, E.F., Brown, S.W. and DuBreuil, S.C. (1997) Womb with a view: beliefs about memory, repression and memory-recovery, in: D.G. Payne and F.G. Conrad (Eds) *Intersections in Basic and Applied Memory Research*, pp. 233–236 (Hillsdale, NJ: Lawrence Erlbaum).

Holland v HM Advocate, Privy Council DRA No. 1 of 2004.

Holland v. HM Advocate (2004) S.L.T. 762.

Hulse, L., Allan, K, Memon, A. and Read, J.D. (2005) Investigating post-stimulus elaboration as a mechanism for emotional arousal effects on memory. Manuscript submitted for publication.

Jacoby, L.L. (1999) Ironic effects of repetition: measuring age-related differences in memory, *Journal of Experimental Psychology: Learning, Memory and Cognition*, 25, pp. 3–22.

Kassin and Sommers (1997) Inadmissible testimony, instructions to disregard, and the jury: Substantive versus procedural considerations, *Personality and Social Psychology Bulletin*, 23, pp. 1046–1054.

Kassin, S., Tubb, A., Hosch, H.M. and Memon, A. (2001) On the 'general acceptance' of eyewitness testimony research: a new survey of experts, *American Psychologist*, 56, pp. 405–416.

Laney, C., Heuer, F. and Reisberg, D. (2003) Thematically-induced arousal in naturally-occurring emotional memories, *Applied Cognitive Psychology*, 17, pp. 995–1004.

Laney, C., Campbell, H.V., Heuer, F. and Reisberg, D. (2004) Memory for thematically arousing events, *Memory and Cognition*, 32, pp. 1149–1159.

Loftus, E. (1980) The impact of expert psychological testimony on the unreliability of eyewitness identification, *Journal of Applied Psychology*, 65, pp. 9–15.

Loftus, E. (2005) Planting information in the human mind: a 30-year investigation of the malleability of memory, *Learning & Memory*, 12, pp. 361–366.

Lindsay, R.C.L., Pozzulo, J.D., Craig, W., Lee, K. and Corber, S. (1997) Simultaneous lineups, and showups: eyewitness identification decisions of adults and children, *Law and Human Behaviour*, 21(4), pp. 391–404.

Lindsay, R.C.L., Nosworthy, G.L, Martin, R. and Martynuck, C. (1994) Using mugshots to find suspects, *Journal of Applied Psychology*, 79, pp. 121–130.

Lindsay, R.C.L., Wallbridge, H. and Drennan, D. (1987) Do the clothes make the man? An exploration of the effect of lineup attire on eyewitness identification accuracy, *Canadian Journal of Behavioral Science*, 19, pp. 463–447.

Maass, A. and Köhnken, G. (1989) Eyewitness identification: simulating the 'weapon effect', *Law and Human Behaviour*, 13, pp. 397–408.

Maass, A., Brigham, J.C. and West, S. (1985) Testifying on eyewitness reliability: expert advice is not always persuasive, *Journal of Applied Social Psychology*, 15, pp. 207–229.

Malpass, R.S. and Devine, P.G. (1984) Research on suggestion in lineups and photospreads, in G.L. Wells and E.F. Loftus (Eds) *Eyewitness Testimony: Psychological Perspectives*, pp. 64–91 (New York: Cambridge University Press).

Meissner, C.A., Brigham, J. and Butz, D. (2005) Memory for own and other-race faces: a dual-process approach, *Applied Cognitive Psychology*, 19, pp. 545–567.

Meissner, C.A., Sporer, S. and Schooler, J. (in press) Person descriptions as eyewitness evidence, in: R. Lindsay *et al.* (Eds) *Handbook of Eyewitness Psychology* (Lawrence Erlbaum & Associates).

Meissner, C.A. and Brigham, J.C. (2001) Thirty years of investigating the own-race bias in memory for faces: a meta-analytic review, *Psychology, Public Policy, & Law*, 7, pp. 3–35.

Memon, A., Gabbert, F. and Hope, L. (2004) The ageing eyewitness, in: J. Adler (Eds) *Forensic Psychology: Debates, Concepts and Practice* (Willan, Forensic Psychology Series).

Memon, A., Hope, L., Bartlett, J. and Bull, R. (2002) Eyewitness recognition errors:

the effects of mugshot viewing and choosing in young and old adults, *Memory and Cognition*, 30, pp. 1219–1227.

Memon, A., Vrij, A. and Bull, R. (2003) *Psychology & Law: Truthfulness, Accuracy and Credibility of Victims, Witnesses and Suspects*, 2nd edn (Chichester: Wiley).

Neil v. Biggers, 409 us 188 (1972).

Phillips, M., McAuliff, B., Kovera, M. and Cutler, B. (1999) Double-blind photoarray administration as a safeguard against investigator bias, *Journal of Applied Psychology*, 84, pp. 940–951.

Pike, G., Brace, N. and Kynan, S. (2002) *The Visual Identification of Suspects: Procedures and Practice*. Home Office, Briefing Note, 2/02.

Pryke, S. and Lindsay, R.C.L. (2001) Multiple independent identification decisions: a radical alternative to current lineup methods. Unpublished Ph.D. thesis, Queen's University, Kingston, Ontario, Canada.

Pryke, S., Lindsay, R.C.L., Dysart, J.E. and Dupuis, P. (2004) Multiple independent identification decisions: a method of calibrating eyewitness identifications, *Journal of Applied Psychology*, 89(1), pp. 73–84.

Rosenthal, R. (1976). *Experimenter Effects in Behavioral Research* (New York: Irvington Press).

R v Turnbull (Launcelot) (1977) 65 Cr App R 242.

Scheck, B. Nuefeld, P. and Dwyer, J. (2000) *Actual Innocence* (New York: Random House).

Searcy, J.H., Bartlett, J.C. and Memon, A. (1999) Age differences in accuracy and choosing in eyewitness identification and face recognition, *Memory and Cognition*, 27, pp. 538–552.

Searcy, J.H., Bartlett, J.C. and Memon, A. (2000) Relationship of availability, lineup conditions and individual differences to false identification by young and older eyewitnesses, *Legal and Criminological Psychology*, 5(2), pp. 219–236

Slater, A. (1994) Identification parades: a scientific evaluation, *Police Research Awards Scheme* (Home Office).

Shaw, J., Garcia, L. and McClure, K. (1999) A lay perspective of the accuracy of eyewitness testimony, *Journal of Applied Social Psychology*, 29, pp. 52–71.

Sporer, S.L. (1992a) An archival analysis of person descriptions. Paper presented at the Biennial Meeting of the American Psychology-Law Society in San Diego, California.

Sporer, S.L. (1992b) Post-dicting eyewitness accuracy: confidence and decision times and person descriptions of choosers and non-choosers, *European Journal of Social Psychology*, 22, pp. 157–180.

Steblay, N.M. (1992) A meta-analytic review of the weapon focus effect, *Law and Human Behaviour*, 16, pp. 413–424.

Steblay, N., Dysart, J., Fulero, S. and Lindsay, R.C.L. (2003) Eyewitness accuracy rates in police showup and lineup presentations: a meta-analytic comparison, *Law and Human Behaviour*, 27, pp. 523–540.

Thomson, D.M., Robertson, S.L. and Vogt, R. (1982) Person recognition: the effects of context, *Human Learning*, 1, pp. 137–154.

Tulving, E. and Thomson, D.M. (1973) Encoding specificity and retrieval processes in episodic memory, *Psychological Review*, 80, pp. 352–373.

Valentine, T. Pickering, A. and Darling, S. (2003) Characteristics of eyewitness identification that predict the outcome of real lineups, *Applied Cognitive Psychology*, 17, pp. 969–993.

Wagstaff, G.F., MacVeigh, J., Boston, R., Scott, L., Brunas-Wagstaff, J. and Cole, J. (2003) Can laboratory findings on eyewitness testimony be generalised to the real world? An archival analysis of the influence of violence, weapon presence and age on eyewitness accuracy, *Journal of Psychology: Interdisciplinary and Applied*, 137, pp. 17–28.

Walker, C. (1999) Miscarriages of justice in Scotland, in: C. Walker and K. Starmer (Eds) *Miscarriages of Justice: A Review of Justice in Error*, pp. 323–353 (London: Blackstone).

Wells, G.L., Lindsay, R. and Tousignant, J. (1980) Effects of expert psychological advice on human performance in judging the validity of eyewitness testimony, *Law and Human Behaviour*, 4, pp. 275–285.

Wells, G.L. and Loftus, E.F. (2002) Eyewitness memory for people and events, in: A. Goldstein (Ed.) *Comprehensive Handbook of Psychology, Volume 11, Forensic Psychology* (New York: Wiley).

Wells, G.L., Small, L., Penrod, S., Malpass, R.S., Fulero, S.M. and Brimacombe, C.A.E. (1998) Eyewitness identification procedures: recommendations for lineups and photospreads, *Law and Human Behaviour*, 22, pp. 603–647.

Wise, R.A. and Safer, M.A. (2004) What U.S. judges know and belief about eyewitness testimony, *Applied Cognitive Psychology*, 18, pp. 427–444.

Wright, D.B. and McDaid, A.T. (1996) Comparing system and estimator variables using data from real lineups, *Applied Cognitive Psychology*, 10, pp. 75–84.

Wright, D.B., Boyd, C.E. and Tredoux, C.G. (2003) Inter-racial contact and the own-race bias for face recognition in South Africa and England, *Applied Cognitive Psychology*, 17, pp. 365–373.

Yarmey, A.D., Yarmey, M.J., Yarmey, A.L. (1996) Accuracy of eyewitness identifications in showups and lineups, *Law and Human Behaviour*, 20(4), pp. 459–477.

Yuille, J.C. and Cutshall, J.L. (1986) A case study of eyewitness memory of a crime, *Journal of Applied Psychology*, 71, pp. 291–301.

Chapter 5

Identification in Court

Andrew Roberts and David Ormerod

Numerous high-profile miscarriages of justice attest to the dangers attending attempts by eyewitnesses to identify other persons (see for example Connors *et al.*, 1996). Those dangers have long been acknowledged by legal systems, and various measures intended to diminish the risk of mistaken identification evidence have been adopted in most criminal justice systems. In many instances, as in England, these safeguards have been informed by law reform agencies' reviews (Devlin Committee, 1976; Law Commission of New Zealand, 1999; Australian Law Reform Commission, 1985; 1987; Scottish Home and Health Department, 1978; Brooks, 1983). While the focus of this chapter is on English criminal procedure, many issues discussed will be common to other jurisdictions.

The title of this chapter might suggest that its scope is limited to events that occur in the courtroom. Where a defendant denies being the person who committed the offences charged, the issue is indeed one for the tribunal fact – either a jury or magistrate. In this sense, disputes as to identification are matters that are always determined 'in court'. However, the information that is proffered at trial in the form of identification evidence will, in the pre-trial stage of proceedings, have been subject to a number of processes or procedures, involving various actors, including police officers, witnesses, defence counsel, prosecutors (see Roberts, 2006).

Any examination of the adequacy of legal safeguards against mistaken identification must be set in a broad procedural context, which extends from the point at which the eyewitness is first drawn into the legal process through to the manner in which the appellate courts' review the safety of any conviction based on disputed identification evidence. It is not possible, within the confines of this chapter, to examine all of this ground. What we offer is a concise account of the deficiencies of the process of procuring identification in the courtroom and of trial-centred safeguards against the risk of wrongful conviction on the basis of mistaken identification. We discuss the relative importance of pre-trial procedures in the context a broad framework of interrelated safeguards.

Identification in Court: The Shortcomings of Trial Proceedings as a Means of Procuring and Scrutinising Identification Evidence

Where a witness has identified an accused in an out-of-court procedure, at an identification parade for example, as a matter of formality the identification should subsequently be verified in court to ensure that the accused is the person to whom the charges relate. However, a process whereby the accused is identified for the first time in the dock in court (a 'dock-identification') is subject to long-standing judicial disapproval (see *R v Cartwright*, 1914), which is hardly surprising given that it is inherently suggestive. Reporting on its review of eyewitness identification evidence in England, the Devlin Committee noted that 'the root of all objections to dock-identification is that it comes as an answer to what is, in effect, if not form, a leading question, that is, a question put in a way which suggests the answer that is expected' (para. 4.99). It has been asserted (Heydon, 2004, p. 84) that a dock identification is of no probative value as 'circumstances conspire to compel the witness to identify the accused in the dock' (*Alexander v R* 1981, p. 427). At the time of writing, the Australian Law Reform Commission ('ALRC') (2005) is undertaking a review of legislation in that jurisdiction, including the issue of whether in-court identifications ought to be prohibited. The position across many jurisdictions is that, although the courts recognise the dangers of, and disapprove of, dock-identification evidence, they remain possible.

Dock Identifications

The trial is traditionally considered the climactic centrepiece of the adversarial criminal process (Damaska, 1997). Although subject to significant qualification, the general principle is that evidence should be tendered to the court through live testimony and be based on each witness's personal recollection of events (see Amina Memon's chapter in this book). Presumptively, this enables the jury or magistrates to assess the reliability of the evidence. While in-court verification of the identification of the accused occurs as a formality, witness testimony regarding identification usually also relates to some previous out-of-court identification. Under this general principle, the in-court verification would be considered the main evidence of identification, with the pre-trial identification being merely a previous consistent statement providing support for the in-court identification. However, it has been suggested that because of the special character of identification evidence, this approach ought to be reversed, so that any out-of-court identification ought to be treated as the principal identification with the subsequent in-court identification serving merely to confirm the accused as the person identified earlier (ALRC, 1985).

If, as the ALRC suggests, in-court identification ought to be regarded merely as confirmation of a principal out-of-court identification, and thereby contingent upon one having occurred, dock-identifications ought not to be permitted. However, in the UK at least, it is clear that a dock-identification is not dependent on the witness having identified the accused at a pre-trial identification parade (line-up). A recent example in Scots law is *Holland v HM Advocate* (see Bromby and Memon, forthcoming). The appellant had been convicted of two counts of robbery and one of possession of an air pistol, arising from separate incidents. Both victims had picked out the appellant from police mugshots. At subsequent identification parades both victims picked out foils, while the first victim's son, having seen the culprits fleeing the scene of the first robbery, identified the appellant. After that identification parade the first victim had been told by police that she 'hadn't done too well'. Subsequently, notwithstanding the failure of both victims to identify Holland at identification parades, the trial judge permitted them both to identify him in the dock. Having been convicted on all counts, Holland appealed on the grounds that the dock-identification was so unfair and unreliable that it was incompatible with his right to a fair trial guaranteed under Article 6 of the European Convention on Human Rights (ECHR). The appellate court found that, exceptionally, a trial judge might conclude that a dock-identification would inevitably render the trial unfair, but the suspect's right to a fair trial would not normally prohibit such evidence. The court specified two factors underpinning its conclusion that Holland did receive a fair trial; (i) that he had been legally represented, and (ii) that his legal representative had been able to cross-examine the witnesses and address the jury on the weaknesses of the evidence.

The judgment is notable in a number of respects. First, although this was a case before a high level appellate court dealing with matters of considerable importance on the issue of eyewitness identification, no reference was made to the established body of psychological research. The second is the court's confidence that cross-examination and the advocate's opportunity to address the jury are sufficient to counterbalance any unfairness in permitting a dock-identification. Although the court referred to the Devlin Committee Report, it did so rather selectively; no reference was made, for example, to the Committee's observations on the inadequacies of the traditional means of assessing the reliability of evidence at trial:

> Our own view is that identification ought to be specially regarded by the law simply because it is evidence of a special character in that its reliability is exceptionally difficult to assess. It is impervious to the usual tests. The two ways of testing a witness are by the nature of his story – is it probable and coherent? – and by his demeanour – does he appear to be honest and reliable? ...in identification evidence there is no story; the issues rests on a single piece of observation ... Demeanour in general is quite useless. The capacity to memorise faces differs enormously from one man to another, but there is no way of finding out in the witness box how much of it the witness has got ... If a man thinks he is a good memoriser and in fact is not, that fact will not show itself in his demeanour.
>
> (Devlin Report 1976, para 4.25)

This raises the broader question of the adequacy of trial mechanisms for evaluating the accuracy of eyewitness identification carried out prior to trial.

Memory, Confidence, and the Sub-Optimal Forensic Environment of the Trial

As the Devlin Committee emphasised, cross-examination alone cannot be relied upon as a tool for uncovering unreliable identification. Cross-examination is ineffective in this respect because the trial will take place months after the events with which it is concerned, and the witness's memory of events may have deteriorated or have been distorted over this period. Obviously, there is a risk with any relevant information that it will be lost as a consequence of such deterioration, and this makes the fact-finding process more difficult. However, in the case of eyewitness identification evidence, there is a more acute challenge to adjudicative accuracy because of the greater risk of contamination and the confidence with which such evidence is presented to the court by an honest witness (see Amina Memon's chapter in this book).

Prior to trial, the witness will typically have recounted his or her information on numerous occasions both in informal conversations and in interviews with police and lawyers (Twining, 1990). However, these encounters will not necessarily involve a one-way flow of information from the witness on relevant matters (Roberts, 2004). Police officers dealing with the eyewitness might, variously or cumulatively, have seen the suspect; spoken to other witnesses who have provided information about the event and offender; formed their own views as to the guilt of the suspect; spoken to other officers who have done either of these things, and so on. Police encounters with witnesses may well be necessary during the course of an investigation, nevertheless, they give rise to the risk that information communicated to the witness will later be recalled by him or her erroneously as having been perceived during observation of the alleged crime. The potential for cross-pollination of inaccurate information, the drawing of false inferences by a witness, and the resultant risk of error is manifest (see Amina Memon's chapter). Furthermore, interactions with others which lend support to a witness's recollection of the events might (unjustifiably) increase his or her confidence in the accuracy of that recollection.

The potential risks of the eyewitness account being corrupted are not restricted to encounters between witnesses and police. Conversations with lawyers who might have seen statements made by other witnesses, or with friends and relatives who might have heard rumours about what had happened and who the culprit might be all increase the risk that the witness's subsequent recollection of events will be coloured by (mis)information acquired from others. As the time between the incident and the trial grows, so the likelihood of such interactions occurring increases, as does the risk of memory distortion, and the task of detecting at trial either a witness's exposure to the risk, or the inherent dangers having been realised, becomes yet more difficult. In *Holland v HM Advocate*, the victim of the first robbery, having picked out one of the foils at an identification parade and been told by a police officer that she had 'not done too well' demonstrated remarkable confidence in the accuracy of her dock-identification of the accused. Having stated that he had 'definitely' been in her house on the night of the robbery, she asserted that her dock-identification of him was more likely to be accurate than her attempt at an identification at the parade. Furthermore, she rejected any suggestion that she might have been mistaken. The fallibility of the human memory was quite vividly illustrated in the testimony of the victim of the second robbery, who after identifying the accused in the dock, erroneously asserted under examination that the accused was the person he had identified at the identification parade.

Pre-trial Identification Procedures: Line-ups, Video Identifications and Identification Parades

Pre-trial Processes and Safeguards

In most jurisdictions, the legal system's response to the risk of wrongful conviction on the basis of mistaken identification has been to establish numerous safeguards, with the most significant being prescribed pre-trial procedures for procuring identification evidence. However, these procedures carry their own risk since the circumstances in which witnesses are invited to attempt to identify a suspect are inherently suggestive: the witness being afforded the opportunity itself implies that the police suspect that a person who appears in the procedure has committed the offence.

In England and Wales, pre-trial identification procedures are the subject of elaborate statutory regulation. The framework is set out in Code D of the Codes of Practice, established by the Police and Criminal Evidence Act 1984. Code D, which is periodically revised and reissued, contains four broad sets of provisions, which (i) prescribe a number of alternative procedures for procuring identifications from witnesses (namely, video identification procedure, identification parade, group identification and confrontation (show-up); (ii) establish a hierarchy among these procedures (as listed previously); (iii) establish when an identification procedure ought to be conducted; and (iv) provide some regulation of street identifications (field show-ups).

Code D establishes video identification as the principal or preferred identification procedure, permitting the police to resort to the other procedures, including a 'live' identification parade, where a video procedure would be impracticable. The provisions stipulating the manner in which the procedures are to be conducted contain various measures designed to ameliorate the inherently suggestive effect of the pre-trial identification process and to minimise the risk of error. The Code provides that the police officer responsible for conducting the procedures must not be involved in the investigation. It requires arrangements to be made to prevent witnesses communicating to one another about the procedure. In respect of an identification parade, for example, the witness should not be permitted to see the parade members before the procedure takes place. At the outset out of the procedure the witness should be told that the culprit may or may not be present and that they should not make a positive identification unless certain. Witnesses should also be prevented from seeing the suspect after the parade. Those provisions of Code D describing how identification parades are to be conducted are mirrored in general terms in the guidelines for US law enforcement officials published by the National Institute of Justice (NIJ) (1999). The publication of *Eyewitness Evidence: A Guide for Law Enforcement* was lauded as a significant achievement. It contains, *inter alia*, recommendations for composing line-ups, instructing witnesses prior to viewing a line-up, conducting identification procedures and recording results.

The effectiveness of particular safeguards, no matter how universal, cannot be evaluated in an atomistic manner. Pre-trial identification procedures are one component of a broad system of safeguards. Taken in isolation, an identification procedure might be considered an important safeguard against wrongful conviction but to a greater or lesser degree the effectiveness of any of the various safeguards is contingent on the effective operation of other measures that also address the dangers.

In this respect there is an important distinction to be drawn between the NIJ Guidelines and Code D. While the former is silent on the circumstances in which an identification parade ought to be conducted, the latter imposes an obligation on the police to conduct one where certain conditions arise. Code D imposes a further duty, 'in the interests of fairness to suspects and witnesses' to arrange an identification procedure as soon as is practicable (para 3.11). The differences in the two approaches might lie in differing perceptions of the purpose that is served by identification parades. The drafters of the NIJ Guidelines appear to regard the parade as providing a procedure designed to ensure the reliability of identification evidence procured by the police for the prosecution case. With a few notable exceptions (e.g. Wells and Lindsay, 1980; Wells and Olson, 2002), little attention appears to have been directed towards the significance of non-identifications in the psychological research concerning identification procedures. Presumably, in this view, any failure by a witness to make an identification is the redundant by-product of the process. However, an identification parade serves a broader forensic purpose. Assuming the general purpose of identification procedures to be the mitigation of the risk of wrongful conviction on the basis of mistaken identification, a parade appears to serve at least two important functions. First, a positive identification on a well-constructed identification parade provides cogent prosecution evidence. In contrast, a failure to make an identification, or the identification of a foil, provides cogent evidence to support a suspect's claim that he or she was not the person involved in the matters under investigation.

Pre-trial Processes as Police Procedures or Safeguards against Miscarriages?

Psychologists' research into the problem of mistaken identification has focused largely on the eyewitness's cognitive processes. Relatively little attention has been paid to police attitudes and decision-making regarding identification procedures. It is perhaps easy to perceive the identification parade to be a 'police procedure', but the English courts have frequently acknowledged that it serves a broader function. In *R v Nicholson* (1999), for example, it was held that an identification parade was 'a service performed impartially for prosecution and defence.' In this view, the police serve as guardians or trustees of the means of procuring evidence that might assist the defence. However, the police are not in a position where they should be expected to act with the probity expected of a trustee. In *R v Forbes* (2001) the court expressed reservations about entrusting decisions concerning the important safeguard of an identification parade to police officers 'whose primary concern will (perfectly properly) be to promote the investigation and prosecution of crime rather than to protect the interest of suspects' (*R v Forbes*, 2001: 696).

Where the prosecution can construct a case against a suspect that would be fit to be left to a jury without the need to conduct an identification parade, the police might regard a parade as presenting an unnecessary risk that the witness will fail to identify the suspect. Such an outcome might lead to the proceedings being discontinued. Alternatively, should matters nevertheless progress to trial, the witness's failure to make an identification might raise sufficient doubt in the mind of the jury for them to conclude that the prosecution has failed to prove its case beyond a reasonable doubt and thus lead them to acquit (although that does not appear to have been the case in *Holland v HM Advocate*). With this in mind, it is important to observe that Code D imposes on the police an obligation to arrange an identification procedure not only where a 'known suspect' disputes an identification, but also where there are witnesses who might be able to identify the culprit but have not been given an opportunity to identify the suspect. In other words, it obliges the police to conduct an identification procedure in circumstances in which the prosecution case does not rely on eyewitness identification evidence and conducting an identification procedure would not significantly advance its case.

Street Identifications (Field Show-ups)

The obligation to arrange an identification procedure under Code D is contingent on there being a 'known suspect'. The Code explains that references to a suspect being 'known' means that the police have sufficient information to justify the arrest of that person for suspected involvement in the offence. The corollary of this is that the police are not obliged to conduct an identification procedure until satisfied that they have established sufficient grounds to arrest the suspect. It is this condition that is often used by the police to justify the use of street identifications.

Street identification procedures generally take place relatively shortly after the commission of a crime. They can occur spontaneously, for example where a witness is taken around the area in which the offence took place in the hope that the culprit remains nearby. They can also take place, more contentiously, where police officers other than those in the company of the witness, act on the witness' description and discover someone resembling that description in the vicinity. In such circumstances a confrontation is immediately arranged between witness and a suspect. These procedures are inherently suggestive and, not surprisingly both the NIJ Guidelines and Code D regulate them. The Guidelines suggest, *inter alia*, that witnesses be kept separate and under instruction not to discuss details of the incident with one another. The witness should always be cautioned that the person he or she is looking at might not be the culprit. Where one witness makes an identification, the police should then consider making the other witnesses perform formal identification procedures. The more prescriptive provisions of Code D prohibit the police from conducting further street identifications in such circumstances. While Code D does provide some regulation of street identifications its general admonishment to police officers that the 'principles applicable to the formal procedures should be followed as far as possible' (para 3.2) is indicative of the fact that these ad hoc procedures do not provide the same level of safeguard afforded by the more formal identification procedures. However, their attraction for the police is obvious. They take place while the event remains fresh in the mind of the witness, and entail none of the resource implications and practical problems associated with arranging formal procedures. Such identifications often provide the cornerstone on which the prosecution case is built. In circumstances, in which the police find a suspect in the vicinity soon after an offence is committed, even where there is sufficient information to justify arrest without immediately arranging a street identification, the opportunity of doing so might prove alluring. The police may consider that the possibility of obtaining an immediate positive street identification, notwithstanding the suggestiveness of the procedure, outweighs the uncertainty of deferring to formal procedures arranged at some future time.

The research concerning show-ups suggests that street identifications procedures should not be used (Levi and Lindsay, 2001; Bromby and Memon, forthcoming). However, as Wells (2001) points out, such a procedure will sometimes be required to establish sufficient grounds (or probable cause) and so trigger the power of arrest. Nonetheless, legitimate concerns have been expressed that street identifications are often used in circumstances in which the police seemingly have sufficient grounds to arrest prior to such a procedure being used (Wolchover and Heaton-Armstrong, 2004). The manner in which police discretion is exercised in this context serves to illustrate quite starkly that the effectiveness of identification parades in safeguarding against mistaken identification lies not only in the design of the procedure but the decision-making of the police (and prosecuting authorities) and the judiciary. It is arguable that police attempts to justify street identifications by pointing to the need to satisfy themselves of the sufficiency of the grounds for arrest, is sometimes an attempt to impart what Reiner (2000, p. 87) describes as 'a respectable gloss to actions undertaken for other reasons' – in our case circumvention of statutory obligations to conduct formal parades (see McKenzie, 2003). Whether or not sufficient information exists to justify the arrest of a person is a question of law and is, therefore, a matter that is ultimately determined by the judiciary. In theory, a judge could find that the arrest condition was satisfied before a street identification was conducted and that performing such a procedure breached Code D. In practice, the courts (too) readily defer to the judgement of the police about the need to conduct street identifications. Indeed, the only circumstances in which the Court of Appeal has been willing to find that a suspect was 'known' prior to a street identification was where he had been formally arrested before the procedure took place! (*R v Lennon*).

It was established in *R v Forbes* that where a suspect has been identified in a street identification he is entitled to test the witness's ability to identify him in a formal identification procedure. From the perspective of the psychologist this might seem pointless as, having identified him in a street identification, the witness is unlikely not to do so in a formal identification procedure. The courts' approach is that if there is a possibility that the witness will fail to identify the suspect he ought to be afforded that opportunity. However, where the police have secured a street identification it appears that failure subsequently to arrange formal identification procedures is a frequent occurrence. In such circumstances there is a tendency to allow the prosecution to adduce evidence of the street identification notwithstanding any breach of Code D or that the street identification has taken place in particularly suggestive circumstances.

Judicial Duties and Discretion

In addition to the safeguards imposed via the regulation of pre-trial procedures, the trial system has also evolved safeguards to combat the risk of wrongful conviction on the basis of mistaken identification. Briefly, these comprise (a) the trial judge's discretion to exclude unreliable evidence and (b) the *Turnbull* Guidelines.

Judicial Discretion

In England and Wales, trial judges have a general discretion to exclude prosecution evidence where its prejudicial effect outweighs its probative value. In addition, section 78 of the Police and Criminal Evidence Act 1984 provides that prosecution evidence may be excluded if 'it appears to the court that ... the admission of the evidence would have such an adverse effect on the fairness of proceedings that it ought not to admit it.' There has been considerable criticism of the application of section 78, principally on the grounds that it is difficult to discern any consistent underlying principles (see Grevling, 1997; Ormerod and Birch, 2004). The discretion ought to operate so as to exclude any unreliable identification evidence on the grounds of fairness.

The statutory scheme including Code D is designed to guard against unfairness and if the police follow its prescriptions it is unlikely that eyewitness identification evidence will be excluded under section 78. However, the provisions of the Code in no way constitute rules of admissibility (Birch, 1991) and a breach of them will not *necessarily* lead to exclusion of evidence. The courts appear willing to exclude evidence only where the police have acted in 'bad faith' and deliberately breached the provisions of the Code. For example, in *R v Nagah* (1991) the suspect had agreed to take part in an identification parade, but the police ensured that the witness was sitting in a car outside the police station at the time the suspect was due to attend. The Court of Appeal held that the trial judge was wrong to have permitted evidence of the witness's identification of the suspect to be adduced in those circumstances.

The reluctance of the judiciary to exercise their discretion to exclude identification evidence, particularly street identifications, has already been noted. A stark and recent illustration of this is *R v Williams* (2003). In that case a man struck up a conversation with a woman at a bus stop. The conversation became more menacing and culminated in a demand for cash and jewellery accompanied by a threat to stab her with a hypodermic needle. She managed to escape, telephone the police and provide a description before going to the house of a nearby relative. She described the culprit as a clean-shaven man with a London accent wearing black or dark blue trousers, a black jacket with black zip and brown shoes. The police making their way to the scene saw and gave chase to a man who was eventually detained on a factory roof. This man spoke with a distinctly different Scottish accent, had two to three days' stubble on his face, was wearing black trousers and a black jacket which had a brass zip, and had black, rather than brown, shoes. The officers who detained the suspect were told of the culprit's threat to stab the victim with a hypodermic needle. As a result he was handcuffed. The victim was driven to a place where she saw the handcuffed suspect standing by a police car surrounded by police officers. She observed him from a distance of about 10 metres and stated that she was positive that he was the culprit. No formal identification procedure was subsequently conducted. At trial the identification evidence of the victim formed the central plank of the prosecution's case. The court accepted that there had been a breach of Code D. It 'mattered not' whether this was because the police had a 'known suspect', in which case formal procedures ought to have been held, or that they had breached the provision stating that 'care must be taken not to direct the witness's attention to any individual unless, taking into account all the circumstances, this cannot be avoided' (Code D, para 3.2(b)). The court acknowledged the suggestiveness of the procedure adopted, stating that 'a clearer way of pointing out to her who it was that the police sought her to identify could not have been imagined' (*R v Williams* 2003, para. 12). Notwithstanding this, it was held that the trial judge's decision not to exclude the evidence was correct and the conviction was safe.

Both *R v Williams* and *Holland v HM Advocate* (and numerous similar cases) ought to raise grave concerns over the (in)effectiveness of the elaborate framework of pre-trial procedures set out in Code D and the failure to apply the judicial discretion to exclude unreliable identification evidence. In Australia, the ALRC claimed that a reading of Australian cases 'left the impression of a reluctance on the part of trial judges to exclude eyewitness identification evidence, however unreliable or weak it may seem' (ALRC 1985, para 424). Similar sentiments, were they to be expressed in respect of the practice in English courts, would not be misplaced. The Australian legislature's response was to establish a statutory rule making the admissibility of eyewitness identification evidence dependent on there having been an identification parade (section 114 Evidence Act (Cth.) 1995).

Turnbull Guidelines

In addition to the discretion to exclude evidence, trial judges in England and Wales have particular duties to protect against unsafe convictions in cases involving disputed identification. The *Turnbull* guidelines, laid down in the eponymous case

R v Turnbull, impose three specific obligations. First, in a trial involving disputed identification, where the prosecution case is based wholly or substantially on eyewitness identification evidence, if the judge considers the identification evidence to be of poor quality, the case *must* be withdrawn from the jury. Where the case is left to the jury the judge must (i) warn the jury of the dangers associated with identification evidence *generally*, and (ii) remind them of specific weaknesses in the evidence in the *particular* case.

The effectiveness of the *Turnbull* guidelines is open to doubt. Dennis (2002, p. 246) points out that the difference between a 'good' and 'poor' quality identification is a matter of degree, and that whether a case is put before a jury, or withdrawn at the close of the prosecution case, may depend on modest increases in the duration of observation and in the quality of the light.

The first of the two jury directions concerns what Redmayne (2001) terms 'group character evidence'. The aim is to warn the jury to treat the identification evidence with caution by explaining, through judicial instruction rather than expert testimony, the reasons why eyewitness identifications are *generally* considered to be unreliable. There is no authority as to the admissibility of expert evidence on issues of eyewitness identification in English law. Space prohibits a rehearsal here of the arguments for and against the admissibility of such testimony. However, the view that a judicial warning as in *Turnbull* alleviates the need for expert evidence concerning the factors that might adversely affect the accuracy of eyewitness identifications has been doubted. Redmayne has asserted that the *Turnbull* warning alone might not be sufficient to prevent a jury attaching inappropriate weight to seemingly weak identification evidence. The *Turnbull* guidance is rudimentary; requiring that the jury be informed of the reason why identification evidence should be treated with caution, but offering little by way of elaboration of the reasons.

There has been some recent judicial acknowledgment that jury directions warning of eyewitness unreliability represent the barest minimum safeguard at trial. In *R v Nash* (2004) the Court of Appeal held that the specimen direction issued to judges by the Judicial Studies Board (JSB) constituted the briefest summary of the dangers inherent in identification evidence that would satisfy the requirements of the *Turnbull* warning. That model direction suggests that the jury be informed that past miscarriages of justice had occurred because of mistaken identification; that a witness who is convinced in his own mind may as a result be a convincing witness but nevertheless be mistaken, and that this might apply to a number of witnesses.

However, this fairly modest warning clearly does not draw on the body of knowledge that an expert witness would rely upon. Nor does it constitute a satisfactory alternative to the more comprehensive, sophisticated and empirically-based testimony that could be offered by an expert witness, and explored in cross-examination. The reason why identification evidence ought to be treated with such caution is that there are various physiological and environmental factors that appear capable of adversely affecting the ability of any witness to make an accurate identification. The JSB specimen direction refers to none of these.

Conclusion

The safeguards imposed at various stages of the criminal process are designed to protect suspects against the risk of wrongful conviction on the basis of mistaken identification. Claims that any of these measures, individually or collectively, are effective in achieving that end are likely to have been made on an inadequate understanding of the interdependency of various safeguards. Twining (1990) has commented that such has been the focus on identification procedures that the perception among researchers appears at times to have been that the problem of mistaken identification is coextensive with defects in those procedures. The problem is one that extends beyond the frailties of witness memory. The judgment in *Holland v HM Advocate*, for example, illustrates the extent to which statutory regulation of pre-trial procedures can be undermined by judicial decisions on admissibility. The legal processes involved in the reception of eyewitness evidence at trial are complex. While efforts to improve particular safeguards are valuable, unless similar attention is extended across all aspects of the treatment of eyewitness identification evidence in legal processes, the returns on those efforts are likely to become increasingly marginal.

References

Alexander v R (1981) 145 Commonwealth Law Reports 395.

Australian Law Reform Commission (1985) *Report No.26, Evidence (Interim), volume 1* (Canberra: Australian Government Publishing Service).

Australian Law Reform Commission (1987) *Report No.38, Evidence (Final)* (Canberra: Australian Government Publishing Service).

Australian Law Reform Commission (2005) *Discussion Paper 69, Review of the Uniform Evidence Acts* (Sydney: ALRC).

Birch, D. (1991) Commentary on R v Oscar, [1991] *Criminal Law Review*, 778.

Bromby, M. and Memon, A. (forthcoming) *Scots Law and the Issue of Dock Identification*.

Brooks, N. (1983) *Law Reform Commission of Canada Study Paper, Pre-trial Eyewitness Identification Procedures* (Ottawa: LRCC).

Connors, E. *et al.* (1996) *Convicted by Juries, Exonerated by Science: Case Studies in the Use of DNA Evidence to Establish Innocence After Trial* (Washington DC: US Justice Department, National Institute of Justice).

Damaska, M. (1997) *Evidence Law Adrift* (London: Yale University Press).

Dennis, I.H. (2002) *The Law of Evidence*, 2nd edn (London: Sweet & Maxwell).

Devlin Committee (1976) *Report to the Secretary of State for the Home Department of the Departmental Committee on Evidence of Identification in Criminal Cases* (London: HMSO).

Grevling, K. (1997) Fairness and the exclusion of evidence under section 78(1) of the Police and Criminal Evidence Act, *Law Quarterly Review*, 113, p. 667.

Heydon, J. (2004) *Cross on Evidence*, 7th Australian edition (Chatswood, NSW: Butterworths).

Holland v HM Advocate (2005) UKPC D1.

Judicial Studies Board Model Directions available from http://www.jsboard.co.uk/criminal_law/cbb/mf_04a.htm#30

Law Commission of New Zealand (1999) Evidence: total recall? The reliability of witness testimony, *Miscellaneous Paper 13* (Wellington: NZLC).

Levi, A.M. and Lindsay, R.C.L. (2001) Lineup and photo spread procedures: issues concerning policy recommendations, *Psychology, Public Policy, and Law*, 7, pp. 776–790.

McKenzie, I. (2003) Eyewitness evidence: will the United States guide for law enforcement make any difference? *International Journal of Evidence and Proof*, 7, p. 237.

National Institute of Justice (1999) *Eyewitness Evidence: A Guide for Law Enforcement* (Washington DC: US Department of Justice).

Ormerod, D. and Birch, D. (2004) The evolution of the discretionary exclusion of evidence, *Criminal Law Review*, 767.

R v Cartwright (1914) 10 Criminal Appeal Reports 219.

R v Lennon (1999) EWCA Crim. 1309.

R v Nagah (1991) 92 Criminal Appeal Reports 344.

R v Nash (2004) EWCA Crim. 2696.

R v O'Brien (2003) EWCA Crim. 1370.

R v Turnbull (1977) Queen's Bench 224.

R v Williams (2003) EWCA Crim. 3200.

Redmayne, M. (2001) *Expert Evidence and Criminal Justice* (Oxford University Press).

Reiner, R. (2000) *The Politics of the Police*, 3rd edn (Oxford University Press).

Roberts, A. (2004) The problem of mistaken identification: some observations on process, *International Journal of Evidence and Proof*, 8, pp. 100–119.

Roberts, A. (2006) Towards a broader perspective on the problem of mistaken identification: police decision-making and identification procedures, in: M. Freeman and B. Brooks-Gordon (Eds) *Current Legal Issues, vol. 9, Law and Psychology* (Oxford University Press).

R v Forbes [2001] 1 AC 473.

R v Nicholson [2000] 1 Cr. App. R. 182.

Scottish Home and Health Department (1978) *Identification Procedure under Scottish Criminal Law* (London: HMSO).

Twining, W. (1990) *Rethinking Evidence* (Northwestern University Press).

Wells, G.L. (2001) Police line-ups: data, theory and policy, *Psychology, Public Policy, and Law*, 7, pp. 791–801.

Wells, G.L and Olson, A. (2002) Eyewitness identification: information gain from incriminating and exonerating behaviors, *Journal of Experimental Psychology: Applied*, 8, p. 155.

Wells, G.L. and Lindsay, R.C.L. (1980) On estimating the diagnosticity of eyewitness non-identifications, *Psychological Bulletin*, 88, pp. 776–784.

Wolchover, D. and Heaton-Armstrong, A. (2004) Ending the farce of staged street identifications, *Archbold News*, 3, p. 5.

Chapter 6

Profiling Evidence in the Courts

Ian Freckelton

Introduction

The insights of profilers and investigative psychologists are increasingly commonly utilised in the course of criminal investigations (see generally Ressler *et al.*, 1988; Canter, 1989; 1994; 2003; Douglas *et al.*, 1993; Holmes and Holmes, 1996; Douglas and Olshaker, 1996; 2000; Ormerod, 1996; Kocsis and Irwin, 1997; Jackson and Bekerian, 1997; Canter and Alison, 1999; 2000a; 2000b; Ainsworth, 2000; Turvey, 2001; Keppel and Birnes, 2003; Alison, 2005; Kocsis, 2006). It has also been contended that because of certain characteristics of a crime scene, inferences can be made about the crime, the offender and the victim. These perceptions have prompted some to attempt to draw profiling from the realm of criminal investigations and to translate its fruits into criminal, civil and coroners' cases in the courts.

Attempts have been made in a number of countries to adduce evidence in the courts that, because of the characteristics of a person, it is either more or less likely that he or she committed a criminal offence. Likewise, it has been argued on the basis of psychological autopsy evidence that a now deceased person was most likely to have been the victim of a crime or, alternatively, committed suicide or was the victim of an accident. Such perspectives can be pertinent in both criminal prosecutions (see Alison *et al.* 2002) and coroners' inquests (see Freckelton and Ranson, 2006).

The argument has been advanced in the courts too that because a certain kind of conduct was foreseeable on the part of a perpetrator, as shown by expert evidence, particular efforts should have been made by the perpetrator to avoid or prevent the conduct and the predictable harm that ensued. This can have ramifications for civil liability, as well as for the terms of coroners' findings and recommendations.

In the United States, a preliminary question arises in the course of criminal investigations in that it is incumbent upon police to establish 'probable cause' to investigate a suspect via measures such as surveillance or property searches (see Meyer and Weaver, 2006). The general approach of the courts has been to utilise profiles created for the purpose of investigations (see for example *People v Genrich*, 928 P 2d 799 (1996); see too *Pennell v State of Delaware*, 602 A 2d 735 (1990).

At the next stage of the criminal justice, after the preferring of criminal charges, for countries in the Anglo-American-Australian tradition, a threshold question arises as to whether profiling evidence can be or should be admitted in spite of the barriers created by the exclusionary rules of evidence (see Kirkpatrick 1998; Meyer 2007).

For countries with other evidentiary traditions, the question is whether significant probative value should be given to the fruits of profiling.

Six major admissibility issues have arisen:

- the status of profiling as an area of expertise, defined by such features as reliability;
- the use that can be made of 'propensity evidence' and 'character evidence';
- whether the probative value of profiling evidence exceeds its prejudicial effect;
- whether profiling evidence is to be classified as precluded evidence of speculation;
- Whether profiling evidence is 'oath-helping' or impermissibly self-serving; and
- whether profiling evidence unacceptably trespasses on the ultimate issue rule.

Thus far, Anglo-American-Australian court decisions have exhibited a disinclination to admit most forms of profiling evidence in criminal trials, whether the attempts to adduce it are by the prosecution or the defence. For the most part, attempts have not been made to utilise it in civil litigation. However, there is Australian authority on the question of admissibility in this context: *Godfrey v New South Wales (No 1)* [2003] NSWSC 160. The greatest uptake of profiling evidence in the courts has been in coroners' hearings where the need has emerged to understand the state of mind of the deceased before his or her death in order to evaluate whether the death was likely to have been because of a deliberate act of the deceased or some other reason (see Freckelton and Ranson, 2006).

This chapter reviews the history of attempts to introduce profiling evidence into the courts and analyses the rationales advanced for its exclusion. It scrutinises case law on the subject in the United Kingdom, Australia, the United States and Canada and argues that it will be some time before profiling evidence is utilized in forums other than coroners' inquests.

Definitional Conundra

The parameters of behavioural profiling have become unclear in the maelstrom of competing claims and critiques (see Kocsis, 2006, pp. 1–3, and also Snook *et al.*, 2007). Canter has tended latterly to subsume it within the rubric of 'investigative psychology' (Canter, 2004), while scholars such as Blau (1994) described it over a decade ago as an 'arcane art' deriving from psychodiagnostic assessment and psychobiography. Kocsis (2006, p. 2) has argued that 'criminal profiling represents a process whereby behaviors and/or actions exhibited in a crime are assessed and interpreted to form predictions concerning the characteristics of the probable perpetrator(s) of the crime. The composite predicted characteristics are often referred to as a criminal profile, the purpose of which is to assist investigators, typically police personnel, in the investigation and thus apprehension of an unknown criminal or criminals.' Canter and Youngs (2003) have argued that personality theory, psychodynamic theory, the career route theory from criminology, social processes and interpersonal narrative theory, provide processes by which 'profiling inferences' can be drawn.

It is important to distinguish between offender profiling, which is a form of investigative psychology and enables inferences to be drawn about a person 'of interest' by reason of their known actions, and other forms of categorisation and classification undertaken on the basis of various forms of psychological assessment (see Canter, 2004; Kocsis, 2006, p. 3). Typically, an offender profile will contain information about a probable offender such as:

- Likely demographics, such as age, gender and, possibly, education;
- Legal history, including antecedents;
- Vocational background;
- Family characteristics;
- Habits and social interests, such as hobbies;
- Mode of transport;
- Geographical background, including residence; and
- Personality characteristics.

As yet, decisions in the courts have gone only a short distance in distinguishing amongst the different modes of classification and in ascribing significance to the differences. They have been preoccupied by the probabilistic nature of offender profiling and its consequential risks by which inappropriate inferences may be drawn by the unwary – such as jurors.

An example of lines that have been robustly drawn is between what Canadian decisions have classified as 'crime scene analysis' and 'criminal profiling', the former exploring what the crime scene shows but the latter analysing why an offence was committed in a particular manner and who is more likely to have committed it (see for example *R v Ranger* (2003) 178 CCC (3d) 375).

This chapter places in context the notion of 'offender profiling' and then scrutinises the form of 'profiling' best known to the courts, namely 'the psychological autopsy', which purports to summarise the characteristics of a known person, now deceased, and infer conduct in which they may have engaged. Another form of evaluation with the potential to cause confusion in a legal context is the assessment undertaken by a mental health professional on the basis of psychometric or other tests, such as plethysmography, in order to determine characteristics or traits of the person. This is better classified as 'psychological profiling' or 'personality profiling'. Each form of 'profiling' is quite conceptually distinct and based upon different methodologies. From the perspective of the courts, there are important differences too in the scientific processes that give rise to professional opinions in respect of each.

Offender Profiling

At the heart of criminal profiling is an informed and probabilistic perspective in relation to the likelihood of a crime having been committed by a particular kind of person. For instance, it is unlikely that persons with one particular kind of personality or sexual orientation will commit certain kinds of crimes. As a corollary, the chances of a person with a different particular kind of personality or sexual orientation having committed a certain kind of crime may be statistically higher. Such considerations can assist both the prosecution and the defence. The question for the courts is whether the assistance in terms of circumstantial evidence that is potentially rendered by such information is of a value that is outweighed by the risk of inappropriate reasoning processes occasioned by the beguiling significance of the evidence.

A classic example is that information relating to a sexual assault may suggest that the offender is likely to be male, to be attracted to young female children, to have a background of having been abused, to live within a certain geographical arc, to be highly fantasy prone and to be obsessive. A person charged with the offence satisfies all such characteristics. Should such information be placed before a jury?

The Psychological Autopsy

A particular form of profiling – the psychological autopsy – is admitted frequently in coroners' courts in an attempt to facilitate understanding of the causes and circumstances of otherwise equivocal deaths. Attempts have also been made to adduce such evidence in criminal proceedings (see *R v Gilfoyle* [2001] 2 Cr App R 57 discussed below).

Shneidman and Collins in 1961 defined the psychological autopsy as 'a retrospective reconstruction of an individual's life that focuses on lethality, that is those features of his life that illuminate his intentions in relation to his own death, clues as to the type of death it was, the degree (if any) of his participation in his own death, and why the death occurred at that time'. With a view to enhancing the information available to coroners, they coined the term while at the Suicide Prevention Center in Los Angeles in 1958.

Non-physical, psychological autopsies are an as yet controversial form of post-mortem investigation. They rely upon interviewing key informants, such as spouses, close family members, work colleagues, treating medical practitioners and relevant others, and analysing pertinent documents, such as suicide notes, diaries and other writings, to determine the mental state of the deceased before his or her death. Other information about the lifestyle and circumstances of the deceased, including behaviours and events preceding death, are also utilised to reconstruct the mental state of the deceased (see Ogloff and Otto, 1993; Schneidman, 1994; Selkin, 1994; Cavanagh *et al.*, 1999; 2003; LaFon, 1999; 2004; Johnstone, 1999; Schneidman and Faberow, 2004; Davis, 2005). McMahon (2002) has observed that, since the original work of Schneidman and his colleagues, research on the psychological autopsy has generally developed in two distinct directions:

- A retrospective form of research into the causes of suicide. Most of the research on the psychological autopsy has been of this type.
- A technique for distinguishing four modes of death: natural causes, accident, suicide, and homicide.

She has argued that 'this application of the psychological autopsy has been much less thoroughly researched, although expert testimony on the psychological autopsy for the purpose of establishing manner of death (murder or suicide) has been admitted in criminal trials since the 1970s'.

As LaFon (1999) has put it, 'Although in use since 1958, the term 'psychological autopsy' and its constituent elements have yet to achieve either consensual validation or operational standardization. This calls into question issues of content validity and reliability when psychological autopsies are used in the field' (see too Bendheim, 1979; Ammon, 1995). Different approaches have become pronounced in relation to the conduct of psychological autopsies. For instance, as part of its criminal profiling work, the FBI developed an approach to the psychological autopsy that has been designated 'equivocal death analysis' (see Poythress *et al.*, 1993). In the investigation of ambiguous deaths, the FBI uses a semi-structured investigative strategy to determine whether a death occurred by reason of natural causes, accident, homicide, or suicide, utilising five factors:

- Victimology: characteristics of the deceased relevant to suicide, probability of being a victim of crime, etc;
- Stressors: variable environmental and personal factors that adversely affect the deceased;
- Medical autopsy information and other information from the death scene, including detailed information on weapons, type and number of injuries, etc;
- Scientific examination: general crime scene analysis, including location and position of body of deceased, etc; and
- Death scene analysis.

This is significantly different from the approach of Professor Canter and colleagues in England (Canter and Allison, 1999, 2000a, 2000b). McMahon (2002) has argued that as yet, psychological autopsies do not rest upon 'a solid and substantial research base. Hence claims that they are scientific must at best be regarded as premature. The problems that continue to bedevil these approaches can be classified into three main categories:

- difficulties inherent in the task
- an inadequate research base; and
- utilisation in the adversarial setting of the criminal trial.'

In turn, this has impacted upon the feasibility of psychological autopsy evidence in the courts.

Several criticisms of psychological profiling have been advanced in the aftermath of its usage in the USS Iowa incident in 1989 (see Poythress *et al.*, 1993; Otto *et al.*, 1993). An explosion took place aboard a United States naval ship. It killed 47 sailors. A Naval Investigative Service inquiry ruled out the possibility of an accidental explosion having caused the deaths. It focused on two sailors – one who had died in the explosion and another who was the beneficiary of the first man's life insurance policy. The inquiry asked behavioural scientists at the FBI to provide an opinion about the likelihood of mass-murder by the surviving sailor; a suicide attempt by the dead sailor to get revenge on the surviving sailor for marrying; and suicide by the dead sailor as a result of a variety of triggers. The FBI analysts favoured the third option but their views, and the way in which they reached them, proved controversial. A peer review panel of 14 psychologists and two psychiatrists was particularly critical. While the panel agreed with many of the inferences drawn by the FBI analysts, they disagreed as to the three options, with the FBI analysts being criticised for adopting negative and stronger conclusions than the members of the panel. The panel recommended that the users of what they termed 'equivocal death analysis' 'should not assert categorical conclusions about the precise mental state or actions of the deceased' (see Poythress *et al.*, 1993, p. 12) and argued that appropriate qualifying statements for any opinions should be expressed.

Notably, there are no formal qualifications that are universally regarded as necessary for conducting psychological autopsies or equivocal death analyses. There is a risk, too, that data-gathering will not be as thorough as it should be (see Ogloff and Otto, 1993) and that it will be biased in favour of a particular hypothesis being explored by the person conducting the autopsy. Interviewee biases, too (see Davis, 2005), have the potential to contaminate the process as surviving relatives and friends may have their own reasons for adopting certain perspectives on the causes of the deceased person's death or on the behaviour of the deceased in the period leading up to his or her death.

The consequence of the level of controversy still existing in relation to the methodology and reliability of psychological autopsies is that their uptake is generally limited to coroners' courts. However, even though coroners are not obliged to apply the rules of evidence strictly, concerns have been raised (see Freckelton and Ranson, 2006) about the risk of inquests uncritically drawing upon psychological autopsy analyses.

The Impediments to Evidentiary Admissibility for Profiling Evidence

A major impediment to the admissibility of offender profiling evidence is whether it is sufficiently reliable to be considered an area of expertise within the terms of the *Frye* rule (*Frye v United States*, 293 F 2d 1013) or under the indicia of *Daubert v Merrell Dow Pharmaceuticals*, 509 US 579; 125 L Ed (2d) 469; 113 S Ct 2786;

43 F 3d 1311 (1993) or to constitute information that can safely be taken into account by courts. Even though the *Frye* and *Daubert* tests are not ubiquitously applied outside the United States (see Freckelton and Selby, 2005), they do provide helpful yardsticks for the exercise of exclusion of evidence under the prejudice/ probative discretion. They do so by focusing both upon the reputation of theories and techniques within the relevant scientific community (the *Frye* test) and the reliability of theories and techniques by reference to factors such as falsifiability, peer review, existence of controls, published literature and views held within the relevant intellectual community (the *Daubert* test). An associated issue is the probative value of such evidence, the potential existing that if the probative value is outweighed by its prejudicial effect, it can be excluded.

A large part of the difficulty is the extent to which the field of offender profiling is profoundly divided, the approaches of the FBI and of Canter and colleagues being exemplary of the differences that pervade approaches (see Kocsis, 2006). In this context, as recently as 2001, Turvey (2001, p. 346) has argued that it cannot yet be said that criminal profiling is 'a science'. He has noted that profiling, as practised by the FBI, has been widely criticised for its failure to test hypotheses and to pass the usual peer review processes.

Generally, it is legally impermissible for the prosecution to adduce evidence that because a person is of a general character, or has a particular propensity or has a particular psychological make-up, this makes it possible or probable that he or she was the perpetrator of a criminal offence. However, it is permissible for the prosecution to adduce evidence of a person having an unnatural passion that makes it more likely that they would sexually assault a person or category of persons. Evidence about particular characteristics possessed by the accused person, which make it more likely than would be the case with random members of the community that they would commit a particular kind of an offence, can be adduced. However, this is subject to the important rider that such evidence is not be significantly more prejudicial than it is probative; such an evaluation is influenced by the scientific reliability of the technique itself.

A significant difficulty in evaluating the admissibility of offender profiling evidence lies in identifying with clarity what use a party to litigation proposes to make of profiling evidence. Circumstantial evidence, sometimes of modest probative value, is commonly admitted in criminal trials, provided that it is not more prejudicial than probative. An important question for trial judges is the kind of reasoning that the party proffering the profiling evidence wishes the trier of fact (such as the jury) to engage in. If it is that the perpetrator of a crime is likely to have had certain characteristics or to have come from a certain vicinity, and the accused has such characteristics or such a provenance, then such evidence has only modest probative value but runs the risk of being mis-estimated in terms of its value. The evidence tends to be excluded because of the imbalance between its probative value and its prejudicial effect.

Ormerod (1996, pp. 865–866) has commented too that definitional difficulties stem from the fact that there is considerable theoretical disagreement about approaches to criminal profiling, describing the process as follows:

> The profiler begins by reconstructing how the crime occurred, on which is based an inference as to why the crime happened, and culminates in an educated guess about the characteristics of the offender. This WHAT to WHY to WHO is seen as the nucleus of the criminal profile. Profiles incorporate many factors, including: evaluations of the crime scene and neighbourhood, post-mortem reports, information as to the victim's movements prior to the crime, the suspect's interaction with the victim, etc. Ideally, the resulting profile should include information as to the age, race, occupational level, marital status, intelligence, educational level, arrest history, military history, family background, social interests, socioeconomic level, residence in relation to the crime and with whom residing, personality characteristics (rigid, passive, manipulative, aggressive), colour, age and description of vehicle, [and] suggested interview techniques for the offender. [Footnotes omitted]

This approach has led the Ontario Court of Appeal to draw a distinction between crime scene analysis or crime scene reconstruction evidence on the one hand and criminal profiling evidence on the other: *R v Ranger* (2003) 178 CCC (3d) 375; *R v Clark* (2004) 182 CCC (3d)1.

For the present, a series of legal difficulties confronts the adducing of profiling evidence – in particular, whether the field of profiling is sufficiently accepted within psychology as an area of scientific expertise; whether it is reliable in its results; and most particularly whether its fruits from a legal point of view are more prejudicial than probative. Another issue that is not entirely clear is whether it makes a difference in terms of admissibility if it is the accused (as against the prosecution) seeking to adduce profiling evidence.

On occasions, profiling evidence has been 'dismissed' as evidence of informed guesswork. Theories and conjectures may be allowed as part of final addresses by legal advocates but courts have been loathe to have them 'legitimised' by being propagated by expert mental health witnesses. In addition, when reduced to its essentials, profiling evidence in some circumstances can be portrayed as 'oath helping' – evidence adduced by the accused in support of his or her protestations of not having engaged in the alleged criminal behaviour. Finally, in jurisdictions such as the United Kingdom, and some parts of Australia, anxieties persist amongst some judges that profiling evidence unduly trespasses into the domain of the fact-finder by breaching the preclusion upon expert evidence concerning ultimate issues.

United Kingdom Caselaw

The decision of the Judicial Committee of the Privy Council in *Lowery v The Queen* [1974] AC 85 illustrates the complexity of the courts' varying decisions in allowing expert evidence about character and what might be described as offender profiling.

The co-accused, Lowery and King, had been convicted in Victoria, Australia, of the murder of a 15-year-old girl. Each had attributed responsibility to the other. One of the witnesses called by King was a psychologist who had interviewed both co-accused and had subjected them to various psychological tests. He gave evidence that King was an immature youth who was likely to have been led and dominated by more aggressive and dominant men and that he might behave aggressively in response to the demands of such people. The psychologist also testified that the tests he had employed showed that Lowery was strongly aggressive and lacked impulse control.

Lowery appealed on the ground that the psychologist's evidence had been wrongly admitted as it tended 'merely' to show disposition. The Privy Council dismissed the appeal, holding that the psychologist's evidence was relevant to King's case in order to show that King's version of events was *more probable* than Lowery's, and the whole substance of Lowery's case placed its admissibility beyond doubt as necessary *to negate* Lowery's evidence. The decision, therefore, relates both to assessment of Lowery's telling the truth on this occasion and to his general disposition and character. The evidence did not relate to particular kinds of offenders but did resort to the psychological profiles of the two accused men in order to evaluate which was the more likely to have been the aggressor and thus which was the more likely to be telling the truth in his accounts of the homicide. While today the psychologist's evidence might well be classified as 'profiling evidence', the term was not employed in 1974.

The first major English case which dealt explicitly with the admissibility of profiling evidence was that of Ognall J in *R v Stagg* (unreported, Central Criminal Court, 14 September 1994; see Ormerod and Sturman, 2005). This occurred in the context of an attempt to introduce profiling evidence against Mr Stagg who had been accused of murder. The profiler, Mr Britton, a psychologist, had guided the criminal investigation from its early stages. He had drafted an initial profile of the killer based upon examination of the crime scene and the characteristics of the victim, her habits, movements and whether or not she had enemies. He then advised on the characteristics of the undercover operative introduced as a confidante to the suspect, Mr Stagg, as well as in relation to correspondence to and from the suspect. The trial of Mr Stagg did not have to determine the admissibility of Mr Britton's opinions but Ognall J commented that the prosecution would have faced 'formidable difficulties' in persuading him that such evidence should be allowed. He observed that he had been provided with no authority that expert evidence about profiling had ever been admitted in proof of identity and suggested that such evidence was no more than evidence of propensity. Ormerod and Sturman (2005, p. 185) have commented:

> profiling rests on the assumptions that behavioural traits or imprints are displayed or reflected in crime scenes, that such imprints are identifiable, that they are unique to the offender, that they remain constant... Profile evidence is potentially very prejudicial when it is being used to draw links between the offender and the accused. Evidence

of discreditable traits of the offender will be transposed in the minds of the jury to the accused.

In words resonant of the *Frye* test from the United States, Ognall J stated that it was 'doubtful' that psychological profile evidence was sufficiently well established or 'generally accepted' as a scientific method to be received as expert evidence. He observed that such a novel technique must satisfy tests such as those articulated in the *Frye* or *Daubert* decisions. He noted too a real risk of unfairness in the investigative process – the suspect was a lonely, sexually inexperienced and socially isolated man who could have been predicted to be vulnerable to the attentions paid to him by the operative orchestrated by the profiler. It may well be that had Stagg made a confession as a result of the interaction with the operative, it would have been classified as involuntary and thereby inadmissible (Ormerod and Sturman, 2005, p. 174). The *Stagg* decision has led to the suggestion that stringent standards for monitoring and review of individual profilers should be introduced, as well as formal accreditation of profilers by the Home Office (Ormerod and Sturman, 2005, pp. 175–176; see too Alison and Canter, 2005; Cox 1999).

The most substantial English analysis of the admissibility of psychological profiling took place in *Gilfoyle* [2001] 2 Cr App R 57. It dealt with the admissibility of profiling evidence by Professor Canter, which took the form of a psychological autopsy. The Court of Appeal declined the evidence, accepting Professor Canter as an expert but finding he had never embarked on evaluating the suicidality of a deceased person previously and on the basis that 'his reports identify no criteria by reference to which the court could test the quality of his opinions: there is no database comparing real and questionable suicides and there is no substantial body of academic writing approving his methodology': (at [67]). It found, too, that Professor Canter's views were based on 'one-sided information' provided by the defendant. It doubted that the signs of unhappiness and arguments about suicide rates were outside the experience of the jury. It noted that there had been 17 occasions in the United States when criminal trial judges had admitted evidence of psychological profiling, on each occasion the decision having been overturned on appeal.

The Court found (at [68]) that there was no conceptual distinction between expert evidence about the profile of a deceased person and about the profile of a defendant:

> In our judgment, the roads of inquiry thus opened up would be unending and of little or no help to a jury. The use of psychological profiling as an aid to police investigation is one thing, but its use as a means of proof in court is another. Psychiatric evidence as to the state of mind of a defendant, witness or deceased falling short of mental illness may, of course, as we have said, be admissible in some cases when based, for example, on medical records and/or recognised criteria. But the academic status of psychological autopsies is not, in our judgment, such as to permit them to be admitted as a basis for expert opinion before a jury.

Australian Caselaw

In the New South Wales civil decision of *Godfrey v New South Wales (No 1)* [2003] NSWSC 160, the issue of criminal profiling arose in a somewhat unusual context: a damages action for psychiatric and physical injury. The plaintiff sought to have the Supreme Court admit evidence from a retired police officer, a Mr Wicks, concerning the likely behaviour of an escaped convict who had held up a newsagency, thereby causing the proprietor to go into premature labour and give birth to a brain-damaged baby. The evidence proposed was to the effect that:

- Escapees will try to go where they know and will seek out relatives and associates for financial assistance and support;
- Almost every escapee commits further crimes while at large;
- If the offender is addicted to heroin, offences such as armed robbery will be 'virtually certain' to be committed by the escapee to obtain money to fund the addiction;
- Responsible law enforcement and prison officials, if they had turned their minds to the question, would have been aware that it was probable and foreseeable that the escapee would proceed to the area in which he had grown up and would probably commit offences in that region to obtain money to satisfy his heroin addiction;
- It was more probable than not that the escapee would commit more serious offences than housebreaking, and would engage in armed robbery, under the influence of his elder brother's career in that form of activity (at [6]).

Justice Shaw held that:

Behavioural profiling of criminal suspects by law enforcement officials is, in my opinion, an organized body of knowledge upon which they legitimately draw in the course of their duties. This is not to raise the predictions of Mr Wicks to a science. Rather, the knowledge of the habits, probable location and likelihood of re-offending of persons who have escaped from gaol is a corpus of knowledge the community would expect of a competent law enforcement agency or officer to have and to utilize in the manner suggested by Mr Wicks, that is, the ability to track or otherwise locate an escaped prisoner. (At [21])

It is unlikely that the decision will be applied in criminal cases. Shaw J noted that, 'in civil cases, every consideration should favour the court having relevant material rather than rejecting it on technical grounds, providing of course that the parties are afforded procedural fairness' (at [24]).

Issues relating to the psychological condition of the deceased were raised in the complex Australian criminal case best known for its conflicting evidence from forensic pathologists: *Velevski v The Queen* (2002) HCA 4; see also *R v Velevski* (1999) NSWCCA 96. The fundamental issue disputed at appellate levels was whether twin babies of three months, their sister of six and their mother, Snezana Velevski, were murdered by their father or whether the deaths were brought about in the course of a murder-suicide in which the mother killed herself. At trial, a psychiatrist was permitted to give expert testimony on behalf of the defence in relation to the mental state of Mrs Velevski prior to her death. The admissibility of this evidence was not challenged. The psychiatrist had not seen the deceased but relied upon her medical records as well as upon interviews with the accused and his parents. He formed the view that Mrs Velevski may have been under stress in the months prior to her death and developed a depressive illness. He concluded that at the relevant time she might have been becoming psychotic with symptoms of confusion, perplexity and lability of mood emerging in the post-partum period following the births of her twins. He referred to Mrs Velevski appearing to be confused and disoriented on the morning of the killings and to her depression concerning the poor state of her marriage. He also noted that her brother experienced a severe depressive illness a few years previously, perhaps indicative of a family propensity to mental illness. He suggested that she killed herself and her children in the course of a psychotically depressive episode.

The testimony of this psychiatrist was not formally described during the course of the trial as a psychological autopsy or an equivocal death analysis, although, as a reconstruction of the mental state of a person prior to her death, it clearly was based on a traditional, clinical version of the psychological autopsy. In a dissenting judgment in the New South Wales Court of Appeal, David Kirby J raised a number of matters which he regarded as inconsistent with the proposition that the deceased woman may have been psychiatrically disturbed and inclined to take her own life: [1999] NSWCCA 96 at [207]-[227]. In the High Court, Gummow and Callinan JJ, who reflected on this aspect of David Kirby J's dissent, found that his Honour's concerns were more properly described as speculation than as a ground for finding a miscarriage of justice to have taken place. The decision highlights the need for expert evidence to be adduced from a suitably qualified profiler and to be grounded in data and published analyses if what is being canvassed is in relation to a psychological autopsy.

Canadian Caselaw

A series of cases has addressed the admissibility of psychological profiling evidence in Canada. The decisions constitute the most important analysis of the admissibility of profiling evidence thus far. Their reasoning is likely to be applied in other jurisdictions.

The most significant of the decisions is the Supreme Court decision of *R v Mohan* [1994] 2 SCR 9; (1994) 89 CCC (3d) 402, arguably Canada's most important decision in relation to the admissibility of expert evidence. The accused was a paediatrician who was charged with a number of sexual assaults upon female patients aged between 13 and 16. The accused sought unsuccessfully at trial to call evidence from a psychiatrist that the perpetrator of the offences alleged to have been committed would be part of a limited and unusual group of individuals and that the accused did not fall within the class because he did not possess the characteristics belonging to members of the group.

In the course of the *voire dire* into the admissibility of the psychiatrist's evidence, the expert explained that there are three general personality groups that have unusual personality traits in terms of their psychosexual profile. The first, he said, encompasses the professional who suffers from major mental illness, such as schizophrenia, and who engages in inappropriate sexual behaviour occasionally. He maintained that the second and largest group contains the sexual deviation types, persons who show distinct abnormalities in terms of the choice of individuals with whom they report sexual excitement and with whom they would like to engage in some type of sexual activity. The third group, he said, is made up of sexual psychopaths, individuals with a callous disregard for people around them, including a disregard for the consequences of their sexual behaviour.

The expert identified paedophiles and sexual psychopaths as examples of members of unusual and limited classes of persons. In response to questions hypothetically encompassing the allegations of the four complainants in respect of whom the accused was charged, the expert stated that the psychological profile of the perpetrator of the first three complaints would be likely to be that of a paedophile, while the profile of the perpetrator of the fourth set of offences would be likely to be that of a sexual psychopath. He said that if the one person was responsible for the offences involving all four of the complainants, he would be likely to be a sexual psychopath, such an individual belonging to a very small, behaviourally distinct category of persons. He said that if the perpetrator was a physician, this would bring him into an even more limited class. It was proposed by the defence that the psychiatrist would go on to testify that the accused did not have the characteristics attributable to any of the three groups into which most sex offenders fall.

The court held that the admission of expert evidence depends on the criteria of:

- relevance;
- necessity in assisting the trier of fact;
- the absence of any exclusionary rule; and
- a properly qualified expert.

It noted a previous decision of the court in *R v Morin* (1988) 44 CCC (3d) 193; [1988] 2 SCR 345; 66 CR (3d) 1 (SCC) (see Kaufman, 1998) where it had been held unanimously that the Crown cannot lead character evidence unless it is relevant to an issue and is not being used merely as evidence of disposition. It held that different considerations apply when the evidence is adduced by the accused who is permitted to call such evidence as to disposition both in his or her own evidence or via evidence: 'The general rule is that evidence as to character is limited to evidence of the accused's reputation in the community with respect to the relevant trait or traits. The accused may rely on specific acts of good conduct': at 415. They noted that evidence from an expert that the accused, by reason of his or her mental make-up or condition of the mind, would be incapable of committing or being disposed to commit the crime, does not fit either of these categories. Referring to the English decision of *R v Chard* (1971) 56 Cr App R 268; *Lowery v The Queen* [1974] AC 85 and *R v Turner* [1975] 1 QB 834, the court noted the English approach of proscribing expert opinion evidence, with the exception of evidence on non-insane automatism, to show the accused's state of mind unless it is contended that the accused is abnormal in the sense of suffering from insanity or diminished responsibility. The court referred to the Canadian decision of *R v Lupien* (1970) 2 CCC 193; 9 DLR (3d) 1; [1970] SCR 263 (SCC) which permitted psychiatric evidence for an accused to show lack of intent that where the accused reacted violently to any form of homosexual activity. Similarly it observed that in *McMillan v The Queen* (1975) 23 CCC (2d) 160; 29 CRNS 191; 7 OR (2d) 750 (Ont CA) the Court had affirmed the admissibility of evidence from a psychiatrist that a third party, the accused's wife, was more likely to have committed a murder of their infant child because she had a psychopathic personality disorder with brain damage.

The court in *R v Mohan* held that, before an expert's opinion is admitted as evidence, the trial judge must be satisfied, as a matter of law, that either the perpetrator of the crime or the accused has 'distinctive behavioural characteristics such that a comparison of one with the other will be of material assistance in determining innocence or guilt. ... The trial judge should consider the opinion of the expert and whether the expert is merely expressing a personal opinion of whether the behavioural profile which the expert is putting forward is in common use as a reliable indicator of membership in a distinctive group' (at 423). Putting the test another way, the court asked (at 423) whether the scientific community had developed:

> a standard profile for the offender who commits this type of crime? An affirmative finding on this basis will satisfy the criteria of relevance and necessity. Not only will expert evidence tend to prove a fact in issue but it will also provide the trier of fact with assistance that is needed. Such evidence will have passed the threshold test of reliability which will generally ensure that the trier of fact does not give it more weight than it deserves. The evidence will qualify as an exception to the exclusionary rule in relation to character evidence provided, of course, that the trial judge is within the field of expertise of the expert witness.

Applying the criteria to the facts of the case, the court in *Mohan* adopted the findings of the trial judge that a person who commits sexual assaults on young women cannot be said to belong to a group possessing behavioural characteristics sufficiently distinctive to be of assistance in identifying the perpetrator of the offences charged. In addition, the court found that the fact that the alleged perpetrator was a physician did not advance the case for reception of the profiling evidence because an acceptable body of evidence that doctors who commit sexual assaults fall into a distinctive class with identifiable characteristics had not been shown to exist. The court also accepted the trial judge's finding that there was no evidence to support the theory that the characteristics of the offending against the fourth complainant identified the perpetrator as a sexual psychopath. It observed that there was no evidence to support a finding that the profile of a paedophile or psychopath 'has been standardized to the extent that it could be said that it matched the supposed profile of the offender depicted in the charges' (at 423). The Supreme Court's decision was that, in the absence of adequate indicia of reliability, 'it cannot be said that the evidence would be necessary in the sense of usefully clarifying a matter otherwise inaccessible, or that any value it may have had would not be outweighed by its potential for misleading or diverting the jury' (at 424). Thus, the court's decision was that the admissibility of the profiling evidence had been correctly rejected.

The issue was revisited in *R v SCB* (1997) 119 CCC (3d) 530 where it was affirmed that psychiatric evidence that an accused person, because of his or her mental make-up, is unlikely to have committed the crime alleged, is generally inadmissible. Again, the problem identified at appellate level was that the mental health expert evidence did no more than indicate that some features of the hypothetical scenario presented to him were consistent with the acts of a sexual sadist or a person with an anti-social personality disorder. The expert did not suggest that others who did not fall within either of these categories could be excluded as possible perpetrators. The profiling evidence was held inadmissible on the basis that it did not address the question of whether the scientific community had developed a standard profile for the offender committing the particular kind of crime. In short, what was being demanded by the court were empirically based data as to the profile of offenders and the fact that the accused also met such a profile – a criterion that contemporary criminal profiling is not even close to being able to satisfy.

A similar approach was taken by the New Brunswick Court of Appeal in *R v Dowd* (1998) 120 CCC (4th) 360 where it had been argued on behalf of a dentist charged with a series of 18 indecent assaults that he should have been allowed to call psychiatric evidence that he did not exhibit the characteristics of the person who would have committed the offences.

In 2000, the Canadian Supreme Court was called upon to review the admissibility of profiling evidence adduced by the defence. In *R v J-LJ* [2000] SCC 51 the court was asked to determine whether a person accused of molesting two children should have been permitted to adduce psychiatric evidence that in all probability a serious sexual deviant with a highly distinctive personality disorder had inflicted the abuse upon the children and that the defendant did not display such personality traits in various tests including penile plethysmography. The court adhered to its settled approach. It applied its reasoning in *Mohan* and held that the trial judge had correctly excluded the profiling evidence. The psychiatrist had testified on *voire dire* that it is not possible to establish a standard profile of individuals with a disposition to sodomise young children but maintained that such people 'frequently' or 'habitually' exhibited distinctive characteristics which can be identified. He said that results from the Minnesota Multiphasic Personality Inventory Test Version Two (the MMPI-2), administered with the monitoring of electromyography (EMG) to measure anxiety, along with the plethysmograph, suggested that the accused did not have such characteristics or a serious sexual disorder.

The accused had been exposed to a range of sexual images and his penis measured by a plethysmograph. The psychiatrist found the accused to have a 'clearly normal profile' with a preference for adult women and a slight attraction for adolescents, but no deviancy in respect of boys in general or specifically prepubescent boys, the category of victim in the case before the court.

The court acknowledged the 'essential role' of expert witnesses in criminal cases and noted the comment of Sopinka J in *Mohan* that:

> Dressed up in scientific language which the jury does not easily understand and submitted through a witness of impressive antecedents, this evidence is apt to be accepted by the jury as being virtually infallible and as having more weight than it deserves.

Justice Binnie (at [25]) commented:

> [T]here is also a concern inherent in the application of this criterion that experts not be permitted to usurp the functions of the trier of fact. Too liberal an approach could result in a trial's becoming nothing more than a contest of experts with the trier of fact acting as a referee in deciding which expert to accept.

He emphasised that, while courts should be extremely cautious in restricting the power of an accused person to call evidence in his or her defence, such evidence must be excluded if it may 'distort the fact-finding process': at [29]. The court found that the psychiatrist's evidence satisfied the first *Mohan* requirement that the subject matter be such that ordinary people are unlikely to form a correct judgment about it, unassisted by persons with specialised knowledge. It noted that what is necessary for evidence of disposition to be admissible is that the particular disposition or tendency be characteristics of a distinctive group: '[T]he term "distinctive" more aptly defines the behavioural characteristics which are a pre-condition to the admission of this kind of evidence.' It applied the *Mohan* determination that 'novel science' should be subject to 'special scrutiny' to determine whether it meets a basic threshold of reliability and whether it is essential in the sense that the trier of fact will be unable to come to a satisfactory conclusion without the assistance of the expert.

The court acknowledged that the penile plethysmograph is generally recognised by the scientific community and is used by well-regarded psychiatric facilities to monitor the result of treatment for sexual pathologies. However, it noted that this was not the situation of the accused and commented (at [35]):

> Dr Beltrami is a pioneer in Canada in trying to use this therapeutic tool as a forensic tool where the problems are firstly to determine whether the offence could only be committed by a perpetrator who possesses distinctive and identifiable psychological traits, secondly to determine whether a 'standard profile' of those traits has been developed, and thirdly to match the accused against the profile.

This meant that his evidence was subject to 'special scrutiny', in particular because of the closeness of the profiler's opinion to the ultimate issue. It held that 'the closer the evidence approaches an opinion on an ultimate issue, the stricter the application of this principle'.

In looking at the 'distinctiveness' criterion, the court held that the offence concerned must be shown only to be committed by members of a distinctive group and then that 'the personality profile of the perpetrator group must be sufficiently complete to identify distinctive psychological elements that were in all probability present and operating in the perpetrator at the time of the offence. Lack of distinctiveness robs the exception of its raison d'être' (at [40]; see also *R v B(SC)* (1997) 119 CCC (3d) 530 at 537 (Ont CA); *R v KB* (1999) 176 NSR (2d) 283 (CA). Binnie J for the court accepted that the level of detail required in the 'standard profile' may vary with the conclusiveness of individual elements (see, for example, necrophilia: *R v Malboeuf* [1997] OJ No 1398 (QL)(CA). However, he held that 'more common personality disorders' are less distinctive and likely to serve as 'badges' to distinguish the perpetrator class from the rest of the population, to the point potentially of being of little assistance: see, for example, *R v Perlett* [1999] OJ No 1695 (QL)(SCJ). Justice Binnie stated (at [44]):

> Between these two extremes, the range and distinctiveness of personality traits attributed to perpetrators of different offences will vary greatly. The requirement of the 'standard profile' is to ensure that the profile of distinctive features is not put together on an ad hoc basis for the purpose of a particular case. Beyond that, the issue is whether the 'profile' is sufficient for the purpose to be served, whether the expert can identify and describe with workable precision what exactly distinguishes the distinctive or deviant perpetrator from other people. If the demarcation is clear and compelling, the fact that the personality portrait cannot be filled in with elements that do not serve to distinguish the perpetrator is not fatal to acceptance of the evidence.

The court accepted that the psychiatrist was an expert but found that his definition of a 'distinctive' group of individuals to commit the 'distinctive crimes' before the court was 'vague'. The court noted that the reliability of the scientific foundations of the theory that certain acts will almost always be done by people having certain distinctive characteristics requires evidence; it cannot simply be assumed: at [49]. It found that the *Mohan* requirement of a standard profile should not be taken to require an exhaustive inventory of personality traits – the profile must confine the class to useful proportions. The court instanced (at [49]) a spectrum of personality disorders stretching from alcoholics to sexual psychopaths as too broad to be useful. It interpreted this to mean that the onus upon the defence is to satisfy the trial court that the underlying principles and methodology of the tests are reliable and, importantly, applicable. In the particular case the defence did not succeed in this regard, the MMPI-2 not being designed for the detection of sexual disorders and not containing any specific probe for unusual sexual preferences. No evidence was called from those who conducted the interviews or administered the plethysmography. Nor were test protocols introduced. Nor was there confirmation that standard procedures for its administration had been followed. Significantly, too, the psychiatrist noted the plethysmograph would detect a sexual deviant only 47.5% of the time. In addition, the judge took account of the fact that the psychiatrist did not explain how, if the basis of the plethysmography was the stimulation of remembrance of past pleasures, the results would vary according to the degree of deviance from some norm. He also took into account that a false negative could be caused by the fact that the visual and auditive scenarios presented to the subject lacked specific elements of stimulation, for example humiliation of the victim. The Supreme Court found (at [55]) that the trial judge had had good reason to be sceptical about the value of the testimony of the psychiatrist:

> [E]ven giving a loose interpretation to the need for a 'standard profile', and passing over the doubts that only a pedophile would be capable of the offence, the evidence of the test error rate in the 'match' of the [accused] with or his 'exclusion' from the 'distinctive class' was problematic. The possibility that such evidence – 'cloaked under the mystique of science' (Beland, at 434) – would distort the fact-finding process, was very real. Moreover, defence evidence of this type can be expected to call forth expert evidence from the Crown in response, with the consequent danger that the trial could be derailed into a controversy on disposition or propensity, with the trial becoming 'nothing more than a contest of experts with the trier of fact acting as referee in deciding which expert to accept' (Mohan, at 24).

The court also had regard to the *Mohan* necessity requirement, commenting (at [56]) that:

> [the] purpose of expert evidence is thus to assist the trier of fact by providing special knowledge that the ordinary person would not know. Its purpose is not to substitute the expert for the trier of fact. What is asked of the trier of fact is an act of informed judgment, not an act of faith.

The court observed that the psychiatrist had not meaningfully explained the facts upon which his opinion had been based. The bottom line was that a conclusory opinion had been offered that, on cross-examination, turned out to be short on demonstrated scientific support.

Moreover, the psychiatrist's evidence was regarded as, in effect, being that the denial of the accused should be believed because he was not the sort of person to offend in such a way. The court noted that this was close to 'oath-helping' in circumstances that did not fit within any legitimate exception. It found, too, that on the basis of a 'cost-benefit' analysis of the necessity requirement, it would have been open to the trial judge to have rejected the psychiatrist's opinion as well.

Crime Scene Analysis Evidence

Two important Ontario Court of Appeal decisions have scrutinised evidence lying on the junction between criminal profiling evidence and evidence analysing a crime scene: *R v Ranger* (2003) 178 CCC (3d) 375; *R v Clark* (2004) 182 CCC (3d) 1. It is likely that their approach and the distinctions that they drew will be followed in other jurisdictions.

In *R v Ranger* (2003) 178 CCC (3d) 375 two sisters were stabbed to death in their home. The accused and his cousin were charged. The prosecution theory was that the accused decided that if he could not have one of the sisters, his former lover, then no one else would. It called Detective Inspector Lines, the Manager of the Behavioural Sciences Section of the Ontario Police Investigative Support Bureau, as an expert in crime scene reconstruction and profiling. She expressed the view that the break-in to the house had been staged and that the person most likely to have been responsible was someone with an association or relationship with the victim and who had no interest in the possessions of the deceased. This pointed a finger squarely toward the accused.

It was put that Detective Inspector Lines had conducted criminal profiling in over 1000 cases, some 500 of which had been homicide investigations. It was also said that about 25 of the cases previously investigated by Detective Inspector Lines had included crime scene staging. Justice of Appeal Charron, writing the leading judgment, noted that the fact that a crime scene may have been staged to look as if the house had been burgled is a piece of circumstantial evidence that may provide some insight into the perpetrator's motivation and, in turn, her or his identity. He accepted that criminal profiling may be a useful, albeit potentially dangerous aid to police investigations, but regarded its use as a means of proof in the courtroom as quite another matter. To this extent, his approach was entirely in conformity with that of *R v Mohan* [1994] 2 SCR 9; (1994) 89 CCC (3d) 402 and *R v J-LJ* [2000] 2 SCR 600; 148 CCC (3d) 487.

He contrasted profiling evidence with crime scene analysis which quite regularly meets the legal requirements for admissibility (at [71]; see Ormerod, 1996):

> A few examples readily come to mind: an expert's opinion in an arson case that a fire was not accidental but, rather, deliberately set; opinion evidence explaining the significance of blood splatters; a pathologist's opinion about the likely cause of death or of injuries observed on a deceased victim; an expert's opinion on how a motor vehicle accident happened. There are many more examples. This kind of evidence assists the trier of fact in understanding WHAT the crime scene shows. The admissibility of that kind of evidence will usually turn on questions of relevance or the witness's particular expertise.

He contrasted (at [72]; see Ormerod, 1996) such evidence with attempts to adduce expert opinion evidence about 'WHY an offence was committed in a particular manner and, more particularly, about WHO is more likely to have committed the offence', which previously had been found in Canada not to be admissible.

Justice Charron for the court found ([at 82]) that Detective Inspector Lines' opinions about the perpetrator's likely motivation for staging the crime scene and his characteristics as a person associated with the victims and having a particular interest in one of the sisters constituted evidence of criminal profiling:

Criminal profiling is a novel field of scientific evidence, the reliability of which was not demonstrated at trial. To the contrary, it would appear from her limited testimony about the available verification of opinions in her field of work that her opinions amounted to no more than educated guesses. As such, her criminal profiling evidence was inadmissible. The criminal profiling evidence also approached the ultimate issue in this case and, hence, was highly prejudicial.

(See, too, *New York v McDonald* 231 AD 2d 647 (1996); *California v Singh* 37 Cal App 4th 1343 (1995); *United States v Yost* 24 F 3d 99 (1994).)

The Ontario Court of Appeal had occasion to consider cognate issues a year later in *R v Clark* (2004) 182 CCC (3d) 1. The accused was convicted of two counts of first degree murder. The victims were found stabbed to death in bed with no sign of a struggle. The accused was shown to have been using the credit card of one of the deceased. The prosecution theory was that the accused had killed the victims in order to silence them.

Once again Detective Inspector Lines was called. Moldaver JA for the court applied the reasoning of Charron JA in *Ranger* but took his analysis further. He found that a properly qualified expert in crime scene analysis can offer opinion evidence about what occurred at the crime scene and about how the crime was committed. He classified such evidence as 'crime scene reconstruction evidence'. He found (at [76]) that, assuming a properly qualified witness, the following three areas will generally require close attention:

- whether the evidence is necessary in the sense that it is likely to fall outside the knowledge or normal experience of the average juror;
- whether the opinion is reliable in the sense that it is anchored in the evidence and not the product of guesswork or speculation; and
- whether there is a real danger that the jury will be overwhelmed by the evidence and give it more weight than it deserves.

He regarded the question of whether a crime scene is 'staged' as a subset of crime scene reconstruction evidence. He found that Detective Inspector Lines' impermissible criminal profiling evidence took two forms. First, in light of her opinion that the crime scene had been staged and her further opinion that people stage crime scenes to divert suspicion from themselves, she had interpreted this to mean that the person responsible for the deaths of the victims would have some knowledge or relationship with them. Applying the approach of the court in *Ranger*, he found this aspect of the profiler's evidence to be impermissible because it went to the motivation and characteristics of the likely perpetrator (see *Ranger* at [82]). He found too that the Inspector was not entitled to testify about the characteristics of the likely offender, characteristics which in the instant case fitted comfortably with the accused man. This was again because it constituted criminal profiling evidence. He held (at [90]), though, that evidence from the Inspector that the crime scene had been staged to make it appear as though a burglary had occurred had been properly admitted at trial on the basis that it was crime scene reconstruction evidence and on the basis that the witness was qualified to express an opinion about staging; that the evidence given by her fell outside the knowledge and experience of the average juror; that her opinion was reliable in the sense that it was anchored in the evidence and not the product of guesswork or speculation; and that the evidence of staging was not so complex or technical that the jury was likely to be overwhelmed by it and give it more weight than it deserved.

The Future for Profiling Evidence

In a number of countries, courts, other than coroners' courts, have exhibited a disinclination to permit evidence that the psychological make-up of a person makes it either more or less likely that it is they who have committed a criminal offence. It is likely that in those countries that do not apply exclusionary evidentiary rules in the Anglo-American-Australian way, circumspection will be exercised in relation to the use made of profiling evidence based upon its current scientific status.

In principle, the Canadian Supreme Court decisions of *R v Mohan* [1994] 2 SCR 9; (1994) 89 CCC (3d) 402 and *R v J-LJ* [2000] 2 SCR 600; 148 CCC (3d) 487 have opened the door to the reception of offender profiling evidence. However, the Supreme Court has not made the reception of such evidence straightforward; empirically grounded advances in profiling research will be necessary as a precondition to admissibility (see Kocsis, 2006).

The challenge lies ahead for witnesses who claim to be able to profile particular kinds of offenders, or even persons who have died (see *Gilfoyle* [2001] 2 Cr App R 57), to show empirically that certain kinds of crimes are only, or even predominantly, committed by persons of a particular psychological make-up. Until that point is reached, it will be very rare for evidence of offender profiling to be permitted on behalf of those accused of criminal conduct and even rarer for it to be able to be adduced on behalf of the prosecution in criminal cases. The potential in the aftermath of the decisions of *R v Ranger* (2003) 178 CCC (3d) 375 and *R v Clark* (2004) 182 CCC (3d) 1 is that evidence may be able to be given from persons interpreting the crime scene provided that they confine themselves to assisting juries to understand what the crime scene shows, rather than *why* an offender behaved in a certain way and what characteristics are likely to have been possessed by the offender. However, even this is not entirely straightforward as it will be incumbent upon the prosecution to establish that interpretation of the crime scene, such as comparative crime scene analysis is reliable.

Thus far, coroners' courts and some civil courts have proved readier to receive psychological profiling evidence than the criminal courts (see for example *Godfrey v New South Wales (No 1)* [2003] NSWSC 160). However, this too is controversial (see Freckelton and Ranson, 2006). Even in the context of inquests, difficult questions of admissibility and evaluation of probative value are raised by the weight that can properly be given to such expert opinion evidence.

References

Ainsworth, P. (2000) *Offender Profiling and Crime Analysis* (Devon: Willan Publishing).

Alison, L.J. (Ed.) (2005) *The Forensic Psychologist's Casebook* (Devon: Willan Publishing).

Alison, L. and Canter, D. (2005) Rhetorical shaping in an undercover investigation, in: Alison, L.J. (Ed.) *The Forensic Psychologist's Casebook* (Devon: Willan Publishing).

Alison, L.J., Bennell, C., Mokros, A. and Ormerod, D. (2002) The personality paradox in offender profiling. Psychology, *Public Policy and Law*, 8, pp. 115–135.

Ammon, J. (1995) The psychological autopsy, *American Journal of Forensic Psychology*, 13(2), p. 39.

Bendheim, O. (1979) The psychiatric autopsy: its legal application, *Bulletin of the American Academy of Psychiatry and Law*, 7, p. 400.

Blau, T.H. (1994) *Psychological Services for Law Enforcement* (New York: Wiley).

Canter, D. (1989) Criminal profiles, *The Psychologist*, 2(1), p. 12.

Canter, D. (1994) *Criminal Profiling* (London: Harper Collins).

Canter, D. (2003) *Mapping Murder: The Secrets of Geographical Profiling* (London: Virgin Books).

Canter, D. (2004) Offender profiling and investigative psychology, *Journal of Investigative Psychology and Offender Profiling*, 1, p. 1.

Canter, D. and Alison, L. (Eds) (1999) *Profiling in Policy and Action* (Dartmouth: Ashgate).

Canter, D. and Alison, L. (Eds) (2000a) *Profiling Property Crimes* (Dartmouth: Ashgate).

Canter, D. and Alison, L. (Eds) (2000b) *The Social Psychology of Crime: Groups, Teams and Networks* (Dartmouth: Ashgate).

Canter, D. and Youngs, D. (2003) Beyond offender profiling: the need for an investigative psychology, in: D. Carson and R. Bull (Eds) *Handbook of Psychology in Legal Contexts* (Chichester: Wiley).

Canter, D.V., Alison, L.J., Alison, E. and Wentink, N. (2004) The organized/disorganized typology of serial murder: myth or model? *Psychology, Public Policy and Law*, 10, p. 293.

Cavanagh, J.T., Owens, D.G. and Johnstone, E.C. (1999) Life events in suicide and undetermined death in south east Scotland: a case control study using the method of psychological autopsy, *Social Psychiatry and Psychiatric Epidemiology*, 34(12), p. 645.

Cavanagh J.T., Carson, A.J., Sharpe, M. and Lawrie, S.M. (2003) Psychological autopsy studies of suicide: a systematic review, *Psychological Medicine*, 33(3), p. 395.

Cox, K. (1999) Psychologists as expert witnesses, in: D. Canter and L. Alison (Eds) *Profiling in Policy and Practice* (Dartmouth: Ashgate).

Davis, M.R. (2005) The psychological autopsy: structured guidelines for conducting equivocal death analyses. Paper presented to the 25th Annual Congress of the Australian and New Zealand Association of Psychiatry, Psychology and Law, Wellington, New Zealand, 5 November 2005.

Douglas, J.E. and Olshaker, M. (1996) *The Anatomy of Motive* (New York: Heinemann).

Douglas, J.E. and Olshaker, M. (2000) *Mindhunter* (New York: Heinemann).

Douglas, J.E., Burgess, A.W., Ressler, A.F. and Ressler, R.K. (1993) *Crime Classification Manual* (New York: Simon & Schuster).

Egger, S.A. (1999) Psychological profiling: past, present, and future, *Journal of Contemporary Criminal Justice*, 15, p. 242.

Freckelton, I. (2006) Untimely death, law and suicidality, *Psychiatry, Psychology and Law*, 12(2), p. 265.

Freckelton, I. and Ranson, D. (2006) *Death Investigation and the Coroner's Inquest* (Melbourne: Oxford University Press).

Freckelton, I. and Selby, H. (2005) *Expert Evidence: Law, Practice, Procedure and Advocacy*, 3rd edn (Sydney: Thomson).

Geberth, V.J. (1990) *Practical Homicide Investigation: Tactics, Procedures and Forensic Techniques* (New York: Elsevier).

Hawton, K., Appleby, L., Platt, S., Foster, T., Cooper, J., Malmberg, A. and Simkin, S. (1998) The psychological autopsy approach to studying suicide: a review of methodological issues, *Journal of Affective Disorders*, 50, p. 269.

Holmes, R.M. and Holmes, S.T. (1996) *Profiling Violent Crimes: An Investigative Tool*, 2nd edn (New York: Sage).

Jackson, J. and Bekerian, D. (1997) *Offender Profiling: Theory, Research and Practice* (New York: Wiley).

Kaufman, F. (1998) *Report of the Commission on Proceedings Involving Guy Paul Martin* (Queen's Printer for Ontario).

Keppel, R.D. and Birnes, W.J. (2003) *The Psychology of Serial Killer Investigations: The Grisly Business Unit* (Elsevier).

Kirkpatrick, L.C. (1998) Profile and syndrome evidence: its use and admissibility in criminal prosecutions, *Secur Jour*, 11, pp. 255–257.

Kocsis, R.N. (1998) Criminal profiling, *Psychiatry, Psychology and Law*, 5(2), p.197.

Kocsis, R.N. (2003) Criminal psychological profiling: validities and abilities, *International Journal of Offender Therapy and Comparative Criminology*, 47, p. 126.

Kocsis, R.L. (2006) *Criminal Profiling: Principles and Practice* (Humana Press).

Kocsis, R.N. and Irwin, H.J. (1997) An analysis of spatial patters in serial rape, arson and burglary, *Psychiatry, Psychology and Law*, 4(2), p. 195.

LaFon, D.S. (1999) The psychological autopsy, in: B. Turvey (Ed.) *Psychological Profiling,* 2nd edn (New York: Academic Press).

LaFon, D.S. (2004) *Psychological Autopsies: Science and Practice* (Boca Raton: CRC Press).

McMahon, M. (2002) Murder or suicide? Expert evidence on psychological autopsies in cases of ambiguous homicide. Paper presented to the Australian and New Zealand Criminology Society Conference, Brisbane, 3 October 2002

Meyer, C.B. (2007), Criminal Profiling as expert evidence, in: R.N. Kocsis (Ed.) *Criminal Profiling: International Theory, Research, and Practice* (Humana Press, in press).

Meyer, R.G. and Weaver, C.M. (2006) *Law and Mental Health: A Case-Based Approach* (New York: Guilford Press).

Ogloff, J.R.P. and Otto, R.K. (1993) Psychological autopsy: clinical and legal perspectives, *Saint Louis University Law Journal*, 37, p. 607.

Ormerod, D.C. (1996) The evidential implications of psychological profiling, *Criminal Law Review*, 863.

Ormerod, D. and Sturman, J. (2005) Working with the courts: advice for expert witnesses, in: L.J. Alison (Ed.) *The Forensic Psychologist's Casebook* (Devon: Willan).

Otto, R.K., Poythress, N., Starr, L. and Darkes, J. (1993) An empirical study of the reports of APA's peer review panel in the congressional review of the USS Iowa incident, *Journal of Personality Assessment*, 61, p. 425.

Poythress, N., Otto, R.K., Darkes, J. and Starr L. (1993) APA's expert panel in the congressional review of the USS Iowa incident, *American Psychologist*, 48, p. 8.

Ressler, J.E., Burgess, A.W. and Douglas, J.E. (1988) *Sexual Homicide: Patterns and Motoives* (New York: Lexington Books).

Schneidman, E. (1994) The psychological autopsy, *American Psychologist*, 75.

Schneidman, E. and Collins, J. (1961) Sample investigations of equivocal deaths, in: N. Faberow and E. Schneidman (Eds) *The Cry for Help* (New York: McGraw-Hill).

Schneidman, E. and Faberow, N. (Eds) (2004) The cry for help, in: E. Schneidman (Ed.) *Autopsy of a Suicidal Mind* (Oxford: Oxford University Press).

Selkin, J. (1994) Psychological autopsy: scientific psychohistory or clinical intuition? *American Psychologist*, 74.

Snook, B., Taylor, P.J. and Bennell, C. (2004) Geographic profiling: the fast, frugal and accurate way, *Applied Cognitive Psychology*, 18, p. 105.

Snook, B., Eastwood, J., Gendreau, P., Goggin, C. and Cullen, R.M. (2007) Taking stock of criminal profiling: a narrative review and meta-analysis, *Criminal Justice and Behavior*, 34(4), 437–453.

Turvey, B. (2001) *Criminal Profiling: An Introduction to Behavioral Evidence Analysis* (New York: Academic Press).

Chapter 7

Implications of Heterogeneity among Individuals with Antisocial Behaviour

Henrik Andershed and Anna-Karin Andershed

We would argue that survey studies in the field of criminology have produced only a scattering of findings that are relevant for practice, either for the administration of juvenile justice or for intervention efforts to prevent or reduce delinquency.

(Loeber and Stouthamer-Loeber, 2002, p. 322)

A central aim for research on antisocial behaviour should be to produce knowledge that can be used to develop and implement effective interventions for people exhibiting antisocial behaviour. For a practitioner seeing a client with a history of antisocial behaviour the task is to find a way to approach the client to achieve a positive change in behaviour. As the practitioner turns to empirical evidence to find the most important aspects to take into account and focus on in this task, would there be sufficient knowledge to provide guidance? In many cases, we would argue that the answer is likely to be no. There are aspects of antisocial behaviour that are either under-researched or not teased apart in a satisfactory way, partly due to the fact that much of existing empirical knowledge has not addressed the heterogeneity among individuals with antisocial behaviour.

The main aim of this chapter is to try to highlight the importance of taking heterogeneity among individuals with antisocial behaviour seriously, and to discuss implications of doing so for research, practice, and the law. We wish to make the point that a considerable part of the limitations of present day knowledge concerning antisocial behaviour stems from the lack of theories and research focusing on teasing apart and understanding the heterogeneity among individuals exhibiting this behaviour. Even though we are far from the first to acknowledge this problem (see for example Farrington, 2005b; Loeber and Stouthamer-Loeber, 2002), we believe the issue is worth emphasizing and expanding on. The ambition of this chapter is not to be comprehensive in reviewing the field of antisocial behaviour but rather to attempt to underscore some examples of concrete problems and limitations of common research approaches used in the field, propose directions for possible ways to move forward, and briefly discuss some implications of considering, or not considering, heterogeneity in theory, research, and practice. We are using the term antisocial behaviour here to refer to deviant, aggressive, normbreaking, criminal behaviour, and offending among children, adolescents, and adults.

To researchers interested in explaining individual antisocial behaviour, a broad question that needs to be addressed and answered is: why do people develop antisocial behaviour? (Farrington, 2005a). This question is concerned with the development of antisocial propensity or potential (i.e. the potential to commit antisocial acts) and why some people exhibit a relatively high potential to commit antisocial acts, while others exhibit a relatively low potential. To answer this question, a correct description of antisocial behaviour is needed to begin with. As stated by Loeber and Stouthamer-Loeber (2002):

> The description of individual differences in criminal careers is a condition sine qua non for the better understanding of factors that can help to explain why some youth become involved in delinquency only marginally and others more deeply.
>
> (Loeber and Stouthamer-Loeber, 2002, p. 320)

In achieving this, one needs to acknowledge that individuals vary in their type of antisocial behaviour displayed, as well in the age of onset, frequency, severity, and duration of their antisocial behaviour. The second step in answering the above question is to understand and identify the causes, risk and protective factors of the antisocial behaviour of individuals with different types and developmental pathways of antisocial behaviour. Here, it seem essential to recognize that some factors and processes are important for some individuals whereas other factors and processes are more important for other individuals in understanding why they engage in antisocial behaviour. As stated by Farrington (2005b):

> From the viewpoint of both explanation and prevention, research is needed to classify types of people according to their most influential risk factors and most important reasons for committing crimes.
>
> (Farrington, 2005b, p. 84)

To a large extent there seems to have been a tendency to disqualify the possibility of heterogeneity in formulating theories and in conducting studies on antisocial behaviour. Although many prominent researchers in the field theoretically acknowledge that people may develop antisocial behaviour in different ways (e.g. Farrington, 2005b; Loeber and Stouthamer-Loeber, 2002; Frick and Morris, 2004; Lahey and Waldman, 2005; Le Blanc, 2005; Moffitt, 1993; 2003), we believe it is fair to say that, with rather few exceptions, both theory and research within psychology and related disciplines focusing on understanding antisocial behaviour have largely failed, or at least been quite limited, in taking heterogeneity into account.

A large number of risk factors on individual, family, and community level have been shown to co-vary or correlate with antisocial behaviour (see for example Farrington and Loeber, 2000; Loeber and Farrington, 2000). An impressive line of research has been very successful in producing a long list of factors that are related to antisocial behaviour and that *potentially* cause antisocial behaviour. However, studies of factors and processes related to antisocial behaviour have often been conducted without explicitly considering that some factors are of importance for explaining antisocial behaviour for one person or groups, while other factors are more crucial for explaining antisocial behaviour for another person or group. Consequently, there is limited knowledge about (1) whether the identified risk factors *actually* cause antisocial behaviour and (2) whether they *apply to all people* who develop antisocial behaviour or just some, and if so, whom. The differential importance of risk and causal factors for different people intersects closely with the concept of *equifinality*, which means that a certain outcome can emerge through several different causal developmental pathways (Cicchetti and Rogosch, 1996). Causes of antisocial behaviour vary across individuals. In addition, it is likely that heterogeneity in terms of causes exists within individuals over time (i.e. different factors are of importance during different periods or developmental stages in life) (e.g. Sampson and Laub, 2005).

Examples of Existing Lines of Research Taking Heterogeneity into Account

In this section we provide some examples of lines of research that seem promising and that underscores the importance of taking heterogeneity seriously in order to gain a better understanding of antisocial behaviour. There are at least four lines of research that in different ways are trying to tease apart heterogeneity within the group of individuals with antisocial behaviour: (1) research focusing on differences in causes and correlates between different ways of expressing antisocial behaviour (e.g. aggressive versus non-aggressive antisocial behaviour); (2) research focusing on identifying different developmental trajectories of antisocial behaviour per se; (3) research focusing on which factors are associated with different developmental trajectories of antisocial behaviour, and; (4) research focusing on subgrouping the population of individuals with antisocial behaviour without initial consideration of form of antisocial behaviour (e.g. by focusing on co-morbid problems in the group of individuals with antisocial behaviour, such as ADHD or psychopathy).

The line of research focusing on differences in causes and correlates between different ways of expressing antisocial behaviour has shown that qualitative aspects of antisocial behaviour are of importance. Antisocial behaviour is a broad and rather heterogeneous behavioural syndrome in itself. Aggressive behaviour is quite different from stealing. We know, for example from research, that genetic influences on aggressive antisocial behaviour are stronger compared to those of non-aggressive antisocial behaviour (e.g. Eley *et al.*, 2003). Furthermore, violence or aggression can be meaningfully subdivided into different subtypes or forms. As noted by Rutter (1978): 'Aggression can take many different forms and it would be unwise to assume that all varieties mean the same thing or have the same causes' (Rutter, 1978, p. 95). In line with this statement, it has for instance been shown that proactive and reactive aggressive behaviours differ in several basic ways (e.g. Dodge and Coie, 1987; Poulin and Boivin 2000).

Research focusing on identifying different developmental trajectories of antisocial behaviour per se is now rather extensive and seems to be growing quite rapidly. Many studies have shown that not all individuals follow the same developmental pathway or trajectory in terms of their antisocial behaviour *per se*, and that variations in these pathways or trajectories are important both for the description and understanding of antisocial behaviour (see for example Broidy *et al.*, 2003; Loeber *et al.*, 1999; Moffitt, 1993; 2003; Nagin and Tremblay, 1999; 2005; Patterson *et al.*, 1992). For example, several studies have shown that there are distinct developmental trajectories of aggressive behaviour during childhood (Broidy *et al.*, 2003; Nagin and Tremblay, 1999; Schaeffer *et al.*, 2003; Shaw *et al.*, 2003; see also Haapasalo and Tremblay, 1994). The number of trajectories found differs somewhat between studies. However, all studies report a trajectory that is characterized by a stable high aggressive behaviour, a trajectory characterized by a stable low aggressive behaviour, and usually one or two additional trajectories going from a medium high or mean level during early childhood to a lower level of aggressive behaviour in late childhood, or remaining on a relatively low level during the entire childhood. The stable high aggressive trajectory is predictive of numerous adjustment problems later in life, such as aggression, delinquency, conduct disorder, number of arrests and Antisocial Personality Disorder (Brame *et al.*, 2001; Broidy *et al.*, 2003; Nagin and Tremblay, 1999; Schaeffer *et al.*, 2003). This line of research clearly illustrates that people seem to follow rather distinctively different developmental pathways of antisocial behaviour.

A third line of research taking heterogeneity into account follows naturally from the previous. Here, the focus is on which risk or causal factors are associated with different developmental trajectories of antisocial behaviour (see for example Colder *et al.*, 2002; Lahey and Waldman, 2005; Moffitt, 1993; 2003; Shaw *et al.*, 2003). A well-known theory within this line of research is Moffitt's (1993, 2003) distinction between individuals with Life Course-Persistent (LCP) and individuals with Adolescence-Limited (AL) antisocial behaviour. The antisocial behaviour of the LCP individuals is initiated in childhood and continues through adolescence and adulthood, while the antisocial behaviour of the AL individuals is not initiated until adolescence and desists before entry into adulthood. These two groups are also thought to differ in terms of etiology (Moffitt, 1993; 2003). On the whole, there is good empirical support for this theory (Moffitt, 2003). However, Moffitt defines only one general type of causal background for the LCP and AL individuals, something that probably should be questioned in line with arguments for equifinality. Another theory focusing on factors related to different developmental trajectories of antisocial behaviour has recently been developed by Lahey and Waldman (2005). They argue that the same set of factors are important for the development of conduct problems for all children (various problematic temperamental dimensions and delays in verbal development), regardless of trajectory. The manifestation of a specific trajectory is decided by different combinations and levels of these factors and the interaction with the environment (Lahey and Waldman, 2005). We believe that this line of research can be taken at least one step further by considering the possibility that individuals within one and the same trajectory of aggressive or antisocial behaviour can have different sets of risk-factors explaining their trail. Put another way, the causal mechanisms behind a specific trajectory of antisocial behaviour may be different for different people.

The fourth line of research focuses on subgrouping the population of individuals with antisocial behaviour without initial consideration of type or form of antisocial behaviour, typically by focusing on some co-morbid psychiatric problem. Two meaningful subgroups that have been identified in research are children and adolescents with antisocial behaviour with co-morbid ADHD (see for example Waschbusch, 2002), or with co-morbid callous-unemotional traits (e.g. Frick, 2004; Frick and Morris, 2004). Both of these subgroups of youths has been shown to differ from other antisocial youths in terms of certain risk factors and risk for future antisocial behaviour. Both subgroups are at higher risk for continuing antisocial behaviour as compared to other youths with antisocial behaviour. In sum, this line of research shows that children with antisocial behaviour or conduct disorder (American Psychiatric Association 2000) constitute a very heterogeneous group. Interestingly, this implies that the current diagnostic subtype of childhood-onset conduct disorder may be too broad and non-specific to be really practically useful. A clear limitation of today's knowledge concerning this line of research is that research on these ways of subgrouping youths with antisocial behaviour largely has been conducted as separate lines of research. Consequently, the knowledge to what extent these ways of subgrouping individuals with antisocial behaviour are independent of or overlapping each other, is limited (see for example Waschbusch *et al.*, 2004). A group of researchers has focused on another co-morbid disorder, namely psychopathic personality disorder or psychopathy, commonly measured with the Hare Psychopathy Checklist-Revised (see Hare, 2003; Patrick, 2006; see also the chapter by David Cooke in the present volume). This subgrouping has been quite successful in identifying individuals with antisocial behaviour that differ in many important respects from other individuals with antisocial behaviour. Antisocial individuals with psychopathy are at higher risk of recidivism in antisocial behaviour, especially violence, and have an earlier onset of antisocial behaviour, as well as more frequent and versatile antisocial behaviour. They also differ from other individuals with antisocial behaviour in that, among other things, they show more specific cognitive deficits, neurobiological abnormalities, and generally seem less responsive to treatment efforts (see Patrick, 2006). Furthermore, although psychopathy is usually treated as a homogeneous construct, evidence from a growing body of theory and research suggests that there may be variants or subtypes of psychopathy (for a review, see Skeem *et al.*, 2003). A subgroup of individuals exhibiting antisocial behaviour reaching the diagnostic cut-off for psychopathy does not recidivate in antisocial behaviour, or does not exhibit specific cognitive deficits, and may be responsive to treatment. Thus, researchers within the field of psychopathy have started to tease apart the heterogeneity within this group of individuals exhibiting antisocial behaviour with the aim of producing more practically useful knowledge (see Hicks *et al.*, 2004; Poythress and Skeem, 2006; Skeem *et al.*, in press; Skeem *et al.*, 2003).

Heterogeneity and Genetic Influences on Antisocial Behaviour

There is now a considerable amount of research showing that there are genetic influences on antisocial behaviour (Rhee and Waldman, 2002). However, the overwhelming evidence stems from adoption and twin-studies, with the consequence that this knowledge is quite non-specific. That is, we know based on these findings that there are, at least in some people, genetically underbuilt risk factors for antisocial behaviour. However, these studies do not tell us what are the actual manifestations of these genetic risk factors or endophenotypes. Hence, we know that there are genetic risk factors for antisocial behaviour, but we do not, as of yet, have a good understanding of which factors they are, or how many there are, although researchers are now beginning to focus on this issue (see for example Caspi *et al.*, 2002; Scourfield *et al.*, 2004; Thapar *et al.*, 2001). Here as well, we would argue that an openness for heterogeneity may be important for a full understanding of how and why antisocial behaviour is partly underbuilt by genetic risks. Following the principle of equifinality, the genetically underbuilt risk factors for antisocial behaviour that evidently exist, are likely to be different and/or manifest in different constellations and levels, in different people. On the biological level, it may be that these potential differences between people in manifested genetic risk factors come from differences between people in complex constellations of genes.

On Analytical Approaches

> While statistical methods that incorporate unobserved heterogeneity are common in other disciplines, not many of these techniques will be in the toolbox of most criminologists.
> (Nagin and Paternoster, 2000, p. 139)

Taking heterogeneity and related theoretical assumptions seriously means that one also should be using research methods that correspond with, and can test, these assumptions. Correlations (i.e. degree of co-variation between two variables), and other statistical methods based on co-variation between variables (e.g. regression analysis and structural equation modelling) are of limited use in producing meaningful and useful knowledge for practice. This is because they hide, rather than reveal possible heterogeneity. Correlations simply do not give answers on the type of questions that the practitioner has (Loeber and Stouthamer-Loeber, 2002). They answer questions about variables, not people. Still, correlations certainly do have a place in the research process. They just do not take us far enough. They can favourably be used as a starting point in answering the basic question of whether a particular variable is a potential causal factor. However, it is not informative on the level of the individual. As stated by Loeber and Stouthamer-Loeber:

> The variable approach does have a place in research. However, for research findings to be practical, analyses of variables should serve to inform analyses of individuals.
>
> (Loeber and Stouthamer-Loeber, 2002, p. 322)

The vast majority of studies to date, looking at factors potentially influencing antisocial behaviour, have indeed focused on between-individual differences, i.e. factors that co-vary with antisocial behaviour, on group-level (Farrington, 2005b). When implications are drawn from these between-individual-based findings for use in interventions, that a change in these identified risk factors should lead to a reduction in antisocial behaviour, we may be wrong (Farrington, 2005b). It can seriously be questioned whether one really can draw valid conclusions about within-individual change from research on between-individual changes in antisocial behaviour. As noted by Farrington (2005b):

> The message is that risk factors that predict antisocial behavior between individuals may not predict offending within individuals, so that implications drawn from the between-individual comparisons about interventions may not be valid.
>
> (Farrington, 2005b, p. 75)

Other prominent researchers in the field, such as Loeber and Stouthamer-Loeber (2002), note this limitation of today's knowledge as well:

> The essential goal of criminal justice interventions is to bring about change in individuals. However, most survey studies concentrate on the study of variables explaining between-group differences or change in group averages over time rather than on factors explaining within-subject change. Similarly, most theories and explanatory models concern relationships between sets of independent variables on the one hand and, usually, one dependent variable on the other. These relationships often are expressed in terms of correlations.
>
> (Loeber and Stouthamer-Loeber, 2002, p. 322)

A conclusion here is that within-individual research seems more compelling than the corresponding between-individual approach in producing really useful knowledge for practice. Without being comprehensive we would like to take the opportunity here to mention briefly some examples of person-oriented statistical methods that can be quite useful for researchers interested in teasing apart individual differences among people developing antisocial behaviour.

A seemingly very promising group-based analytical technique for identifying different developmental trajectories over time of a variable, such as antisocial behaviour, has been developed by Nagin (see Nagin 1999, 2005; see also Nagin and

Tremblay, 1999, 2005, for relevant empirical examples). Other methods are more pattern-oriented, in which the variables under study gain their meaning through the configuration that they form together in the individual (see for example Bergman, 2001). These methods focus on the identification of individuals with similar patterns across variables of interest. There are many useful pattern-oriented statistical methods that place the individuals rather than the variables in focus. A method known to many is cluster analysis, used to identify individuals with similar constellations across the variables of interest. An interesting and useful alternative to common exploratory cluster analysis is the so-called model-based cluster analysis (see Banfield and Raftery, 1993; Fraley and Raftery, 2002, see also Hicks et al., 2004; Skeem et al. in press, for examples of application). Model-based cluster analysis avoids some of the problems inherent in common cluster analysis, for example the dilemma of choosing the number of clusters. Other examples of useful research methods focusing on persons rather than variables include Configural Frequency Analysis (CFA; von Eye, 1990), and EXACON (Bergman and El-Khouri, 1987). Both methods provide the possibility to look at patterns or combinations of values on discrete variables, and test the probability of a frequency of a pattern or combination to be more frequent (called Types) or less frequent (called Antitypes) than what could be expected by chance (Bergman, 1998). Both CFA and EXACON are modules of the statistical package Sleipner, version 2.1 (Bergman and El-Khouri, 2002), which exclusively includes various individual-oriented statistical methods (Sleipner can be downloaded for free at www.psychology.su.se/sleipner).

Implications for Research, Practice and the Law

We believe that there are several implications of our argument in this chapter for practice and the law. To reach a greater understanding of antisocial behaviour and individuals with antisocial behaviour and thus facilitating more effective interventions and correct and effective interactions with the law, we argue that researchers within psychology and related disciplines interested in antisocial behaviour need to develop and empirically test more specific theories that take into account the heterogeneity that exists within the group of individuals with antisocial behaviour. In terms of the law, we believe that there are at least three organizational units where much could be gained with an increased knowledge about heterogeneity: the police force (e.g. for the purposes of profiling – see Canter, 2000 – interrogation and preliminary investigation), court organizations (e.g. for the purposes of prosecution and sentencing), and correctional organizations (e.g. for the purposes of risk assessment, placement issues, management and treatment).

Furthermore, the fact that there are interventions that have proven effective for prevention and treatment of antisocial behaviour at group-level, does not automatically mean that they are effective for everyone (Frick, 2001, 2004). The effects of interventions that focus on single risk factors will likely be limited for the great majority of individuals with antisocial behaviour (Frick, 2004). In addition, interventions that are implemented without considering which individuals with antisocial behaviour would benefit from the specific programme at hand are likely to fail. One way in which intervention practice could improve is to move away from a 'one size fits all'-model, toward an adjustment of interventions to relevant subgroups of individuals with antisocial behaviour where factors such as unique patterns of risk and co-morbidity are considered. Hence, the effectiveness of specific interventions will be limited to the individuals displaying the risk factors which the intervention is aimed at reducing. For prevention and treatment to be effective, programming needs to be based on updated knowledge of risk- and protective-factors, and relevant contextual circumstances. A consideration of heterogeneity within the population of individuals with antisocial behaviour is crucial for the creation and implementation of successful interventions (e.g. Frick, 2001, 2004; Shirk *et al.*, 2000).

When it comes to the area of assessment of risk for recidivism in antisocial behaviour and violence, an important implication of our argumentation is that one cannot simply apply a general risk model on individuals based on the current state of knowledge. For each individual, one needs to decide whether each single risk factor, is really relevant (criminogenic) for that particular individual or not. For example, a problematic use of alcohol or drugs has shown to be a risk factor for recidivism in antisocial behaviour. However, based on existing empirical knowledge, we cannot say that this problem, if observed in an individual with antisocial behaviour, is related to an increased risk for recidivism in that particular individual. One needs to investigate for each individual whether the particular evidence-based risk factor observed in an individual is criminogenic or not. An example of a structured risk assessment instrument that seriously and systematically takes this into account is the Risk for Sexual Violence Protocol (RSVP; Hart *et al.*, 2003), in which the evaluator is asked to rate the relevance of each risk factor to the development of future management strategies.

Summary and Concluding Comments

The purpose of this chapter was to point out areas of theory, research, and practice where a consideration of heterogeneity is of importance. We also wanted to highlight limitations within these areas, which prohibit an appropriate and effective handling of the individual with antisocial behaviour.

Many researchers have argued and shown that people commit antisocial acts for different reasons and in different ways. The underlying patterns of risk factors and mechanisms, the developmental trajectories toward antisocial behaviour, and the patterns of antisocial behaviour and related difficulties are not the same for every delinquent child, antisocial adolescent, or adult individual with antisocial behaviour. In other words, there are several parameters in the process of describing, understanding, predicting, and preventing antisocial behaviour that require a consideration of heterogeneity within the population of individuals with antisocial behaviour.

With regard to theory, it is important to note that we do not want to argue here that a theory is only useful and sufficient if it includes all potential causal pathways to antisocial behaviour. Furthermore, it is probably not the case that different causal pathways are 100% distinct. It is probably more realistic to expect that some risk- or causal factors or processes are similar across different causal pathways whereas others are unique. We think that it is important to be open to the possibility of causal heterogeneity or equifinality even within one and the same antisocial behaviour-trajectory. That is, not all children on the stable high aggressive pathway will have the same causal background. We think that a practically useful theory needs to be aware of, and able to relate to, the fact that all risk factors and causal processes may not be similar for all people. In addition, we think it is important that researchers testing theories use analytical methods that are individual- or person-based in order to take heterogeneity into account. The common study of between-individual differences gives little information about the within-individual variations in patterns of antisocial behaviour that form the basis of the heterogeneity within the group of individuals with antisocial behaviour. More research is needed on the relationship between within-individual changes in risk factors and within-individual changes in antisocial behaviour (Farrington, 2005b).

It should be noted here that not all researchers interested in understanding antisocial behaviour would fully agree with our position (see for example Gottfredson and Hirschi, 1990; Sampson and Laub, 2005). For example, although Sampson and Laub (2005) clearly acknowledge that different causal factors can be of importance in different stages of life, which would be supportive of heterogeneity within individuals, they have stated that: '...our theory implies that offender subdivision is not warranted and that general mechanisms should in the first instance be sought for explaining crime at each age' (Sampson and Laub, 2005, p. 175). They also argue that this is based on findings from their long-term longitudinal study: '... we do not find good evidence that there are causally distinct groups with causally distinct trajectories' (Sampson and Laub, 2005, p. 175). Another example is Gottfredson and Hirschi's (1990) general theory of crime in which they argue that causes of antisocial behaviour are basically invariant with the age of the individual and that similar causes or constellations of causes operate at each developmental stage. However, this idea goes against several research findings, including the finding that the genetic influences are stronger on childhood-onset antisocial behaviour than on adolescent-onset antisocial behaviour (Taylor *et al.*, 2000).

People display antisocial behaviour in different ways and the causes of their antisocial behaviour can be quite different as well. We have tried to argue in this chapter that this kind of heterogeneity is crucial to tease apart in order to produce more meaningful, practically useful, and precise knowledge. We think that this can be done if a larger number of researchers develop and test new theories, or integrate existing theories that have their starting points in heterogeneity-principles such as equifinality. Scholars have already started to do this, and it seems very important that this research continues, and even accelerates, because of the considerable potential it holds for improving the understanding and prevention of antisocial behaviour.

References

American Psychiatric Association (2000) *Diagnostic and Statistical Manual of Mental Disorders*, 4th edn, Text Revision (Washington, DC: American Psychiatric Association).

Banfield, J.D. and Raftery, A.E. (1993) Model-based Gaussian and non-Gaussian clustering, *Biometrics*, 49, pp. 803–821.

Bergman, L.R. (1998) A pattern-oriented approach to studying individual development, in: R.B. Cairns, L.R. Bergman and J. Kagan (Eds) *Methods and Models for Studying the Individual*, pp. 83–121 (Thousand Oaks, California: Sage).

Bergman, L.R. (2001) A person approach in research on adolescence: Some methodological challenges, *Journal of Adolescent Research*, 16, pp. 28–53.

Bergman, L.R. and El-Khouri, B. (1987) EXACON: A FORTRAN 77 program for the exact analysis of single cells in a contingency table. *Educational and Psychological Measurement*, 47, pp. 155–161.

Bergman, L.R. and El-Khouri, B.M. (2002) *Sleipner – A statistical package for pattern-oriented analyses, vs. 2.1* (Stockholm: Department of Psychology, Stockholm University).

Brame, B., Nagin, D.S. and Tremblay, R.E. (2001) Developmental trajectories of physical aggression from school entry to late adolescence, *Journal of Child Psychology and Psychiatry and Allied Disciplines*, 42, 503– 512.

Broidy, L.M., Nagin, D.S., Tremblay, R.E., Bates, J.E., Brame, B., Dodge, K.A., Fergusson, D., Horwood, J.L., Loeber, R., Laird, R., Lynam, D.R., Moffitt, T.E., Pettit, G.S. and Vitaro, F. (2003) Developmental trajectories of childhood disruptive behaviors and adolescent delinquency: a six-site, cross-national study. *Developmental Psychology*, 39, pp. 222–245.

Canter, D. (2000) Offender profiling and criminal differentiation, *Legal and Criminological Psychology*, 5, pp. 23–46.

Caspi, A., McClay, J., Moffitt, T.E., Mill, J., Martin, J., Craig, I.W., Taylor, A. and Poulton, R. (2002) Role of genotype in the cycle of violence in maltreated children. *Science*, 297, pp. 851–854.

Cicchetti, D. and Rogosch, F.A. (1996) Equifinality and multifinality in developmental psychopathology, *Development and Psychopathology*, 8, pp. 597–600.

Cicchetti, D. and Toth, S.L. (1992) The role of developmental theory in prevention and intervention, *Development and Psychopathology*, 4, pp. 489–493.

Coie, J.D., Watt, N.F., West, S.G., Hawkins, D.J., Asarnow, J.R., Markman, H.J., Ramey, S.L., Shure, M.B. and Long, B. (1993) The science of prevention: a conceptual framework and some directions for a national research program, *American Psychologist*, 48, pp. 1013–1022.

Colder, C.R., Mott, J.A. and Berman, A.S. (2002) The interactive effects of infant activity level and fear on growth trajectories of early childhood behavior problems, *Development and Psychopathology*, 14, pp. 1–23.

Dodge, K.A. and Coie, J.D. (1987) Social-information-processing factors in reactive and proactive aggression in children's peer groups, *Journal of Personality and Social Psychology*, 53, pp. 1146–1158.

Eley, T.C., Lichtenstein, P. and Moffitt, T.E. (2003) A longitudinal behavioral genetic analysis of the etiology of aggressive and nonaggressive antisocial behavior, *Development and Psychopathology*, 15, pp. 383–402.

Farrington, D.P. (2005a) Introduction to integrated developmental and life-course theories of offending, in: D.P. Farrington (Ed.) *Integrated Developmental & Life-Course Theories of Offending – Advances in Criminological Theory*, Vol. 14, pp. 1–14 (New Brunswick: Transaction Publishers).

Farrington, D.P. (2005b) The integrated cognitive antisocial potential (ICAP) theory, in: D.P. Farrington (Ed.) *Integrated Developmental & Life-Course Theories of Offending – Advances in Criminological Theory*, Vol. 14, pp. 73–92 (New Brunswick: Transaction Publishers).

Fraley, C. and Raftery, A. E. (2002) MCLUST: software for model-based clustering, density estimation and discriminant analysis. *Technical report No. 415*, Department of Statistics, University of Washington.

Frick, P.J. (2001) Effective interventions for children and adolescents with conduct disorder, *The Canadian Journal of Psychiatry*, 46, pp. 26–37.

Frick, P.J. (2004) Developmental pathways to conduct disorder: implications for serving youth who show severe aggressive and antisocial behavior, *Psychology in the Schools*, 41, pp. 823–834.

Frick P.J. and Ellis, M.L. (1999) Callous-unemotional traits and subtypes of conduct disorder, *Clinical Child and Family Psychology Review*, 2, pp. 149–168.

Frick, P.J. and Morris, A.S. (2004) Temperament and developmental pathways to conduct problems, *Journal of Clinical Child and Adolescent Psychology*, 33, pp. 54–68.

Gottfredson, M.R. and Hirschi, T. (1990) *A General Theory of Crime* (Stanford: Stanford University Press).

Haapasalo, J. and Tremblay, R.E. (1994) Physically aggressive boys from ages 6 to 12: family background, parenting behavior, and prediction of delinquency, *Journal of Consulting and Clinical Psychology*, 62, pp. 1044–1052.

Haapasalo, J., Tremblay, R.E., Boulerice, B. and Vitaro, F. (2000) Relative advantages of person- and variable-based approaches for predicting problem behaviors from kindergarten assessments, *Journal of Quantitative Criminology*, 16, pp. 145–168.

Hare, R.D. (2003) *The Hare Psychopathy Checklist – Revised*, 2nd edn (Toronto, ON: Multi-Health Systems).

Harris, G.T. and Rice, M.E. (2006) Treatment of psychopathy: a review of empirical findings in: C.J. Patrick (Ed.) *Handbook of Psychopathy*, pp. 555–572 (New York: The Guilford Press).

Hart, S.D., Kropp, R.P., Laws, R.D., Klaver, J., Logan, C. and Watt, K.A. (2003) *The Risk for Sexual Violence Protocol (RSVP): Structured Professional Guidelines for Assessing Risk of Sexual Violence* (Vancouver: Pacific Psychological Assessment Corporation and the British Columbia Institute).

Hicks, B.M., Markon, K.E., Patrick, C.J., Krueger, R.F. and Newman, J.P. (2004) Identifying psychopathy subtypes on the basis of personality structure, *Psychological Assessment*, 16, pp. 276–288.

Hinshaw, S.P. (2002) Intervention research, theoretical mechanisms, and causal processes related to externalizing behavior patterns, *Development and Psychopathology*, 14, pp. 789–818.

Lahey, B.B. and Waldman, I.D. (2005) A developmental model of the propensity to offend during childhood and adolescence, in: D.P. Farrington (Ed.) *Integrated Developmental & Life-Course Theories of Offending – Advances in Criminological Theory*, Vol. 14, pp. 15–50 (New Brunswick: Transaction Publishers).

Le Blanc, M. (2005) An integrative personal control theory of deviant behavior: answers to contemporary empirical and theoretical developmental criminology issues, in: D.P. Farrington (Ed.) *Integrated Developmental & Life-Course Theories of Offending – Advances in Criminological Theory*, Vol. 14, pp. 125–164 (New Brunswick: Transaction Publishers).

Loeber, R. and Stouthamer-Loeber, M. (2002) The development of offending, in: S. Cote (Ed.) *Criminological Theories – Bridging the Past to the Future*, pp. 318–323 (Thousand Oaks, CA: Sage).

Loeber, R., Wei, E., Stouthamer-Loeber, M., Huizinga, D. and Thornberry, T. (1999) Behavioral antecedents to serious and violent juvenile offending: joint analyses from the Denver Youth Study, Pittsburgh Youth Study, and the Rochester Development Study, *Studies in Crime and Crime Prevention*, 8, pp. 245–263.

Lynam, D.R. (1996) Early identification of chronic offenders: who is the fledgling psychopath? *Psychological Bulletin*, 120, pp. 209–234.

Moffitt, T.E. (1993) Adolescent-limited and life-course-persistent antisocial behavior: a developmental taxonomy, *Psychological Review*, 100, pp. 674–701.

Moffitt, T.E. (2003) Life-course persistent and adolescence-limited antisocial behavior: a 10-year research review and a research agenda, in: B.B. Lahey, T.E. Moffitt and A. Caspi (Eds) *Causes of Conduct Disorder and Juvenile Delinquency*, pp. 49–75 (New York: Guilford Press).

Nagin, D.S. (1999) Analyzing developmental trajectories: a semi-parametric, group-based approach, *Psychological Methods*, 4, pp. 139–157.

Nagin, D.S. (2005) *Group-Based Modeling of Development over the Life Course* (Cambridge, MA: Harvard University Press).

Nagin, D. and Paternoster, R. (2000) Population heterogeneity and state dependence: state of the evidence and directions for future research, *Journal of Quantitative Criminology*, 16, pp. 117–144.

Nagin, D.S. and Tremblay, R.E. (1999) Trajectories of boys' physical aggression, opposition, and hyperactivity on the path to physically violent and nonviolent juvenile delinquency, *Child Development*, 70, pp. 1181–1196.

Nagin, D.S. and Tremblay, R.E. (2005) Developmental trajectory groups: fact or fiction? *Criminology*, 43, pp. 873–904.

Patrick, C.J. (2006) *Handbook of Psychopathy* (New York: Guilford Press).

Patterson, G.R., Crosby, L. and Vuchinich, S. (1992) Predicting risk for early police arrest, *Journal of Quantitative Criminology*, 8, pp. 333–355.

Patterson, G.R., Reid, J.B. and Dishion, T.J. (1992) *Antisocial Boys* (Eugene, OR: Castalia).

Poythress, N. G. and Skeem, J. L. (2006) Disaggregating psychopathy: where and how to look for subtypes. in C.J. Patrick (Ed.) *Handbook of Psychopathy*, pp. 172–192 (New York: Guilford Press).

Poulin, F. and Boivin, M. (2000) Reactive and proactive aggression: evidence of a two-factor model, *Psychological Assessment*, 12, pp. 115–122.

Rhee, S.H. and Waldman, I.D. (2002) Genetic and environmental influences on antisocial behavior: a meta-analysis of twin and adoption studies, *Psychological Bulletin*, 128, pp. 490–529.

Rutter, M. (1978) Family, area and school influences in the genesis of conduct disorders, in L.A. Hersov and M. Berger (Eds) *Aggression and Anti-social Behaviour in Childhood and Adolescence*, pp. 95–113 (Oxford: Pergamon Press).

Sampson, R.J. and Laub, J.H. (2005) A general age-graded theory of crime: lessons learned and the future of life-course criminology, in: D.P. Farrington (Ed.) *Integrated Developmental & Life-Course Theories of Offending – Advances in Criminological Theory*, Vol, 14 pp. 165–182 (New Brunswick: Transaction Publishers).

Schaeffer, C.M., Petras, H., Ialongo, N., Poduska, J. and Kellam, S. (2003) Modeling growth in boys' aggressive behavior across elementary school: links to later criminal involvement, conduct disorder, and antisocial personality disorder, *Developmental Psychology*, 39, pp. 1020–1035.

Scourfield, J., Martin, N., Eley, T.C. and McGuffin, P. (2004) The genetic relationship between social cognition and conduct problems, *Behavior Genetics*, 34, pp. 377–383.

Shaw, D.S., Gilliom, M., Ingoldsby, E.M. and Nagin, D.S. (2003) Trajectories leading to school-age conduct problems, *Developmental Psychology*, 39, pp. 189–200.

Shirk, S., Talmi, A. and Olds, D. (2000) A developmental psychopathology perspective on child and adolescent treatment policy, *Development and Psychopathology*, 12, pp. 835–855.

Skeem, J.L., Johansson, P., Andershed, H., Kerr, M. and Eno Louden, J. (in press) Two subtypes of psychopathic violent offenders that parallel primary and secondary variants, *Journal of Abnormal Psychology.*

Skeem, J.L., Poythress, N., Edens, J.F., Lilienfeld, S.O. and Cale, E.M. (2003) Psychopathic personality or personalities? Exploring potential variants of psychopathy and their implications for risk assessment, *Aggression and Violent Behavior*, 8, pp. 513–546.

Taylor, J., Iacono, W.G. and McGue, M. (2000) Evidence for a genetic etiology for early-onset delinquency, *Journal of Abnormal Psychology*, 109, pp. 634–643.

Thapar, A., Harrington, R. and McGuffin, P. (2001) Examining the comorbidity of ADHD-related behaviours and conduct problems using a twin study design, *British Journal of Psychiatry*, 179, 224–229.

Tolan, P.H. and Gorman-Smith, D. (2002) What violence prevention research can tell us about developmental psychopathology, *Development and Psychopathology*, 14, pp. 713–729.

von Eye, A. (1990) *Introduction to Configural Frequency Analysis: The Search for Types and Antitypes in Cross-classifications* (Cambridge: Cambridge University Press).

Waschbusch, D.A. (2002) A meta-analytic examination of comorbid hyperactive-impulsive-attention problems and conduct problems, *Psychological Bulletin*, 128, pp. 118–150.

Waschbusch, D.A., Porter, S., Carrey, N., Kazmi, S.O., Roach, K.A. and D'Amico, D.A. (2004) Investigation of disruptive behaviour in elementary-age children, *Canadian Journal of Behavioural Science*, 36, pp. 97–112.

Chapter 8

From Crime to Tort: Criminal Acts, Civil Liability and the Behavioral Science

Daniel B. Kennedy and Jason R. Sakis, J.D.

Introduction

Premises liability for negligent security is one of the fastest growing areas of tort litigation in the United States[1] and is expected to become an emerging basis of civil liability worldwide.[2] Negligent security is a theory of premises liability law, which is asserted by victims of crime against owners and occupiers of land for failing to prevent foreseeable and avoidable attacks from occurring.

This theory of civil liability may be asserted when an individual is attacked while he or she is visiting property owned by another. While business owners are not the guarantors of safety for these visitors, a legal duty is imposed upon them to exercise reasonable care to prevent foreseeable criminal attacks. The rationale underlying the imposition of a legal duty upon these business owners is that they are in the best possible position to prevent such criminal attacks from taking place on their premises. More importantly, society has determined that individuals should be relatively safe in their apartments, schools, shopping areas, restaurants, entertainment venues, and workplaces. For these two reasons, the general duty to provide protection for visitors and others legitimately upon the premises is recognized in the United States.

With the expansion of tort litigation in other parts of the world, it would not be unreasonable to expect this theory of liability to spread. A review of the literature suggests that this will occur, given that various forms of contingent legal fees have been adopted and are currently being adopted in the remainder of the developed world.[3] While some critics fear that these arrangements encourage unnecessary

---

1   Much of this growth can be attributed to the large verdicts and settlements these victims have been able to recover, a number of them exceeding $10 million (Bates, 2004).

2   According to the findings of a recent survey, insurance companies are becoming increasingly concerned about the growth of tort litigation in Europe (Insurance Leadership Institute 2004).

3   The Lithuanian Parliament, for instance, has enacted contingent legal fee legislation which authorizes attorneys to charge their clients a percentage of the recovery as an attorney fee (Klimas, 2000). Other countries have also adopted conditional fees. A conditional fee is a premium attorney fee paid if a case is won, but the premium is not related to the total recovery

litigation, it cannot reasonably be denied that they provide access to the court system for those citizens who would not otherwise be able to afford litigation. Regardless of who is correct, premises liability lawsuits alleging negligent security will become more common as these forms of attorney fee agreements are utilized.

In the United States, the explosive growth of negligent security litigation has spawned a new generation of forensic experts necessary for the prosecution and defense of these intricate lawsuits. These experts are needed because judges and juries are usually unfamiliar with criminological, sociological, and psychological theories as well as available security measures. Criminologists, psychiatrists, psychologists, sociologists, and security experts satisfy this role. Their contributions are required in order to establish the likelihood of crime occurring at a particular location, appropriate standards of care to be taken by owners and occupiers of land to prevent criminal attacks, the feasibility of security measures, and the psychological conditions of, and treatment recommendations for, crime victims. All of these expert contributions will be discussed in the second part of this treatise. In the first part, however, negligent security litigation will be examined in the context of a traditional negligence case.

Establishing Negligence/Negligent Security Cases

Negligence comprises four parts: (a) duty, (b) breach, (c) causation, and (d) damages. All of these parts, which are referred to as elements, must be established by a preponderance of the evidence by the party who initiates the lawsuit and requests relief. Essentially, the claimant is required to show that he or she was exposed to an unreasonable risk of harm by the alleged tort-feasor (e.g. landlord), who either acted in a manner inconsistent with the law or refrained from acting in a manner consistent with the law. Affirmatively proving that there was a legal duty on the part of the alleged tort-feasor is the first element of a negligence tort. This involves an examination of whether or not the harm that resulted from the action or inaction was reasonably foreseeable without the benefit of hindsight.

The breadth of such legal duties is as diverse as the factual circumstances to which they relate. Attorneys, judges, and juries should therefore rely upon the analysis of trained experts to determine the foreseeability of harm given a specific set of facts. Various tests for determining foreseeability in negligent security cases have been adopted in different jurisdictions. Some of them may be defined as conservative in nature and others as more liberal. This essentially means that foreseeability, in this context, depends entirely upon the test being applied since the tests themselves dictate the nature of the evidence that may be considered or is required (Kaminsky, 2001).

(Emons and Garoupa, 2004). Conditional fees have now been adopted in the United Kingdom, Belgium, and the Netherlands, the latter now considering the possibility of formally allowing contingency fees. Spain, Italy, and Portugal are also contemplating the adoption of conditional fees (Emons and Garoupa, 2004). Similarly, in France, attorneys are now accepting lower billing rates in exchange for success fees (Fleming, 2004).

Legal Duty/Foreseeability Tests

As a general proposition, business owners do not have a legal duty to protect visitors against the criminal attacks of third parties. When a special relationship exists between the parties, however, a duty may be imposed upon owners and occupiers of land to exercise reasonable care to prevent crime (American Law Institute, 1977). A number of relationships are deemed special because of the limited amount of control visitors have over their safety. These relationships include, but are not in any way limited to, innkeeper/guest, landlord/tenant, common carrier/passenger, university/ student, and business owner/patron. Regardless of the type, legal duty is limited to protecting against only those criminal acts that are foreseeable.

There are five basic foreseeability tests used in premises liability for negligent security cases: (a) the prior similar acts test, (b) the doctrine of specific harm aka the imminent danger rule, (c) the totality of the circumstances test, (d) the balancing test, and (e) the sliding scale test.[4]

Foreseeability under the prior similar acts model requires only that the general risk of attack, not the exact sequence of events that resulted in the criminal attack, be anticipated by the business. However, the evidence must reveal previous criminal acts of a similar nature on or near the premises in order to appropriately establish legal foreseeability (*Texas Real Estate Holdings, Inc. v. Quach* 2002). This approach has been criticized by some scholars as allowing the business owner to avoid civil liability for the first crime. Conversely, it has been praised by those who feel that the imminent danger rule is too restrictive.

The most conservative of these tests, known as the specific harm test and/or the imminent danger rule, requires notice of specific dangers to specifically identifiable visitors just prior to or during an attack (*Burns v. Johnson* 1995). Under this test, legal duty is often limited to summoning the police. Beyond contacting the police, very little is required on the part of the owner and/or occupier of land. While this test is advocated by some for the promotion of business in underdeveloped areas, the opposite effect might occur because most individuals do not want to frequent unsafe environments.

As premises security law has developed, foreseeability tests have become more intricate. One of the more liberal is the totality of the circumstances test. Under this particular approach, all of the factual circumstances are considered in the analysis. Although prior criminal attacks may be the most significant circumstance tending to demonstrate foreseeability under this approach, several other factors are also considered. These factors often include the crime rates in surrounding areas, environmental characteristics which may or may not make the premises an attraction to criminals, and the appropriateness of any security measures adopted (*Storts v.*

---

4   Some courts do not use any special formula for foreseeability in negligent security cases and choose to merely apply traditional negligence principles (*L.A.C. v. Ward Parkway Shopping Center Company, L.P.* 2002).

Hardee's Food Systems, Inc. 1998).[5] Many of the other issues relative to this test will be addressed in the behavioral sciences discussion.

The balancing test approach is basically a variation of the totality of the circumstances test. This test and the totality of the circumstances test are flexible methods of considering foreseeability which were conceived in response to the more rigid prior similar acts and imminent danger tests. With the balancing test, the foreseeable risk of criminal attack is compared to the business owner's ability and burden of abating unsafe conditions (*Smith v. Dodge Plaza Limited Partnership* 2002). In other words, the scope of the duty is determined by balancing the foreseeability of the harm against the legal duty to be imposed. The final foreseeability test, the sliding scale approach, appears to be an even more flexible hybrid of the balancing test. When there is a higher degree of foreseeability, the burden on the business owner to protect its visitors is commensurately higher (*Workman v. United Methodist Committee* 2003). Although numerous other variations of these standard tests have been utilized and adopted, the core principles are based upon one of the five main approaches.

Breach of Duty/Standards of Care

Once a legal duty to protect has been established, the victimized litigant must prove that there was a breach of some standard of conduct. On this issue, the forensic expert ordinarily explains what was or was not appropriate under the circumstances for the specific business or industry in question. Suffice it to say at this point that a number of industry standards have been adopted over the years. Without addressing any specific standards, it is important to enunciate clearly the general duty: a business owner's duty is to act as a reasonably prudent owner would under all of the circumstances. Civil liability will thus attach for a business owner's failure to exercise at least that amount of care.

Proximate Causation

The third element is proximate causation. This requires the victim of an attack to show a close connection between his or her assault and the business owner's failure to exercise reasonable care.[6] Presenting this argument is difficult because the harm inflicted upon an innocent victim is always the result of an intentional act of the criminal. Realizing this fact, owners and operators of land defend these lawsuits by arguing that their own actions or inactions have not caused the victim's injuries;

---

5   Generally speaking, violent crimes are foreseeable if the premises has been the site of other prior violent crimes, including robbery, assault, burglary, robbery, arson, abduction, murder, sexual assault, and rape (*Madden v. C & K Barbecue Carryout, Inc* 1988).

6   While various tort claims may be asserted directly against the perpetrators of these crimes, the reality is that these tort-feasors frequently lack the resources to compensate the victims.

business owners frequently attempt to limit blame to those who actually committed the crime itself. However, the law does not require crime victims to prove that their injuries were solely caused by the business owner's actions or inactions. Plaintiffs are merely required to show that a business owner's failure to provide protection was *a* proximate cause, not *the sole proximate cause*, of the harm. To be sure, the test is not whether proper security measures would have absolutely prevented an attack, but whether it was more likely than not that the attack would have been prevented absent the business owner's negligence (*Sandoval v. Bank of America, NT & SA* 2002).

Damages/Apportionment of Fault

In negligent security cases, the damage or harm to the victim can be significant because the attack often involves a rape, aggravated assault, or killing. For this reason, it is not uncommon for large verdicts to be awarded in these cases (e.g. *Hendry v. Zelaya* 2003).[7] Economic damages for lost income, earning capacity, and employment benefits are part of the compensation available to these individuals. Non-economic damages for physical pain and suffering, mental anguish, and denial of social pleasures are also available. Proving and disproving the damages element ordinarily requires expert testimony.

Negligent tort-feasors have traditionally been held responsible for all of the resulting damages caused by their culpable conduct. However, in negligent security cases, a different wrinkle arises because a third party intentionally causes the harm. To solve this problem, some courts have adopted an apportionment model of assigning responsibility to criminals, landowners, and even plaintiffs themselves (Leighton, 2003). These are known as comparative fault systems. Other courts, however, have refused to allow the negligent conduct of a landholder to be compared with the intentional conduct of a criminal.

Contributions of the Behavioral Sciences

It stands to reason that different criminal attacks will be characterized by different factual scenarios. Accordingly, the theories utilized by social scientists to interpret, understand, and explain foreseeability, standards of care, causation, and harm would depend on the facts of each case. Furthermore, social scientists may choose varying levels of explanation from which to launch their inquiry, ranging from a broader, grand scale approach through theories of the middle range to ad hoc explanations

---

7   An award of $4.5 million for past and future pain and suffering to a hotel bar patron, who was struck in the head with a beer bottle by a second patron, did not warrant a new trial. The award was supported by the evidence where the injured patron suffered brain damage, migraine headaches, and depression (*Hendry v. Zelaya* 2003).

that are highly idiographic in nature.[8] For example, there are numerous theories at various levels of abstraction and generality that can be applied to the question of foreseeability.

Legal Duty/Foreseeability Tests

Routine activity theory can be utilized to orient juries to the foreseeability issues of a security case. In essence, crime would be foreseeable where motivated offenders come together in time and place with suitable targets in the absence of capable guardians (Cohen and Felson, 1979). Thus, criminals might be attracted to the parking lot of a shopping center at night during the holiday shopping season where many female shoppers burdened with packages are returning to their cars. To the extent there are insufficient guardians in the form of visible patrols and where poor lighting and multiple hiding places abound, a criminal attack may be foreseeable.

Neighborhoods characterized by high density, poverty, mixed use, transience, and dilapidation are known to attract and/or generate criminal behavior (Stark, 1987). To the extent a defendant would be expected to be aware of these conditions, particularly if supported by census or other socioeconomic data (and given the correlation between crime and unemployment, poverty, etc), foreseeability of criminal attack may be established or refuted. Social scientists have also documented the relationship between certain types of land use and crime. Thus, properties that are located close to bars (Roncek and Maier, 1991), public housing (Roncek and Francik, 1981) and schools (Laub, 1987; Roncek and Lobosco, 1983) might be more vulnerable to crime, particularly if there has been any history of criminal attack.[9] On the other hand, although Sherman's research on 'hot spots' can be used to suggest that crime foreseeability increases with each instance of crime at an address, this same research established that many properties in high crime areas never experience a criminal incursion (Sherman *et al.*, 1989).[10]

Of course, what people are known to actually do in an area is of critical importance. Goldstein (1985) has shown the relationship between cocaine and economic, systemic, and psychopharmacological violence. The developing literature

---

8   See Kennedy (1984) for an early attempt to apply the knowledge of social and behavioral scientists to security practices.

9   Journey-to-crime research and further investigations of the distance-decay principle constitute analytic tools which can clarify the relationship between criminal attack and proximity to a source of criminals (Gore and Pattavina, 2004; Paulsen and Robinson, 2004). It would be quite helpful for any forensic expert to be familiar with the potential contributions of environmental criminology to issues of crime foreseeability (Brantingham and Brantingham, 1984; 1998; Kennedy, 1990).

10   Criminologists are very helpful in civil litigation due to their ability to interpret prior criminal activity at a location through an analysis of police calls for service and police narrative incident reports. Just as an individual's past behavior often forecasts future behavior, a location's past experience with crime is often used to assess future likelihood of crime.

on crime attractors and crime generators (Brantingham and Brantingham, 1995a) or, more generally, crime magnets (Ratcliffe and McCullagh, 1999) can also be used to assess the criminogenic qualities, if any, of a neighborhood.[11]

There is much in the criminological literature that would help jurors understand the foreseeability of hate crimes around gay bars (Comstock 1989; Harry 1982; Miller and Humphreys, 1980; Sagarin and MacNamara, 1975), and the attraction of pedophiles to playgrounds, video arcades, and roller skating rinks (Goldstein, 1999; van Dam 2001). In recent years, behavioral scientists have also generated forensically useful research identifying the extent of sexual abuse of elderly females in assisted living and nursing home facilities (Groth and Birnbaum, 1979; Safarik *et al.*, 2000), criminal proclivities among subsets of illegal immigrant populations (Ward, 2000), and the possibilities of increased violence among the mentally ill homeless who are also substance abusers (Hodgins, 1993; Snow *et al.*, 1989; Swanson *et al.*, 1990).[12] The foreseeability of an Alzheimer's patient wandering away from a nursing home and meeting an unfortunate death has also been an issue in litigation (Kennedy, 1993).

The problem of workplace violence has received much attention in both the US and Europe of late. As Type III worker-on-worker violence (Merchant and Lundell 2001) has attracted the attention of both the media and civil litigators, law enforcement and security executives along with behavioral scientists and mental health professionals have developed threat assessment models in their efforts to examine targeted violence (Borum *et al.*, 1999; Pynchon and Borum, 1999) and to conduct fitness for duty (Stone, 2000) and other protective evaluations (Calhoun and Weston, 2003; Corcoran and Cawood, 2003; Meloy, 2000).

Just as civil litigation involving security issues has grown in the US, more and more lawsuits are filed against criminal justice agencies for their failure to prevent arguably foreseeable behavior. For example, several hundred lawsuits are filed in the US each year claiming that a prisoner's suicide in custody was foreseeable, yet no treatment or preventive measures were provided. Although behavioral scientists understand the role of gender, social isolation, depression, hopelessness, and ideation in suicidality, the problem of false positives greatly complicates effective correctional response (Joiner *et al.*, 2005; Kennedy and Homant, 1988).

---

11 In some jurisdictions, social scientists are informed by case law what factors the courts will consider in their evaluation of foreseeability. In Texas, USA, for example, a crime may be foreseeable depending on the proximity, recency, frequency, similarity, and publicity of prior crimes. See *Timberwalk Apartments, Partners, Inc. v. Cain* (1998).

12 Even the foreseeability of crime committed by heavily tattooed individuals has not escaped the attention of criminologists and behavioral scientists (Sanders 1989). Consider also the use of demographic and behavioral characteristics to establish 'profiles' of drug couriers, terrorists (Heumann and Cassak, 2003), and school shooters (Mohandie, 2000). The degree to which racial profiling may have determined certain arrests is frequently debated (Harris, 2002) along with contrary arguments that 'soft' profiling can be indicative of good police work (MacDonald, 2003).

How foreseeable is bilateral ocular self-enucleation by an inmate who has not yet been diagnosed as schizophrenic but who had presented at sick call on a few occasions with scratches around the eyes (Favazza, 1998; Jones 1990; Patton 2004)? If an individual in custody is diagnosed as suicidal, might he also be expected to be homicidal (Nock and Marzuk, 1999)? Should police officers have foreseen that there would be a murder-suicide when they escorted an abused wife back to her home to retrieve personal belongings (Marzuk *et al.*, 1992)? Has the spate of DNA exonerations in the US (Scheck *et al.*, 2001) revealed a widespread pattern of stress-induced false confessions (Leo and Ofshe, 1998; but, see Cassell, 1998a). Finally, many police shootings have resulted in civil litigation when plaintiffs argue that an individual should have been identified as likely to try to force responding officers to shoot him in their own self-defense. The phenomenon of 'suicide-by-cop' (Kennedy *et al.*, 1998; Lindsay and Lester, 2004) has been argued both by plaintiff experts to establish liability and by defense experts to refute it. Clearly, the issue of foreseeability plays as much of a significant role in civil justice cases arising out of the criminal justice system (see, for example, Hughes, 2001; Novak *et al.*, 2003; Vaughn *et al.*, 2001) as it does in premises liability litigation.

As disparate as these examples may seem, all have arisen in the context of civil litigation. Such theories and the questions they generate assist jurors in arriving at their decisions concerning the foreseeability of criminal or otherwise problematic behavior.[13] Such questions represent the wide ranging nature of police and security-related litigation requiring input from the research of social and behavioral scientists.

Breach of Duty/Standards of Care

After considering the question of foreseeability, and thus the issue of duty, criminologists and other behavioral scientists generally turn their attention to the question of breach of duty. The plaintiff hopes to show that the defendant's actions in a certain case were negligent and in violation of the appropriate standard of care. In other words, the defendant's actions were not reasonable under the circumstances. Here, criminologists and security specialists should research any standards promulgated by various professional associations, the defendant's own policies, community practices, and learned treatises.[14] For example, the expert might consider reference to pertinent material published by the American Society

---

13 It is important to note that, while many cases have numerous elements in common with others, each case must be appreciated as unique and must be approached as such. Often seemingly minor characteristics of an offender's MO or signature can be important. All hotels are not designed or protected in the same fashion, not all convenience stores present the same risk of robbery, and not all victims respond similarly either during a crime or in its aftermath.

14 See Kennedy (in press) for a more extensive discussion of the various types of security standards and their sources.

for Industrial Security International, the National Fire Protection Association, the American Correctional Association, and the Commission on Accreditation for Law Enforcement Agencies. The publications of more specialized industry groups such as the International Association for Healthcare Safety and Security and the International Association of Campus Law Enforcement Administrators might also be referenced. As shall be noted, however, even those measures considered to constitute a standard of care because of their crime prevention value may not always prove effective.

Contrary to lay opinion, the question of the efficacy of several commonly employed security measures is far from settled. For example, while many people might assume increased lighting readily serves as a crime deterrent, early research (Tien *et al.*, 1977) called such an assumption into question. More recently, Welsh and Farrington (2004) have argued for the crime deterrent benefits of lighting, but even these findings have already been challenged (Marchant, 2004). Further discussions concerning certain counterintuitive arguments about lighting can be found in Brantingham and Brantingham (1995b), Purpura (1979), and Mellard (1997).

The crime prevention benefits of general preventive patrol were first called into serious question by the Kansas City study (Kelling *et al.*, 1974), yet other research has extolled the virtues of aggressive patrols (Wilson and Boland, 1978). While CCTV may be said to be effective under certain conditions, particularly for property crime (Painter and Tilley, 1999; Welsh and Farrington, 2003), it may be less effective than its proponents had hoped (Gill and Spriggs, 2005). Even the crime deterrent benefits of so basic a measure as fencing or gating a property are far from settled (Blakely and Snyder, 1997).

As an example of the debates surrounding the appropriate standards of care to be applied to a given industry, consider the question of convenience store security. Sometimes referred to as 'stop and rob' stores, many robberies and murders have been perpetrated therein. As a result, some jurisdictions have mandated such preventive measures as requiring at least two clerks to be on duty during certain hours. The convenience store industry has responded by commissioning criminological research challenging the value of these and other measures (Erickson, 1998; National Association of Convenience Stores, 1991; see also, Hunter, 1999).

Consider also the widely extolled crime prevention virtues of defensible space (Newman, 1972) and its progeny, *Crime Prevention through Environmental Design* (Crowe, 2000). Just as plaintiff attorneys may argue that a crime occurred because a property was built and designed contrary to these 'established' principles (i.e. standard of care), defense attorneys may learn from their consulting criminologists that defensible space theory and CPTED are not always effective (Merry, 1981). The upshot would be, of course, that a crime prevention theory or practice that is not consistently effective should not constitute a standard of care.

Standard of care issues are not limited to questions of physical security as discussed above but can also involve specific practices. For example, loss prevention operatives often engage in interrogation of employees and shoppers suspected of internal and external theft. Widely advocated interview and interrogation techniques

(Inbau *et al.*, 2001; Zulawski and Wicklander, 1993) have also been challenged as productive of false confessions. While Leo and Ofshe (1998) and Kassin (2005) have called into question certain interrogative procedures, Cassell (1998a; 1998b) has been more defensive of them.

There are many public sector policies and procedures that have also become the subject of litigation. Social and behavioral scientists can contribute to an understanding of standard of care issues by framing the questions properly and applying directly relevant or even tangentially-related research findings to the issues. For example, should suicidal inmates be kept in seclusion in a suicide gown so they can be watched closely, or would this sort of sterile, inactive environment contribute to their decompensation? Should other inmates be used to help monitor the potential suicide, or is this too important a task to be left to inmates? As careful analysis will often reveal, for many policy positions, there are often compelling counterarguments (Kennedy, 1994).[15]

Fortunately, there is guidance available to forensic, social, and behavioral scientists hoping to work with standard of care issues. Over the past several years, rational choice theory and situational crime prevention techniques have been applied to any number of crime and security issues with refreshing clarity (Clarke, 1980, 1995, 1997). The objective and empirical approach to crime prevention issues embodied in rational choice theory and situational crime prevention is buttressed by the move toward evidence-based crime prevention (Sherman, 2003; Sherman *et al.*, 1997) and the burgeoning efforts of the Campbell Collaboration (Farrington and Petrosino, 2001) to assess a wide variety of intervention efforts.

A number of cautions are in order, however. The forensic social scientist must remember that any case to be evaluated may share characteristics with other cases, yet no two are the same. A burglary/rape in location A involving perpetrator B and victim C can be substantially different than burglary/rape D involving perpetrator E and victim F. Different foreseeability issues may arise that invoke more nuanced standards of care and, as will be seen, the question of causation may also be affected. A problem arises when the expert's testimony in one case varies from his or her testimony in a prior, seemingly similar case. The opposing attorney will attempt to impeach the expert with his own 'prior inconsistent testimony.' Thus, the expert

---

15 Consider also the question of police pursuits. To limit the speeds at which police may pursue could simply inspire eluders to drive faster so that officers will break off the chase sooner. To restrict pursuits only to serious felonies may tempt youth to drive in an even more careless fashion, thus increasing the risk of accidental death and encouraging the development of road rage (Galovski and Blanchard, 2004) in others, which can lead to even more deaths. Given the amount and intensity of litigation concerning police pursuits, particularly when innocents are injured, the forensic criminologist would do well to consult research on pursuit practice, policy, and law (Alpert and Dunham, 1990; Chemerinsky, 2001; Kennedy *et al.*, 1992).

must be prepared to point out how the subtle differences between two superficially similar cases account for disparate opinions.[16]

Proximate Causation

Even if a crime was reasonably foreseeable at a given location and a defendant landlord did not meet the applicable standard of care, the plaintiff must still establish that the defendant's negligence more likely than not substantially contributed to the plaintiff's injury. Quite frequently, the defendant will argue, through the testimony of social and behavioral scientists, that something other than the defendant's alleged negligence compelled the perpetrator's actions or that the perpetrator would have committed the crime even if the defendant had acted as the plaintiff argues he should have.

For example, consider the shooting of one young man by another in the parking lot of a public housing project wherein earlier in the day the 'victim' had delivered a beating to the shooter. During the early morning hours of the next day, while standing in the parking lot, the plaintiff was injured in a drive-by shooting. It is quite likely the shooting was retaliatory (Black, 1983; Jacobs, 2004) and had nothing to do with the condition of the property, or that the shooting was really the product of a risky lifestyle (Fattah, 1991; Hindelang *et al.*, 1978; Miethe *et al.*, 1987). Consider also the plight of an Asian American shopkeeper abducted from her place of business and taken to her home where she was robbed and raped by two Asian American males who came to the shop with duct tape, plastic cuffs, and a detailed knowledge of her home. Is it more likely this crime occurred because of insufficient parking lot patrol or because she was another victim in a series of specifically targeted home invasions in an Asian American community (Burke and O'Rear, 1990; Dunlap, 1997).

Criminologists and psychologists have also considered the perpetrator's behavior style and personality characteristics in assessing the question of causation. Based on an analysis of the crime itself, the expert may conclude the criminal was acting in a highly impulsive or expressive manner, rather than in a more rational, instrumental fashion (McGuire, 2004; Meloy, 1997; Webster and Jackson, 1997). It may be argued that the criminal characterized by the former response style will less likely be deterred by conventional security measures than the more cautious, reasoning criminal. We might also consider the nature of a known criminal, one who was captured and convicted and whose crime constituted the reason for the premises liability litigation. If the defense expert can establish the psychopathic nature of the perpetrator, she can explain how his lack of fear, unconditionability, and impulsivity

---

16 See Brodsky (1991, 2004) for excellent treatises addressing an expert's optimal approaches to courtroom testimony and attorney tactics. A discussion of expert witness law and practice may be found in Malone and Zwier (1999). See Godwin and Godwin (1984) and Hollien (1990) for a discussion of expert witness ethics. Kennedy and Homant (1996) discuss the overall role of the criminologist as a consulting and testifying expert in negligent security cases.

(Hare, 1999; Millon *et al.*, 1998) made it unlikely he would have been deterred by ordinarily effective crime prevention measures once he spotted his target.

Consider also the possible contributions of profiling to the question of causation in civil litigation. Retrospective profiling involves the attribution of personal and behavioral characteristics to a criminal based on his behavior during and after a particular crime (Ainsworth, 2001; Canter, 2000, 2004; Turvey, 2002). In the US, a number of former FBI 'profilers' have taken to opining on the likely deterrability of a given criminal based on details of the crime itself. While such testimony has a certain juror appeal, there are some inherent problems with the application of profiling to every matter under litigation (Kennedy and Homant, 1997), and *Daubert* considerations may tend in some cases to moderate application of the various schools of profiling to civil litigation (Alison *et al.*, 2004; Dahir *et al.*, 2005).[17] As a general proposition, however, any behavioral scientist interested in working within the forensic arena would be well advised to review the criminological literature dealing with crime deterrence (Nagin, 1998).

Another example of causation issues concerns the all too-prevalent crime of rape, an injury frequently motivating premises liability litigation. Criminologists have identified at least four rapist types: power reassurance, power assertive, anger retaliatory, and anger excitation (Hazelwood, 1999; Keppel and Walter, 1999).[18] Power reassurance rapists tend to refrain from gratuitous violence and generally surprise the victim by, for example, sneaking into her bedroom. On the other hand, the anger retaliatory rapist tends to overwhelm the victim with a sudden blitz of excessive violence even in such open settings as parking lots or stairwells. Most criminologists would opine that the power reassurance rapist would be more deterrable by conventional security measures than the anger retaliation rapist. As with every typology, of course, there are exceptions. This is just another reminder that each case must be evaluated on its own merits.

There are many other instances wherein causation issues are quite important in civil litigation, only a few of which can be reported here. For example, did a

---

17 The US Supreme Court case of *Daubert v. Merrell Dow Pharmaceuticals, Inc.* (1993) resulted in federal case law compelling judges to assess the reliability of scientific testimony before allowing it to reach the jury. The purpose behind the ruling is to keep 'junk science' out of the courtroom (Faigman, 1995, 2000; Milloy and Gough, 1998). Thus far, the contributions of social and behavioral scientists have not been adversely impacted, signaling a generally receptive attitude toward our work (Groscup, 2004; Shuman and Sales, 1999). Although many of the world's leading social and behavioral scientists are certainly not subjected to Daubert limitations, objectivity and skepticism would be well served by a review of Daubert principles.

18 A more recent and perhaps more scientific typology is offered by Knight (1999) who identifies nine rapist subtypes. More controversial notions about the etiology of rape have recently entered the literature. While this is not the place for an elaboration of their work, or for an adequate discussion of the evolutionary theory of rape, see Thornhill and Palmer (2001).

rape really occur, or did it occur under quite the same circumstances as reported by the plaintiff (Aiken *et al.*, 1999)? Was a hospital truly negligent in caring for an infant, or is a mother's Munchausen Syndrome by Proxy condition a valid defense available to the hospital (Schreier and Libow, 1993)? In cases of supposed positional asphyxiation by police officers, did a subject die because of police officers 'piling on,' or did he die due to excited delirium and/or a rage-induced adrenalin surge taxing his already pathological system (Chan *et al.*, 1998; Ross, 1997, 1998)? Did a police officer commit a supposedly negligent act because of his own predispositions or does the fundamental attribution error blind the plaintiff to the situational pressures which actually validate his decision (Vander Zanden, 1987)?

Damages/Apportionment of Fault

For a common law tort to have occurred, the plaintiff must establish that the defendant's negligence actually caused some harm to be suffered. The remedy, of course, is generally monetary damages since the actual act cannot be undone. Emotional pain and suffering probably constitute forensic subject matter most familiar to psychiatrists, psychologists, social workers, and other mental health professionals. However, most behavioral scientists who address issues of foreseeability, standards of care, and causation do not generally testify about damages as well. This may be because of different skill sets, or it may be that it is best not to stretch one's expertise over too wide a range of subjects for trial purposes.

Nevertheless, social and behavioral scientists can offer several observations to the trial attorney. Many crime victims are likely to claim Post Traumatic Stress Disorder (PTSD) as evidence of their emotional injuries (Litz and Roemer, 1996).[19] Since its articulation after the Vietnam War, PTSD has been expanded in definition and application such that it may have lost its discriminatory value in that, at least of late, for damages purposes virtually any stress symptom may be taken as probative of PTSD (McNally, 2003; Rosen, 1995; 1996; Schouten, 1994). A balanced review of the literature, however, will reveal that most victims of crime do not develop PTSD. In fact, most victims of disastrous events do not emerge emotionally crippled for life, a tribute to the remarkable human capacity for resilience. On the other hand, sexual assault is potentially devastating to victims (Kilpatrick *et al.*, 1989), whether complicated by anticipated social reactions or not (Holmstrom and Burgess, 1979). The point here, of course, is to educate the attorney or jury about the realities of

---

19 There are, of course, more focused syndromes arguably related to specific crimes such as Rape Trauma Syndrome (Burgess and Holmstrom, 1974; Frazier and Borgida, 1992), Battered Woman Syndrome (Schuller and Vidmar, 1992) and Child Sexual Abuse Accommodation Syndrome (Summit 1983). See Edwards (1998), Freckelton (1994), and Richardson *et al.* (1995) for critical discussions of several such syndromes.

PTSD, including the potential for malingered PTSD, particularly when considered in a forensic setting.[20]

Although behavioral scientists may be generally familiar with the clinical issues contributing to the sequelae of criminal attack, the study of victimology can introduce an epidemiological perspective which can be useful to a jury in assessing monetary damages. Under a theory of comparative negligence, the degree to which a victim contributed to his own victimization could diminish commensurately the amount to be awarded him.

For example, although early victimology has been criticized for 'blaming the victim' (Bard and Sangrey, 1986; Ryan, 1971), modern victimology takes a more balanced approach to the victim's causal role in his own victimization. Social scientists can point out the distinctions between victim facilitation, victim precipitation, and victim provocation (Karmen, 2001) in order to assist a jury in deciding whether comparative negligence should be an issue in assessing damages. In addition, the fact that many victims have a tendency toward self-blame can be misunderstood by judges and juries alike. Thus, a rape victim whose self-imposed guilt comes across during her courtroom testimony might be awarded lesser damages because jurors consciously or unconsciously believe, based on her own testimony and demeanor, that she actually invited sexual relations with her attacker.

In one case, a jail social worker made a rational and well-reasoned decision to return an inmate to the general population from an observation cell due to his greatly diminished suicidal ideation. When he subsequently hung himself, she felt responsible because it was she, partially based on his own entreaties, who took him off suicide watch. Even though the decision was quite supportable professionally, her own reactions to the suicide almost led a jury to conclude she had acted negligently.

Behavioral scientists can also provide attorneys with an understanding of jury psychology concerning damage awards. The 'ideal' victim, in terms of anticipated jury awards, would be one who is vulnerable (e.g. young, old, female), who is engaged in an innocent activity in a legitimate location, and who is a stranger to a notably bad individual (Kennedy and Sacco, 1998). Other victimologists have observed that some jury members will be less likely to sympathize with certain crime victims if to do so would acknowledge their own susceptibility to victimization under similar circumstances (Coates *et al.*, 1979). The conditions under which juror backgrounds interact favorably or otherwise with victim characteristics are only beginning to be understood and constitute a fertile research agenda for social and behavioral scientists.

There are many ways in which an understanding of victim patterns and victim psychology can inform the civil justice process. Some criminologists and victimologists study the nature of injuries caused by violent crime (Simon *et al.*

---

20 According to the DSM-IV-TR, malingering is certainly a possibility in a medicolegal context (e.g. the person is referred by an attorney to a clinician for examination). The presence of Antisocial Personality Disorder also suggests the possibility of malingering.

2001) whereas others assess the costs to both the individual and society (Miller *et al*. 1996). While some scholars attempt to estimate the dollar value of victim pain and suffering (Cohen, 1988), still others study jury dynamics in order to understand the attribution of blame for compensable accidents and other injuries (Feigenson, 2000). Just as importantly, of course, it is also possible to apply our knowledge of past victimization in order to improve crime prevention skills for the purpose of victimization avoidance (Davis and Smith, 1994). As further proof that victimology can play an integral role in premises liability actions, leading victimology textbooks often provide comprehensive discussion of victims' rights litigation (Doerner and Lab, 2002; Wallace, 1998).

Conclusion

From a policymaking standpoint, who should properly bear the responsibility of providing medical treatment, psychotherapy, and monetary awards to catastrophically injured crime victims suffering serious and permanent disabilities as a result of criminal attacks occurring upon privately owned property? Because the perpetrators of these crimes themselves are often not apprehended or do not have the ability to provide such compensation, should the financial responsibility be borne by the business or property owner who is often in the best position to know about prior crimes and to prevent future crimes from occurring? Or should the burden fall upon society as a whole because such injured victims are not able to care for themselves? Those countries that have not yet confronted the issue of premises liability for negligent security may eventually have to consider the nature and extent of damages allowable for such claims. Should the victims of these crimes be limited to recovering economic damages or should they also be permitted to recover compensation for their emotional distress and physical pain? These difficult questions and others, like the test for legal foreseeability, will certainly be the topic of much debate.

It cannot be debated, however, that negligent security claims are spreading at a fast pace in several jurisdictions and will undoubtedly reach the doorsteps of other developed nations within a short period of time if they have not already. Because the issues of foreseeability, standard of care, causation, and damages relate to a number of specialized disciplines, forensic experts in criminology, security, sociology, psychology, and psychiatry are frequently needed for the prosecution and defense of premises liability lawsuits involving negligent security. Numerous mainstream theories have been applied by these experts and continue to be conceived by them to explain the circumstances surrounding criminal attacks of innocent victims. In the final analysis, those attorneys and experts familiar with the multidisciplinary intersection of these theories will be better suited for the task.

References

Aiken, M., Burgess, A. and Hazelwood, R. (1999) False rape allegations, in: R. Hazelwood and A. Burgess (Eds) *Practical Aspects of Rape Investigation*, 2nd edn, pp. 219–240 (Boca Raton: CRC Press).

Ainsworth, P. (2001) *Offender Profiling and Crime Analysis* (Cullompton, Devon: Willam Publishing).

Alison, L., West, A. and Goodwill, A. (2004) The academic and the practitioner: Pragmatists' views of offender profiling, *Psychology, Public Policy, and Law*, 10, pp. 71–101.

Alpert, G. and Dunham, R. (1990) *Police Pursuit Driving: Controlling Responses to Emergency Situations* (New York: Greenwood Press).

American Law Institute (1977) *Restatement of the law: Torts* 2d (St. Paul, MN: American Law Institute Publishers).

Bard, M. and Sangrey, D. (1986) *The Crime Victim's Book*, 2nd edn (New York: Brunner/Mazel Publishers).

Bates, N. (2004) *Major Developments in Premises Security Liability III* (Sudbury, MA: Liability Consultants).

Black, D. (1983) Crime as social control, *American Sociological Review*, 48, pp. 34–45.

Blakely, E. and Snyder, M. (1997) *Fortress America: Gated Communities in the United States* (Washington, DC: Brookings Institution).

Borum, R., Fein, R., Vossekuil, B. and Berglund, J. (1999) Threat assessment: defining an approach for evaluating risk of targeted violence, *Behavioral Sciences and the Law*, 17, pp. 323–337.

Brantingham, P.J. and Brantingham, P.L. (1984) *Patterns in Crime* (New York: Macmillan).

Brantingham, P.L. and Brantingham, P. J. (1995a) Criminality of place: crime generators and crime attractors, *European Journal on Criminal Policy and Research*, 3, pp. 5–26.

Brantingham, P.J. and Brantingham, P.L. (1995b) Understanding and controlling crime and fear of crime: conflicts and trade-offs in crime prevention planning. Paper presented at the Academy of Criminal Justice Sciences Conference, Boston.

Brantingham, P.J. and Brantingham, P.L. (1998) Environmental criminology: From theory to urban planning practice, *Studies on Crime and Crime Prevention*, 7, pp. 31–60.

Brodsky, S. (1991) *Testifying in Court: Guidelines and Maxims for the Expert Witness* (Washington, DC: American Psychological Association).

Brodsky, S. (2004) *Coping with Cross-examination and other Pathways to Effective Testimony* (Washington, DC: American Psychological Association).

Burgess, A. and Holmstrom, L. (1974) Rape trauma syndrome, *American Journal of Psychiatry*, 131, pp. 981–986.

Burke, T. and O'Rear, C. (1990) Home invaders: Asian gangs in America, *Police Studies*, 13, pp. 154–156.

Burns v. Johnson, 458 S.E.2d 448 (Va. 1995).

Calhoun, F. and Weston, S. (2003) *Contemporary Threat Management* (San Diego: Specialized Training Services).

Canter, D. (2000) *Criminal Shadows: The Inner Narratives of Evil* (Irving, TX: Authorlink Press).

Canter, D. (2004) Offender profiling and investigative psychology, *Journal of Investigative Psychology and Offender Profiling*, 1, pp. 1–15.

Cassell, P. (1998a) The guilty and the 'innocent': an examination of alleged cases of wrongful conviction from false confessions, *Harvard Journal of Law & Public Policy*, 22, pp. 523–603.

Cassell, P. (1998b) Protecting the innocent from false confessions and lost confessions – and from Miranda, *Journal of Criminal Law and Criminology*, 88, pp. 497–556.

Chan, T., Vilke, G. and Neuman, T. (1998) Re-examination of custody restraint position and positional asphyxia, *The American Journal of Forensic Medicine and Pathology*, 19, pp. 201–205.

Chemerinsky, E. (2001) High-speed chases, *Trial*, 37 (February), pp. 24–27.

Clarke, R. (1980) Situational crime prevention: theory and practice, *British Journal of Criminology*, 20, pp. 136–147.

Clarke, R. (1995) Situational crime prevention, in: M. Tonry and D. Farrington (Eds) *Building a Safer Society: Strategic Approaches to Crime Prevention*, pp. 91–150 (Chicago: University of Chicago Press).

Clarke, R. (1997) *Situational Crime Prevention*, 2nd edn (Guilderland, NY: Harrow and Heston).

Coates, D., Wortman, C. and Abbey, A. (1979) Reactions to victims, in: I. Frieze, D. Bar-Tal and J. Carroll (Eds) *New Approaches to Social Problems*, pp. 21–52 (San Francisco: Jossey-Bass).

Cohen, C. and Felson, M. (1979) Social change and crime rate trends: a routine activities approach, *American Sociological Review*, 44, pp. 588–608.

Cohen, M. (1988) Pain, suffering, and jury awards: a study of the cost of crime to victims, *Law and Society Review*, 22, pp. 537–555.

Comstock, G. (1989) Victims of anti-gay/lesbian violence, *Journal of Interpersonal Violence*, 4, pp. 101–106.

Corcoran, M. and Cawood, J. (2003) *Violence Assessment and Intervention: The Practitioner's Handbook* (Boca Raton: CRC Press).

Crowe, T. (2000) *Crime Prevention Through Environmental Design*, 2nd edn (Woburn, MA: Butterworth-Heineman).

Dahir, V., Richardson, J., Ginsburg, G., Gatowski, S., Dobbin, S. and Merlino, M. (2005) Judicial application of *Daubert* to psychological syndrome and profile evidence: a research note, *Psychology, Public Policy, and Law*, 11, pp. 62–82.

Daubert v. Merrell Dow Pharmaceuticals, Inc.,113 S.Ct. 2786 (1993).

Davis, R. and Smith, B. (1994) Teaching victims crime prevention skills: can individuals lower their risk of crime? *Criminal Justice Review*, 19, pp. 56–68.

Doerner, W. and Lab, S. (2002) *Victimology*, 3rd edn (Cincinnati: Anderson Publishing Company).

Dunlap, R. (1997) Asian home invasion robbery, *Journal of Contemporary Criminal Justice*, 13, pp. 209–319.

Edwards, C. (1998) Behavior and the law reconsidered: psychological syndromes and profiles, *Journal of Forensic Science*, 43, pp. 141–150.

Emons, W. and Garoupa, N. (2004) The economics of US-style contingent fees and UK-style conditional fees. Discussion paper 04.07, University of Bern (Mai 2004), revised June 2005 http://www-vwi.unibe.ch/theory/papers/emons/cfees.pdf.

Erickson, R. (1998) *Convenience Store Security at the Millennium* (Alexandria, VA: National Association of Convenience Stores).

Faigman, D. (1995) The evidentiary status of social science under *Daubert*, *Psychology, Public Policy, and Law*, 1, pp. 960–979.

Faigman, D. (2000) *Legal Alchemy: The Use and Misuse of Science in the Law* (New York: W.H. Freeman).

Farrington, D. and Petrosino, A. (2001) The Campbell collaboration crime and justice group, *Annals of the American Academy of Political and Social Science*, 578, pp. 35–49.

Fattah, E. (1991) *Understanding Criminal Victimization* (Scarborough, Ont: Prentice-Hall Canada).

Favazza, A. (1998) The coming of age of self-mutilation, *The Journal of Nervous and Mental Disease*, 186, pp. 259–268.

Feigenson, N. (2000) *Legal Blame: How Jurors Think and Talk about Accidents* (Washington, DC: American Psychological Association).

Fleming, C. (2004) Europe learns litigious ways, *Wall Street Journal*, 24 February, pp. A16–A17.

Frazier, P. and Borgida, E. (1992) Rape trauma syndrome: a review of case law and psychological research, *Law and Human Behavior*, 16, pp. 293–311.

Freckelton, I. (1994) Contemporary comment: when plight makes right – The forensic abuse syndrome, *Criminal Law Journal*, 18, pp. 29–49.

Galovski, T. and Blanchard, E. (2004) Road rage: a domain for psychological intervention? *Aggression and Violent Behavior*, 9, pp. 105–127.

Gill, M. and Spriggs, M. (2005) *Assessing the Impact of CCTV* (Home Office Research Study 252) London: Home Office.

Godwin, F. and Godwin, D. (1984) Expert witnesses: hired guns or purveyors of knowledge, *Journal of Security Administration*, 7, pp. 39–49.

Goldstein, P. (1985) The drugs–violence nexus: a tripartite conceptual framework. *Journal of Drug Issues*, 39, pp. 143–174.

Goldstein, S. (1999) *The Sexual Exploitation of Children*, 2nd edn (Boca Raton: CRC Press).

Gore, R. and Pattavina, A. (2004) Applications for examining the journey-to-crime using incident-based offender residence probability surfaces, *Police Quarterly*, 7, pp. 457–474.

Groscup, J. (2004) Judicial decision-making about expert testimony in the aftermath of *Daubert* and *Kumho, Journal of Forensic Psychology Practice*, 4, pp. 57–66.

Groth, N. and Birnbaum, H. J. (1979) *Men who Rape: The Psychology of the Offender* (Cambridge: Perseus Publishing).

Hare, R. (1999) *Without Conscience: The Disturbing World of the Psychopaths among Us* (New York: The Guilford Press).

Harris, D. (2002) *Profiles in Injustice* (New York: The New Press).

Harry, J. (1982) Derivative deviance: the cases of extortion, fag-bashing, and shakedown of gay men, *Criminology*, 19, pp. 546–564.

Hazelwood, R. (1999) Analyzing the rape and profiling the offender, in: R. Hazelwood and A. Burgess (Eds) *Practical Aspects of Rape Investigation*, 2nd edn, pp. 155–181 (Boca Raton: CRC Press).

Hendry v. Zelaya, 841 So.2d 572, 574 (Fla. 2003).

Heumann, M. and Cassak, L. (2003) *Good Cop, Bad Cop: Racial Profiling and Competing Views of Justice* (New York: Peter Lang).

Hindelang, M., Gottfredson, M. and Garofalo, J. (1978) *Victims of Personal Crime: An Empirical Foundation for a Theory of Personal Victimization* (Cambridge, MA: Ballinger).

Hodgins, S. (Ed.) (1993) *Mental Disorder and Crime* (Newbury Park, CA: Sage).

Hollien, H. (1990) The expert witness: ethics and responsibilities, *Journal of Forensic Sciences*, 35, pp. 1414–1423.

Holmstrom, L. and Burgess, A. (1979) Rape: the husband's and boyfriend's initial reactions, *The Family Coordinator*, 28, pp. 321–330.

Hughes, T. (2001) Police officers and civil liability: 'The ties that bind,' *Policing*, 24, pp. 240–262.

Hunter, R. (1999) Convenience store robbery revisited: a review of prevention results. *Journal of Security Administration*, 22, pp. 1–13.

Inbau, F., Reid, J., Buckley, J. and Jayne, B. (2001) *Criminal Interrogation and Confessions*, 4th edn (Gaithersburg, MD: Aspen Publishers).

Insurance Leadership Institute. (2004) *European Executive Survey 2004*, September (Overland Park, KS: GE Insurance Solutions).

Jacobs, B. (2004) A typology of street crime retaliation, *Journal of Research in Crime and Delinquency*, 10, pp. 295–323.

Joiner, T., Brown, J. and Wingate, L. (2005) The psychology and neurobiology of suicidal behavior, *Annual Review of Psychology*, 56, pp. 287–314.

Jones, N. (1990) Self-enucleation and psychosis, *British Journal of Ophthalmology*, 74, pp. 571–573.

Karmen, A. (2001) *Crime Victims: An Introduction to Victimology*, 4th edn (Belmont, CA: Wadsworth).

Kaminsky, A. (2001) *A Complete Guide to Premises Security Litigation*, 2nd edn (Chicago: American Bar Association).

Kassin, S. (2005) On the psychology of confessions: does *innocence* put *innocents* at risk? *American Psychologist*, 60, pp. 215–228.

Kelling, G., Pate, T., Dieckman, D. and Brown, C. (1974) *The Kansas City Preventive Patrol Experiment: A Summary Report* (Washington, DC: The Police Foundation).

Kennedy, D. (1984) Contributions of the social sciences to security education and practice, *Journal of Security Administration*, 7, pp. 7–24.

Kennedy, D. (1990) Facility site selection and analysis through environmental criminology, *Journal of Criminal Justice*, 18, pp. 239–252.

Kennedy, D. (1993) Precautions for the physical security of the wandering patient, *Security Journal*, 4, pp. 170–176.

Kennedy, D. (1994) Rethinking the problem of custodial suicide, *American Jails*, 7 (January–February), pp. 41–45.

Kennedy, D. (in press) Forensic security and the law, in: M. Gill (Ed.) *Handbook of Security* (Leicester: Perpetuity Press).

Kennedy, D. and Homant, R. (1988) Predicting custodial suicides: problems with the use of profiles, *Justice Quarterly*, 5, pp. 401–416.

Kennedy, D. and Homant, R. (1996) Role of the criminologist in negligent security cases, in: Wiley Law Publications Staff (Eds) *1996 Wiley Expert Witness Update*, pp. 151–166 (New York: Wiley).

Kennedy, D. and Homant, R. (1997) Problems with the use of criminal profiling in premises security litigation, *Trial Diplomacy Journal*, 20, pp. 223–229.

Kennedy, D., Homant, R. and Hupp, T. (1998) Suicide by cop, *FBI Law Enforcement Bulletin*, 67 (August), pp. 21–27.

Kennedy, D., Homant, R. and Kennedy, J. (1992) A comparative analysis of police vehicle pursuit policies, *Justice Quarterly*, 9, pp. 227–246.

Kennedy, L. and Sacco, V. (1998) *Crime Victims in Context* (Los Angeles: Roxbury).

Keppel, R. and Walter, R. (1999) Profiling killers: a revised classification model for understanding sexual murder, *International Journal of Offender Therapy and Comparative Criminology*, 43, pp. 417–437.

Kilpatrick, D., Saunders, B., Amick-McMullan, A., Best, C., Veronen, L. and Resnick, H. (1989) Victim and crime factors associated with the development of crime-related Post-Traumatic Stress Disorder, *Behavior Therapy*, 20, pp. 199–214.

Klimas, T. (2000) New Lithuanian law on contingency fees. Retrieved May 25, 2005, from http://jurist.law.pitt.edu/world/lithucor1.htm

Knight, R. (1999) Validation of a typology for rapists, *Journal of Interpersonal Violence*, 14, pp. 303–330.

L.A.C. v. Ward Parkway Shopping Center Company, 75 S.W.3d 247, 258 (Mo. 2002).

Laub, J. (1987) Rediscovering the importance of cities, neighborhoods, and crime. *Journal of Qualitative Criminology*, 3, pp. 83–93.

Leighton, J. (2003) Apportionment of fault in inadequate security cases, *Victim Advocate*, 4 (Fall), pp. 3–6.

Leo, R. and Ofshe, R. (1998) The consequences of false confessions: deprivations of liberty and miscarriages of justice in the age of psychological interrogation, *Journal of Criminal Law and Criminology*, 88, pp. 429–496.

Lindsay, M. and Lester, D. (2004) *Suicide by Cop: Committing Suicide by Provoking Police to Shoot You* (Amityville, NY: Baywood).

Litz, B. and Roemer, L. (1996) Post-Traumatic Stress Disorder: an overview, *Clinical Psychology and Psychotherapy*, 3, pp. 153–168.

MacDonald, H. (2003) *Are Cops Racist?* Chicago: Ivan R. Dee.

Madden v. C & K Barbecue Carryout, Inc., 758 S.W.2d 59 (Mo. 1988).

Malone, D. and Zwier, P. (1999) *Expert Rules*, Revised edn (Notre Dame, IN: National Institute for Trial Advocacy).

Marchant, P. (2004) A demonstration that the claim that brighter lighting reduces crime is unfounded, *British Journal of Criminology*, 44, pp. 441–447.

Marzuk, P., Tardiff, K. and Hirsch, C. (1992) The epidemiology of murder-suicide, *Journal of the American Medical Association*, 267, pp. 3179–3183.

McGuire, J. (2004) *Understanding Psychology and Crime* (Berkshire, UK: Open University Press).

McNally, R. (2003) Progress and controversy in the study of Post-Traumatic Stress Disorder, *Annual Review of Psychology*, 54, pp. 229–252.

Mellard, R. (1997) A light to remember, *Security Management*, 41 (July), pp. 38–43.

Meloy, J. (1997) *Violent Attachments* (Northvale, NJ: Jason Aronson).

Meloy, J. (2000) *Violence Risk and Threat Assessment* (San Diego: Specialized Training Services).

Merchant, J. and Lundell, J. (2001) *Workplace Violence: A Report to the Nation* (Iowa City: The University of Iowa Injury Prevention Research Center).

Merry, S. (1981) Defensible space undefended: social factors in crime control through environmental design, *Urban Affairs Quarterly*, 16, pp. 397–422.

Miethe, T., Stafford, M. and Long, S. (1987) Social differentiation in criminal victimization: a test of routine activities/lifestyle theories, *American Sociological Review*, 52, pp. 184–194.

Miller, B. and Humphreys, L. (1980) Lifestyles and violence: homosexual victims of assault and murder, *Qualitative Sociology*, 3, pp. 169–185.

Miller, T., Cohen, M. and Wiersema, B. (1996) *Victim Costs and Consequences: A New Look* (Washington, DC: U.S. Department of Justice).

Millon, T., Simonsen, E., Birket-Smith, M. and Davis, R. (Eds) (1998) *Psychopathy: Antisocial, Criminal and Violent Behavior* (New York: the Guilford Press).

Milloy, S. and Gough, M. (1998) *Silencing Science* (Washington, DC: Cato Institute).

Mohandie, K. (2000) *School Violence Threat Management* (San Diego: Specialized Training Services).

Nagin, D. (1998) Criminal deterrence research at the outset of the twenty-first century, in: M. Tonry (Ed.) *Crime and Justice: A Review of Research*, Vol. 23, pp. 1–42 (Chicago: The University of Chicago Press).

National Association of Convenience Stores (1991) *Convenience Store Security: Report and Recommendations* (Alexandria, VA: Author).

Newman, O. (1972) *Defensible Space* (New York: Macmillan).

Nock, M. and Marzuk, P. (1999) Murder-suicide: phenomenology and clinical implications, in: D. Jacobs (Ed.) *Guide to Suicide Assessment and Intervention*, pp. 188–209 (San Francisco: Jossey-Bass Publishers).

Novak, K., Smith, B. and Frank, J. (2003) Strange bedfellows: civil liability and aggressive policing, *Policing*, 26, pp. 352–368.

Painter, K. and Tilley, N. (Eds) (1999) *Surveillance of Public Space: CCTV, Street Lighting, and Crime Prevention*, Vol. 10 (New York: Criminal Justice Press).

Patton, N. (2004) Self-inflicted eye injures: a review, *Eye*, 18, pp. 867–872.

Paulsen, D. and Robinson, M. (2004) *Spatial Aspects of Crime: Theory and Practice* (Boston: Allyn & Bacon).

Purpura, P. (1979) Police activity and the full moon, *Journal of Police Science and Administration*, 7, pp. 350–353.

Pynchon, M. and Borum, R. (1999) Assessing threats of targeted gang violence: contributions from social psychology, *Behavioral Sciences and the Law*, 17, pp. 339–355.

Ratcliffe, J. and McCullagh, M. (1999) Hot beds of crime and the search for spatial accuracy, *Journal of Geographical Systems*, 1, pp. 385–398.

Richardson, J., Ginsburg, G., Gatowski, S. and Dobbin, S. (1995) The problems of applying *Daubert* to psychological syndrome evidence, *Judicature*, 79, pp. 10–16.

Roncek, D. and Francik, J. (1981) Housing projects and crime, *Social Problems*, 29, pp. 151–166.

Roncek, D. and Lobosco, A. (1983) The effect of high schools on crime in their neighborhoods, *Social Science Quarterly*, 64, pp. 598–613.

Roncek, D. and Maier, P. (1991) Bars, blocks, and crimes revisited: linking the theory of routine activities to the empiricism of 'hot spots', *Criminology*, 29, pp. 725–754.

Rosen, G. (1995) The *Aleutian Enterprise* sinking and Post-Traumatic Stress Disorder: misdiagnosis in clinical and forensic settings, *Professional Psychology: Research and Practice*, 26, pp. 82–87.

Rosen, G. (1996) Post-Traumatic Stress Disorder, pulp fiction, and the press, *Bulletin of the American Academy of Psychiatry and the Law*, 24, pp. 267–269.

Ross, D. (1997) Medical risk factors of sudden in-custody deaths, *The Police Marksman*, 22 (November/December), pp. 42–47.

Ross, D. (1998) Examining the liability factors of sudden wrongful deaths in police custody, *Police Quarterly*, 1, pp. 65–91.

Ryan, W. (1971) *Blaming the Victim* (New York: Vintage).

Safarik, M., Jarvis, J. and Nussbaum, K. (2000) Elderly female serial sexual homicide, *Homicide Studies*, 4, pp. 294–307.

Sagarin, E. and MacNamara, D. (1975) The homosexual as a crime victim, *International Journal of Criminology and Penology*, 3, pp. 13–25.

Sanders, C. (1989) *Customizing the Body: The Art and Culture of Tattooing* (Philadelphia: Temple University Press).

Sandoval v. Bank of America, NT & SA, 94 Cal.App.4th 1375 (Cal. 2002).

Scheck, B., Neufeld, P. and Dwyer, J. (2001) *Actual Innocence: When Justice goes Wrong and How to Make it Right* (New York: Signet).

Schouten, R. (1994) Distorting Post-Traumatic Stress Disorder for court, *Harvard Review of Psychiatry*, 2, pp. 171–173.

Schreier, H. and Libow, J. (1993) *Hurting for Love: Munchausen by Proxy Syndrome* (New York: Guilford Press).

Schuller, R. and Vidmar, N. (1992) Battered woman syndrome evidence in the courtroom: a review of the literature, *Law and Human Behavior*, 16, pp. 273–291.

Sherman, L. (2003) Misleading evidence and evidence-led policy: making social science more experimental, *Annals of the American Academy of Political and Social Science*, 589, pp. 6–19.

Sherman, L., Gartin, P. and Buerger, M. (1989) Hot spots of predatory crime: routine activities and the criminology of place, *Criminology*, 27, pp. 27–55.

Sherman, L., Gottfredson, D., MacKenzie, D., Eck, J., Reuter, P. and Bushway, S. (1997) *Preventing Crime: What Works, What Doesn't, What's Promising* (Washington, DC: US Department of Justice).

Shuman, D. and Sales, B. (1999) The impact of *Daubert* and its progeny in the admissibility of behavioral and social science evidence, *Psychology*, *Public Policy, and Law*, 5, pp. 3–15.

Simon, T., Mercy, J. and Perkins, C. (2001) *Injuries from Violent Crime, 1992–1998* (Washington, DC: US Department of Justice).

Smith v. Dodge Plaza Limited Partnership, 811 A.2d 881, 891 (Md. 2002).

Snow, D., Baker, S. and Anderson, L. (1989) Criminality and homeless men: an empirical assessment, *Social Problems*, 36, pp. 532–549.

Stark, R. (1987) Deviant places: a theory of the ecology of crime, *Criminology*, 25, pp. 893–909.

Stone, A. (2000) *Fitness for Duty: Principles, Methods and Legal Issues* (Boca Raton: CRC Press).

Storts v. Hardee's Food Systems, Inc., 210 F.3d 390 (10th Cir. 2000).

Summit, R. (1983) The child sexual abuse accommodation syndrome, *Child Abuse and Neglect*, 7, pp. 177–193.

Swanson, J., Holzer, C., Ganju, V. and Jono, R. (1990) Violence and psychiatric disorder in the community: evidence from the epidemiological catchment area surveys, *Hospital and Community Psychiatry*, 41, pp. 761–770.

Texas Real Estate Holdings, Inc. v. Quach, 95 S.W.3d 395 (Tex. 2002).

Timberwalk Apartments, Partners, Inc. v. Cain, 972 S.W.2d 749 (Tex. 1998).

Thornhill, R. and Palmer, C. (2001) *A Natural History of Rape: Biological Bases of Sexual Coercion* (Cambridge, MA: MIT Press).

Tien, J., O'Donnell, V., Barnett, A. and Mirchandani, P. (1977) *Street Lighting Projects: National Evaluation Program, Phase I Summary Report* (Washington, DC: National Institute of Law Enforcement and Criminal Justice).

Turvey, B. (2002) *Criminal Profiling: An Introduction to Behavioral Evidence Analysis*, 2nd edn (San Diego: Academic Press).

van Dam, C. (2001) *Identifying Child Molesters* (New York: Haworth Press).

Vander Zanden, J. (1987) *Social Psychology* (New York: Random House).

Vaughn, M., Cooper, T. and del Carmen, R. (2001) Assessing legal liabilities in law enforcement: Police chiefs' views, *Crime and Delinquency*, 47, pp. 3–27.

Wallace, H. (1998) *Victimology: Legal, Psychological, and Social Perspectives* (Boston: Allyn and Bacon).

Ward, R. (2000) The internationalization of criminal justice, in: C. Friel (Ed.) *Criminal Justice* 2000, *Boundary Changes in Criminal Justice Organizations*, pp. 267–321 (Washington, DC: US Department of Justice).

Webster, C. and Jackson, M. (Eds) (1997) *Impulsivity: Theory, Assessment, and Treatment* (New York: The Guilford Press).

Welsh, B. and Farrington, D. (2003) Effects of closed-circuit television on crime, *Annals of the American Academy of Political and Social Science*, 587, pp. 110–135.

Welsh, B. and Farrington, D. (2004). Surveillance for crime prevention in public space: results and policy changes in Britain and America, *Criminology and Public Policy*, 3, pp. 497–526.

Wilson, J. and Boland, B. (1978) The effect of police on crime, *Law and Society Review*, 12, pp. 367–384.

Workman v. United Methodist Committee, 320 F.2d 259 (D.C. Cir. 2003).

Zulawski, D. and Wicklander, D. (1993) *Practical Aspects of Interview and Interrogation* (Boca Raton, FL: CRC Press).

Chapter 9

The Consequences of Prison Life: Notes on the New Psychology of Prison Effects

Craig Haney

Elsewhere I have argued that psychology and related disciplines now explicitly acknowledge the importance of social contextual influences on behavior (Haney, 2002). As a result, the psychological impact of especially powerful social settings and situations – including prisons – should be recognized more fully and assessed more carefully in future policy-related decisions. 'Prison effects' – the psychological impact of prison conditions themselves – once again have become the topic of serious study and debate (e.g. Haney, 2006; Irwin, 2005; Liebling and Maruna, 2005; Petersilia, 2003). Perhaps, in response, the mindless clamoring for 'more prisons' and 'harsher punishment' will finally diminish. Indeed, policymakers, politicians, and members of the public may begin to reflect on the way in which living conditions inside the huge network of prisons that we have created over the last several decades adversely shape and affect prisoner behavior – inside prison and beyond. As I will show in this chapter, adapting to the harsh realities of prison life may negatively change a prisoner's habits of thinking and acting, in ways that can persist long after his or her incarceration has ended.

This new perspective represents a turnaround of sorts, a move away from the apparent consensus that emerged in the closing decades of the 20th century, when the era of mass incarceration was in full swing. Specifically, the notion that imprisonment per se inflicted relatively little measurable psychological harm appeared to be widely accepted – tacitly agreed upon in some circles, openly touted in others. This assertion – and the related suggestion that most corrections experts shared the view – served as implicit reassurance that the punitive policies of the day really had no downside. That is, if prison did no real damage to the sturdy souls whom we sent there, then locking up the most people we could for the longest possible periods of time would inflict little or no lasting harm.

Among other things, these notions reflected the resurgent individualism of the times, when ascribing exclusively personal responsibility for bad acts as well as economic misfortune became a kind of political rallying cry. Despite the macroeconomic shifts that buffeted them about, and the radically refocused crime control policies that targeted certain crimes (and therefore, certain criminals) out of proportion to the harm they caused, even the most disempowered and marginalized groups in society were once again portrayed as the captains of their own destiny. Surely these ruggedly free and autonomous decision-makers could stand up to the rigors of prison life, no matter how cruelly it was structured. In the same way that politicians argued that prisoners' intractable characters were difficult if not impossible to change for the better, they also implied that this same toughness protected them from the damaging effects of harsh prison conditions. A 'nothing works' critique of prison programming begat a 'nothing hurts' view of prison effects.

The minimizing of prison effects also seemed to represent a form of defensive, wishful thinking. It was made useful (if not necessary) by the extraordinary influx of prisoners who were crowded into our prisons over the last several decades. After all, once a society committed itself to policies of mass imprisonment, evidence of the harmful effects of incarceration – effects now being inflicted on unprecedented numbers of people for unprecedented lengths of time – was painful and problematic to contemplate. Instead, we took comfort in the view that Hans Toch (1981, p. 3) accurately summarized, at the outset of the era of overincarcertaion – that '[t]hough *some* inmates experience tangible stress, which is destructive and disabling for them, most inmates somehow adapt to prison and remain comparatively healthy and sane behind walls'.

However, even then the debate over the psychological effects of imprisonment revolved around how much *harm* was inflicted rather than how much benefit was produced (e.g. Bukstel and Kilmann, 1980; Bonta and Gendreau, 1990). Thus, as the policies of mass incarceration persisted and intensified, some commentators celebrated the reassuring fact that prisons did not irreparably harm literally everyone who was confined in them, that imprisonment was not 'uniformly devastating,' and it did not seem 'inevitably' to damage all of the persons subjected to it (Porporino 1990, p. 36). To be sure, even ardent proponents of the prison status quo nonetheless were forced to admit that prison life *could* take a heavy toll: '[R]elationships with family and friends can be severed... particular vulnerabilities and inabilities to cope and adapt can come to the fore in the prison setting, [and] the behavior patterns and attitudes that emerge can take many forms, from deepening social and emotional withdrawal to extremes of aggression and violence' (Porporino, 1990, p. 36).

Of course, there are now unprecedented numbers of incarcerated persons throughout the world who are exposed to the pains of imprisonment. They are at risk of suffering their ill effects. Fortunately, as I say, we have a much firmer grasp of the importance of context and situation in shaping behavior and, by implication, the potentially long-term psychological consequences of exposure to harsh and extreme environmental conditions. It is proving increasingly difficult to ignore the significant cost that the intensely, exclusively punitive approach to crime control has exacted. The time has come to step back and examine the implications of what we have done over the last several decades, and how we might approach the next stage of crime control and prison policy more effectively and more humanely.

Methodological Constraints on the Study of Prison Pain

The empirical consensus that prisons inflicted relatively little overall psychological harm was not driven entirely by ideological concerns or amplified by political interest groups alone. Several methodological challenges help to account for the belief – one genuinely-held among many scholars – that prison had only minimal effects on prisoners. For one, there was a persistent tendency to talk about prisons as if they were all the same – as some sort of Weberian ideal type. This meant that the absence of negative prison effects in a relatively well-run institution that was not plagued by overcrowding and violence (perhaps the very ones most amenable to research) was generalized to others, including ones that were overrun with prisoners, plagued by widespread idleness, and wracked with conflict.

Obviously, prisons vary along a variety of highly important dimensions that determine whether and how harmful they actually are. Not all prisons are equally benign, some are extremely toxic to the mental (as well as physical) well-being of the prisoners, and the effects of confinement in one kind of facility cannot automatically be generalized to another. Referring to very different kinds of institutions simply as 'prisons' has blurred critically important distinctions. This simple, basic insight has led more recently to a careful assessment of particular prison settings and a franker acknowledgement that certain conditions of confinement do much more damage than others.[1]

Beyond the problem of imprecision, the task of actually measuring prison effects – including subjective states that prisoners are motivated to modify and be reticent about expressing – has proven especially challenging. Thus, empirical studies have been limited by the lack of meaningful techniques with which to calculate precisely the real pains of imprisonment. Because the human psyche abhors the sensation of constant pain, people tend to adapt over time to the suffering they endure. Like all people, prisoners, too, can tolerate only so much suffering before attempting to transform the experience to reduce its painfulness. This greatly complicates attempts to document the harmful effects of long-term imprisonment and the chronic cruelty of prison life.

When prisoners have been able to mute or dampen the chronic pain of imprisonment – if only to survive it better – long-term exposure to even very cruel conditions may eventually lead to less self-reported psychological suffering. Of course, it is difficult to argue that this numbing process does not come at a significant

---

1   To avoid inadvertently falling prey to precisely this methodological problem, I should make clear that most of the comments that follow are intended to apply to what are termed medium and maximum security prisons in the United States. Wherever possible, I will try to specify the precise aspect of imprisonment or the particular conditions of confinement whose effects I am discussing, rather than generalizing to 'prisons' at large. The final section of the chapter that summarizes some of the 'new psychology of prison effects' illustrates the heightened focus on the ways that *specific* dimensions of the prison experience – rather than prison itself – influence and affect prisoner psychology.

psychological cost. Yet, the inability to capture this phenomenon with the techniques commonly used to measure suffering helps to account for some of the masking of long-term prison effects – the argument that, somehow, most people do manage to 'adjust,' more or less.

In addition, most studies of the effects of long-term imprisonment assess its effects in the very context where prisoners literally have been forced to adapt and where they must strive to achieve a minimally tolerable state of mind – inside prison itself. Arguably, a more meaningful test of the various ways that imprisonment transforms prisoners would occur *after* their release, when the full impact of this atypical and severe environment would be more apparent. Historically, high rates of recidivism have served as a reminder that imprisonment in general does little to eliminate criminal behavior. Until recently, however, there has been little attention given to the range of negative psychological effects of imprisonment that persist after prisoners are released or to the ways these prison effects compromise their ability to survive in the free world. As I will suggest later in this chapter, research focusing on *that* point in the process now suggests that the experience of imprisonment is anything but benign.

Moreover, a number of the studies that concluded that prison had few if any negative effects focused largely if not exclusively on quantitative indices of suffering (e.g. Bonta and Gendreau, 1990). Yet, there is no reason to assume that numerical measurements of the pains of imprisonment *necessarily* produce more valid representations of prison effects. This is one area of research where what psychologists gained in precision often came at the expense of real meaning. Indeed, there are some subtle yet profound changes that may occur in prison settings that more interpretive researchers – ones who employ observation and interview methodologies – are better positioned to document. These kinds of studies can provide more textured and 'thick' descriptions of prison environments and their effects, and include observations of changes that occur over time, in the course of induced and enforced institutional adjustment. In addition, field researchers are often better able to gain prisoners' trust, and to obtain more candid responses about a range of sensitive issues. Especially in light of the complex interpersonal dynamics and politically-charged demand characteristics that often come into play inside many prisons – where, for example, few prisoners want to 'cop out' and admit to suffering or pain to persons who are viewed as part of 'the system' – it is difficult to know what to make of studies purporting to show no effects from exposure to conditions that appear to be extremely psychologically invasive and would cause pain and harm in other contexts.

The fact that empirical psychology still lacks the means to quantify precisely some of the most subtle, negative psychological effects of imprisonment does not mean that the prison experience fails to produce them. Nor does it mean that they cannot be accurately described and thoughtfully analyzed. Indeed, sociological and ethnographic accounts of prison life represent important supplemental sources of information about the complex personal transformations that occur during imprisonment. They add context and depth to more systematic psychological studies.

In fact, even some first-hand, autobiographical accounts of prison life – written by persons whose experiences appear to have profoundly transformed them – contain important insights about the pains of imprisonment and their lasting effects. In some instances, the published stories themselves were conceived by their authors as one way to exorcise the demons that they felt prison had instilled in them. Victor Serge, for example, wrote that prison 'burdened me with an experience so heavy, so intolerable to endure' that, long after his release, he felt compelled to write his first book 'to free myself from this inward nightmare' (Serge, 1969, p. xii). In it, Serge remembered what he called the 'icy moment' of arrest years after it happened. He crossed what he termed, 'the invisible boundary,' after which: 'I was no longer a man but a man in prison. An inmate' (Serge, 1969, p. 4).

Past Psychological Research on Negative Prison Effects

As I noted in passing above, although some commentators minimized the risk of negative prison effects – even as the numbers of prisoners grew dramatically – few researchers doubted that the pains of imprisonment could have real consequences. In fact, many of the psychological studies of the effects of prison life conducted during this period confirmed precisely this. That is, although psychologists and other experts sometimes expressed the view that prisons were relatively benign (e.g. Suedfeld, 1978), and these views at least indirectly appeared to promote or condone the unprecedented expansion of the prison system itself (e.g. Wilson, 1975), psychological research never uniformly supported this view.

Indeed, even one widely cited literature review – generally interpreted as a defense of then-current expansionist prison policies – concluded that there were many harmful psychological consequences produced by less than ideal prison conditions. Thus, for example, Bonta and Gendreau (1990, p. 353) summarized prison crowding research by noting that: 'physiological and psychological stress responses... were very likely [to occur] under crowded prison conditions' and that 'a correlation [has been found] between population density and misconduct [when age is used as a moderator variable]'. The same reviewers also acknowledged that as 'exposure to crowded situations increase so does the risk for misconduct,' that there was 'a significant relationship between crowding and post-release recidivism,' and that 'high inmate turnover [in some prisons has been found to predict] inmate disruptions' (Bonta and Gendreau, 1990, p. 354).

Similarly, they cited research showing that, in certain instances, *long-term* incarceration had adverse psychological effects; that is, it led to 'increases in hostility and social introversion... and decreases in self-evaluation and evaluations of work and father' (Bonta and Gendreau, 1990, p. 357), that such imprisonment produced 'deteriorating community relationships over time' (Bonta and Gendreau, 1990, p. 359) as well as 'unique difficulties' with 'family separation issues and vocational skill training needs' (Bonta and Gendreau, 1990, p. 360), and that inmates may undergo a 'behavioral deep freeze' during incarceration such that 'outside-world behaviors that led the offender into trouble prior to imprisonment remain until release' (Bonta and Gendreau, 1990, p. 359).

Thus, even though researchers and commentators might have disagreed over how to interpret the magnitude and significance of these negative effects, few psychologists doubted that prison was an extremely stressful environment. Indeed, most understood the damaging effects that came about as a result of prolonged exposure to such extreme levels of stress. For example, Frederick Hocking's classic review of the psychological consequences of exposure to extreme environmental stress led him to conclude that it 'may result in permanent psychologic disability' (Hocking 1970). And, although persons varied in their ability to adjust to and tolerate different amounts of stress, 'subjection to prolonged, extreme stress results in the development of "neurotic" symptoms in virtually every person exposed to it...' (Hocking, 1970, p. 23). Individual difference variables – 'constitutional factors, patterns of child rearing, and pre-existing personality characteristics' – appeared to influence how long a person could withstand prolonged, extreme stress, not whether they eventually succumbed. In fact, psychologists working in other arenas helped to develop the concept of post-traumatic stress disorder ('PTSD') to describe a range of long-term trauma-related symptoms that occurred after exposure to extreme stress. PTSD symptoms include depression, emotional numbing, anxiety, isolation, hypervigilance, and related reactions (e.g. Wilson and Raphael, 1993).

Thus, it was generally understood that the psychological mechanisms employed in response to high levels of prison stress could take a severe psychological toll, and the longer the duration and the more intense the stressful conditions to which prisoners were required to adapt, the greater the consequences. Severely overcrowded conditions, high levels of idleness, inadequate mental health care, and the like – all of which became widespread in many prison systems over the last several decades – combined to increase the levels of prison stress with which many prisoners were forced to cope. Although what prison legal scholar Fred Cohen (2004) termed 'naked physical brutality' (Cohen, 2004, p. 421) certainly was not as commonplace as it had been in earlier times (when, for example, American courts literally refused to intervene behind prison walls), many prisoners nonetheless were still being subjected to forms of extreme degradation, humiliation, and even physical mistreatment.

In addition, prison researchers knew that many prisoners continued to devote a substantial portion of their day-to-day existence to minimizing the very real risks and dangers of imprisonment. Vivid accounts of life inside prisons in the United States written over the last several decades in which the prisons filled with unprecedented numbers of prisoners acknowledged that many of these institutions had become truly dangerous and frightening places (e.g. Branham, 1992; Bowker, 1980; Martin and Eckland-Olson, 1987; Morris 1988; Rideau and Wikberg, 1992). Not surprisingly, many prisoners were intensely focused on their own personal safety, and in a state of constant hypervigilance to defend against victimization.

Indeed, research documented the ways in which many prisoners had learned to project a tough convict veneer to others at a distance. As prison researcher Richard McCorkle put it, many prisoners had come to 'believe that unless an inmate can convincingly project an image that conveys the potential for violence, he is likely to be dominated and exploited throughout the duration of his sentence' (McCorkle, 1992, p. 161). As would be expected, under these circumstances, studies showed that fear played a major role in shaping the lifestyles of prisoners inside many penal institutions, as they adopted various behavioral strategies to avoid victimization in the dangerous environment around them. For example, McCorkle's (1992) own study found that large numbers of prisoners frequently adverted to fear-related concerns in their day-to-day lives (e.g. almost three-quarters of the prisoners reported that they had been forced to 'get tough' with another inmate to avoid victimization, and more than a quarter kept a 'shank' or other weapon nearby with which to defend themselves).

Of course, shaping such an outward image of toughness would require prisoners carefully to monitor, dampen, and control their emotional responses as they struggled to suppress their visible reactions to events around them. However, suppressing emotional reactions, especially in a tense and provocative environment like prison, could easily intensify rather than reduce the stress of confinement. For example, David d'Atri (1981) found that prisoners who suppressed hostile feelings (by, among other things, reporting that they never felt irritable or felt like fighting) and those who described their stay in prison in uniformly positive terms (for example, by characterizing their conditions of confinement as very comfortable and pleasant and the guards as good-natured) had higher blood pressure levels than those who did the opposite. D'Atri interpreted this in terms of the repression of natural feelings of aggression in response to the frustrations of prison life.

Psychologists also understood that prisoners who labored at both an emotional and behavioral level to develop a 'prison mask' that was unrevealing and impenetrable also risked alienation from themselves and others. Thus, researchers have observed that prisoners may develop an emotional flatness that becomes chronic and debilitating in social interactions and in their personal relationships. Indeed, some research indicated that the prison experience led some prisoners to withdraw from authentic social interactions altogether (e.g. Jose-Kampfner, 1990; Sapsford, 1978).

This kind of self-isolating dynamic is exacerbated by the enormous strain that imprisonment places on familial and other personal relationships (e.g. Crosthwaite, 1975; Fishman and Alissi, 1979). Financial and interpersonal hardships that are imposed on loved ones, and the significant practical difficulties that are encountered in the course of most prison visiting (that can range from mere inconvenience to outright humiliation) may take a significant and sometimes decisive toll on already fragile connections to family members, intimates, and the outside world in general (e.g. Friedman and Esselstyn, 1965; Hairston, 1988; 1991; Harris and Miller, 2006; Schneller, 1975). For some prisoners, self-imposed isolation – pushing others away – functions as a defensive reaction to the anticipated loss of social support.

Accounts of life in prison also revealed the way in which idleness and inactivity paradoxically often lead to chronic tiredness or lethargy. Prisoners have often talked about 'pulling time,' as if it were a weight; among other things, the heaviness to which they refer comes from the lack of meaningful activities in which to engage and the monotony of their surroundings and daily routine. Victor Serge (1969) was especially sensitive to the disjuncture between the weight of prison time and the pace of the free world and he thought he could make the latter more closely match the former: 'The contrast between this vacant, empty prison time and the intense rhythm of normal life is so violent that it will take a long and painful period of adaptation to slow down the pulse of life…' (Serge, 1969, p. 10).

In extreme cases, idleness, inactivity, and the loss of personal autonomy that imprisonment imposes can lead not only to lethargy but also to depression. Not surprisingly, long-term prisoners are particularly vulnerable to this kind of despondency. Indeed, at the outset of the period during which incarceration rates began their dramatic increase, Taylor (1961, p. 373) wrote that the long-term prisoner 'shows a flatness of response which resembles slow, automatic behavior of a very limited kind, and he is humorless and lethargic'. In fact, Jose-Kampfner (1990) analogized the plight of long-term women prisoners to that of persons who were terminally-ill, whose experience of this 'existential death is unfeeling, being cut off from the outside… [and who] adopt this attitude because it helps them cope' (Jose-Kampfner, 1990, p. 123).

Other researchers concentrated on the fact that imprisonment forced most prisoners to negotiate tensions between their pre-prison identity, the person who they had to appear to be in prison and, finally, the one they eventually would become when they were released (e.g. Schmid and Jones, 1991). Not surprisingly, these complicated identity shifts were difficult to manage successfully. Moreover, some researchers – writing as the policies that swelled the prison population were being vigorously pursued – identified a troublesome relationship: the ability to adapt successfully to certain prison contexts appeared to be *inversely* related to subsequent adjustment in the community. That is, as one study showed: '[I]nmates who adjusted most successfully to a prison environment actually encountered the most difficulty making the transition from institutional life to freedom' (Goodstein, 1979, p. 265).

Indeed, no careful reading of the literature on prison effects published over the last several decades could have led thoughtful analysts to conclude that prisons were psychological healthy places in which to confine persons for long periods of time. Clearly, then, the increased public and political tolerance of the harmful consequences of imprisonment did *not* come about because prison conditions had improved significantly, or that there was new and convincing scientific evidence to show that imprisonment did little or no damage to the persons who were subjected to it.

On Prisonization as Coping

As I suggested above, previous research on prison effects identified several patterns of coping with the stress of confinement, including hypervigilance, projecting a tough convict veneer, suppressing outward signs of emotion, and becoming generally distrustful of others. Viewed collectively, as they occur over time, these patterns are part of an overall process of forced adjustment or adaptation. The term 'institutionalization' has been used to describe ways in which inmates are shaped and transformed by the institutional environments in which they live. The process is by no means limited to prisoners (e.g. Goffman, 1961). George Herbert Mead (1956) once noted that 'a person is a personality because he belongs to a community, because he takes over the institutions of that community into his own conduct' (Mead, 1956, p. 239). If so, then a prisoner's personality is shaped by the institutional contingencies to which the community of prison requires him to adapt.

Called 'prisonization' when it occurs in correctional settings, this process has been studied extensively by sociologists, psychologists, psychiatrists, and others (e.g. Goodstein, 1979; Homant, 1984; Irwin, 1981; Peat and Winfree, 1992; Thomas and Peterson, 1981). In his classic formulation, sociologist Donald Clemmer (1958, p. 299) defined 'prisonization' as 'the taking on in greater or less degree of the folkways, mores, customs, and general culture of the penitentiary', but there are important psychological components to the process as well. Just as with the coping mechanisms discussed above, these changes are natural and normal adaptations made by prisoners in response to the unnatural and abnormal conditions of prison life. Of course, even these normal responses may become problematic if they are taken to extremes, or become so chronic and deeply internalized that they persist even though surrounding conditions have changed. Moreover, like most gradual transformations, prisonization does not require conscious awareness; prisoners do not have to make a 'choice' to allow themselves be changed or transformed.

Not surprisingly, during the initial period of incarceration, most prisoners find the harsh and rigid institutional routine, deprivations of privacy and liberty, stigmatized status, and sparse living conditions to be stressful, unpleasant, and difficult to tolerate. As prison researcher Edward Zamble (1992, p. 420) put it simply: 'It would appear that the beginning of the term [of imprisonment] induces considerable psychological discomfort…'. However, over time, they come to accept the many aspects of prison life that they cannot change. Indeed, as Zamble (1992, p. 420) noted, 'the constancy of the prison environment leads to a slow and gradual amelioration'.

The process of gradually 'ameliorating' is not necessarily neutral or benign. Zamble and others have suggested that this process 'does not induce widespread behavior change,' but instead results in a kind of 'behavioral deep freeze' (Zamble, 1992, p. 420). However, once prisoners have adapted to these contingencies, many find that their new behavior patterns are not easily 'unfrozen.' Moreover, the benign sounding term, 'amelioration,' does not necessarily capture the painfulness of the process, the losses that occur in the course of the transformation, or the distortions in the habits of thinking and acting that are required to bring it about. Prisoners who try actively to resist the process may be severely sanctioned by the prison administration or even by other inmates, and their very psychological survival may be placed at risk. In any event, widespread and deep-seated behavior change certainly occurs; it is the very purpose of the process.

Moreover, there is reason to believe that these transformations impede adjustment to free society once prisoners are released. Prison systems rarely acknowledge the negative psychological consequences of prison adjustment, of course, and there are few if any in-prison programs designed to reverse these effects as a prisoner's release date approaches. Even in the rare prison system where reintegrative services or after-care programs are available, the lingering effects of prisonization are typically ignored.

Several of the most important dimensions of prisonization can be summarized. Among other things, penal institutions typically force people to give up the power to make most of their own choices and decisions. This practice – a seemingly reasonable way to efficiently manage large numbers of people – is taken to extreme lengths in most prisons. Thus, prisoners must relinquish control over the most basic and mundane aspects of their daily existence. Indeed, most of the countless day-to-day decisions that citizens in the free world make on a routine basis, and naturally take for granted, are made for them, by others, in prison. Prisoners typically feel infantalized by this loss of control. However, over time, by 'ameliorating' to the erosion of personal autonomy, the fact that others routinely decide these things begins seem increasingly 'natural.' As the process of prisonization continues, prisoners come to *depend* on institutional decision-makers to make choices for them, and to rely on the structure and routines of the institution to organize their daily activities.

Most prisons deny prisoners basic privacy rights, especially in large correctional facilities that place an extremely heavy emphasis on security and control. In the United States, maximum and medium security prisons are typically surrounded by high double fences or walls, with armed guards in observation towers, and increasingly sophisticated surveillance technology at their disposal to monitor and control prisoner behavior. In addition to the external physical constraints, all prisons implement a network of rules and use structures, devices (locks, grills, handcuffs, chains, and the like), and control mechanisms of all sorts to keep behavior inside the institution in check. Over time, however, prisoners can become dependent on these limiting structures and procedures to constrain their actions. Rather than relying on internal organization, or what is commonly referred to as 'self control' to guide and restrain their conduct, institutions force prisoners to shape and structure their decision making around – or in response to – external limits and constraints.

Prisonization creates so much dependency on external limits and constraints that internal controls may atrophy or, in the case of especially young inmates, fail to develop at all. Like the ability to initiate behavior, the capacity to exercise self-control diminishes under conditions where it is rarely used or needed. If and when the external limits on which prisoners are forced to become dependent are removed, however, they may find that are less able to make appropriate choices, exercise personal judgment, or refrain from behavior that ultimately is harmful or self-destructive.

Prisoners also must adjust to extremely deprived and diminished living conditions. They typically live in small, cramped, sparsely furnished, and sometimes badly deteriorating and poorly maintained living spaces. Many prisons are old, with antiquated facilities that cannot easily accommodate the large numbers of people who use them. Plumbing, heating, ventilation and other systems needed to maintain overall living conditions often break down under the strain of overcrowding. Prisoners are double-celled in spaces designed for one, or housed in densely packed dormitories that afford little or no privacy and compromise safety.

Obviously, prisoners must learn to tolerate the very intimate daily contact that living in such extremely close quarters requires and negotiate the interpersonal conflicts and compromises it engenders. Although few of them are confined around-the-clock in these cramped spaces, high levels of overcrowding and the lack of rehabilitation programs have combined to further reduce already limited opportunities for meaningful out-of-cell activities in maximum security prisons. Moreover, in prisons that are plagued by violent conflict, prisoners are 'locked down' in their cells and they may remain there continuously – sometimes for months at a time – until normal movement is restored.

The degraded conditions under which prisoners live serve as constant reminders of their compromised and stigmatized social status and role. A diminished sense of self-worth and personal value may result. In extreme cases of prisonization, the symbolic meaning that can be inferred from this externally imposed substandard treatment and these degraded circumstances is internalized. That is, prisoners may come to think of themselves as the kind of person who deserves no more than the degradation and stigma to which they have been subjected while incarcerated (e.g. Homant, 1984; Irwin, 1970; McCorkle and Korn, 1954; Thomas and Peterson, 1981; Tittle, 1972; and Wulbert, 1965). This degraded identity may be difficult or impossible to relinquish upon release from prison. Of course, if prisoners return to communities where they continue to be marginalized or stigmatized by others, then the degraded identity is more likely to persist.

Prisons also are characterized by elaborate informal rules and norms that are part of an unwritten but essential culture and 'code.' Like the formal rules of the institution, these too must be abided; there are very real and often severe consequences when violations occur. Some prisoners, eager to defend themselves against what they perceive as constant dangers and deprivations of the surrounding environment, may fully embrace and internalize as many of these informal norms as possible. The norms of the prisoner culture can be harsh, exploitative, and even predatory. Especially in poorly run maximum security prisons, where the informal prisoner culture may become especially powerful, many prisoners – those who cannot somehow devise an improbable strategy to appear aloof and uninvolved – perceive a stark choice between becoming a victim or victimizer.

Ironically, in prisons where institutional treatment is particularly severe, in which there is a heightened concern for security and control, and where the day-to-day deprivations of prison life are especially extreme, the competing power and importance of the informal prisoner culture may be intensified. That is, the less access prisoners have to meaningful programming opportunities and other institutionally sanctioned activities in which to become invested and engaged, the more likely an alternative and oppositional prisoner culture is to emerge. Among other things, this means that some prisoners will rely on prison gangs or 'cliques' to provide support, comradeship, protection, and access to activities and other 'goods and services' that they perceive cannot be obtained in any other way. An informal gang culture may emerge. As it grows stronger, the choice to refrain or completely withdraw from – or 'drop out' after the fact – is more difficult for individual prisoners to make.

Signs of weakness or vulnerability may invite exploitation in many prisons, and prisoners are reluctant to show genuine emotion or interpersonal intimacy as a result. Prisoner culture strongly reinforces this norm, and helps to turn it into a self-fulfilling prophecy as well as a survival strategy. That is, in many prison settings, the failure to exploit weakness is itself seen as a sign of weakness and an invitation to exploitation by others. In men's prisons especially, these values and orientations may promote a kind of hypermasculinity in which force and domination are glorified.

Not surprisingly, prisoners who internalize these habits, values, and perspectives are likely to encounter extremely difficult transitions back to free-world norms. A tough veneer that precludes seeking help for personal problems, the generalized mistrust that comes from the fear of exploitation, or a tendency to strike out in response to minimal provocations are highly functional in many prison contexts but problematic virtually everywhere else. In interactions with persons who know nothing about the norms and psychological effects of the places from which they have come, prisoners may be perceived as unfeeling, distant or aloof or cold, needlessly suspicious or even paranoid, and capable of impulsive, dangerous overreactions.

Finally, because prisonization occurs gradually and many of the psychological changes take place subtly over time, prisoners often are unaware of the depth and magnitude of the transformations that they have undergone. Because many prisoners have learned to ignore or, at least, to mask their internal feelings and reactions, they struggle to locate the source of whatever anxiety and interpersonal disjunctures that they may experience during the transition back to the free world. Because they have learned to conceal emotions, problems, and vulnerabilities – even to themselves – it is often difficult for them to acknowledge these things once they leave prison. An outwardly projected image of post-prison adjustment may belie a great deal of inner turmoil, stress, and fear that can jeopardize their successful return to the free world.

The New Psychology of Prison Effects

Consistent with the contextual model of behavior around which much of my analysis has been structured, there is an emerging 'new psychology of prison effects' that documents the painfulness of prison and its long-term harmful – even criminogenic – effects. This research is characterized by its recognition of the power of prison environments to shape and transform its inhabitants, and to do so in ways that may have immediate and long-lasting adverse effects. Much of the research represents an advance over earlier research in part because of its careful attention to the specific psychological dimensions of conditions of confinement. Indeed, in many instances, measuring those dimensions and assessing their impact on the well-being of prisoners is the very purpose of the empirical analysis. Moreover, some of this new research takes the important additional step of assessing the impact of prison-induced change on post-prison adjustment.

I noted earlier that few informed psychological researchers really doubted the adverse consequences that long-term exposure to the punitive excesses and extremes of prison confinement could engender. In fact, many of them began to conceptualize exposure to extreme prison conditions as a form of trauma – in some instances, trauma severe enough that it could result in PTSD. Thus, Judith Herman (1992a,b) and others proposed that the diagnostic category of post-traumatic stress disorder be restructured to include what she termed 'complex PTSD,' a disorder created by 'prolonged, repeated trauma or the profound deformations of personality that occur *in captivity*' (Herman, 1992a, p. 119, emphasis added).

Unlike classic PTSD – which is thought to arise from relatively circumscribed traumatic events – complex PTSD occurs in response to more chronic exposure that is more closely analogous to the experience of imprisonment. Complex PTSD can result – as the long-term psychological costs of adapting to an oppressive situation – in protracted depression, apathy, and the development of a profound sense of hopelessness. As Herman (1992b, p. 382) wrote: 'The humiliated rage of the imprisoned person also adds to the depressive burden... During captivity, the prisoner can not express anger at the perpetrator; to do so would jeopardize survival'.

A number of systematic empirical studies have assessed the various ways that more general prison conditions affect the mental states of prisoners. For example, Claudia Kesterman (2005) and her colleagues analyzed the social contextual correlates of depressive symptoms among male prisoners in the correctional systems of several Baltic countries. Building on the basic notion that unhealthy prisons can have unhealthy psychological effects on prisoners, Kesterman, Frieder Dunkel, and the others involved in this project have concluded that there are a variety of specific conditions of confinement associated with certain adverse emotional reactions. Thus, the researchers found that poor relations with staff and other prisoners (i.e. perceived rejection), the presence of environmental stress factors, the experience of victimization, the lack of respect by staff, and the absence of home and/or work release at the facility were all significant predictors of whether prisoners manifested depression.

An especially impressive body of research conducted by Alison Liebling and her colleagues showed that the measured levels of distress in the prisons they studied were 'extraordinarily high' (Liebling *et al.*, 2005). In fact, in 11 of the 12 facilities on which the researchers focused, the mean distress score recorded among prisoners was above the threshold that ordinarily triggers an inquiry into whether a patient is suffering from a treatable emotional or psychological illness. Furthermore, the levels of distress varied in predictable ways, in part as a function of the quality of life in the prison environment (or the prisoners' experience of it). Thus, prisons whose 'moral performance' was poor – ones rated low on social climate and other measures – also produced higher levels of distress among prisoners.

A number of the conclusions reached by Liebling and her colleagues – that context-related factors help to account for emotional distress and even suicide in prison settings – have been confirmed by others. For example, Huey and McNulty (2005) used nationwide data to examine the effects of deprivation and overcrowding on prison suicide in the United States. The research was premised on the basic notion around which the new psychology of prison effects is structured – that 'individual actions are embedded in social contexts' (Huey and McNulty, 2005, p. 491). Huey and McNulty hypothesized that higher rates of suicide would occur in prisons that kept prisoners under more 'deprived' conditions – maximum security facilities that increased the 'social isolation experienced by inmates, both within the prison itself and from loved ones on the outside' (Huey and McNulty, 2005, p. 492). In addition, they speculated that the stress of overcrowding – including the 'struggles for resources, space, and personal autonomy' that accompanied it – would 'create atmospheres that impeded inmate adaptation to prison life and increase the likelihood of suicide' (Huey and McNulty, 2005, p. 494).

In fact, they found that both variables – deprivation and overcrowding – increased suicide rates. For example, the likelihood of suicide was 'significantly higher in maximum-security facilities' compared with minimum and medium security (Huey and McNulty, 2005, p. 505), and also was higher in prisons that experienced greater degrees of overcrowding. Indeed, the overcrowding effect appeared powerful enough to override the advantage that came from being in a prison that enjoyed lower levels of deprivation, such that 'the buffer against suicide provided by lesser deprivation in minimum-security facilities may be erased under conditions of high overcrowding' (Huey and McNulty, 2005, p. 504).

In addition to research on the effects of the general social climate of prison, and special environmental stress factors (such as deprived and overcrowded conditions of confinement) that too often characterize many contemporary prison systems, some recent studies have focused on the psychological consequences of particular forms of prison trauma. For example, researchers have examined the adverse psychological effects of a relatively new form of prison confinement – in long-term solitary or so-called 'supermax' units. The use of these facilities – which impose extreme forms of isolation on prisoners for what often are extremely long periods of time – has grown in the United States since the start of the 1990s.

My own study of the adverse emotional and behavioral consequences of such extreme and prolonged forms of isolation (Haney, 2003) found many of the same problems identified by other researchers, leading me to voice many of the same serious concerns about this practice that other commentators have expressed – for example, that 'mental health and psychiatric issues might be among the most important and problematic aspects of supermaxes' (Kurki and Morris, 2001, p. 394).

Specifically, long-term confinement in supermax-type facilities has been implicated in the development or exacerbation of hypertension, uncontrollable anger, hallucinations, emotional breakdowns, chronic depression, and suicidal thoughts and behavior. A representative sample of supermax prisoners at the notorious California facility that I studied manifested a range of symptoms of psychological trauma as well as the psychopathological effects of prolonged isolation. Prevalence rates were extremely high, with well over half to three-quarters of prisoners reporting anxiety, a sense of an impending breakdown, irrational anger, confused thought processes, social withdrawal, chronic depression, emotional flatness, and violent fantasies (Haney, 2003).

Of course, not only do prisons vary widely in terms of the kinds of experiences they create for prisoners – as I noted earlier, not all prisons are equally benign, painful, or capable of inflicting harm – but prisoners themselves vary in terms of how they experience the same environments and how harmful and disabling the same prison experience proves to be for different prisoners over the long-term (e.g. Hemmens and Marquart, 1999; Toch and Adams, 2002). This insight, too, has become part of the more sophisticated way that prison effects are now being acknowledged and assessed.

For example, Robert Guthrie (1998) found a high prevalence of post-traumatic stress – 30% – in the sample of federal prisoners he evaluated. He concluded that these high levels were attributable not only to the prisoners' histories of having been exposed to trauma before they entered prison but also to the traumatic prison experiences to which they were subjected once incarcerated. Another study of prison distress (Hochstetler *et al.*, 2004), focused on the degree to which having been victimized in prison – subjected to 'theft, con games and scams, robbery, destruction of property, assault, and serious threats of bodily injury' (Hochstetler *et al.*, 2004, p. 444) – led to depression and symptoms of post-traumatic stress. These researchers concluded not only that 'prison victimization contributes to the occurrence of depressive and [post-traumatic stress] symptoms' (Hochstetler *et al.*, 2004, p. 448) but also that a history of having been exposed to trauma and violence prior to coming to prison helped to explain the resulting level of prison distress. Thus, the experience of being victimized in prison *added* to the pains of the pre-existing events to which the prisoner had been exposed. Especially because of the potentially disabling post-prison consequences of PTSD symptoms, the authors recommended that '[r]ehabilitative efforts should help inmates recover from trauma occurring inside *and* outside prison' (Hochstetler *et al.*, 2004, p. 448, emphasis added).

In a related vein, Huey and McNulty (2005) proposed the 'reasonable hypothesis' that some prisoners suffered from pre-existing mental health problems that were 'especially affected by conditions such as overcrowding, perhaps accounting in part for their heightened risk of suicide' (Huey and McNulty, 2005, p. 508). In fact, this interactionist model – acknowledging that some prisoners are uniquely vulnerable to the environmental stress of prison confinement in ways that may exacerbate its negative effects – has been incorporated in some legal decisions that apply to solitary or supermax confinement. Thus, some US federal courts have ruled that prisoners suffering from certain kinds of psychological disorders must be excluded from supermax confinement (*Jones El v. Berge*, 2001; *Madrid v. Gomez*, 1995; and *Ruiz v. Johnson*, 1999).

Insights from the new psychology of prison effects also can be used proactively, to improve and reform otherwise hurtful and harmful prison conditions. Thus, as I noted earlier, Alison Liebling and her colleagues have found that the overall distress levels among the prisoners they studied tended to be very high. However, distress levels varied as a function of how the prisoners were treated in prison. In particular, Liebling found that the measurable quality of life and nature of prisoner treatment in prison could compound *or* alleviate the vulnerabilities with which persons entered prison. Prisoners who were confined in safe and caring facilities and who experienced fair treatment during incarceration experienced a greater sense of well being and were less likely to suffer negative outcomes (such as suicide) during incarceration (see, Liebling, 2002; 2004 and Liebling *et al.*, 2005).

Similarly, Paul Gendreau and his colleagues (Gendreau and Keyes, 2001) have concluded that, because serious disruptions in prison are often caused by 'situational elements' inside the prison, prevention and control of these kinds of behaviors are possible through the monitoring and improvement of certain aspects of the 'institutional climate.' Further, they argued that in-prison behavior and post-prison success could be improved through prison programming, especially programming that was 'appropriate' to the prisoners in question – that is, directed to their particular needs.

Finally, evidence that high levels of prison distress and trauma translate into lasting problems for the prisoners who suffer them comes from a variety of sources. As Hans Toch and Kenneth Adams have acknowledged, the 'dictum that prisons are stressful cannot be overestimated' (Toch and Adams, 2002, p. 230). In addition, as I noted earlier, prisoners have little choice but to attempt to adapt to prison life. Yet, mastering the psychological challenges that prisoners confront in prison does little to facilitate their successful reintegration into the free world. Moreover, stress that is extreme and endured on a long-term basis is more than unpleasant; we now know that it can result in psychological damage that persists beyond imprisonment itself.

For example, in Adrian Grounds' (2005) psychiatric assessments of a group of long-term prisoners who were exonerated and subsequently released from custody, he recognized that the most serious psychological problems many prisoners would face were likely to occur after they left prison. In fact, Grounds' assessments uncovered a pattern of disabling symptoms and severe psychological problems that plagued ex-prisoners long after they had re-entered the free world. Thus, he found evidence of personality change and adjustment difficulties similar to those described 'in clinical studies of others who have experienced chronic psychological trauma,' including 'marked features of estrangement, loss of capacity for intimacy, moodiness, inability to settle, loss of a sense of purpose and direction, and a pervasive attitude of mistrust toward the world,' being 'withdrawn, unable to relate to the world,' manifesting the diagnostic criteria for post-traumatic stress disorder, suffering depressive disorders, and encountering a whole range of serious problems with family contact, social adjustment, and employment (Grounds, 2005, p. 21–41). Indeed, Grounds (2005, p. 15) concluded that the 'extent of the suffering was profound'.

It is likely that exposure to adverse conditions of confinement will compromise post-prison adjustment in a variety of different ways. Joan Petersilia (2003) summarized the results of research on the plight of persons released from typically overcrowded, punishment-oriented prisons by noting that nowadays the 'average inmate' likely returns home from unusually long prison sentences 'more disconnected from family and friends,' lacking badly needed education and the job skills needed to find employment, and suffering from 'a higher prevalence of substance abuse and mental illness' than previous cohorts of ex-convicts. She also observed that '[e]ach of these factors is known to predict recidivism, yet few of these needs are addressed while the inmate is in prison or on parole' (Petersilia, 2003, p. 53).

John Irwin (2005) reached many of the same conclusions about the medium security prisoners he studied at a California penal institution. Irwin encountered many 'long-termers' who had been 'living in crowded conditions without privacy, reduced options, arbitrary control, disrespect, and economic exploitation' (Irwin 2005, p. 168). He speculated that the predictable psychological reactions to years of exposure to these deprived conditions – '[a]nger, frustration, and a burning sense of injustice' – would have an equally predictable effect once the prisoners were released – it would 'significantly reduce the likelihood that [the prisoners would] pursue a viable conventional, non-criminal life after release' (Irwin, 2005, p. 168).

In fact, when Paul Gendreau and his colleagues conducted a comprehensive meta-analytic study of the relationship between incarceration, length of confinement, and recidivism, they concluded that doing time in prison actually had a criminogenic effect (Smith *et al.*, 2004). That is, not only did going to prison increase the chances of re-offending but also, the more time served, the greater the effect. Although the overall effects were modest in size, Gendreau and his colleagues concluded that 'the enormous costs accruing from the excessive use of prison may not be defensible,' and that the long-term cost – in terms of increased amounts of crime produced by more people going to prison for longer amounts of time – was particularly problematic 'given the high incarceration rates currently in vogue in North America' (Smith *et al.*, 2004, p. 20).

Other research suggests that, in addition to the length of imprisonment, the harshness of the conditions of confinement has an adverse impact on the amount and nature of recidivism. Specifically, Chen and Shapiro (2002, p. 12) found that 'harsher prison conditions induce not only increased but systematically worse crimes'. It may be that the negative effects of harsher forms of imprisonment result in part from the greater difficulties that prisoners who are housed in these especially punitive facilities encounter in maintaining family ties and establishing connections to employers before they are released. That is, harsher prisons may not only 'harden' the persons confined in them but also harden the nature of the social world to which they return.

Indeed, the negative consequences that imprisonment has on recidivism are likely to be the joint result of a number of factors, only some of which are psychological in nature. For example, in addition to the direct negative effects of imprisonment on prisoners themselves, there is much evidence that prison directly and adversely affects subsequent employment opportunities. Not surprisingly, perhaps, ex-convicts have higher rates of unemployment and earn lower wages when they do find jobs (e.g. Western *et al.*, 2001). The long periods of time from which prisoners are removed from the job market (during which they are provided with opportunities to acquire few if any marketable skills), and the stigma that employers attach to their having done prison time contribute to these employment effects. In fact, Pettit and Western (2004, p. 155) characterized imprisonment as 'an illegitimate timeout that confers enduring stigma'. As they observed, this stigma deters employers from offering even low wage jobs, and a prison record also can create formal legal barriers that prohibit ex-convicts from entering certain skilled and licensed occupations.

Although there is certainly no systematic empirical proof for the proposition that all prisons are criminogenic, these studies underscore the fact there is a strong crime control rationale for positively transforming these institutions, reducing the magnitude of the pain that they inflict, and reducing the number of people who experience it. As one veteran prison administrator acknowledged: 'I now think that my colleagues and I initially underestimated the negative effect of custody. We are now much more willing to say that even the research findings on recidivism affirm a widely shared belief that custody is best viewed as the last resort' (Andrews, 1995, p. 48).

Conclusion

Over the last decade, a new psychology of prison effects has emerged to give more careful and sustained attention to the negative psychological consequences of penal confinement. This research has identified the various ways in which prisoners are changed and transformed by their prison experience, especially in a range of adverse and problematic correctional environments. The willingness to tolerate or ignore these negative consequences that characterized the era of mass incarceration appears to have ended. Armed with more sophisticated conceptual frameworks, this research makes it increasingly difficult to advocate policies of increased punishment without simultaneously acknowledging the potential human costs. Indeed, Gendreau and Keyes (2001) have lamented the fact that '[s]adly, there are repeated calls to make prison living conditions even tougher,' and termed the current 'growth industry [in] the use of various prison segregation environments' that came about over the last decade and a half 'appalling' (Gendreau and Keyes, 2001, p. 124).

The core notion that 'context matters' – in prison and beyond – has far reaching implications for prison policy and crime control strategies (Haney, 2006). It certainly implies, as I noted earlier in this chapter, that not only can and should we fully assess the psychological costs of incarceration, but also that we are better positioned to advocate a vision of prison reform that is based on accurate knowledge about which prison programs and environments are the most humane and truly effective.

In addition, there are important implications for contexts outside prison. Thus, the recent, appropriate, and long overdue attention being given to the important issue of prisoner reintegration takes an explicitly social contextualist perspective into account (e.g. Maruna and Immarigeon, 2004; Travis *et al.*, 2001). Moreover, recognizing the ways in which people's behavior is influenced by their surrounding contexts implies that criminal justice policy 'should focus more intently on the underlying causes of criminal behavior... [including] family, community, school, and peer processes' (Huey and McNulty, 2005, p. 508). Indeed, these interrelated aspects of this emerging psychological perspective provide a framework with which to fundamentally alter the direction in which criminal justice policy has moved over the last several decades.

References

Andrews, D. (1995) The psychology of criminal conduct and effective treatment, in: J. McGuire (Ed.) *What Works: Reducing Reoffending*, pp. 35–62 (New York: Wiley).

Bonta, J. and Gendreau, P. (1990) Reexamining the cruel and unusual punishment of prison life, *Law and Human Behavior*, 14, 347–372.

Bowker, L. (1980) *Prison victimization* (New York: Elsevier).

Branham, L. (1992) *The Use of Incarceration in the United States: A Look at the Present and the Future* (Chicago, IL: American Bar Association).

Bukstel, L. and Kilmann, P. (1980) Psychological effects of imprisonment on confined individuals, *Psychological Bulletin*, 88, 469–493.

Bureau of Justice Statistics (1986) *Population Density in State Prisons* (Washington, DC: US Department of Justice).

Chen, K. and Shapiro, J. (2002) Does prison harden inmates? A discontinuity-based approach. Unpublished manuscript, Yale University.

Clemmer, D. (1958) *The Prison Community* (New York: Holt, Rinehart & Winston).

Cohen, F. (2004) The limits of the judicial reform of prisons: what works, what does not, *Criminal Law Bulletin*, 40, pp. 421–465.

Cooper, C. and Berwick, S. (2001) Factors affecting psychological well-being of three groups of suicide prone prisoners, *Current Psychology*, 20, pp. 169–182.

Crosthwaite, A. (1975) Punishment for whom? The prisoner or his wife, *International Journal of Offender Therapy*, 19, pp. 275–284.

d'Atri, D. (1981) Measuring prison stress, in: D. Ward and K. Schoen (Eds) *Confinement in Maximum Custody: Last Resort Prisons in the United States and Western Europe*, pp. 27–38 (Lexington, MA: D.C. Heath).

Durose, M. and Langan, P. (2005) *State Court Sentencing of Convicted Felons, 2002: Statistical Tables*. NCJ 208910 (Washington, DC: US Department of Justice).

Fishman, S. and Alissi, A. (1979) Strengthening families as natural support systems for offenders, *Federal Probation*, 43, pp. 16–21.

Friedman, S. and Esselstyn, T. (1965) The adjustment of children of jail inmates, *Federal Probation*, 29, pp. 55–59.

Gendreau and D. Keyes, D. (2001) Making prisons safer and more humane environments, *Canadian Journal of Criminology*, 43, pp. 123–130.

Goodstein, L. (1979) Inmate adjustment to prison and the transition to community life, *Journal of Research on Crime and Delinquency*, 16, pp. 246–272.

Goffman, E. (1961) *Asylums: Essays on the Social Situation of Mental Patients and other Inmates* (New York: Anchor Books).

Grounds, A. (2005) Understanding the effects of wrongful imprisonment, in: M. Tonry (Ed.) *Crime and Justice: A Review of Research*, Vol. 32, pp. 1–58 (Chicago: University of Chicago Press).

Guthrie, R. (1998) The prevalence of posttraumatic stress disorder among federal prison inmates. Unpublished doctoral dissertation, West Virginia University, Morgantown, West Virginia.

Hairston, C. (1988) Family ties during imprisonment: do they influence future criminal activity? *Federal Probation*, 52, pp. 48–52.

Hairston, C. (1991) Family ties during imprisonment: important to whom and for what? *Journal of Sociology and Social Welfare*, 18, pp. 87–104.

Haney, C. (2002) Making law modern: toward a contextual model of justice, *Psychology, Public Policy and Law*, 7, pp. 3–63.

Haney, C. (2006) *Reforming Punishment: Psychological Limits to the Pains of Imprisonment* (Washington, DC: American Psychological Association Books).

Haney, C. (2003) Mental health issues in long-term solitary and 'supermax' confinement, *Crime & Delinquency*, 49, pp. 124–156.

Harris, O. and Miller, R. (Eds) (2006) *Impacts of Incarceration on the African American Family* (New Brunswick, NJ: Transaction Books).

Hemmens, C. and Marquart, J. (1999) Straight time: inmate's perceptions of violence and victimization in the prison environment, *Journal of Offender Rehabilitation*, 28, pp. 1–21.

Herman, J. (1992a) *Trauma and Recovery* (New York: Basic Books).

Herman, J. (1992b) Complex PTSD: a syndrome in survivors of prolonged and repeated trauma, *Journal of Traumatic Stress*, 5, pp. 377–391.

Hochstetler, A., Murphy D. and Simons, R. (2004) Damaged goods: exploring predictors of distress in prison inmates, *Crime & Delinquency*, 50, pp. 436–457.

Hocking, F. (1970) Extreme environmental stress and its significance for psychopathology, *American Journal of Psychotherapy*, 24, pp. 4–26.

Homant, R. (1984) Employment of ex-offenders: the role of prisonization and self-esteem, *Journal of Offender Counseling, Services and Rehabilitation*, 8, pp. 5–23.

Huey, M. and McNulty, T. (2005) Institutional conditions and prison suicide: conditional effects of deprivation and overcrowding, *The Prison Journal*, 85, pp. 490–514.

Irwin, J. (1970) *The Felon* (Englewood Cliffs, NJ: Prentice-Hall).

Irwin, J. (1981) Sociological studies of the impact of long-term confinement, in D. Ward and K. Schoen (Eds) *Confinement in Maximum Custody* (Lexington, MA: Lexington Books).

Irwin, J. (2005) *The Warehouse Prison: Disposal of the New Dangerous Class* (Los Angeles, CA: Roxbury Publishing).

Jones 'El v. Berge, 164 F. Supp. 2d 1096 (2001).

Jose-Kampfner, C. (1990) Coming to terms with existential death: an analysis of women's adaptation to life in prison, *Social Justice*, 17, pp. 110–125.

Kesterman, C. (2005) Prison life: factors affecting health and rehabilitation. Paper presented at the European Conference on Psychology and Law, July, Vilnius, Lithuania.

Keve, P. (1974) *Prison Life and Human Worth* (Minneapolis, MN: University of Minnesota Press).

Kurki, L. and Morris, N. (2001) The purposes, practices and problems of supermax prisons, in M. Tonry (Ed.) *Crime and Justice: A Review of Research*, Vol. 28, pp. 385–424 (Chicago: University of Chicago Press).

Liebling, A. (2002) Suicide and the safer prisons agenda, *Probation Journal*, 49, pp. 140–150.

Liebling, A. (2004) *Prisons and their Moral Performance: A Study of Values, Quality And Prison Life* (Oxford, UK: Clarendon Press).

Liebling, A. and Maruna, S. (Eds) (2004) *The Effects of Imprisonment* (Portland, OR: Willan).

Liebling, A., Durie, L., van den Beukel, A., Tait, S. and Harvey, J. (2005) Revisiting prison suicide: the role of fairness and distress, in: A. Liebling and S. Maruna (Eds) *The Effects of Imprisonment*, pp. 209–232 (Cullompton, UK: Willan).

Madrid v. Gomez, 889 F. Supp. 1146 (1995).

Martin, S. and Ekland-Olson, S. (1987) *Texas Prisons: The Walls Came Tumbling Down* (Austin, TX: Texas Monthly Press).

Maruna, S. and Immarigeon, R. (Eds) (2004) *After Crime and Punishment: Pathways to Offender Re-integration* (Cullompton: Willan).

Mauer, M., Kind, R. and Young, M. (2004) *The Meaning of 'Life': Long Prison Sentences in Context* (Washington, DC: The Sentencing Project).

McCorkle, R. (1992) Personal precautions to violence in prison, *Criminal Justice and Behavior*, 19, pp. 160–173.

McCorkle, L. and Korn, R. (1954) Resocialization within walls, *The Annals*, 293, pp. 88–98.

Mead, G. (1956) *The Social Psychology of George Herbert Mead* (Chicago: Phoenix Books).

Morris, R. (1988) *The Devil's Butcher Shop: The New Mexico Prison Uprising* (Albuquerque, NM: University of New Mexico Press).

Peat, B. and Winfree, T. (1992) Reducing the intra-institutional effects of 'prisonization': a study of a therapeutic community for drug-using inmates, *Criminal Justice and Behavior*, 19, pp. 206–225.

Petersilia, J. (2003) *When Prisoners Come Home: Parole and Prisoners Reentry* (New York: Oxford University Press).

Pettit, B. and Western, B. (2004) Mass imprisonment and the life course: race and class inequality in U.S. incarceration, *American Sociological Review*, 69, pp. 151–169.

Phillips, J. (2001) Cultural construction of manhood in prison, *Psychology of Men & Masculinity*, 2, pp. 13–23.

Porporino, F. (1990) Difference in response to long-term imprisonment: implications for the management of long-term offenders, *The Prison Journal*, 80, pp. 35–36.

Rideau, W. and Wikberg, R. (1992) *Life Sentences: Rage and Survival Behind Bars* (New York: Time Books).

Ruiz v. Estelle, 503 F. Supp. 1265 (S.D. Tex. 1980), aff'd in part, vacated in part, 679 F.2d 1115 (5th Cir. 1982), cert. Denied, 460 U.S. 1042 (1982).

Ruiz v. Johnson, 37 F. Supp. 2d 855 (1999).

Sabol, W. and McGready, J. (1999) *Time Served in Prison by Federal Offenders, 1986–1997*. Bureau of Justice Statistics Special Report, June. NCJ 170032 (Washington, DC: US Department of Justice).

Sapsford, R. (1978) Life sentence prisoners: psychological changes during sentence, *British Journal of Criminology*, 18, pp. 128–145.

Schmid, T. and Jones, R. (1991) Suspended identity: identity transformation in a maximum security prison, *Symbolic Interaction*, 14, pp. 415–432.

Schneller, D. (1975) Prisoners' families: a study of some social and psychological effects of incarceration of the families of Negro prisoners, *Criminology*, 12, pp. 402–412.

Serge, V. (1969) *Men in Prison*. R. Greeman trans. (Garden City, NY: Doubleday).

Smith, P., Goggin, C. and Gendreau, P. (2004) The effects of prison sentences and intermediate sanctions on recidivism: general effects and individual differences. Unpublished Manuscript, Department of Psychology, University of New Brunswick.

Stephan, J. and Karberg, J. (2003) *Census of State and Federal Correctional Facilities, 2000*. NCJ 198272 (Washington, DC: Bureau of Justice Statistics).

Suedfeld, P. (1978) Beyond sentimentality, *International Journal of Offender Therapy and Comparative Criminology*, 22, pp. 49–55.

Taylor, A. (1961) Social isolation and imprisonment, *Psychiatry*, 24, pp. 373–376.

Thomas, C. and Peterson, D. (1981) A comparative organizational analysis of prisonization, *Criminal Justice Review*, 6, pp. 36–43.

Tittle, C. (1972) Institutional living and self-esteem, *Social Problems*, 20, pp. 65–77.

Toch, H. (1981) A revisionist view of prison reform, *Federal Probation*, 3–9.

Toch, H. (1982) The role of the expert on prison conditions: the battle of footnotes in *Rhodes v. Chapman, Criminal Law Bulletin*, 18, pp. 38–49.

Toch, H. and Adams, K. (2002) *Acting Out: Maladaptive Behavior in Confinement* (Washington, DC: American Psychological Association).

Travis, J., Solomon, A. and Waul, M. (2001) *From Prison to Home: The Dimensions and Consequences of Prisoner Reentry* (Washington DC: The Urban Institute).

Western, B., Kling, J. and Weiman, D. (2001) The labor market consequences of incarceration, *Crime and Delinquency*, 47, pp. 410–427.

Wilson, J. (1975) *Thinking about Crime* (New York: Basic Books).

Wilson, J. and Raphael, B. (Eds) (1993) *International Handbook of Traumatic Stress Syndromes* (New York: Plenum).

Wolff v. McDonnell, 418 U.S. 539 (1974).

Wormith, J. (1995) The controversy over the effects of long-term incarceration, in: T. Flanagan (Ed.) *Long-term Imprisonment: Policy, Science and Correctional Practice*, pp. 53–63 (Thousand Oaks, CA: Sage).

Wulbert, R. (1965) Inmate pride in total institutions, *American Journal of Sociology*, 71, pp. 1–9.

Zamble, E. (1992) Behavior and adaptation in long-term prison inmates: descriptive longitudinal results. *Criminal Justice and Behavior*, 19, pp. 409–425.

Chapter 10

Psychopathy as an Important Forensic Construct: Past, Present and Future

David J. Cooke

Psychopathy is a personality disorder, that is, a chronic disturbance in an individual's relations with self, others and their environment, which results in distress or failure to fulfil social roles and obligations (Cooke and Hart, 2004). Personality disorders affect how individuals think, feel and behave. Psychopathic personality disorder is a particular form of personality disorder that is characterised by three broad dimensions, an interpersonal style that is dominant, forceful, deceptive and grandiose, by an affective deficiency evidenced by a failure to experience remorse or guilt, and by behaviour that can be described as impulsive and reckless.

Past Conceptualisation of Psychopathic Personality Disorder

The constellation of personality characteristics that today is labelled as psychopathic has long been recognised, both across time and across cultures. The psalmist identified key features central to contemporary accounts of the disorder: wickedness or immoral behaviour, pride, vanity, grievousness, a sense of invulnerability, deceitfulness and manipulation. This pattern was associated with extreme violence (Psalms, 10, v2–8). Other historical sources, including the Icelandic Sagas, identified a similar pattern (Hoyersten, 2001): they distinguished between the merely antisocial and the psychopathic.

The pattern has been recognised in many societies: Murphy (1976), in her classic anthropological study, identified psychopathy in two pre-industrial societies, the Inuit of North West Alaska and the Yoruba tribe of Nigeria. Members of these groups could distinguish psychopathy from other forms of mental disorder – in particular schizophrenia, and they had specific terms for the disorder – Kulangeta and Aranakan respectively – and specific management strategies.

Although thought to be more prevalent in men, psychopathy has long been described in women. From Greek mythology to contemporary cinema (e.g. Médée, Salomé, Manon Lescaut), *les femmes fatale* harmed others by being seductive, manipulative, cruel, egocentric, callous, affectionless and unfaithful. Using their sensuality and sexuality, they controlled and dominated others (Forouzan and Cooke, 2005).

The clinical description of this disorder can be traced back to the case studies of Pinel and Pritchard (Berrios, 1996). Their contribution was twofold. First, they demonstrated that mental disorder can exist even when reasoning is intact, and second, they argued that incorrigible behaviour may be a consequence of such disorder. These and other influential alienists described mental disorders characterised by a disturbance of emotion or volition, which they gave names such as *manie sans delire*, *monomanie*, *moral insanity*, and *folie lucide* (Millon, 1981).

Interestingly, the motivation for describing these disorders was forensic. To ensure that their testimony would be relevant, the alienists of the 19th century had to extend their expertise beyond the realm of 'total insanity'. Even 200 years ago it was argued that a mental disorder whose symptomatology includes antisocial behaviour is a moral judgement that is open to abuse in forensic settings (Berrios, 1996). It is also tautological with past social deviance being used to diagnose a mental disorder, which in turn is used to predict future social deviance. The role of antisocial behaviour in diagnosis remains contentious; this is an issue to which I will return below.

The first half of the 20th century saw a narrowing of the concept of psychopathy to refer only to personality disorder. Little consensus existed about the specific forms of personality disorder, nonetheless a consensus emerged about the existence of an important cluster of symptoms related to aggression, impulsivity and antisocial behaviour (Berrios, 1996). In Scotland, Henderson (1939) had a tripartite taxonomy, he described the 'predominantly aggressive psychopath', the 'inadequate psychopath' and the 'creative psychopath'; Kahn described the 'impulsive,' 'weak,' and 'sexual' psychopath; and Schneider, the 'labile', 'explosive,' and 'wicked' psychopath (Berrios, 1996).

The second half of the last century saw a further narrowing of the construct of psychopathy, to a disorder defined by specific interpersonal, affective, and behavioural features. Rich clinical descriptions – such as those of Arieti (1963), Cleckley (1988), Gough (1948) and the McCords (McCord and McCord, 1964) – have provided a framework for describing these individuals. There is broad agreement that interpersonally, psychopathic individuals are dominant, forceful, arrogant, and deceptive; affectively, they lack appropriate emotional responses, with any emotional responses being limited and short lived; and behaviourally, they are impulsive, reckless and lack 'planfullness'. There is also broad agreement that criminal behaviour, while being associated with psychopathy, is not a core defining feature (Blackburn, 2005).

Current work suggests that clinicians experienced with this group of patients have a more sophisticated view of the disorder, adding further domains including problems of self, attachment, and cognitive processing (e.g. Cooke *et al.*, 2006c; and below).

In summary, it is evident that the construct of psychopathy has been recognised across time and across cultures both in formal and informal descriptions; it, or cognate constructs, has had a central importance in forensic thinking for over two centuries;

and over time, clinical descriptions have become more specific, with the importance of antisocial behaviour as a marker of the disorder remaining controversial.

Current Concerns and Controversies regarding Psychopathic Personality Disorder

The diagnosis of psychopathy has always been a contentious diagnosis. Toch (1998), for example, argued that the diagnosis is a form of counter-transference – a label given to patients that a therapist does not like. However, Mullen (1992), while acknowledging the pejorative connotations of the term, argued that there is a group of individuals for which this, or some other, descriptive term is required. Evidence for the validity of the construct has improved dramatically over the last decade with evidence from the genetic, developmental, neuropsychological, neurochemical, psychometric, clinical and forensic – amongst other – domains becoming available (e.g. Cooke *et al.*, 1996; Patrick, 2006).

A major step towards fuller understanding of this disorder over the last two decades has been the development of the Hare's Psychopathy Checklist-Revised (PCL-R; Hare 2001, 2003). This currently remains the instrument of choice for measuring psychopathy (Stone, 1995). However, as will be demonstrated, the procedure does suffer from some significant psychometric and conceptual limitations (Cooke *et al.*, 2006a, 2006b; Skeem *et al.*, 2006).

The PCL-R is a construct rating scale in which 20 symptoms are considered to be diagnostic of psychopathy (e.g. grandiosity, impulsivity and lack or remorse); these symptoms are rated on the basis of an interview with the patient, but most importantly, by a systematic review of file information regarding the patient. The assessor uses all this information to understand life-time patterns of behaviour in order to demonstrate that the symptoms are persistent, pervasive and pathological. The greater the number of symptoms present the closer the patient is to the prototypical psychopath. The PCL-R has helped to clarify some issues; it has also served to confuse others.

In the remainder of this section I will consider three current controversies, first, the structure of the PCL-R, and by inference what this tells us about the structure of the construct of psychopathy; second, the association between the core traits of psychopathy and antisocial behaviour; and third, the cross-cultural variability of the disorder.

The Measurement Model Underpinning the PCL-R

Psychology is interested in unobservable characteristics – or constructs – such as intelligence, neuroticism, conformity, etc; these constructs cannot be examined directly but have to be inferred by using fallible measures. By exploring the structure of our measures we can gain insight into the nature of our constructs (Smith *et al.*, 2003). It is important that constructs and measures are not confused (Campbell, 1960). A danger that the field now faces is operationalism, i.e. PCL-R scores are now being confused with the construct of psychopathy (see Skeem *et al.*, 2006). This forecloses on the possibility of examining the mapping of the theoretical construct (psychopathy) onto the empirical observation (PCL-R scores).

Traditionally, the PCL-R has been considered to be underpinned by two distinct but related factors; factor one measuring both the interpersonal and affective features of the disorder, and factor two measuring the behavioural features (Harpur *et al.*, 1989). Recent research, using Confirmatory Factor Analysis (CFA), cluster analytic and Item Response Theory (IRT) approaches, indicated that this conceptualisation of the PCL-R is inadequate and based on a misunderstanding of statistical methods (Cooke and Michie, 2001). The PCL-R (and indeed other related instruments) has a hierarchical structure in which a superordinate 'Psychopathy' factor overarches three subordinate factors we have labelled as, Arrogant and Deceitful Interpersonal Style; Deficient Affective Experience; and Impulsive and Irresponsible Behavioural Style (Cooke and Michie, 2001). This model has been cross-validated across cultures and across measures (Cooke *et al.*, 2005a, 2005b). It suggests that the disorder is best assessed by considering personality traits rather than distinct behaviours such as criminal behaviour. Additionally, support for the three factor model has been obtained from independent samples and/or independent researchers (e.g. Cooke *et al.*, 2001a; Johansson *et al.*, 2002b; Skeem *et al.*, 2003).

Some have argued that this model is controversial (Salekin *et al.*, in press). Hare (2003) and his colleagues (Hare and Neumann, 2005; Neumann *et al.*, in press) have recently argued against the three-factor model measurement model of the PCL-R and have proposed a number of four-factor models. Essentially, within these models the three factors of Cooke and Michie (2001) are supplemented with a fourth 'factor' comprising five items related to criminal behaviour, i.e. Poor behavioural controls; Early behaviour problems; Juvenile delinquency; Revocation of conditional release; and Criminal versatility. Previously, Hare and his colleagues have argued 'psychopathy and criminality are distinct but related constructs' (Hart *et al.*, 1995; emphasised in original) and that psychopathy should not be confused with antisocial and criminal behaviour (Hare, 1999). More recently, Hare and Neumann (2005, p. 62) have argued that PCL-R items that capture antisocial tendencies, including criminality, are important psychopathic traits, asserting that the 'real core of psychopathy has yet to be uncovered'. This approach to the conceptualisation of the disorder leads to tautological thinking well illustrated by the following quotation. 'Why has this man done these terrible things? Because he is a psychopath. And how do you know that he is a psychopath? Because he has done these terrible things' (Ellard, 1988, p. 387). As Blackburn (1988, p. 507) noted, 'The contribution of personality characteristics to antisocial behaviour is an empirical question that can only be answered if the two are identified independently'.

Hare and colleagues observe that the three factor model's exclusion of antisocial behaviour decreases the utility of the PCL-R in predicting violence and aggression (see Skeem *et al.*, 2003), and thus, 'current findings suggest that the four-factor model has incremental validity over the three-factor one in predicting important external correlates of psychopathy' (Neumann *et al.*, in press, p. 22). This logic is confused: adding variables, for example gender, age or a history of substance abuse, would also improve prediction. However, such an improvement would not imply that these characteristics are core to psychopathic personality disorder. A measure's validity in representing the construct of psychopathy should not be confused with its utility in predicting deviant behaviour (Skeem *et al.*, 2003).

My colleagues and I have argued elsewhere that there are good reasons to reject the contention that criminal behaviour should play a central role in diagnosing psychopathy; instead, such behaviour is best viewed as a secondary feature, sequelae, or consequence of the disorder (Cooke *et al.*, 2004, 2006a, 2006b; Skeem *et al.*, 2006). What is the basis of this position? First, classical clinical descriptions of the disorder do not include antisocial behaviour as a core feature, second, there are theoretical reasons to assume that the core traits increase the likelihood that someone will engage in antisocial behaviour, third, antisocial behaviour is associated with many mental disorders and thus lacks specificity, and fourth, the risk factors for antisocial behaviour are very broad, personality pathology being only one.

The controversy can be addressed by empirical analysis. Factor analysis is a tool that can assist the mapping of constructs onto measures, given the explicit recognition that all measures are fallible indicators of constructs; manifest variables (measures) are the product both of latent variables (constructs) and error. Factor analytic approaches assume that latent variables *produce* the thoughts, feelings, and modes of behaviour that are measured or recorded by item scores plus error (Edwards and Bagozzi, 2000). Factor analysis can partition the variance associated with each item into two parts; *common variance*, or variance associated with specific latent variables, and *unique variance*, or variance specific to an item together with random error. Factor analysis thus explicates the multivariate relationships amongst the latent variables (constructs) that together influence the item ratings (empirical observations). Factor analysis, like all analytic strategies, can be misused and can mislead.

We have recently explored the methodological and conceptual problems that underpin the claims that antisocial behaviour forms a fourth component of the construct of psychopathy (Cooke *et al.*, 2006b). Many of these problems relate to the improper application of factor analytic techniques. There are three major issues to do with analytic strategy, first, the use of underpowered studies, second, the confusion between hierarchical and correlated factor models, and third, the use of inappropriate statistical techniques including parcelling.

The Use of Underpowered Studies

Many of the attempts to explore the structure of the PCL measures have been seriously underpowered in terms of sample size, with samples at, or even well below, 150 individuals (e.g. Hill *et al.*, 2004; Jackson *et al.*, 2002a; Salekin *et al.*, in press; Vitacco *et al.*, 2005). Kline (1998) provides guidance on the issue, indicating that

20 cases per free parameter is desirable, 10:1 is just acceptable and the statistical stability with 5:1 must be regarded as suspect. Thus, for the simplest models of the PCL-R the minimum sample size should be between 360 and 720, while for the more complex models more than 820 would be regarded as the minimum. The publication of underpowered studies merely serves to confuse the field.

The Confusion between Hierarchical and Correlated Models

The work of Hill *et al.* (2004) highlights the field's emerging difficulty with distinguishing between hierarchical and non-hierarchical models (see Hare and Neumann 2005; Neumann *et al.* 2005). This leads to significant conceptual confusion.

A key feature of a hierarchical model is the demonstration that the higher order construct of interest can be regarded as sufficiently unidimensional to be regarded as a coherent psychopathological syndrome. Two or three factor models are inherently hierarchical in that correlated factor models are mathematically equivalent to models with a superordinate factor overarching subordinate factors. With four or more factors this is no longer the case: it is necessary explicitly to compare a four factor hierarchical model with a four factor correlated model. This has conceptual importance. The hierarchical model implies some general latent trait underpinned by distinct facets of the disorder; the four factor correlated model could be merely a hodgepodge of related domains that are not unified by an overarching latent trait.

An example might assist. Psychopathy has been observed to be associated with body building, tattoos, steroid use, and body piercing; it is plausible that a 'Body enhancement' factor specified by these characteristics could emerge. We would argue it does not make conceptual sense to assume that body building and tattoos are primary symptoms of psychopathy, given that the frequency of these activities is clearly influenced by norms that vary across cultures – and across time within cultures. If it is assumed that this is not a core feature of the disorder then the hierarchical model will not fit whereas the correlated factor may.

This is equally true for the inclusion of items that are essentially counts of antisocial behaviours in the model; however, this has more important theoretical ramifications for our understanding of the association between psychopathy and antisocial behaviour. If measures of antisocial behaviour could be shown to fit a hierarchical model with the core three factors of psychopathy then it could be argued that antisocial is a core feature of the disorder. If the measure of antisocial behaviour fits a correlated model then it merely implies that antisocial behaviour is correlated with psychopathy, an essentially trivial observation.

A major problem in the 3- versus 4-factor debate has been the failure of many of the proponents of the 4-factor model to compare their models directly with the 3-factor model. When this is done it is clear that there is no evidence that a 4-factor model fits PCL-R data (Cooke *et al.* 2005a, 2005b; Cooke *et al.* 2006b).

The Inappropriate Use of Parcelling

In structural equation modelling (SEM) a parcel is an aggregate level indicator derived by combining individual items (e.g. adding individual PCL-R items to derive a new manifest variable, see Little *et al.* 2002). This is a controversial technique (Bandalos 2002; Little *et al.* 2002). Essentially, the variability in the items is ignored and they are all assumed to be equally relevant for the measurement of the underlying latent trait. It has been argued elsewhere that this procedure should not be used for modelling the structure of tests such as the PCL-R (Cooke *et al.* 2006a). It is possible to demonstrate empirically that items can be parcelled into the wrong factors and a 'perfect fit' can be achieved; the inappropriate use of parcelling leads to nonsensical results (Cooke *et al.* 2006a).

In conclusion, it would appear that there are three main dimensions of psychopathic personality that can be extracted from the PCL-R. The inclusion of what are essentially counts of criminal and other antisocial behaviour leads to tautological thinking. It is likely that more clinically sensitive measures of the disorder will result in more dimensions of the disorder being uncovered. This remains in the future. I will now turn to the second current controversy, the link between psychopathy and criminal behaviour.

Modelling the Relations between Psychopathy and Antisocial Behaviour

Having identified the three key dimensions underpinning the PCL-R we decided that there was merit in trying to understand the relations between these dimensions and other constructs being measured by the PCL-R (Cooke *et al.* 2004). Further analysis of large datasets of PCL-R ratings indicated the presence of two other distinct constructs underpinning certain PCL-R ratings: namely, *Criminal Behaviour* and *Relationship Lability*. The first is underpinned by three PCL-R items, *Juvenile Delinquency*, *Revocation of conditional release* and *Criminal versatility*, the second by two PCL-R items; *Promiscuous sexual behaviour* and *Many short-term marital relationships*. These additional traits are not core features of psychopathy but correlates.

The separation of the distinct conceptual domains of personality and social deviance has two major potential advantages. First, from a theoretical perspective, it undermines the tautology whereby past social deviance is used to diagnose a mental disorder, which in turn is used to predict future social deviance. Indeed, the notable power of the PCL-R to predict future offending (e.g. Hart *et al.* 1988; Hemphill *et al.* 1998) may reflect, in part, the test's high saturation with social deviance (e.g. Skeem and Mulvey 2001). A purified measure of psychopathy would facilitate further validation of the construct. Second, from a practical perspective, separating personality and social deviance allows both constructs to be measured separately and included as distinct factors in clinical decision-making. For example, the clinical-forensic practice of violence risk assessment may be improved if it is possible to develop purified measures of important risk factors such as psychopathy and antisocial behaviour (e.g. Monahan *et al.* 2001).

We attempted to model the relationships amongst the three core factors of psychopathy and *Criminal Behaviour* and *Relationship Lability* using Structural Equation Modeling (SEM) (Cooke *et al.* 2004). The final model is presented in Figure 10.1 This model suggests that *Relationship Lability* is associated with the Arrogant and Deceptive Interpersonal Style factor while *Criminal Behaviour* is associated with the Impulsive and Irresponsible Behavioural Style factor. The paths were moderate to large in magnitude (Kline 1998).

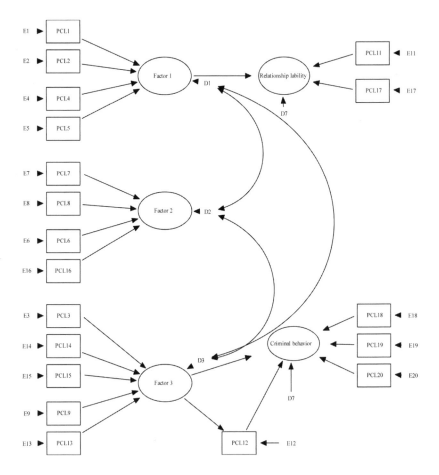

Figure 10.1   Structural equation model mapping the paths between the 3-factor model of psychopathy and two putative outcomes: Criminal behaviour and relationship lability

Why are these constructs related? In the absence of clear theory any account must be speculative; however, these speculations may illustrate how this type of modelling approach can be applied to refine our understanding of the links between psychopathy and social deviant behaviours of all types.

The Link between Arrogant and Deceitful Interpersonal Style and Relationship Lability

A core aspect of the interpersonal style facet is grandiosity. This grandiosity can be considered to be pathological dominance and is expressed by a preoccupation with seeking and exerting status, by exercising control and influence over others. Other individuals are viewed as status objects rather than love or attachment objects (Harpur *et al.*, 1994; Hart and Hare 1994; Kernberg 1998); the manipulativeness inherent in the disorder facilitates the exercising of pathological dominance.

There is a strong association between the Arrogant and Deceitful Interpersonal Style facet of psychopathy and *Relationship Lability*. It is implausible that this relationship can be explained by predictor-criterion contamination in that information about *Many short-term marital relationships* and *Promiscuous sexual behaviour* is irrelevant to the ratings of the four items that define the Arrogant and Deceitful Interpersonal Style facet.

This association suggests interesting theoretical interpretations. Mealey (1995) argued that primary psychopathy is not a disorder but a life strategy based on manipulation and predatory sexual behaviour; in particular, it is a life strategy characterised by high *mating effort* (effort expended in obtaining sexual intercourse with members of the preferred gender) and low *parental effort* (investment in mate and offspring) (Harris *et al.*, 1994; Quinsey 2001). The *Relationship Lability* facet can be viewed as a composite of high *mating effort* and low *parental effort*. The ability to charm, lie, con and manipulate (all aspects of this facet of psychopathy) would facilitate high mating effort. This finding can be regarded as being consistent with Mealey's theory.

Ratings of *Promiscuous sexual behaviour* include any history of coercive sexual behaviour. The sense of entitlement associated with a *Grandiose sense of self worth*, therefore, may also contribute to this link. Pathological dominance frequently leads to suspiciousness regarding the motives of others (Kernberg, 1998). For example, many sexually aggressive men perceive women as untrustworthy, communicating the exact opposite of what they intend in sexual situations (Malamuth and Brown 1994).

It is noteworthy that neither of the other facets of psychopathy are linked to *Relationship Lability* and that the association between *Relationship Lability* and *Criminal Behaviour* can be accounted for completely by the mutual associations of these variables with psychopathy.

The Links between Impulsive and Irresponsible Behavioural Style and Criminal Behaviour

The Impulsive and Irresponsible Behavioural Style facet of psychopathy encapsulates an amalgam of lower order traits including boredom susceptibility, unreliability, novelty seeking, adventuresomeness, sensation seeking, risk taking, lack of planning and lack of forethought (Hart and Dempster 1997). Two pathways between the Impulsive and Irresponsible Behavioural Style facet and *Criminal Behaviour* were required to explain the relationships in the PCL-R data; one a direct path the other mediated by the PCL-R item *Early behavioural problems*. The direct link between this facet and offending is understandable in terms of lack of forethought, risk taking and lack of concern for the future.

The finding of the mediated path is consistent with the evidence that there is a group of individuals who display consistent antisocial behaviour across the life-span. Life-course persistent offenders have been identified in a range of countries (Hodgins 1994; Kratzer and Hodgins 1999; Moffitt 1993); as few as 5% of males may be responsible for the majority of all criminal acts (Stattin and Magnusson 1991; Kratzer and Hodgins 1996). Early onset of conduct problems is a key indicator.

In summary, the structural model can serve as a basis for theoretical speculations about why these constellations of personality traits may affect the likelihood of future offending. These must remain speculation until other forms of psychological research is carried out to examine the validity or otherwise of these speculations.

I will now turn to the third current controversy, the stability or otherwise of psychopathy across cultures.

Psychopathy across Cultures

Mental disorders vary in the extent to which they are influenced by culture. Some have a strong pan-cultural core, whereas others are specific to a certain culture or vary considerably across cultures (Alaracon *et al.*, 1998; Draguns, 1973, 1986; Kitayama and Markus, 1994; Lopez and Gaurnaccia, 2000; Mezzich *et al.*, 1996; Rogler, 1993, 1996, 1999). Because personality is inherently relational in nature, manifested largely – some would argue even primarily – in the interpersonal sphere, it is likely that culture influences personality disorders more than other forms of mental disorder (Alaracon *et al.* 1998; Cross and Markus, 1999, Triandis and Suh, 2002).

The impact of culture on psychopathy has been discussed by several commentators (Cooke, 1996, 1998; Lykken, 1995; Paris, 1998). Cross-cultural differences in the assessment of psychopathy are theoretically important, but also may be of considerable practical importance. Previous research suggests that psychopathy, as assessed using the Psychopathy Checklist-Revised (PCL-R; Hare 1991), is an important risk marker for criminal and violent behaviour (Hart 1998; Hart and Hare, 1997; Hemphill *et al.*, 1998; Salekin *et al.*, 1996). Because of this, the PCL-R is now used routinely in forensic decision-making in many jurisdictions around the world. It plays a role in such things as criminal sentencing, including decisions regarding indefinite commitment and capital punishment; institutional placement and treatment; conditional release; juvenile transfer; and indeterminate civil commitment (e.g. Cooke *et al.* 2001b; Fitch and Ortega 2000; Hart 2001; Hemphill and Hart 2002; Lyon and Ogloff 2000; Zinger and Forth 1998). But if there are systematic differences across cultures in the assessment of psychopathy using the PCL-R, it may be dangerous to assume that research findings – especially those based on raw PCL-R scores – are generalisable. Thus, to assume results obtained in Canada and the US apply in Scotland, Sweden or Spain is a dangerous assumption; to my knowledge we do not know whether the apparent predictive power of the PCL-R would apply in Lithuania.

What do we know about cross-cultural variations in psychopathy? A series of empirical studies by Cooke, Michie and colleagues (e.g. Cooke *et al.* 2001a, 2005a, 2005b; Cooke and Michie 1997, 1999, 2001;) has examined cross-cultural differences in psychopathy among adult male offenders and forensic psychiatric patients, assessed by the Hare Psychopathy Checklist-Revised (Hare 1991). Two major findings have emerged from these studies. First, there is little evidence of measurement bias across ethnocultural groups within dominant cultures. For example, research using Confirmatory Factor Analysis (CFA) and Item Response Theory (IRT) methods has found structural and metric invariance of PCL-R ratings from Canada versus the United States (Cooke and Michie 1997, 2001); from White versus African-American offenders within the United States (Cooke *et al.* 2001a); from Scotland versus England and Wales within the United Kingdom (Cooke *et al.* 2005a); and from the United Kingdom versus various countries of continental Europe (Cooke *et al.* 2005b). In particular, the 3-factor model found to underlie the PCL-R demonstrated structural equivalence in a large number of samples from Europe and North America. In other words the same symptoms defined the disorder in the same way in all these countries or cultures.

The second major finding from these studies is evidence of small but robust cross-cultural differences in the assessment of psychopathy. Research comparing PCL-R ratings from North America and Europe has found structural invariance but not metric invariance (Cooke *et al.* 2005b; Cooke and Michie 1999). Metric variance occurs when the scores on a test do not bear the same relationship with the underlying construct being measured in two different groups. For example, we can measure temperature using either Centigrade or Fahrenheit scales; what we are measuring is the same but the scale points and the zero points are not the same. Specifically, IRT analyses indicated that, given equivalent standing on the latent trait of psychopathy, offenders from North America – specifically, the United States and Canada, both of which have been characterised as having dominant cultures that are vertically individualistic – received total scores on the PCL-R that were between 2 and 3 points higher than their counterparts from Europe, whose cultures have been characterised as more horizontally individualistic. The cross-cultural differences were largest for interpersonal and behavioural symptoms of psychopathy and smallest for affective symptoms. This has led us to suggest that Defective affective experience may be the pan-cultural core of the disorder.

A difference in 2 or 3 points may not seem great (the maximum score possible is 40), however, at the individual level it can make the difference between indefinite detention or not. At the aggregate level it can virtually double the number of individuals defined as psychopaths in prisons in the UK; this has significant implications for the services that have to be provided (Cooke *et al.* 2005a).

Although these cross-cultural metric differences appear to be relatively robust, their source is not yet clear. Do they reflect the pathoplastic effects of culture? Or, alternatively, are they merely in the eyes of beholders? Put differently, do cross-cultural metric differences reflect differences in the *expression* or the *perception* of psychopathic symptoms? To test these competing hypotheses, we conducted a study in which raters from Canada and Scotland made PCL-R ratings of offenders from Canadian and Scottish prisons on the basis of videotaped interviews and summaries of file information (Cooke *et al.*, 2005a). This study found that raters of both nationalities rated prisoners of both nationalities in the same way, suggesting that the perceived differences were not due to the eye of the beholder but were more likely to be in the expression of the disorder.

In summary, cross-cultural differences are important for both practical and theoretical reasons. Within the western countries studied, the same symptoms coalesce to form the same sub-components of the disorder, however, there are important variations in the degree of expression of certain key symptoms, particularly interpersonal symptoms. These appear to be genuine differences that are not merely in the eye of the beholder.

Psychopathic Personality Disorder: Some Future Directions

Our understanding of this disorder has grown – and continues to grow. There is a need to continue the exploration of the genetic, developmental, neuropsychological, neurochemical, psychometric, clinical and forensic domains in relation to this important disorder. From the perspective of forensic clinical psychology there are two important steps that require to be taken to improve our understanding. First, both conceptual and empirical work is required to move beyond the simple observation that psychopathy is associated with antisocial behaviour towards a greater understanding of *why* these pathological traits increase the likelihood of offending. Such an understanding is necessary to allow more effective clinical intervention. Second, more comprehensive and clinically focused measures of the disorder are required. It is these issues that I will consider in the final section of this chapter.

The Missing Links

Our structural model was an early step on this path. A major limitation of this study is that socially deviant behaviour is only operationalised using PCL-R items; while useful, these items only provide limited coverage of the domain of socially deviant behaviour. Other measures may reveal further links between facets of psychopathy and aspects of socially deviant behaviour, indeed, further links would be expected from theoretical arguments.

A link between *Arrogant and deceitful interpersonal style* and less impoverished measures of criminal behaviour might be expected. The status needs of psychopaths can be gratified through criminal activities. Criminal activities, in particular violent crime – in overt defiance of authority – promotes the psychopath's feeling of superiority over victims, criminal peers and members of the criminal justice system. Status may be enhanced both through the plaudits of criminal peers and concrete rewards including money and goods. The status needs of psychopathic individuals may lead to suspiciousness and a tendency to construe maleficent motives underpinning the behaviour of others (Serin, 1991). They are overly sensitive to challenges to their perception of high status. Aggression is a common response to such challenges (Baumeister *et al.* 1996; Blackburn, 1993; Blair *et al.*, 1995; Hart and Hare, 1996; Serin, 1991).

Blackburn (1992, 1998) has provided the most detailed and rigorous articulation of the links between the rigid and inflexible interpersonal style of the psychopath and criminal activity. He has argued that the psychopathic individuals make consistent, rigid and inflexible interpersonal responses that may be characterised as falling within the dominant and hostile quadrant of the interpersonal circumplex. Rigid and inflexible interpersonal behaviour leads to dysfunctional relations. Blackburn (1998) reported that *Glibness/superficial charm* and *Grandiose sense of self-worth* were closely linked to the dominant-submissive dimension of the interpersonal circle in a sample of male mentally disordered offenders. In a further sample (Blackburn and Renwick 1996) demonstrated that a coercive interpersonal style was associated with persistent criminality indeed, Blackburn (1998, p. 292) argued 'It is therefore likely that these findings represent a causal relation between interpersonal style and criminality'. Kosson *et al.* (1997) provided additional evidence of the importance of interpersonal features: they found that the Interpersonal Measure of Psychopathy (IM-P) contributed uniquely, over and above the traditional factor 1 and factor 2 of the PCL-R, in the prediction of reported fights as an adult.

Violent crime may be shaped by the interpersonal belief that others will dominate or exploit them; specific forms of violence, e.g. sadism, may be founded on the desire to control, demean and humiliate others (Hare *et al.* 1999). There are a number of plausible mechanisms that could link core traits of psychopathy and criminal behaviour.

Theory predicts a link between Deficient affective experience and *criminal behaviour* (Hume 1966; Miller and Eisenberg 1988) found that empathic and sympathetic responses were associated negatively with both general antisocial behaviour and violence. Affects such as empathy, guilt and fear that generally inhibit criminal behaviour, in general – and violent behaviour, in particular – are notably absent in those high in this dimension (e.g. Hart and Hare, 1997; Hoffman 2000;

Patrick *et al.* 1997; Rice *et al.* 1994). The failure to find a link in the structural model may reflect the breadth and inadequacy of the *criminal behaviour* measure. The three items that define this latent trait are heterogeneous in terms of the criminal behaviours covered including drugs offences, violence, dishonesty and failure to conform to norms. Purer measures of violence may be required.

Future Research

To progress this field requires different methods; if we are to avoid predictor criterion contamination (Pedhazur and Schmelkin 1991) we should not rely on the PCL-R to measure both psychopathy and social deviance. To allow adequate tests of models of this type it is necessary to collect new data using new methods. First, psychopathy and criminality must be operationalised in distinct ways that avoid criterion contamination.

Cornell *et al.*'s (1996) approach is a good example of how to limit predictor-criterion contamination; they examined the link between psychopathy and instrumental violence. Videotaped interviews and file reviews were edited to ensure that all information pertaining to criminal history was removed. The non-criminal items of the Psychopathy Checklist Screening Version (PCL:SV; Hart *et al.* 1995) were assessed using this information. Ratings of instrumental violence were completed by different researchers based solely on criminal behaviour and without access to any other file or interview information. This paradigm would have utility in improving our understanding of the links amongst aspects of psychopathy and aspects of social deviance.

For progress to be made, the measurement of social deviance and criminality requires improvement (Patrick *et al.* 1997). Lack of clarity within just one domain of criminality – that of violence – illustrates the conceptual and measurement problem. Monahan and Steadman (1994, p. 10) argued '[A] recurring problem in risk assessment research is the lack of precision produced by not disaggregating criterion violence into meaningful subtypes. The predictors of one form of violence may be quite different than the predictors of another'. Michie and Cooke (2006) empirically disaggregated violence into two forms of violence and demonstrated that these two forms are differentially associated with other variables. *Violence Based on Weapon Use* was particularly associated with psychopathy, a history of childhood violence and the frequency of aggressive fantasies, whereas *Violence without Weapon Use* was particularly associated with level of anger as measured by the Novaco Anger Scale (Part A) (Novaco, 1994) and inversely related with age.

A New Measure of Psychopathy: The Comprehensive Assessment of Psychopathic Personality Disorder

Stephen Hart, Caroline Logan, Christine Michie and I were commissioned by the Home Office in England and Wales to develop a measure of psychopathy that would have the potential to measure change should change be achieved in their innovative treatment programme for high risk offenders (Attril 2006). The measure has been developed by reviewing the extensive literature on the construct of psychopathy, by reviewing all instruments that attempt to measure this construct and finally by carrying out detailed interviews with clinicians who work with such offenders. This led to the development of a six-dimensional conceptual model focused within the domain of personality pathology. The conceptual model is inherently hierarchical with the assumption – as yet untested – that an underlying higher order latent trait 'produces' these distinct but related expressions of the disorder.

The *Attachment* domain reflects difficulties with interpersonal affiliation, such as the failure to form close, stable emotional bonds with others. It focuses on the intimacy and acceptance by others that people attempt to achieve in interpersonal exchanges.

The *Behavioural* domain reflects problems with organisation of goal-directed activities, such as the tendency to be impulsive and sensation-seeking. It focuses on behaviour regulation, including the failure to establish adaptive strategies to deal with life tasks in a systematic, consistent, or planned manner.

The *Cognitive* domain reflects problems with mental flexibility and adaptability, such as the tendency to be distractible, intolerant, and suspicious. It focuses on mental actions and processes, including how the person focuses and allocates attention, encodes and processes information, organises thoughts, and makes attributions.

The *Dominance* domain reflects difficulties with interpersonal agency, such as excessive status-seeking and assertiveness. It focuses on the degree of power or control that people try to take in interpersonal exchanges.

The *Emotionality* domain reflects problems with mood regulation, such as the tendency to experience shallow, labile emotions. It focuses on the tone, depth, and appropriateness of people's affective responses.

The *Self* domain reflects problems with identity or individuality, such as being self-centred and self-aggrandising. It is concerned with people's accurate consciousness of their own identities, including appreciation of their personality traits and schemas; and an appreciation of their salient abilities, qualities and desires. Additionally, the self influences social roles and relations with others.

In many respects, the domains of PPD symptomatology described here correspond closely to basic dimensions identified in more general theoretical and empirically-derived models of normal and abnormal personality (Widiger 1998). This model is currently being tested empirically and hopefully will yield, with appropriate modifications, a more comprehensive model of this important disorder.

In conclusion, this work is a beginning; it suggests an approach and a method rather than providing a full resolution of the problem faced by those who strive to understand this important disorder and the links between severe personality pathology and social deviance. Clearly, the PCL-R has firmly established itself in the history of research on personality disorder and in the armamentarium of forensic practitioners. However, it is now time to extend our understanding of this important forensic construct by developing more comprehensive and clinically informed measures. Failure to do so will mean the field will move further into a conceptual and methodological cul-de-sac.

Author's Notes

David Cooke received support from the Research and Development Directorate of the Greater Glasgow Primary Care NHS Trust to prepare this manuscript. He would like to thank Brian Rae for his continued support. This chapter summarises work that David Cooke has carried out with a number of valued colleagues over the last few years. He would like to thank Christine Michie, Stephen Hart, Caroline Logan and Jennifer Skeem for their support, guidance and sagacity during their collaboration.

References

Alaracon, R.D., Foulks, E.F. and Vakkur, M. (1998) *Personality Disorders and Culture: Clinical and Conceptual Interactions* (New York: Wiley).

Arieti, S. (1963) Psychopathic personality: Some views on its psychopathology and psychodynamics, *Comprehensive Psychiatry*, 4, pp. 301–312.

Attrill, G. (2006) Chromis: An intervention designed for psychopathic offenders (unpublished work).

Bandalos, D.L. (2002) The effects of item parceling on goodness-of-fit and parameter estimate bias in structural equation modeling, *Structural Equation Modelling*, 9, pp. 78–102.

Baumeister, R.F., Smart, L. and Boden, J.M. (1996) Relation of threatened egotism to violence and aggression: the dark side of self – esteem, *Psychological Review*, 103, pp. 5–33.

Berrios, G.E. (1996) *The History of Mental Symptoms: Descriptive Psychopathology Since the Nineteenth Century* (Cambridge: Cambridge University Press).

Bibiak, P. (2000) Psychopathic manipulation at work, in: C.B. Gacono (Ed.) *The Clinical and Forensic Assessment of Psychopathy: A Practitioner's Guide*, pp. 287–311 (Mahwah: NJ: Lawrence Erlbaum Associates Publishers).

Blackburn, R. (1988) On moral judgement and personality disorders: the myth of psychopathic personality revisited, *British Journal of Psychiatry*, 153, pp. 505–512.

Blackburn, R. (1992) Criminal behaviour, personality disorder, and mental illness: the origins of confusion, *Criminal Behaviour and Mental Health*, 2, pp. 66–77.

Blackburn, R. (1993) *The Psychology of Criminal Conduct: Theory, Research and Practice*, 1st edn (Chichester: Wiley).

Blackburn, R. (1998) Psychopathy and personality disorder: implications of interpersonal theory, in D.J. Cooke, A.E. Forth and R.D. Hare (Eds) *Psychopathy:*

Theory, Research and Implications for Society, pp. 269–301 (Dordrecht, The Netherlands: Kluwer Academic).

Blackburn, R. (2005) Psychopathy as a personality construct, in: S. Strack (Ed.) *Handbook of Personology and Psychopathology*, pp. 271–291 (New York: Wiley).

Blackburn, R. and Renwick, S. (1996) Rating scales for measuring the interpersonal circle in forensic psychiatric patients, *Psychological Assessment*, 8, pp. 76–84.

Blair, R., Jones, L., Clark, F. and Smith, M. (1995) Is the psychopath morally insane? *Personality and Individual Differences*, 19, pp. 741–752.

Campbell, D.T. (1960) Recommendations for APA test standards regarding construct, trait or discriminant validity. American psychologist, 15, pp. 546–553.

Cleckley, H. (1988) *The Mask of Sanity*, 5th edn (St Louis: Mosby).

Cooke, D.J. (1996) Psychopathic personality in different cultures: what do we know? What do we need to find out? *Journal of Personality Disorders*, 10, pp. 23–40.

Cooke, D.J. (1998) Cross-cultural aspects of psychopathy, in: T. Millon, E. Simonsen, M. Birket-Smith and R. D. Davis (Eds) *Psychopathy: Antisocial, Criminal and Violent Behavior*, pp. 260–276 (New York: Guilford).

Cooke, D.J. (2006) Exploring the construct of psychopathy: themes and variation. The invited address to the American Psychology and Law Society, Annual Conference, Hilton Hotel, St Petersburg, Florida, 1– 5 March, 2006.

Cooke, D.J. and Hart, S.D. (2004) Personality disorders, in: E. Johnstone, L. Owens, M. Sharpe and C. Freeman (Eds) *Companion to Psychiatric Studies*, 7th edn, pp. 502–526 (Edinburgh: Elsevier).

Cooke, D. J. and Michie, C. (1997) An item response theory evaluation of Hare's psychopathy checklist, *Psychological Assessment*, 9, pp. 2–13.

Cooke, D.J. and Michie, C. (1999) Psychopathy across cultures: North America and Scotland compared, *Journal of Abnormal Psychology*, 108, pp. 55–68.

Cooke, D.J. and Michie, C. (2001) Refining the construct of psychopathy: towards a hierarchical model, *Psychological Assessment*, 13, pp. 171–188.

Cooke, D.J., Forth, A. E. and Hare, R.D. (1996) *Psychopathy: Theory, Research and Implications for Society*, 1st edn (Dordrecht: Kluwer Academic).

Cooke, D.J., Michie, C., Hart, S.D. and Hare, R.D. (1998) The functioning of the screening version of the Psychopathy Checklist–Revised: an item response theory analysis, *Psychological Assessment*, 11, pp. 3–13.

Cooke, D.J., Kosson, D.S. and Michie, C. (2001a) Psychopathy and ethnicity: structural, item and test generalizability of the Psychopathy Checklist Revised (PCL–R) in Caucasian and African – American participants, *Psychological Assessment*, 13, pp. 531–542.

Cooke, D.J., Michie, C. and Ryan, J. (2001b) *Evaluating Risk for Violence: A Preliminary Study of the HCR – 20, PCL – R and VRAG in a Scottish Prison Sample* (Edinburgh: Scotland Office).

Cooke, D.J., Michie, C., Hart, S.D. and Clark, D. (2004) Reconstructing psychopathy: clarifying the significance of antisocial and socially deviant behavior in the diagnosis of psychopathic personality disorder, *Journal of Personality Disorders*, 18, 337–356.

Cooke, D.J., Michie, C. Hart, S.D. and Clark, D. (2005a) Assessing psychopathy in the United Kingdom: concerns about cross-cultural generalisability, *British Journal of Psychiatry*, 186, pp. 339–345.

Cooke, D.J., Michie, C. Hart, S.D. and Clark, D. (2005b) Searching for the pan-cultural core of psychopathic personality disorder: continental Europe and North America compared, *Personality and Individual Differences*, 39, pp. 283–295.

Cooke, D.J., Michie, C. and Hart, S.D. (2006a) Facets of clinical psychopathy: towards clearer measurement, in C. Patrick (Ed.) *Handbook of Psychopathic Personality Disorder* (Guilford: New York).

Cooke, D.J., Michie, C. and Skeem, J.L. (2006b) Understanding the structure of the Psychopathy Checklist – Revised: an exploration of methodological confusion, *British Journal of Psychiatry*, Ref Type: Unpublished Work.

Cooke, D.J., Hart, S.D., Logan, C. and Michie, C. (2006c) Evaluating the construct of psychopathic personality disorder: The development of a comprehensive clinical assessment (in preparation).

Cornell, D.G., Warren, J., Hawk, G., Stafford, E., Oram, G. and Pine, D. (1996) Psychopathy in instrumental and reactive violent offenders, *Journal of Consulting and Clinical Psychology*, 64, pp. 783–790.

Cross, S.E. and Markus, H.R. (1999) The cultural constitution of personality, in L.A. Pervin and P.O. John (Eds) *Handbook of Personality*, pp. 378–396 (New York: Guilford).

Draguns, J.G. (1973) Comparison of psychopathology across cultures: issues, findings, directions, *Journal of Cross-cultural Psychology*, 4, pp. 9–47.

Draguns, J.G. (1986) Culture and psychopathology: what is known about their relationship, *Australian Journal of Psychology*, 38, pp. 329–338.

Edwards, J.R. and Bagozzi, R.P. (2000) On the nature and direction of relationships between constructs and measures, *Psychological Methods*, 5, pp. 155–174.

Ellard, J. (1988) The history and present status of moral insanity, *Australian and New Zealand Journal of Psychiatry*, 22, pp. 383–389.

Fitch, W.L. and Ortega, R.J. (2000) Law and the confinement of psychopaths, *Behavioral Sciences and the Law*, 18, pp. 663–678.

Forouzan, E. and Cooke, D.J. (2005) Figuring out la femme fatale; conceptual and assessment issues concerning psychopathy in females, *Behavioural Science and the Law*, 23, pp. 765–778.

Forth, A.E., Brown, S.L., Hart, S.D. and Hare, R.D. (1996) The assessment of psychopathy in male and female noncriminals: reliability and validity, *Personality and Individual Differences*, 20, pp. 531–543.

Gough, H.G. (1948) A sociological theory of psychopathy, *American Journal of Sociology*, 53, pp. 359–366.

Gustafon, S.B. and Ritzer, D.R. (1995) The dark side of normal: a psychopathy-linked pattern called aberrant self-promotion, *European Journal of Personality*, 9, pp. 147–183.

Hare, R.D. (1991) *Manual for the Revised Psychopathy Checklist*, 1st edn (Toronto: Multi-Health Systems).

Hare, R.D. (1999) Psychopathy as a risk factor for violence, *Psychiatric Quarterly*, 70, pp. 181–197.

Hare, R.D. (2003) *Manual for the Revised Psychopathy Checklist*, 2nd edn (Toronto: Multi-Health Systems).

Hare, R.D. and Neumann, C. S. (2005) Structural models of psychopathy, *Current Psychiatric Reports*, 7, pp. 57–64.

Hare, R.D., Cooke, D.J. and Hart, S.D. (1999) Psychopathy and sadistic personality disorder, in: T. Millon, P.H. Blaney and R.D. Davies (Eds) *Oxford Textbook of Psychopathology*, 1st edn, pp. 555–584 (Oxford: Oxford University Press).

Hare, R.D., Clark, D., Grann, M. and Thornton, D. (2002) Psychopathy and the predictive validity of the PCL-R: an international perspective, *Behavioral Sciences and the Law*, 18, pp. 623–645.

Harpur, T.J., Hare, R D. and Hakstain, A.R. (1989) Two-factor conceptualisation of psychopathy: construct validity and assessment implications, *Psychological Assessment: A Journal of Consulting and Clinical Psychology*, 62, pp. 387–397.

Harpur, T.J., Hart, S.D. and Hare, R.D. (1994) Personality of the psychopath, in: P.T. Costa and T.A. Widiger (Eds) *Personality Disorders and the Five-Factor Model of Personality*, pp. 149–173 (Washington DC, USA: American Psychological Association).

Harris, G.T., Rice, M.E. and Quinsey, V.L. (1994) Psychopathy as a taxon: evidence that psychopaths are a discrete class. *Journal of Consulting and Clinical Psychology*, 62, pp. 387–397.

Hart, S.D. (1998) Psychopathy and risk for violence, in: D.J. Cooke, A.E. Forth and R.D. Hare (Eds) *Psychopathy: Theory, Research and Implications for Society*, pp. 355–374 (Utrecht: Kluwer Academic).

Hart, S.D. (2001) Assessing and managing violence risk, in K. S. Douglas, C. D. Webster, S.D. Hart, D. Eaves, and J.R.P. Ogloff (Eds) *HCR – 20 violence risk Management Companion Guide*, pp. 13–25 (Burnaby, British Columbia: Mental Health, Law and Policy Institute, Simon Fraser University, and Department of Mental Health, Law and Policy, Florida Mental Health Institute, University of South Florida).

Hart, S.D. and Dempster, R.J. (1997) Psychopathy: assessment and association with criminal conduct, in: D.M. Stoff, J. Brieling and J. Maser (Eds) *Handbook of Antisocial Behavior*, pp. 22–35 (New York: Wiley).

Hart, S.D. and Hare, R.D. (1994) Psychopathy and the big five: correlations between observers' ratings of normal and pathological personality, *Journal of Personality Disorders*, 8, pp. 32–40.

Hart, S.D. and Hare, R.D. (1996) Psychopathy and risk assessment, *Current Opinion in Psychiatry*, 9, 380–383.

Hart, S.D. and Hare, R.D. (1997) Psychopathy: Assessment and association with criminal conduct, in: D.M. Stoff, J. Maser and J. Brieling (Eds) *Handbook of Antisocial Behaviour* (New York: Wiley).

Hart, S.D., Kropp, P.R. and Hare, R.D. (1988) The performance of male psychopaths following conditional release from prison, *Journal of Personality Disorders*, 8, pp. 32–40.

Hart, S.D., Cox, D.N. and Hare, R.D. (1995) *The Hare Psychopathy Checklist: Screening Version*, 1st edn (Toronto: Multi-Health Systems Inc).

Hemphill, J.F., Hare, R.D. and Wong, S. (1998) Psychopathy and recidivism: a review, *Legal and Criminological Psychology*, 3, pp. 139–170.

Hemphill, J.F. and Hart, S.D. (2002) Motivating the unmotivated: psychopathy, treatment, and change, in M. McMurran (Ed.) *Motivating Offenders to Change: A Guide to Enhancing Engagement in Therapy*, pp. 193–220 (Chichester: Wiley).

Henderson, D.K. (1939) *Psychopathic States* (New York: W. W. Norton).

Hill, C.D., Neumann, C.S. and Rogers, R (2004) Confirmatory factor analysis of the Psychopathy Checklist: screening version in offenders with Axis I disorders, *Psychological Assessment*, 16, pp. 90–95.

Hodgins, S. (1994) Status at age 30 of children with conduct problems, *Studies on Crime and Prevention*, 3, pp. 41–61.

Hoffman, M.L. (2000) *Empathy and Moral Development: Implications for Caring and Justice* (Cambridge: Cambridge University Press).

Hoyersten, J.G. (2001) The Icelandic Sagas and the idea of personality and deviant personalities in the Middle Ages, *History of Psychiatry*, xii, pp. 199–212.

Hume, D. (1966) *Enquiries Concerning the Human Understanding and Concerning the Principles of Morals*, 2nd 1777 original work published edn (Oxford, UK: Clarendon Press).

Jackson, R.L., Rogers, R., Neumann, C.S. and Lambert, P.L. (2002) Psychopathy in female offenders: an investigation of its underlying dimensions, *Criminal Justice and Behavior*, 29, pp. 692–704.

Johansson, P., Andershed, H., Kerr, M. and Levander, S. (2002) On the operationalization of psychopathy: further support for a three-faceted personality oriented model, *Acta Psychiatrica Scandanavica*, 106, pp. 81–83.

Kernberg, O.F. (1998) The psychotherapeutic management of psycopathic, narcissistic, and paranoid transferences, in T. Millon, E. Simonsen, M. Birket-Smith and R.D. Davis (Eds) *Psychopathy, Antisocial, Criminal and Violent Behavior*, 1st edn, pp. 372–392 (New York: Guilford).

Kitayama, S. and Markus, H.R. (1994) Introduction to cultural psychology and emotion research, in: S. Kitayama and H.R. Markus (Eds) *Emotion and Culture: Empirical Studies of Mutual Influence*, 1st edn, pp. 1–22 (Washington: American Psychological Association).

Kline, R.B. (1998) *Principles and Practice of Structural Equation Modeling* (New York: Guilford).

Kosson, D.S., Stuerwald, B.L., Forth, A.E. and Kirkhart, K.J. (1997) A new method for assessing the interpersonal behaviour of psychopathic individuals: preliminary validation studies, *Psychological Assessment*, 9, pp. 89–101.

Kratzer, L. and Hodgins, S.E. (1996) Patterns of crime and characteristics of female as compared to male offenders. Paper presented at the Life History Research Society Meeting, London UK.

Kratzer, L. and Hodgins, S.E. (1999) A typology of offenders: A test of Moffitt's theory among males and females from childhood to age 30, *Criminal Behaviour and Mental Health*, 9, pp. 57–73.

Little, T.D., Cunningham, W.A., Shahar, G. and Widaman, K.F. (2002) To parcel or not to parcel: exploring the question, weighing the merits, *Structural Equation Modelling*, 9, pp. 151–173.

Lopez, S.T. and Gaurnaccia, P.J.J. (2000) Cultural psychopathology: uncovering the social world of mental illness, *Annual Review of Psychology*, 5, pp. 571–598.

Lykken, D.T. (1995) *The Antisocial Personalities*, 1st edn (Hillsdale: Lawrence Erlbaum).

Lyon, D. and Ogloff, J.R.P. (2000) Legal and ethical issues in psychopathy assessment, in: C.B. Gacono (Ed.) *The Clinical and Forensic Assessment of Psychopathy*, pp. 139–173 (Mahwah, NJ: Lawrence Erlbaum).

Malamuth, N. and Brown, A.J. (1994) Sexually aggressive men's perceptions of women's communications: testing three explanations, *Journal of Personality and Social Psychology*, 67, pp. 699–712.

McCord, W. and McCord, J. (1964) *The Psychopath: an Essay on the Criminal Mind*, 1st edn (Princeton NJ: Van Nostrand).

Mealey, L. (1995) The sociobiology of sociopathy: An integrated evolutionary model, *Behavioral and Brain Sciences*, 18, pp. 523–599.

Mezzich, J.E., Kleinman, A., Fabrega, H. and Parron, D.L. (1996) *Culture & Psychiatric Diagnosis: a DSM–IV Perspective*, 1st edn (Washington: American Psychiatric Association).

Michie, C. and Cooke, D.J. (2006) The structure of violent behaviour: a hierarchical model, *Criminal Justice and Behavior* (in press).

Miller, P.A. and Eisenberg, N. (1988) The relation of empathy to aggressive and externalizing/antisocial behavior, *Psychological Bulletin*, 103, pp. 324–344.

Millon, T. (1981) *Disorders of Personality* (New York: Wiley).

Moffitt, T.E. (1993) Adolescence – limited and life – course – persistent antisocial behavior: a developmental taxonomy, *Psychological Review*, 100, pp. 674–701.

Monahan, J. and Steadman, H. (1994) Towards a rejuvenation of risk assessment research, in: J. Monahan and H.J. Steadman (Eds) *Violence and Mental Disorder: Developments in Risk Assessment*, pp. 1–17 (Chicago: The University of Chicago Press).

Monahan, J., Steadman, H.J., Silver, E., Appelbaum, P.S., Robbins, P.C. Mulvey, E.P., Roth, L.H., Grisso, T. and Banks, S (2001) *Rethinking Risk Assessment: The MacArthur Study of Mental Disorder and Violence* (New York: Oxford University Press).

Mullen, P.E. (1992) Psychopathy: a developmental disorder of ethical action, *Criminal Behaviour and Mental Health*, 2, pp. 234–244.

Murphy, J.M. (1976) Psychiatric labeling in cross – cultural perspective: similar kinds of disturbed behaviour appear to be labeled abnormal in diverse cultures, *Science*, 191, pp. 1019–1028.

Neumann, C.S., Kosson, D.S. and Salekin, R.T. (2005) Exploratory and confirmatory factor analysis of the psychopathy construct: methodological and conceptual issues, in H. Herve and J.C. Yuille (Eds) *Psychopathy, Theory, Research and Social Implications* (New York: Lawrence Erlbaum).

Neumann, C.S., Kosson, D.S. and Salekin, R.T. (2005) Exploratory and confirmatory factor analysis of the psychopathy construct: methodological and conceptual issues, in: H. Herve and J.C. Yuille (Eds) *Psychopathy, Theory, Research and Social Implications* (New York: Lawrence Erlbaum).

Novaco, R.W. (1994) Anger as a risk factor for violence among the mentally disordered, in: J. Monahan and H.J. Steadman (Eds) *Violence and Mental Disorder: Developments in Risk Assessment*, 1st edn, pp. 21–59 (Chicago: The University of Chicago Press).

Paris, J. (1998) Personality disorders in sociocultural perspective, *Journal of Personality Disorders*, 12, pp. 289–301.

Patrick, C. (2006) *Handbook of Psychopathy* (New York: The Guilford Press).

Patrick, C.J., Zempolich, K.A. and Levenston, G.K. (1997) Emotionality and violent behaviour in psychopaths, in A. Raine, P. Brennan, D. Farrington and S.A. Mednick (Eds) *Biosocial Bases of Violence*, pp. 145–161 (New York: Plenum).

Pedhazur, E.J. and Schmelkin, L.P. (1991) *Measurement, Design and Analysis: An Integrated Approach* (Hillsdale, NJ: Lawrence Erlbaum).

Quinsey, V.L. (2001) Evolutionary theory and criminal behaviour, *Legal and Criminological Psychology*, 7, pp. 1–13.

Rice, M.E., Chaplin, T.C., Harris, G.T. and Coutts. J. (1994) Empathy for the victim and sexual arousal among rapists and nonrapists, *Journal of Interpersonal Violence*, 9, pp. 435–449.

Rogler, L.H. (1993) Culturally sensitizing psychiatric diagnosis: a framework for research, *Journal of Nervous and Mental Disease*, 191, pp. 401–408.

Rogler, L.H. (1996) Framing research on culture in psychiatric diagnosis: the case of the DSM–IV, *Psychiatry*, 49, pp. 145–155.

Rogler, L.H. (1999) Methodological sources of cultural insensitivity in mental health, *American psychologist*, 54, pp. 424–433.

Salekin, R.T., Rogers, R. and Sewell, K.W. (1996) A review and meta-analysis of the Psychopathy Checklist and Psychopathy Checklist – Revised: predictive validity of dangerousness, *Clinical Psychology: Science and Practice*, 3, pp. 203–215.

Salekin, R.T., Branner, D., Zalot, A., Leistico, A. and Newmann, C (in press) Factor structure of psychopathy in youth: testing the applicability of the new four factor model, *Criminal Justice and Behaviour.*

Serin, R.C. (1991) Psychopathy and violence in criminals, *Journal of Interpersonal Violence*, 6, pp. 423–431.

Skeem, J.L. and Mulvey, E.P. (2001) Psychopathy and community violence among civil psychiatric patients: results from the MacArthur violence risk assessment study, *Journal of Consulting and Clinical Psychology*, 15, pp. 467–477.

Skeem, J., Mulvey, E. and Grisso, T. (2003) Applicability of traditional and revised models of psychopathy to the Psychopathy Checklist: Screening Version (PCL – SV) *Psychological Assessment*, 15, pp. 41–55.

Skeem, J., Cooke, D.J. and Michie, C. (2006) Is antisocial behaviour essential to psychopathy? Conceptual directions for resolving the debate. Unpublished manuscript.

Smith, G.T., Fischer, S. and Fister, S. (2003) Incremental validity principles in test construction, *Psychological Assessment*, 15, pp. 467–477.

Stattin, H. and Magnusson, D. (1991) Stability and change in criminal behaviour up to age 30: findings from a prospective, longitudinal study in Sweden, *British Journal of Criminology*, 31, pp. 327–346.

Stone, G.L. (1995) Review of the Hare Psychopathy Checklist – revised, in: J.C. Conoley and J.C. Impara (Eds) *Twelfth Mental Measurement Yearbook*, pp. 454–455 (Lincoln: Buros Institute).

Toch, H. (1998) Psychopathy or antisocial personality in forensic settings, in: T. Millon, E. Simonsen, M. Birket-Smith, and R.G. Davi (Eds) *Psychopathy, Antisocial, Criminal and Violent Behavior*, 1st edn, pp. 144–158 (New York: Guilford).

Triandis, H.C. and Suh, E.M. (2002) Cultural influences on personality, *Annual Review of Psychology*, 53, pp. 133–160.

Vitacco, M., Rogers, R., Neumann, C.S., Harrison, K.S. and Vincent, G.M. (2005) A comparison of factor models on the PCL-R with mentally disordered offenders, *Criminal Justice and Behavior*, 32, pp. 526–545.

Widiger, T.A. (1998) Psychopathy and normal personality, in: D.J. Cooke, A.E. Forth, and R.D. Hare (Eds) *Psychopathy: Theory, Research and Implications for Society*, pp. 47–68 (Kluwer Academic).

Widom, C.S. (1977) A methodology for studying non-institutionalized psychopaths, *Journal of Consulting and Clinical Psychology*, 45, pp. 674–683.

Zinger, I. and Forth, A.E. (1998) Psychopathy and Canadian criminal proceedings: the potential for human rights abuses, *Canadian Journal of Criminology*, 40, pp. 237–276.

Chapter 11

Key Considerations and Problems in Assessing Risk for Violence

Michael R. Davis and James R. P. Ogloff

The assessment of an individual's risk of committing future acts of violence is a prominent issue in all areas of mental health practice (Mullen 2000). Regardless of whether they work in a forensic setting, the concern that a patient may harm others is a considerable source of anxiety for any treating team (Otto 2000). Furthermore, in many jurisdictions such assessments are required by law (see Ogloff and Davis 2005, for discussion of Australian legislation). Indeed, in the criminal context, the question of accuseds' or offenders' 'dangerousness' is naturally central to many decisions that are made throughout the criminal justice process. Decisions involving whether someone will be granted bail, whether someone will be incarcerated or granted probation, where one will be incarcerated, whether one will be granted parole, and conditions of release from custody may all be affected by the perceived level of risk for violence of the offender. Similar questions arise in the context of young offenders and for them the additional question of whether they should be proceeded against in adult court as compared to youth court (or some variant) can be affected again by their deemed level of risk for violence. Furthermore, questions of whether an adult prisoner poses an 'unacceptable risk to the community' to be released from prison may also occur as post-sentence detention of prisoners is now permissible in many jurisdictions throughout the world, particularly with regard to sexual offenders (Covington 1997; Ogloff and Davis, 2005; Wollert 2006).

In this chapter, we will outline key considerations and problems that clinicians must be cognisant of when performing such assessments. We begin by briefly discussing the history and feasibility of violence risk assessment. We then discuss considerations regarding training, the clinician's role with the individual, the purpose of the assessment, appropriate tools, and idiosyncratic issues. Finally, we describe several problems that assessors may face and provide a framework for conducting risk assessments that are defensible and empirically based, whilst still being sensitive to the individual case.

The Feasibility of Violence Risk Assessment

It is important to note that only three decades ago there was very little evidence that the prediction of what was then called 'dangerousness' was an activity that mental health professionals should even be attempting. Two judicial decisions in the United States (i.e. *Baxstrom v. Herold*, 1966; *Dixon v. Attorney General of the Commonwealth of Pennsylvania*, 1971) resulted in the large scale release of patients from hospitals for the criminally insane. This provided an unprecedented opportunity to test the recidivism of patients that had, at some stage, been considered dangerous. In both cases less than 20% of these patients were found to be violent after four years (Douglas and Webster 1999; Monahan 1981; Steadman and Cococozza 1974; Steadman and Halfon 1971; Thornberry and Jacoby 1979). While this illustrates a severe over-prediction of violence ('false positive' errors), Cocozza and Steadman (1976) showed that 'false negative' errors (i.e., assessing someone as not dangerous who is subsequently violent) were also prevalent, although not nearly to the same extent.[1] They followed 257 indicted defendants in the state of New York who had been found incompetent to stand trial during the years 1971 and 1972. Sixty percent had been assessed by psychiatrists as dangerous. Of those released into the community, only 14% of the dangerous group and 16% of the not-dangerous group were rearrested for violent offences. Accordingly, Cocozza and Steadman (1976, p. 1084) concluded that there was 'clear and convincing evidence' of mental health professionals' inability to forecast violence accurately.

The view that predicting dangerousness was a seemingly futile practice was particularly prominent amongst the mental health professions themselves. Taskforces of the American Psychiatric Association in 1974 and the American Psychological Association in 1978 argued that their members were not qualified to make such predictions (see Monahan 1981; Steadman 2000). Nevertheless, the courts continued to see mental health professionals as the only group of people even remotely qualified to perform the task. Indeed, in the death penalty case of *Barefoot v. Estelle* (1983), the United States Supreme Court noted that, despite the poor research findings, 'it makes little sense, if any, to subject that psychiatrists, out of the entire universe of persons who might have an opinion on this issue, would know so little about the subject that they should not be permitted to testify' (*Barefoot v. Estelle* 1983, pp. 896–897; see Melton *et al.* 1997, for discussion).

The beginning of the modern study of violence risk assessment can be traced to Monahan's seminal 1981 monograph *Predicting Violent Behaviour: An Assessment of Clinical Techniques*. After reviewing the available literature he concluded that:

> psychiatrists and psychologists are accurate in no more than one out of three predictions of violent behavior over a several-year period among institutionalized populations that

---

1   The tendency for clinicians to over-predict violence may stem from the fact that the consequences of the two types of error are far from equal. A false negative prediction of violence may well invoke community outcry, whereas a false positive prediction would rarely lead to widespread condemnation because it cannot be proven false if a patient is not released. Thus, the consequences are diametrically opposed and clinicians may understandably err on the side of caution (Ogloff and Davis 2005).

had both committed violence in the past (and thus had high base rates for it) and who were diagnosed as mentally ill. (Monahan, 1981, pp. 47, 49).

Monahan (1981, p. 63) made two specific recommendations – 'an increased emphasis on using statistical concepts in clinical prediction, and a heightened sensitivity to environmental and contextual variables'. The former recommendation has since been followed with much fervour in the literature and many subsequent advances have been made. The dichotomous trait-like concept of 'dangerousness' has been replaced with the more probabilistic construct of 'risk.' Furthermore, many appropriate predictor variables have been identified. These include static (generally unchangeable) and dynamic (potentially changeable) risk factors. Accordingly, there are now numerous formal tools for assessing risk for violence (Douglas and Skeem 2005). These include both strictly mechanical actuarial tools and structured professional guidelines. This increase in research activity has led to greatly increased predictive power. In fact, the effect size for violence risk assessment is now superior to that of many other medical and psychological practices. For example, Douglas *et al.* (1999a) compared the standardised effect sizes (Cohen's *d*) of a variety of common health-care activities.[2] The effect size for violence risk assessment – at that time – ranged from 0.91 to 1.19 across studies. This was superior to the effect of chemotherapy on breast cancer ($d = 0.08$–0.11), the effect of bypass surgery on angina ($d = 0.80$), psychotherapy in general ($d = 0.76$), or the effect of electroconvulsive therapy on depression ($d = 0.80$). While violence risk assessment is far from infallible, it can now be considered a feasible activity that can be made with at least a modicum of accuracy (Douglas *et al.* 1999a; Ogloff and Davis 2005). We will now turn our discussion toward key clinical considerations when conducting violence risk assessments.

Key Considerations

Training and Qualifications

One obvious conclusion from the early literature on violence risk assessment is that simply being a mental health professional, even a forensic mental health professional, does not qualify one to assess or predict violence. Clinical experience is no substitute for specialist training, particularly in a field where clinical judgement has historically proven so poor and the empirical literature is capacious (see also Harris 2003). Indeed, Dietz (1985, p. 98) noted that 'psychiatrists and psychologists who have no knowledge of crime have no more business predicting crime than other citizens'.

---

2   Cohen's *d* reports the size of an effect as the difference between two groups in terms of their pooled standard deviation (i.e. $[M1 - M2]/\sigma_{pooled}$, where $\sigma_{pooled} = \sqrt{[(\sigma1^2 + \sigma2^2)/2]}$. Thus, a d value of 1.00 refers to a difference between groups on the criterion variable of one standard deviation. A d of 0.80 or higher is considered to be large, 0.50 moderate, and 0.20 small (see Cohen 1988, 1992).

Somewhat harsher in their view of clinicians' judgements were Grove and Meehl (1996, p. 302) who argued that 'clinical experience is only a prestigious synonym for anecdotal evidence when the anecdotes are told by somebody with a professional degree and a license to practice a healing art'. Accordingly, Douglas *et al.* (1999a) discussed a model curriculum for training in violence risk assessment. Much like the development of other clinical skills, their proposed module includes observation, reading, mock assessments, supervised experience, and finally a supervised clinical caseload.

While it is difficult to establish firm base requirements for asserting who should or should not be conducting violence risk assessments, it is sensible in our view that the individual have a post-graduate degree in psychology, training in psychiatry, or advanced post-graduate training in another mental health profession (e.g., social work). Some of the risk assessment tools contain items that require assessment by a licensed psychiatrist or psychologist. As such, the assessor ought to be a licensed mental health professional. Next, the assessor must have clinical expertise in working with the class of persons being assessed (e.g., psychiatric patients, prisoners, forensic psychiatric patients). Beyond mere credentials and experience, it is most important that the individual have an expert level of knowledge of the risk assessment literature. This should be attained to a level equivalent to post-graduate level knowledge of the field. The individual should then work with one who is established in the area who can provide proper clinical supervision to assist the assessor to develop applied clinical expertise in the area. We suggest this should begin with the individual sitting in on assessments conducted by the supervisor followed by occasions where the supervisor sits in on assessments conducted by the novice. Following this process, conventional supervision should commence (beyond having a supervisor simply reading and editing reports!). Surely, this is not too much to ask with assessments that may very well influence the life events of offenders and perhaps future victims.

Dual Role Conflicts

It is important for clinicians to be aware of the biasing effects of dual-role conflicts and avoid them wherever possible. The most difficult area, and one in which forensic clinicians may find themselves without necessarily engaging in unethical conduct, is in the role of therapist and risk assessor. While a treating clinician should generally not act as a forensic evaluator[3] with the same client, they should still be encouraged to routinely assess their clients' potential for violence, just as they would in regard to suicide. Furthermore, in some jurisdictions, the treating clinician is requested by the courts to comment on their forensic patients' perceived level of risk. This is misguided. Any risk assessment conducted by a treating clinician is prone to

---

3   The term forensic evaluator is used here to refer to the individual doing a formal forensic evaluation for the courts or some other administrative decision making tribunal (e.g. parole board).

additional biases caused by the somewhat incompatible features of the clinician's therapeutic role with their assessing role. This bias has been termed *treating clinician myopia* (see Davis and Ogloff 2005a; Ogloff and Davis 2005) and may lead to an increase in false negative predictions. Of course, among the information collected by the forensic evaluator should be information from the treating clinician, including information about attention paid by the clinician to the individual's level of risk. Formal risk assessment schemes, completed by independent forensic evaluators, are likely to counter the possibility of clinician myopia, by drawing attention away from therapeutic variables unrelated to risk, and focusing attention on appropriate risk factors.

Clarify the Purpose of the Assessment

It is important for assessing clinicians to determine the purpose of the risk assessment, as the focus may differ substantially. Heilbrun (1997; see also Heilbrun and Kramer 2001) differentiated between *prediction* and *management* models of risk assessment. The former emphasises overall accuracy of prediction and is perhaps most relevant to assessments for the purpose of commitment. Such assessments have a greater focus upon static risk factors with high predictive power. Conversely, the management model is more concerned with identifying dynamic risk factors that can be targeted for treatment and management (see also Douglas and Skeem 2005). Many assessments will request a combination of the two, where the clinician must indicate a level of risk and also detail how this risk can be best contained and managed. This would appear to be the future focus in violence risk assessment, as our goal as clinicians should be to prevent violence rather than merely predict it (Hart 1998; Wong and Gordon 2006).

Choosing Appropriate Tools

As previously noted, a wide array of formal schemes now exist for assessing risk for general violence and other more specific offences. These can be divided into two broad camps: actuarial prediction and structured professional judgement.

Actuarial prediction In contrast to traditional *unstructured* clinical decision making, actuarial prediction 'involves a formal, algorithmic, objective procedure (e.g., equation) to reach the decision' (Grove and Meehl, 1996, pp. 293–294). Actuarial tools are based upon the statistical relationship between a range of predictive factors and the likelihood of violence. These schemes are used mechanically to place the individual into a particular category of risk. Aside from the clinical judgement required to obtain the information for each predictor, the final assessment of risk is purely mechanical when using an actuarial approach (Davis and Ogloff, 2005b; Ogloff and Davis 2005; Quinsey *et al.* 1998, 2006). The development of these tools was greatly influenced by the merits of actuarial prediction in the wider decision-making literature (e.g. Meehl 1954, 1957, 1986; Sarbin, 1943), in which the mechanical prediction of just about any outcome was generally superior to the unstructured judgement of clinicians (see Grove *et al.* 2000, for a meta-analysis). This has also proven to be the case for the prediction of violence (Bonta *et al.* 1998; Hanson and Bussière, 1998; Harris *et al.* 2002).

Structured professional judgement   In contrast to purely actuarial prediction, structured professional judgement consists of professional guidelines for clinical assessment. These instruments include a number of risk factors, derived rationally from consideration of the literature, that the evaluator must carefully score from an administration manual. However, the clinician is not advised to sum the items in a mechanical fashion. After completing the tool they make what is considered to be a structured clinical opinion of low, moderate, or high risk. The term 'structured professional judgement' indicates that the resulting opinions are not mechanical but are qualitatively distinct from the traditional unstructured use of clinical judgement. There is no specified method for making the structured rating (Boer *et al.* 1997; Douglas and Ogloff, 2003; Webster *et al.* 1997). This reflects the opinion that interactions between risk factors are likely to be non-linear and idiographic (Davis and Ogloff 2005b; Hart *et al.* 2003). It also allows for the consideration of case-specific risk factors that the clinician feels are relevant, but which were too rare to be identified and included in the instrument[4] (Davis and Ogloff, 2004; de Vogel *et al.* 2004; Monahan, this volume; West 2001). Despite often heated debate in the literature, both the actuarial and structured professional judgement approaches have offered comparable predictive validity.

We will now briefly describe some of the most prevalent risk assessment tools currently in use. This is by no means an exhaustive review. It is important to note that different tools have been developed for the assessment of risk for general violence, sexual violence, and spousal violence, and that clinicians should choose an appropriate tool, or tools, for the individual case.

Tools for Assessing Risk for General Violence

The Violence Risk Appraisal Guide (VRAG). The VRAG (Harris *et al.* 1993; Quinsey *et al.* 1998, 2006) is arguably the apotheosis of pure actuarial prediction. It is a 12-item tool comprised almost exclusively of static variables. Each variable is differentially weighted based upon the strength of the item in predicting the outcome. One such

---

4   These rare, idiosyncratic variables are often particularly relevant in regard to targeted violence. For example, the first author once conducted an assessment in which the patient described a wish to kill his previous victim should he be released. He subsequently provided considerable detail regarding his plans. Regardless of this patient's omnibus risk level, which was moderate, the author understandably considered the risk of targeted violence toward this one person to be high, despite the fact that specific threats are generally not included in formal schemes due to their low occurrence.

variable is a score on the Psychopathy Checklist-Revised (PCL-R; Hare 1991, 2003). Based upon their VRAG score, individuals are placed into nine categories, each with a documented probability of recidivism after seven and 10 years.[5] The instrument has demonstrated validity with forensic psychiatric (Harris *et al.* 2002; Rice and Harris, 1997), correctional (Loza *et al.* 2002), and civil psychiatric (Harris *et al.* 2004) samples. A modification of the VRAG exists for assessing the risk of general violence amongst sex offenders (not sexual recidivism *per se*). This 14-item variant is known as the Sex Offender Risk Appraisal Guide (SORAG; Quinsey *et al.* 1998, 2006).

The Historical-Clinical-Risk Management-20 (HCR-20) The HCR-20 (Webster *et al.* 1997) is the leading instrument of the structured professional judgement approach. As the name suggests, the instrument is comprised of 20 items on three scales. The Historical scale comprises ten static factors that form the foundation of the assessment. As with the VRAG, the PCL-R or Psychopathy Checklist: Screening Version (PCL:SV; Hart *et al.* 1995) is required to score a psychopathy item. The Clinical scale consists of five dynamic items relating to current functioning. Finally, the Risk Management scale consists of five dynamic items that relate to future adjustment and contextual considerations. Each item is scored on a three-point scale (0 = no evidence; 1 = possible or partial evidence; and 2 = definite evidence).

A growing body of research confirms that the HCR-20 is reliable and validly predicts violence across forensic psychiatric (Dernevik *et al.* 2001; Douglas *et al.* 2003; Strand *et al.* 1999), correctional (Belfrage *et al.* 2000), and civil psychiatric samples (Douglas *et al.* 1999b; Nicholls *et al.* 2004). Importantly, structured judgements outperform the use of the HCR-20 in a mechanical, actuarial fashion (de Vogel and de Ruiter 2005; Douglas *et al.* 2003, 2005). Furthermore, because half of the items in the HCR-20 are dynamic they can also serve as risk management targets and a risk management companion guide has been published (Douglas *et al.* 2001).

The Classification of Violence Risk (COVR) The COVR (Monahan *et al.* 2005; see also Monahan, this volume) is a computer-assisted actuarial tool that uses a multiple-model iterative classification tree approach to classify involuntarily hospitalised psychiatric patients into five categories with a documented probability of recidivism after 20 weeks. The COVR includes 40 static and dynamic variables across 10 empirical models; however, due to the decision-tree approach, not all of these are utilised in each assessment. The COVR was developed and validated with involuntarily hospitalised civil psychiatric patients in the United States and has demonstrated a very high degree of predictive validity in these samples.

---

5   It must be emphasised that actuarial and structured professional judgment measures do not predict an individual's level of risk per se. Rather, they provide information regarding the group into which the individual falls (see Hart *et al.* in press).

The Violence Risk Scale (VRS)   The VRS (Wong and Gordon 1998, 2006) is a 26-item structured instrument that integrates risk assessment, prediction, and treatment. The VRS includes six static items and 20 dynamic items. The 20 dynamic items enable identification of treatment targets using a modified stages-of-change model. Furthermore, the VRS includes a pre- and post-treatment version of the dynamic scale, such that positive treatment changes can be assessed quantitatively. Recent empirical work indicates considerable predictive validity in a correctional sample (Wong and Gordon 2006). A variant known as the Violence Risk Scale – Sex Offender Version (Wong *et al.* 2004) has also been developed.

Tools for Assessing Risk for Sexual Violence

The Static-99   The Static-99 (Hanson and Thornton 1999; Harris *et al.* 2003) is a ten-item actuarial tool that is the most widely used tool for assessing long-term risk of sexual recidivism and has been found to be a reliable and valid instrument. It was created from the variables of two previous sex offender risk assessment measures, the Rapid Risk Assessment for Sex Offence Recidivism (RRASOR; Hanson 1997) and the Structured Anchored Clinical Judgement (SACJ-Min; Grubin 1998). As the name suggests, it is comprised exclusively of static risk factors. Static-99 scores place the individual into four categories with a documented probability of recidivism after five, 10, and 15 years.

That Static-99 has a relatively high level of predictive validity; however, given the low base rate of sexual re-offending across samples, even those individuals who fall into the 'high' risk for sexual re-offending category have relatively low absolute levels of sexual recidivism (i.e. 39% over 5 years, 45% over 10 years, and 52% over 15 years). While these levels of recidivism are roughly twice those of the low risk groups, still a majority of those in the 'high risk' groups in fact did not re-offend over five or 10 years and then just over half re-offended over 15 years (Hanson and Thornton 1999). The Static-99 is also affected, as other measures would be, with factors such as aging and length of time in the community offence-free. With respect to aging, for example, Hanson (2005) reported that the level of recidivism dropped across age groups. Across all age groups, the recidivism rate of those in the 'high risk' category over five years was 31.6%. It reduced to 25.7% for those between 40 and 49 years of age and to 24.3% for those who were aged 50 to 59 years of age. In individuals over the age of 60 years, the five year recidivism was 9.1%. Thus, the clinician must carefully factor individual differences into the final risk judgements being made.

The Sexual Violence Risk-20 (SVR-20)   The SVR-20 (Boer *et al.* 1997) is a structured professional judgement tool for assessing risk of sexual violence. It comprises 20 items that are divided into three scales: psychosocial adjustment (11 items), sexual offences (seven items), and future plans (two items). Each item is scored on a three-point scale of no, maybe, or yes, which is analogous to the 0-1-2 scheme on the HCR-20. Similar to the HCR-20, the PCL-R or PCL:SV is required to score a psychopathy item. The SVR-20 has been found to have considerable predictive validity, with structured judgements also outperforming the use of the tool as a mechanical instrument (see de Vogel *et al.* 2004).

The Risk for Sexual Violence Protocol (RSVP)   The RSVP (Hart *et al.* 2003) is a 22-item structured professional judgement tool that is in many ways a revision of the SVR-20. The RSVP features five categories of risk factors and each item is scored on three 'no, maybe, yes' scales that relate to past presence, recent presence, and future relevance of the risk factor. The categories are sexual violence history (five items), psychological adjustment (five items), mental disorder (five items), social adjustment (four items), and manageability (three items). The RSVP has expanded the structured professional judgement model to include the identification of risk scenarios and case management strategies. Predictive validity is thus far unknown, although the close similarity to the SVR-20 suggests that it may well possess predictive validity.

Tools for Assessing Risk for Spousal Violence

The Ontario Domestic Assault Risk Assessment (ODARA)   The ODARA (Hilton *et al.* 2004) is a 13-item actuarial tool developed primarily for use by police. It comprises dichotomous variables that are primarily static in nature. Good predictive validity has been reported for both development and cross-validation analyses (Hilton *et al.* 2004).

The Spousal Assault Risk Assessment Guide (SARA)   The SARA (Kropp *et al.* 1994, 1999) is a 20-item structured professional judgement tool, which features four scales of static and dynamic risk factors: criminal history (three items), psychosocial adjustment (seven items), spousal assault history (seven items), and alleged/most recent offence (three items). Each item is scored on the same 0-1-2 format as other structured schemes. While the SARA is a structured professional judgement scheme, norms are provided and clinicians are asked to justify any differences between their structured judgement and the number of identified risk factors. Nonetheless, the literature suggests that structured judgements add incremental validity to the total scores on the instrument (Kropp and Hart 2000).

Choosing Appropriate Tools

In this section, we shall review how the clinician may choose appropriate risk assessment measures. We begin with a brief note on the actuarial versus structured professional judgement measures. We next discuss the (in)advisability of combining risk measures in the search for higher degrees of overall predictive validity. Finally, we note that the choice of risk assessment measures is often influenced by considerations of the prediction of risk over some time period.

In our view, both actuarial and structured professional judgement instruments are suitable for establishing one's level of risk over some time period (dependent on the nature of the assessment instruments employed). This is what Heilbrun (1997; Heilbrun and Kramer 2001) referred to as a prediction model of risk assessment. However, the actuarial instruments, which are typically based on static or unchangeable risk factors, are not sensitive to change over time and are not useful for risk management models of risk assessment (i.e. using risk information to manage an individual's level of risk) (Douglas and Skeem 2005).

There is another important message in the use of violence risk measures – that using more than one of them does not necessarily produce an increase in the level of predictive accuracy. Like so many things, clinicians seem to believe that if one measure works moderately well, then using several measures will somehow increase the level of predictive accuracy. For example, Seto (2005) conducted a study to investigate whether combining some combination of actuarial risk assessment measures (the VRAG, SORAG, RRASOR and the Static-99) produced greater degrees of predictive accuracy than the strongest individual predictor. No combination of measures improved prediction beyond the single best predictor. Thus, if they are going to employ actuarial measures, clinicians are advised to use a single actuarial measure that has been proven to have acceptable predictive validity. Then, rather than simply adding additional actuarial measures, it is advisable to employ a structured professional judgement measure to review both static and dynamic risk variables over time.

The time period that the risk assessment refers to is often a crucial consideration for the assessing clinician. As noted above, some actuarial tools provide estimates of recidivism for some time in the next five years. While this is undeniably useful in gauging an individual's baseline level of risk, it is also important to have some indication of risk in the short-term. Dynamic risk factors are arguably more relevant in the short-term and several tools have been developed for the purpose of short-term risk assessment.

The Short Term Assessment of Risk and Treatability (START; Webster *et al.* 2004) is a structured professional judgement tool comprising 20 dynamic items that are scored on both a risk scale and a strength scale. The START is not unlike an expanded version of the C- and R-scales of the HCR-20 and is designed to complement an assessment of historical information (such as the H-scale of the HCR-20 or the VRAG). It assesses short- to medium-term risk across seven domains: violence to others, self-harm, suicide, unauthorised leave, substance abuse, self-neglect, and victimisation. Recent empirical validation with forensic psychiatric inpatients suggested moderate to moderate/large relationships with the various overlapping risks (Nicholls *et al.* 2006).

The Dynamic Appraisal of Situational Aggression: Inpatient Version (DASA; Ogloff and Daffern 2004, 2006) is a seven-item structured professional judgement tool that is also comprised entirely of dynamic risk factors. It is designed for very short-term risks, of approximately 24 hours, in an inpatient setting. The DASA has shown excellent predictive validity for use in forensic and general psychiatric hospitals.

Idiosyncratic Issues and Caveats

With a large number of risk assessment tools available, it is important for the assessing clinician to be aware of the limitations of each tool so that they are not used in an inappropriate fashion. At present some violence risk assessment schemes have only been validated in North America. As such, a clinician cannot know how valid the instrument will be in other parts of the world and must offer appropriate caveats in their report if they decide to use such a tool in their jurisdiction. Generalisability of a risk assessment tool may also be threatened by the composition of the construction and validation samples. For example, the COVR was developed and validated on large samples of involuntarily committed civil psychiatric patients in the United States. However, only 26% of the sample had a primary diagnosis of schizophrenia (Monahan *et al.* 2001). This would likely be considerably different in other jurisdictions, such as Australia or Britain, and the generalisability of the instrument could suffer.

The applicability of a risk assessment instrument to an individual case may also be lessened in regard to the client or patient's age. As noted, recent publications in the sexual offending literature have suggested that the base rates of sex offending drop considerably with advanced age (Hanson 2005). Moreover, Wollert (2006) applied Bayes' theorem to agewise sexual recidivism rates with a range of current actuarial tools and was quite pessimistic about their validity with older offenders. Similarly, Hanson (2006) suggested that clinicians using the Static-99 should consider advanced age when making an overall assessment of risk.

One difficulty that clinicians may face when conducting a risk assessment is the unenviable situation in which the subject of the assessment will not agree to be interviewed. This poses considerable difficulty, but, in many cases, an estimate of risk may still be required. Although less than ideal, some tools can be completed without an interview if appropriate file information is available (e.g. HCR-20, VRAG, Static-99). Nonetheless, it is crucial that the clinician documents this non-standard completion of the particular scheme and notes appropriate caveats. Perhaps more likely is a situation where the subject of the assessment agrees to the interview but totally denies any culpability in the index offence. In such situations it is difficult to complete some of the more involved risk assessment schemes and the clinician must document this difficulty. Attention to such details is congruent with the various ethical codes to which mental health professionals ascribe. For example, Ethical Standard 9.01(b) of the American Psychological Association (1992) requires psychologists to note the limitations of the reliability and validity of their opinions if made without a direct examination of the individual. Given the possible consequences of a risk assessment these standards are arguably even more important than in other areas of practice.

Key Problems for the Assessor

Errors and Cognitive Limitations

In his early analysis of the risk assessment literature, Monahan (1981) identified several errors that appeared to be endemic in clinical predictions of violence. These included a lack of specificity in defining the outcome that was being predicted, ignoring statistical base rates of violence, relying upon illusory correlations (i.e. variables that actually had little or no relationship with violence), and failing to incorporate environmental or contextual information into assessments of risk. It can be argued that biases from the wider decision-making literature also play a role in risk assessment, such as overweighting or ignoring variables, overconfidence (Arkes *et al.* 1986; Baron 2000), and 'cognitive overload' when faced with a range of possible contributing risk factors (Kleinmuntz 1990). Assessing clinicians must be cognisant of these common limitations. The use of a structured or actuarial scheme may certainly help to overcome such errors. Formal schemes focus upon variables with actual relationships with violence and ensure that important variables are considered. They also usually include a definition of violence as a criterion. Furthermore, structured tools encourage assessors to provide contextualised assessments that include the likely imminence, nature, and severity of any predicted harm (Hart *et al.* 2003).

Assessment-specific Problems

Some situations, such as the client refusing to be interviewed, are largely beyond the control of the clinician. Nonetheless, there are several other problematic situations in which the assessing clinician has much more control and must be vigilant. The first of these is the requirement for adequate collateral information. Clinicians should attempt, wherever possible, to obtain information about the individual in question from multiple sources (Heilbrun 2001). Police records, treatment reports, criminal history, and interviews with family members and treating clinicians should take place where possible. A valid violence risk assessment cannot take place on the basis of an interview alone.

A potential problem that can occur is to neglect or underemphasise historical information and static risk factors (Webster 1997). Earlier in this chapter we described the concept of 'treating clinician myopia,' in which treating a patient's non-criminogenic issues can erroneously affect ones view of their risk. However, this is also possible when the focus of treatment is to ameliorate dynamic risk factors. It cannot be forgotten that the foundation of any violence risk assessment must be in the historical risk factors. The old aphorism that past behaviour is the best predictor of future behaviour (Thorndyke 1911) has considerable merit in regard to violence. Therefore, substantial change in some dynamic risk factors may still result in an individual who poses a concerning risk for violence.

Despite the need for a foundation based on historical risk factors, the clinician must not fail to individualise and contextualise the assessment. For all of their predictive power, static risk factors are largely nomothetic. It is important for the assessor to consider the phenomenology of the individual's previous offending. A detailed examination of the antecedents, circumstances, and contexts of previous violence to identify repetitive themes is known as *anamnestic assessment* (Borum *et al.* 1996; Davis and Ogloff 2005c; Miller and Morris 1988; Otto 2000). While there is no empirical evidence for the validity of anamnestic assessment as a standalone approach, it can be invaluable for providing context and for understanding how the more nomothetic risk factors, both static and dynamic, apply to the individual in question (Davis and Ogloff 2005c). This is particularly important because formal risk assessment schemes largely neglect the consideration of situational variables at the expense of dispositional constructs. Risk management considerations naturally flow from a more informed assessment.

Assessment Framework

The issues discussed in this chapter need to be considered as part of a consistent, reliable framework. We would strongly recommend that all violence risk assessments begin with a thorough review of collateral information prior to a clinical interview (where possible). Clinicians need to consider the purpose of the assessment and choose an appropriate risk assessment tool or tools. Options include a purely actuarial instrument or a structured professional judgement scheme. Some clinicians may choose to anchor their assessment in an actuarial tool that is laden with static factors, yet also use a structured scheme to consider dynamic variables. Regardless of the choice of tool, what is needed is a systematic assessment using a validated scheme that is grounded in empirical knowledge (Webster *et al.* 1997). A thorough report will also individualise the assessment by means of anamnestic appraisal. The final risk judgement should eschew any dichotomous conclusions in favour of probabilistic reporting that outlines particular conditions and scenarios in which the individual is likely to be most at risk of violence. Such judgements should flow into risk management considerations.

Conclusion

Despite its less than stellar origins, the field of violence risk assessment has seen considerable progress over the past three decades. The dichotomous concept of 'dangerousness' has been replaced by the probabilistic notion of risk. Reliability and validity has been greatly enhanced by adopting an empirical focus by means of actuarial prediction tools and structured professional judgement schemes. Modern-day risk assessment is now a feasible activity with predictive validity that rivals that of many other medical and psychological practices. In this chapter we have provided an overview of pertinent issues, problems, and caveats that clinicians should consider when conducting such appraisals and have placed these into a structured assessment framework that is grounded in empirical evidence, yet flexible and attentive to the case at hand. Such an approach reflects the state of knowledge at this point in the field's development. In our view, given the liberty and public safety matters that are at stake in many situations where mental health professionals are called upon to make assessments of violence risk, it is ethically imperative that the clinician be particularly well trained and that they rely upon a validated risk assessment protocol.

References

American Psychological Association (1992) Ethical principles of psychologists and code of conduct, *American Psychologist*, 47, pp. 1597–1611.

Arkes, H.R., Dawes, R.M. and Christensen, C. (1986) Factors influencing the use of a decision rule in a probabilistic task, *Organizational Behavior and Human Decision Processes*, 37, pp. 93–110.

Barefoot v. Estelle, 463 U.S. 880 (1983).

Baron, J. (2000) *Thinking and Deciding*, 3rd edn (Cambridge: Cambridge University Press).

Baxstrom v. Herold, 383 U.S. 107 (1966).

Belfrage, H., Fransson, G. and Strand, S. (2000) Prediction of violence using the HCR-20: A prospective study in two maximum-security correctional institutions, *Journal of Forensic Psychiatry*, 11, pp. 167–175.

Boer, D.P., Hart, S.D., Kropp, P.R. and Webster, C.D. (1997) *Sexual Violence Risk-20: Professional Guidelines for Assessing Risk of Sexual Violence* (Vancouver, British Columbia: British Columbia Institute on Family Violence and Mental Health, Law, and Policy Institute, Simon Fraser University).

Bonta, J., Law, M. and Hanson, K. (1998) The prediction of criminal and violent recidivism among mentally disordered offenders: a meta-analysis, *Psychological Bulletin*, 123, pp. 123–142.

Borum, R., Swartz, M. and Swanson, J. (1996) Assessing and managing violence risk in clinical practice, *Journal of Practical Psychiatry and Behavioral Health*, 2, pp. 205–215.

Cocozza, J. and Steadman, H. (1976) The failure of psychiatric predictions of dangerousness: clear and convincing evidence, *Rutgers Law Review*, 29, pp. 1084–1101.

Cohen, J. (1988) *Statistical Power Analysis for the Behavioral Sciences*, 2nd edn (Hillsdale, NJ: Lawrence Erlbaum).

Cohen, J. (1992) A power primer, *Psychological Bulletin*, 112, pp. 155–159.

Covington, J.R. (1997) Preventive detention for sex offenders, *Illinois Bar Journal*, 85, pp. 493–498.

Davis, M.R. and Ogloff, J.R.P. (2004, June) Broken leg countervailings and violence risk assessment: the views of practicing clinicians. Paper presented at the Fourth Annual Conference of the International Association of Forensic Mental Health Services (IAFMHS), Stockholm, Sweden.

Davis, M.R. and Ogloff, J.R.P. (2005a) Treating clinician myopia: the need for structured violence risk assessments in therapeutic practice. Paper presented at the Fifth Annual Conference of the International Association of Forensic Mental Health Services (IAFMHS), Melbourne, Australia, April.

Davis, M.R. and Ogloff, J.R.P. (2005b) Identifying the sources of actuarial superiority in violence risk assessment: Meehl's 'Clinical versus statistical prediction' revisited. Paper presented at the 15th European conference on Psychology and Law, Vilnius, Lithuania, June.

Davis, M.R. and Ogloff, J.R.P. (2005c) Anamnestic violence risk assessment: A contextual bridge between nomothetic and idiographic risk appraisal. Paper presented at the annual conference of the Royal Australian and New Zealand College of Psychiatrists Section of Forensic Psychiatry, Gold Coast, Australia, August.

de Vogel, V. and de Ruiter, C. (2005) The HCR-20 in personality disordered female offenders: a comparison with a matched sample of males, *Clinical Psychology and Psychotherapy*, 12, pp. 226–240.

de Vogel, V., de Ruiter, C., van Beek, D. and Mead, G. (2004) Predictive validity of the SVR-20 and Static-99 in a Dutch sample of treated sex offenders, *Law and Human Behavior*, 28, pp. 235–251.

Dernevik, M., Grann, M. and Johansson, S. (2001) Violent behaviour in forensic psychiatric patients: risk assessment and different risk-management levels using the HCR-20, *Psychology, Crime, and Law*, 8, pp. 1–19.

Dietz, P.E. (1985) Hypothetical criteria for the prediction of individual criminality, in: C.D. Webster, M.H. Ben-Aron and S.J. Hucker (Eds) *Dangerousness: Probability and Prediction, Psychiatry and Public Policy*, pp. 87–102 (New York: Cambridge University Press).

Dixon v. Attorney General of the Commonwealth of Pennsylvania, 325 F.Supp. 966 (M.D. Pa. 1971).

Douglas, K.S. and Ogloff, J.R.P. (2003) Multiple facets of risk for violence: the impact of judgmental specificity on structured decisions about violence risk, *International Journal of Forensic Mental Health*, 2, pp. 19–34.

Douglas, K.S. and Webster, C.D. (1999) Predicting violence in mentally and personality disordered individuals, in: R. Roesch, S.D. Hart and J.R.P. Ogloff (Eds) *Psychology and Law: The State of the Discipline*, pp. 175–239 (New York: Kluwer Academic/Plenum Publishers).

Douglas, K.S. and Skeem, J.L. (2005) Violence risk assessment: getting specific about being dynamic, *Psychology, Public Policy, and Law*, 11, pp. 347–383.

Douglas, K.S., Cox, D.N. and Webster, C.D. (1999a) Violence risk assessment: science and practice, *Legal and Criminological Psychology*, 4, pp. 149–184.

Douglas, K.S., Ogloff, J.R.P., Nicholls, T.L. and Grant, I. (1999b) Assessing risk for violence among psychiatric patients: the HCR-20 violence risk assessment scheme and the Psychopathy Checklist: Screening Version, *Journal of Consulting and Clinical Psychology*, 67, pp. 917–930.

Douglas, K.S., Webster, C.D., Hart, S.D., Eaves, D. and Ogloff, J.R.P. (Eds) (2001) *HCR-20 Violence Risk Management Companion Guide* (Burnaby, BC: Mental Health Law and Policy Institute, Simon Fraser University).

Douglas, K.S., Ogloff, J.R.P. and Hart, S.D. (2003) Evaluation of a model of violence risk assessment among forensic psychiatric patients, *Psychiatric Services*, 54, pp. 1372–1379.

Douglas, K.S., Yeomans, M. and Boer, D.P. (2005) Comparative validity analysis of multiple measures of violence risk in a sample of criminal offenders, *Criminal Justice and Behavior*, 32, pp. 479–510.

Grove, W.M. and Meehl, P.E. (1996) Comparative efficiency of informal (subjective, impressionistic) and formal (mechanical, algorithmic) prediction procedures: the clinical-statistical controversy, *Psychology, Public Policy, and Law*, 2, pp. 293–323.

Grove, W.M., Zald, D.H., Lebow, B.S., Snitz, B.E. and Nelson, C. (2000) Clinical versus mechanical prediction: a meta-analysis, *Psychological Assessment*, 12, pp. 19–30.

Grubin, D. (1998) *Sex Offending Against Children: Understanding the Risk*, Police Research Series, Paper 99 (London, UK: Home Office).

Hanson, R.K. (1997) *The Development of a Brief Actuarial Scale for Sexual Offence Recidivism* (Ottawa: Department of the Solicitor General of Canada).

Hanson, R.K. (2005) *The Validity of Static-99 with Older Sexual Offenders* (Ottawa: Department of Public Safety and Emergency Preparedness Canada).

Hanson, R.K. (2006) Does Static-99 predict recidivism among older sexual offenders? *Sexual Abuse: A Journal of Research and Treatment*, 18, pp. 343–355.

Hanson, R.K. and Bussière, M.T. (1998) Predicting relapse: a meta-analysis of sexual offender recidivism studies, *Journal of Consulting and Clinical Psychology*, 66, pp. 348–362.

Hanson, R.K. and Thornton, D. (1999) *Static-99: Improving Actuarial Risk Assessments for Sex Offenders* (Ottawa: Department of the Solicitor General of Canada).

Hare, R.D. (1991) *The Hare Psychopathy Checklist-Revised* (Toronto, Ontario, Canada: Multi-Health Systems).

Hare, R.D. (2003) *The Hare Psychopathy Checklist-Revised*, 2nd edn (Toronto, Ontario, Canada: Multi-Health Systems).

Harris, G. (2003) Men in his category have a 50% likelihood, but which half is he in? Comments on Berlin, Galbreath, Geary, and McGlone, *Sexual Abuse: A Journal of Research and Treatment*, 15, pp. 389–392.

Harris, G.T., Rice, M.E. and Quinsey, V.L. (1993) Violent recidivism of mentally disordered offenders: the development of a statistical prediction instrument, *Criminal Justice and Behavior*, 20, pp. 315–335.

Harris, G.T., Rice, M.E. and Cormier, C.A. (2002) Prospective replication of the *Violence Risk Appraisal Guide* in predicting violent recidivism among forensic patients, *Law and Human Behavior*, 26, pp. 377–394.

Harris, A., Phenix, A., Hanson, R.K. and Thornton, D. (2003) *Static-99 Coding Rules Revised – 2003* (Ottawa: Department of the Solicitor General of Canada).

Harris, G.T., Rice, M.E. and Camilleri, J.A. (2004) Applying a forensic actuarial instrument (the *Violence Risk Appraisal Guide*) to nonforensic patients, *Journal of Interpersonal Violence*, 19, pp. 1063–1074.

Hart, S.D. (1998) The role of psychopathy in assessing risk for violence: conceptual and methodological issues, *Legal and Criminological Psychology*, 3, pp. 121–137.

Hart, S.D., Cox, D. and Hare, R.D. (1995) *The Hare Psychopathy Checklist: Screening Version (PCL:SV)* (Toronto, Ontario, Canada: Multi-Health Systems).

Hart, S.D., Kropp, P.R. and Laws, D.R. (2003) *The Risk for Sexual Violence Protocol (RSVP): Structured Professional Guidelines for Assessing Risk of Sexual Violence* (Vancouver, British Columbia: Mental Health, Law, and Policy Institute, Simon Fraser University and British Columbia Institute on Family Violence).

Hart, S.D., Michie, C. and Cooke, D.J. (in press) The precision of actuarial risk assessment instruments: evaluating the 'margins of error' of group versus individual predictions of violence, *British Journal of Psychiatry*.

Heilbrun, K. (1997) Prediction versus management models relevant to risk assessment: the importance of legal decision-making context, *Law and Human Behavior*, 21, pp. 347–359.

Heilbrun, K. (2001) *Principles of Forensic Mental Health Assessment* (New York: Kluwer Academic/Plenum Publishers).

Heilbrun, K. and Kramer, G.M. (2001) Update on risk assessment in mentally disordered populations, *Journal of Forensic Psychology Practice*, 1, pp. 55–63.

Hilton, N.Z., Harris, G.T., Rice, M.E., Lang, C., Cormier, C.A. and Lines, K.J. (2004) A brief actuarial assessment for the prediction of wife assault recidivism: the Ontario Domestic Assault Risk Assessment, *Psychological Assessment*, 16, pp. 267–275.

Kleinmuntz, B. (1990) Why we still use our heads instead of formulas: toward an integrative approach, *Psychological Bulletin*, 107, pp. 296–310.

Kropp, P.R. and Hart, S.D. (2000) The Spousal Assault Risk Assessment (SARA) Guide: reliability and validity in adult male offenders, *Law and Human Behavior*, 24, pp. 101–118.

Kropp, P.R., Hart, S.D., Webster, C.D. and Eaves, D. (1994) *Manual for the Spousal Assault Risk Assessment Guide* (Vancouver, BC: The British Columbia Institute on Family Violence).

Kropp, P.R., Hart, S.D., Webster, C.D. and Eaves, D. (1999) *Spousal Assault Risk Assessment Guide: User's Manual* (Toronto: Multi-Health Systems Inc).

Loza, W., Villeneuve, D.B. and Loza-Fanous, A. (2002) Predictive validity of the Violence Risk Appraisal Guide: a tool for assessing violent offender's recidivism, *International Journal of Law and Psychiatry*, 25, pp. 85–92.

Meehl, P.E. (1954) *Clinical Versus Statistical Prediction: A Theoretical Analysis and a Review of the Evidence* (Minneapolis: University of Minnesota Press).

Meehl, P.E. (1957) When shall we use our heads instead of the formula? *Journal of Counseling Psychology*, 4, pp. 268–273.

Meehl, P.E. (1986) Causes and effects of my disturbing little book, *Journal of Personality Assessment*, 50, pp. 370–375.

Melton, G.B., Petrila, J., Poythress, N.G. and Slobogin, C. (1997) *Psychological Evaluations for the Courts: A Handbook for Mental Health Professionals and Lawyers*, 2nd edn (New York: The Guilford Press).

Miller, M. and Morris, N. (1988) Predictions of dangerousness: an argument for limited use, *Violence and Victims*, 3, pp. 263–270.

Monahan, J. (1981) *Predicting Violent Behavior: An Assessment of Clinical Techniques* (Beverly Hills, CA: Sage).

Monahan, J. (2008) Computer-assisted violence risk assessment among people with mental disorder, in D.V. Canter and R. Žukauskienė (Eds) *Psychology, Crime and Law: Bridging the Gap* (Aldershot, UK: Ashgate).

Monahan, J., Steadman, H.J., Silver, E., Appelbaum, P., Robbins, P.C., Mulvey, E.P. *et al.* (2001) *Rethinking Risk Assessment: The MacArthur Study of Mental Disorder and Violence* (Oxford: Oxford University Press).

Monahan, J., Steadman, H.J., Appelbaum, P.S., Grisso, T., Mulvey, E.P., Roth, L.H., *et al.* (2005) *Classification of Violence Risk (COVR)* (Lutz, FL: Psychological Assessment Resources).

Mossman, D. (1994) Assessing predictions of violence: being accurate about accuracy, *Journal of Consulting and Clinical Psychology*, 62, pp. 783–792.

Mullen, P.E. (2000) Dangerousness, risk, and the prediction of probability, in M. G. Gelder, J.J. Lopez-Ibor and N. Andreasen (Eds) *New Oxford Textbook of Psychiatry: Vol. 2*, pp. 2066–2078 (Oxford: Oxford University Press).

Nicholls, T.L., Ogloff, J.R.P. and Douglas, K.S. (2004) Assessing risk for violence among male and female civil psychiatric patients: the HCR–20, PCL:SV, and McNiel and Binder's screening measure, *Behavioral Sciences and the Law*, 22, pp. 127–158.

Nicholls, T.L., Brink, J., Desmarais, S.L., Webster, C.D. and Martin, M. (2006) The Short-Term Assessment of Risk and Treatability (START): a prospective validation study in a forensic psychiatric sample, *Assessment*, 13, pp. 313–327.

Ogloff, J.R.P. and Daffern, M. (2004) Dynamic Appraisal of Situational Aggression: Inpatient Version (Fairfield, Victoria, Australia: Centre for Forensic Behavioural Science, Monash University and Forensicare).

Ogloff, J.R.P. and Daffern, M. (2006) The dynamic appraisal of situational aggression: an instrument to assess risk for imminent aggression in psychiatric inpatients, Behavioral Sciences and the Law, 24, pp. 799–813.

Ogloff, J.R.P. and Davis, M.R. (2005) Assessing risk for violence in the Australian context, in D. Chappell and P. Wilson (Eds) *Crime and Justice in the New Millennium*, pp. 301–338 (Chatswood: Lexis Nexis Butterworths).

Otto, R.K. (2000) Assessing and managing violence risk in outpatient settings, *Journal of Clinical Psychology*, 56, pp. 1239–1262.

Quinsey, V.L., Rice, M.E., Harris, G.T. and Cormier, C.A. (1998) *Violent Offenders: Appraising and Managing Risk* (Washington, DC: American Psychological Association).

Quinsey, V.L., Rice, M.E., Harris, G.T. and Cormier, C.A. (2006) *Violent Offenders: Appraising and Managing Risk*, 2nd edn (Washington, DC: American Psychological Association).

Rice, M. and Harris, G. (1997) Cross-validation and extension of the *Violence Risk Appraisal Guide* for child molesters and rapists, *Law and Human Behavior*, 21, pp. 231–241.

Sarbin, T.R. (1943) A contribution to the study of actuarial and individual methods of prediction, *American Journal of Sociology*, 48, pp. 593–602.

Seto, M. (2005) Is more better? Combining actuarial risk scales to predict recidivism among adult sex offenders, *Psychological Assessment*, 17, pp. 156–167.

Steadman, H.J. (2000) From dangerousness to risk assessment of community violence: taking stock at the turn of the century, *Journal of the American Academy of Psychiatry and the Law*, 28, pp. 265–271.

Steadman, H. and Cocozza, J. (1974) *Careers of the Criminally Insane* (Lexington, MA: Lexington Books).

Steadman, H. and Halfon, A. (1971) The Baxstrom patients: backgrounds and outcome, *Seminars in Psychiatry*, 3, pp. 376–386.

Strand, S., Belfrage, H., Fransson, G. and Levander, S. (1999) Clinical and risk management factors in risk prediction of mentally disordered offenders: more important than actuarial data? *Legal and Criminological Psychology*, 4, pp. 67–76.

Thornberry, T. and Jacoby, J. (1979) *The Criminally Insane: A Community Follow-up of Mentally Ill Offenders* (Chicago: University of Chicago Press).

Thorndyke E.L. (1911) *Animal Intelligence* (New York: Macmillan).

Webster, C.D. (1997) A guide for conducting risk assessments, in C.D. Webster and M. A. Jackson (Eds) *Impulsivity: Theory, Assessment, and Treatment*, pp. 343–358 (New York: The Guilford Press).

Webster, C.D., Douglas, K.S., Eaves, D. and Hart, S.D. (1997) *HCR-20: Assessing Risk for Violence*, version 2 (Burnaby, BC: Mental Health, Law, and Policy Institute, Simon Fraser University).

Webster, C. D., Martin, M., Brink, J. and Middleton, C. (2004) *Short-term Assessment of Risk and Treatability* (Hamilton, Canada: St. Joseph's Healthcare and Forensic Psychiatric Services Commission).

West, A. G. (2001) Current approaches to sex-offender risk assessment: a critical review, *British Journal of Forensic Practice*, 3, pp. 31–41.

Wollert, R. (2006) Low base rates limit expert certainty when current actuarials are used to identify sexually violent predators: an application of Bayes's theorem, *Psychology, Public Policy, and Law*, 12, pp. 56–85.

Wong, S. C. P. and Gordon, A. (1998) *Violence Risk Scale* (Saskatoon, Saskatchewan, Canada: Department of Psychology, University of Saskatchewan).

Wong, S. C. P. and Gordon, A. (2006) The validity and reliability of the Violence Risk Scale: a treatment-friendly violence risk assessment tool, *Psychology, Public Policy, and Law*, 12, pp. 279–309.

Wong, S. C. P., Olver, M. E., Nicholaichuk, T. and Gordon, A. (2004–2006) *Violence Risk Scale – Sex Offender Version* (Saskatoon, Saskatchewan, Canada: Department of Psychology, University of Saskatchewan).

Chapter 12

Computer-assisted Violence Risk Assessment among People with Mental Disorder

John Monahan

After three decades of largely depressing research on the abilities of mental health professionals at predicting violence among people with mental disorder, the journals have become replete with guardedly optimistic studies indicating that actuarial instruments may succeed where unstructured clinical judgment has failed. For the first time, relatively accurate assessments of the risk of violence that a patient poses may be within the realm of science rather than science fiction.

The general superiority of statistical over clinical risk assessment in the behavioral sciences has been known for almost half a century (Meehl 1954; Swets *et al.* 2000). Despite this, and despite a long and successful history of actuarial risk assessment in bail and parole decision making in criminology (Champion 1994), there have been few attempts until recently to develop actuarial tools for the specific task of assessing risk of violence to others among people with mental disorder. For example, Steadman and Cocozza (1974), in an early study of mentally disordered offenders, developed a Legal Dangerousness Scale based on the presence or absence of a juvenile record and a conviction for a violent crime, the number of previous incarcerations, and the severity of the current offense. This scale, along with the patient's age, was significantly associated with subsequent violent behavior.

More recently, the Violence Risk Appraisal Guide (VRAG) was developed from a sample of over 600 men from a maximum-security hospital in Canada (Quinsey *et al.* 1998). All had been charged with serious criminal offenses. Approximately 50 predictor variables were coded from institutional files. The criterion measure used to develop the actuarial instrument was any new criminal charge for a violent offense, or return to the institution for a similar act, over a time at risk in the community that averaged approximately seven years after discharge. A series of analyses identified 12 variables for inclusion in the instrument. These 12 variables were used to place patients into one of nine categories reflecting their actuarial risk of future violence. In a prospective replication of this research with 347 male forensic patients, 11% of the patients who scored in category 1 on the VRAG were later found to commit a new violent act, compared with 42% of the patients in category 5, and 100% of the patients in category 9 (Harris *et al.* 2002).

   In this chapter, I will describe the most recent attempt to develop a comprehensive actuarial procedure to assess the risk that a person being discharged from a mental health facility will be violent to others in the next several months. This actuarial instrument, called the Classification of Violence Risk (COVR), is the first empirically-grounded software-based procedure for violence risk assessment. First, I will describe the development of the actuarial instrument. Second, I will describe its validation. Third, I will address the issue of cut-off scores. Finally, I will reflect on the role of clinical judgment in actuarial risk assessment.

The Development of the Classification of Violence Risk

The MacArthur Risk Assessment Study (Steadman *et al.* 1994; Monahan *et al.* 2001) assessed a large sample of male and female acute civil patients at several facilities on a wide variety of variables believed to be related to the occurrence of violence. The risk factors fall into four domains. One domain, 'dispositional' variables, refers to the demographic factors of age, race, gender, and social class, as well as to personality variables (e.g., impulsivity and anger control) and neurological factors (e.g., head injury). A second domain, 'historical' variables, includes significant events experienced by subjects in the past, such as family history, work history, mental hospitalization history, history of violence, and criminal and juvenile justice history. A third domain, 'contextual' variables, refers to indices of current social supports, social networks, and stress, as well as to physical aspects of the environment, such as the presence of weapons. The final domain, 'clinical' variables, includes types and symptoms of mental disorder, personality disorder, drug and alcohol abuse, and level of functioning. Community violence is measured during interviews with the patients and with a collateral conducted post-discharge in the community, as well as from a review of official records. Data are available for two time periods, the first 20-weeks after discharge, and the first year after discharge. First, I will address a number of risk factors for violence (Kraemer *et al.* 1997) on their own merits, and then consider the risk factors in combination.

   Variables are highlighted here based on their clinical and theoretical prominence in the field of violence risk assessment. Variables considered include both those that have long been considered in the criminological literature to be prime risk factors for violence, as well as those whose status as important risk factors for violence has been advanced by clinicians.

Gender

Findings from the MacArthur research that men are no more likely to be violent than women over the course of the one-year follow-up differ dramatically from results generally found in the criminological literature, but not from findings of other studies of men and women with a mental disorder. While the overall prevalence rates are similar for women and men, there are some substantial gender differences in the quality or context of the violence committed (Robbins *et al.* 2003). Men are more likely to have been drinking or using street drugs, and less likely to have been adhering to prescribed psychotropic medication, prior to committing violence. Women are more likely to target family members and to be violent in the home. The violence committed by men is more likely to result in serious injury – requiring treatment by a physician – than the violence committed by women.

Prior Violence and Criminality

The MacArthur data suggest quite clearly that, regardless of how the measure is obtained, prior violence and criminality are strongly associated with the post-discharge violent behavior of psychiatric patients.

Childhood Experiences and Violence

Although prior *physical* abuse as a child was associated with post-discharge violence, prior *sexual* abuse was not. While patients' reports of deviant behaviors by fathers and mothers, such as excessive alcohol and drug use were associated with increased rates of post-discharge violence, having lived with either the father or the mother prior to age 15 was associated with a decreased rate of violence.

Neighborhood Context

The MacArthur findings suggest that research efforts aimed at assessing violence risk among discharged psychiatric patients may benefit from specifying a role for the neighborhood contexts into which patients are discharged, in addition to measuring their individual characteristics. That is, violence by persons with mental disorders may be, in part, a function of the high-crime neighborhoods in which they typically reside. The association between race and violence, for example, was rendered insignificant when statistical controls were applied to the crime rate of the neighborhoods in which the patients resided.

Diagnosis

The presence of a co-occurring diagnosis of substance abuse or dependence was found to be a key factor in the occurrence of violence. A diagnosis of a major mental disorder was associated with a lower rate of violence than a diagnosis of an 'other' mental disorder, primarily a personality or adjustment disorder. Further, within the major mental disorders, a diagnosis of schizophrenia was associated with lower rates of violence than a diagnosis of depression or of bipolar disorder, as several other studies have found (e.g., Gardner *et al.* 1996; Quinsey *et al.* 1998).

Psychopathy

Despite the low base rate of psychopathy per se, as measured by scores on the Hare Psychopathy Checklist: Screening Version (Hare PCL:SV) among the civil psychiatric patients studied, limited traits of psychopathy and antisocial behavior were predictive of future violence. The Hare PCL:SV added incremental validity to a host of covariates in predicting violence, including recent violence, criminal history, substance abuse, and other personality disorders. However, most of the Hare PCL:SV's basic *and* unique predictive power is based upon its 'antisocial behavior' factor, rather than the 'emotional detachment' factor (cf. Skeem *et al.* 2005).

Delusions

The MacArthur data suggest that the presence of delusions does not predict higher rates of violence among recently discharged psychiatric patients. This conclusion remains accurate even when the type of delusions and their content (including violent content) is taken into account. In particular, a relationship between 'threat/control-override' delusions and violence (Link and Stueve 1994) were not confirmed in the MacArthur study. On the other hand, non-delusional suspiciousness – perhaps involving a tendency toward misperception of others' behavior as indicating hostile intent – does appear to be linked with subsequent violence, and may account for the findings of previous studies.

Hallucinations

Although command hallucinations per se did not elevate violence risk, if the voices commanded violent acts, the likelihood of their occurrence over the subsequent year was significantly increased. These results should reinforce the tendency toward caution that clinicians have always had when dealing with patients who report voices commanding them to be violent.

Violent Thoughts

The MacArthur results indicate that when patients report violent thoughts during hospitalization, there is indeed a greater likelihood that they will engage in violent acts during the first 20 weeks and during the year following discharge. It was especially increased for patients who continued to report imagined violence after discharge.

Anger

Patients with high scores on the Novaco Anger Scale at hospitalization were twice as likely as those with low anger scores to engage in violent acts after discharge. The effect, although neither highly predictive nor large in absolute terms, was statistically significant.

A few of the variables from the MacArthur Study examined here were quite predictive of violence, as expected (e.g., prior violence). Contrary to expectations, other variables were found not to be 'risk factors' for violence at all in our sample (e.g., delusions, schizophrenia). Most criminological and clinical variables we examined, however, had a complex relationship to violence. The complexity of the findings reported here underscores the difficulty of identifying *main-effect* or *univariate* predictors of violence – variables that are across-the-board risk factors for violence in all populations. This complexity is no doubt one of the principal reasons why clinicians, relying on a fixed set of individual risk factors, have had such difficulty making accurate risk assessments. It suggests the need to take an *interactional* approach to violence risk assessment, such that the same variable could be a positive risk factor for violence in one group, unrelated to violence in another group, and a protective factor against violence in a third group. Such an interactional strategy for violence risk assessment was the one adopted in the MacArthur Study.

Risk Factors in Combination

The MacArthur Study developed what the researchers called an 'Iterative Classification Tree,' or ICT. A classification tree approach to violence risk assessment is predicated upon an interactive and contingent model of violence, one that allows many different combinations of risk factors to classify a person as high or low risk. Whether a particular question is asked in any clinical assessment grounded in this approach depends on the answers given to each prior question by the person being evaluated. Based on a sequence established by the classification tree, a first question is asked of all persons being assessed. Contingent on the answer to that question, one or another second question is posed, and so on, until each person is classified into a category on the basis of violence risk. This contrasts with the usual approach to actuarial risk assessment in which a common set of questions is asked of everyone being assessed and every answer is weighted and summed to produce a score that can be used for purposes of categorization.

In the first test of the ICT method (Steadman *et al.* 2000) focused on how well the method performed in making violence risk assessments under ideal conditions (i.e., with few constraints on the time or resources necessary to gather risk factors). For example, the risk factor that most clearly differentiated high risk from low risk groups was the Hare Psychopathy Checklist: Screening Version (Hare PCL:SV) (Hart *et al.* 1995). Given that the full Hare PCL-R requires several hours for data gathering and administration – the Screening Version alone takes over 1 hour to administer – resource constraints in many non-forensic clinical settings will preclude its use. Monahan *et al.* (2000) sought to increase the utility of this actuarial method for real-world clinical decision-making by applying the method to a set of violence risk factors commonly available in clinical records or capable of being routinely assessed in clinical practice. Results showed that the ICT partitioned three-quarters of a sample of psychiatric patients into one of two categories with regard to their risk of violence toward others during the first 20 weeks after discharge. One category consisted of groups whose rates of violence were no more than half the base-rate of the total patient sample (i.e., equal to or less than 9% violent). The other category consisted of groups whose rates of violence were at least twice the base-rate of the total patient sample (i.e., equal to or greater than 37% violent). The actual prevalence of violence within individual Risk Groups varied from 3% to 53%.

Finally, rather than pitting different risk assessment models against one another and choosing the one model that appears 'best', Monahan *et al.* (2001) adopted an approach that integrates the predictions of many different risk assessment models, each of which may capture a different but important facet of the interactive relationship between the measured risk factors and violence. Using this 'multiple models' approach, these researchers ultimately combined the results of five prediction models generated by the Iterative Classification Tree methodology. By combining the predictions of several risk assessment models, the multiple models approach minimizes the problem of data overfitting that can result when a single 'best' prediction model is used. Monahan *et al.* (2001) were able to place all patients into one of five risk classes for which the prevalence of violence during the first 20 weeks following discharge into the community varied between 1% and 76%, with an area under the Receiver Operating Characteristic curve (Swets *et al.* 2000) of 0.88.

Validating the Classification of Violence Risk

After the results of the MacArthur Violence Risk Assessment had been published and all the data placed on the web for public use,[1] a National Institute of Mental Health grant was obtained that allowed not only the development of software for violence risk assessment, but also the prospective validation of that software (Monahan *et al.* 2005b). The newly developed software was administered to independent samples of acute civil inpatients at two sites (total *n* = 157). Patients classified by the software as high or low risk of violence were followed in the community for 20 weeks after discharge. Expected rates of violence in the low and high risk groups were 1% and 64%, respectively. Observed rates of violence in the low and high risk groups were 9% and 35%, respectively, when a strict definition of violence was used, and 9% and 49%, respectively, when a slightly more inclusive definition of violence was used. These results indicated that software incorporating the multiple ICT models may be helpful to clinicians who are faced with making decisions about discharge planning for acute civil inpatients (Monahan *et al.* 2005a).[2]

---

1   www.macarthur.virginia.edu
2   The software is available at www.parinc.com.

The Choice of Cut-off Scores in Actuarial Risk Assessment

To trigger an intervention to manage – i.e., to reduce – violence risk, as in the mental health or criminal justice interventions described above, it is necessary to apply a cut-off or 'decision threshold' (Swets *et al.* 2000) to the estimates that risk assessments generate: if the risk estimate is below the decision threshold, then the contemplated action to manage risk is foregone, and if the estimate is at or above the decision threshold, then the contemplated action commences. The choice of decision threshold for managing risk, of course, is itself a decision, and one that in many circumstances belongs to policy makers, and not to the psychologists or psychiatrists who are assessing the risk.

Monahan and Silver (2003) reported a study that directly asked one set of policy makers – judges – where they would set the threshold for one type of risk management decision: whether or not to institute short-term civil commitment as a 'danger to others' of a non-offender with a serious mental disorder. The survey was conducted in the context of an actual violence risk assessment project, the Classification of Violence Risk software, described above.

Judges enrolled in the Graduate Program for Judges at the University of Virginia served as subjects. The judges had a mean of ten years experience on the bench. Approximately 90% sat on state appellate courts at the time of the research (and many had been trial judges in the past).

The MacArthur Study was briefly described to the judges, and they were presented with the findings on the five final 'risk classes' reported in that research. The judges were then asked the question:

> If this violence risk assessment software were administered to a person who was mentally disordered, and if the mental health professional who administered the software agreed with the estimate it produced, *what is the lowest likelihood of violence to others that you would accept* as fulfilling the 'dangerousness' criterion for authorizing short-term civil commitment?

The response categories they were given to check off were the same five categories as in the actual Classification of Violence Risk software: Group 1 (1% probability of violence), Group 2 (8% probability of violence), Group 3 (26% probability of violence), Group 4 (56% probability of violence), and Group 5 (76% probability of violence).

The results were clear: judges in this study drew a line between Risk Classes 2 and 3 as their cut-off for the risk management activity being contemplated. In the terms proposed by Swets *et al.* (2000), they chose Risk Class 3 – a 26% likelihood of committing a violent act – as their decision threshold for short-term civil commitment as dangerous to others. That is, on average, the judges were of the view that people with a serious mental disorder whose risk was assessed by the MacArthur instrument as being in Risk Classes 1 or 2 did not qualify for commitment, and that people with a serious mental disorder whose assessed risk placed them in Risk Classes 3, 4, or 5 did qualify for commitment. Of course, if the decision presented to the subjects had been different from short-term civil commitment (e.g., outpatient commitment), or if the type of violence being predicted had been different from the given illustration of battery with injury (e.g., sexual violence), or if the person had also been convicted of a crime, other decision thresholds might have been chosen.

The choice of a decision threshold has many and varied consequences. For example, if one applied the decision threshold of Risk Class 3 or higher to the data produced in the MacArthur Study, the risk assessment upon which the contemplated risk management activity was predicated (short-term civil commitment, in this case) would have a true positive rate of 44.0% (and therefore a false positive rate of 56.0%), a true negative rate of 96.1% (and therefore a false negative rate of 3.9%), a sensitivity of 86.9 and a specificity of 74.4. Slightly over three-quarters of the sample (76.8%) would be correctly classified as violent or non-violent. If the risk management activity was completely successful at preventing the predicted violence, then 91.1% of all the violence committed by this sample of patients would be prevented. To accomplish this, however, it would be necessary to intervene in the lives of 37.1% of the patients (of whom more than half (56.0%) would not have been violent even without the intervention). To the extent that the risk management activity was less than completely successful, the percentage of all violence prevented would decline.

The Clinical Use of Actuarial Estimates

Should actuarial risk assessment such as the COVR used to supplant clinical judgment of violence risk? Or, is actuarial risk assessment best considered a tool – a very powerful tool – to support the exercise of clinical judgment regarding violence risk? The question is not easily or unambiguously answered (cf. Quinsey *et al.* 1998).

Two primary reasons are given in support of allowing clinicians the option to use their judgment to review, and perhaps to discard, actuarial violence risk assessment estimates. The first reason can be termed questionable validity generalization and the second rare risk or protective factors.

Questionable Validity Generalization

The COVR was validated on a sample that consisted of civilly hospitalized patients in the United States, who were between 18 and 60 years old. Is the considerable predictive validity of the COVR generalizable to forensic patients, or to people in Lithuania, or to people who are less than 18 or more than 60 years old, or to the assessment of people who have not recently been hospitalized? The predictive validity of this instrument may generalize widely. Yet there comes a point at which the sample to which an actuarial instrument is being applied appears so fundamentally dissimilar to the sample on which it was validated that one would be hard pressed to castigate the evaluator who took the actuarial estimate as advisory rather than conclusive.

Rare Risk or Protective Factors

The second reason often given in defense of allowing a clinician the option to review and revise actuarial risk estimates is that the clinician may note the presence of rare risk or protective factors in a given case, and that these factors – precisely because they are rare – will not have been properly taken into account in the construction of the actuarial instrument. This issue has been termed broken leg countervailings by Grove and Meehl (1996, following Meehl, 1954). The story is simple: a researcher has developed an actuarial instrument that predicts with great accuracy when people will go to the movies, and the instrument yields an estimate of 0.80 that a given individual, Professor Smith, will go to the movies tomorrow. But the researcher then learns that Professor Smith has just broken his leg and is immobilized in a hip cast. 'Obviously, it would be absurd to rely on the actuarial prediction in the face of this overwhelmingly prepotent fact' (Grove and Meehl 1996, p. 307). While Grove and Meehl (1996, p. 307) call the countervailing of actuarial risk estimates by rare events 'one of the few intellectually interesting concerns of the antistatistical clinicians', they are skeptical about its applicability to areas such as violence risk assessment. In the broken leg story, they state, there is 'an almost perfectly reliable ascertainment of a fact [a broken leg] and an almost perfect correlation between that fact and the kind of fact being predicted [going to the movies]. Neither one of these delightful conditions obtains in the usual kind of social science prediction of behavior from probabilistic inferences' (Grove and Meehl 1996, p. 308).

In the context of actuarial instruments for assessing violence risk, the most frequently mentioned 'broken leg' is a direct threat, that is, an apparently serious statement of intention to do violence to a named victim. Assuming that most minimally rational people who do not want to be in a hospital can consciously suppress the verbalization of such intentions while they are being evaluated, direct threats are presumably rare, and for that reason will not emerge as items on an actuarial instrument. Yet as Hanson (1998, p. 61), in the context of predicting violence among sex offenders, has stated, 'Although I am aware of no study that has examined the relationship between behavioral intentions and sexual offense recidivism, it would be foolish for an evaluator to dismiss an offender's stated intention to reoffend'.

Consider the example of delusions. The MacArthur Study found that the presence of delusions was not generally a risk factor for violence (see above). Yet Appelbaum *et al.* (2000) have cautioned against ignoring delusions in a given case:

> Even on their face, [these data] do not disprove the clinical wisdom that holds that persons who have acted violently in the past on the basis of their delusions may well do so again. Nor do they provide support for neglecting the potential threat of an acutely destabilized, delusional person in an emergency setting, in which the person's past history of violence and community supports are unknown. (Appelbaum *et al.* 2000, p. 571)

It may be instructive in thinking about this difficult issue, as it has been in thinking about other topics in this area (Monahan and Steadman 1996), to analogize violence prediction to weather prediction. The National Weather Service (NWS) routinely collects data on 'risk factors' (e.g., barometric pressure) known to be predictors of one or another type of weather. This information is analyzed by computer programs that yield what the NWS refers to as 'objective' (what would here be called actuarial) predictions of various weather events. These predictions are given at regular intervals to meteorologists in local areas. The local meteorologists – who refer to the actuarial estimates as 'guidance, not gospel' – then review and, if they believe necessary, revise them. For example, a local meteorologist might temper an objective prediction of 'sunny and dry' for the forecast area if he or she looked out the window and saw threatening clouds approaching. A 'subjective' (what would here be called clinical) prediction is then issued to the media.

Weather forecasting is one area in which the clinical review and revision of actuarial risk estimates has been empirically studied (for others, see Grove and Meehl 1996; Quinsey *et al.* 1998). Clinical involvement actually increases, rather than decreases, predictive accuracy in the meteorological context. The clinically revised predictions of temperature and precipitation are consistently more valid than the unrevised actuarial ones (Carter and Polger 1986).

Will clinical review and revision increase the validity of actuarial predictions of violence, as they increase the validity of actuarial predictions of the weather? Reasonable people will differ on the aptness of the weather analogy. As with validity generalization, above, the advisability of allowing clinicians to take into account rare risk or protective factors is ultimately an empirical question. A careful study of (a) how often, when they review actuarial risk estimates, clinicians feel it necessary to revise those estimates; (b) why clinicians feel it necessary to revise the actuarial estimates (e.g., the specific reason that the validity of the actuarial instrument is believed not to generalize, or the specific rare risk or protective factor that is believed to be present); and (c) how much clinicians want to revise actuarial risk estimates, would be invaluable. Pending such research, we believe that actuarial instruments (including, among others, the multiple-ICT presented here) are best viewed as 'tools' for clinical assessment – tools that support, rather than replace, the exercise of clinical judgment.

Conclusion

A computer-assisted tool to assist clinicians to assess violence risk among people hospitalized for mental disorder has recently been developed and validated in the United States. Whether the validity of this Classification of Violence Risk software can be generalized to other people (e.g., people without mental disorder, people outside the United States) or to other settings (e.g., outpatient settings, criminal justice settings) awaits further empirical research.

References

Appelbaum, P., Robbins, P. and Monahan, J. (2000) Violence and delusions: data from the MacArthur Violence Risk Assessment Study, *American Journal of Psychiatry*, 157, pp. 566–572.

Carter, G. and Polger, P. (1986) *A 20–year Summary of National Weather Service Verification Results for Temperature and Precipitation*, Technical Memorandum NWS FCST 31 (Washington, DC: National Oceanic and Atmospheric Administration).

Champion, D. (1994) *Measuring Offender Risk: A Criminal Justice Sourcebook* (Westport, CT: Greenwood Press).

Gardner, W., Lidz, C., Mulvey, E. and Shaw, E. (1996) A comparison of actuarial methods for identifying repetitively violent patients with mental illness, *Law and Human Behavior*, 20, pp. 35–48.

Grove, W. and Meehl, P. (1996) Comparative efficacy of informal (subjective, impressionistic) and formal (mechanical, algorithmic) prediction procedures: the clinical–statistical controversy, *Psychology, Public Policy, and Law*, 2, pp. 293–323.

Hanson, R. (1998) What do we know about sex offender risk assessment? *Psychology, Public Policy, and Law*, 4, pp. 50–72.

Harris, G., Rice, M. and Cormier, C. (2002) Prospective replication of the Violence Risk Appraisal Guide in predicting violent recidivism among forensic patients, *Law and Human Behavior*, 26, pp. 377–394.

Hart, S., Cox, D. and Hare, R. (1995) *The Hare Psychopathy Checklist: Screening Version. Multi-Health Systems* (Niagara, New York).

Kraemer, H., Kazdin, A., Offord, D., Kessler, R., Jensen, P. and Kupfer, D. (1997) Coming to terms with the terms of risk, *Archives of General Psychiatry*, 54, p. 337.

Link, B. and Stueve, A. (1994) Psychotic symptoms and the violent/illegal behavior of mental patients compared to community controls, In J. Monahan and H. Steadman (Eds) *Violence and Mental Disorder: Developments in Risk Assessment*, pp. 137–159 (Chicago, IL: The University of Chicago Press).

Meehl, P. (1954) *Clinical Versus Statistical Prediction: A Theoretical Analysis and a Review of the Evidence* (Minneapolis; University of Minnesota).

Monahan, J. and Silver, E. (2003) Judicial decision thresholds for violence risk management, *International Journal of Forensic Mental Health*, 2, pp. 1–6.

Monahan, J. and Steadman, H. (1996) Violent storms and violent people: how meteorology can inform risk communication in mental health law, *American Psychologist*, 51, pp. 931–938.

Monahan, J., Steadman, H., Appelbaum, P., Robbins, P., Mulvey, E., Silver, E., Roth, L., and Grisso, T. (2000) Developing a clinically useful actuarial tool for assessing violence risk, *British Journal of Psychiatry*, 176, pp. 312–319.

Monahan, J., Steadman, H., Silver, E., Appelbaum, A., Robbins, P., Mulvey, E., Roth, L., Grisso, T. and Banks, S. (2001) *Rethinking Risk Assessment: The MacArthur Study of Mental Disorder and Violence* (New York: Oxford University Press).

Monahan, J., Steadman, H., Appelbaum, P., Grisso, T., Mulvey, E., Roth, L., Robbins, P., Banks, S. and Silver, E. (2005a) *The Classification of Violence Risk* (Lutz, FL: Psychological Assessment Resources).

Monahan, J, Steadman, H., Robbins, P., Appelbaum, P., Banks, S., Grisso, T., Heilbrun, K., Mulvey, E., Roth, L. and Silver, E. (2005b) An actuarial model of violence risk assessment for persons with mental disorders, *Psychiatric Services*, 56, pp. 810–815.

Quinsey, V., Harris, G., Rice, M. and Cormier, C. (1998) *Violent offenders: Appraising and managing risk.* Washington, DC: American Psychological Association.

Robbins, P., Monahan, J. and Silver, E. (2003) Mental disorder and violence: The moderating role of gender, *Law and Human Behavior*, 27, pp. 561–571.

Skeem, J., Miller, J., Mulvey, E., Tiemann, J. and Monahan, J. (2005) Using a Five Factor lens to explore the relation between personality traits and violence in psychiatric patients, *Journal of Consulting and Clinical Psychology*, 73, pp. 455–465.

Steadman, H. and Cocozza, J. (1974) *Careers of the Criminally Insane* (Lexington, MA: Lexington Books).

Steadman, H., Monahan, J., Appelbaum, P., Grisso, T., Mulvey, E., Roth, L., Robbins, P., and Klassen, D. (1994) Designing a new generation of risk assessment research, in: J. Monahan and H. Steadman (Eds) *Violence and Mental Disorder: Developments in Risk Assessment*, pp. 297–318 (Chicago: University of Chicago Press).

Steadman, H., Silver, E., Monahan, J., Appelbaum, P., Robbins, P., Mulvey, E., Grisso, T., Roth, L. and Banks, S. (2000) A classification tree approach to the development of actuarial violence risk assessment tools, *Law and Human Behavior*, 24, pp. 83–100.

Swets, J., Dawes, R. and Monahan, J. (2000) Psychological science can improve diagnostic decisions, *Psychological Science in the Public Interest*, 1, pp. 1–26.

Chapter 13

Does the Law Use Even a Small Proportion of What Legal Psychology has to Offer?

Viktoras Justickis

Introduction

The resources of modern psychology are really huge. They include multiple branches, dealing with practically all areas of life. Several focus upon psychological problems of the law, while all the others are open for use in solving legal problems. Does the law use even a small proportion of what psychology has to offer? How much psychology does the law demand and how much does it use? What precludes the law from using it more?

These are questions this chapter focuses on.

The chapter consists of four parts. The first tries to answer the question of how much psychology the law needs. The second compares this need with reality. The third part reviews reasons that restrain the use of psychology in the law. Current explanations of 'resistance' of the law against psychology are critically reviewed and alternatives are proposed. The final part deals with ways in which these 'incompatibility' problems can be resolved.

How much Psychology the Law ought to Use

We shall refer to this as the 'demand of law for psychology', a situation when a legal problem can be solved more efficiently by using psychological knowledge. For example, the testimony of a witness can be examined without any modern witness psychology; however, it can be done much better with this knowledge.

Modern law is a huge empire consisting of many single 'kingdoms' – branches of law: civil, criminal, church, labor, constitutional, international, European, environmental, etc. Their numbers are different in different countries (see, for example, Table 1, which shows the most popular branches). Each kingdom – a branch – is 'populated' with many legal regulations (laws and by-laws). Their numbers also can be very different: from a few hundred to many thousands.

Table 13.1   Some branches of law

Administrative law	Church (canonic) law
Civil law	Commercial law
Company law	Constitutional (State) law
Environmental protection law	European law
Executive law	Financial and tax law
Intellectual property law	International criminal law
International private law	Law of land
Marital law	Mass media law
Medicine law	Police law
Space law	Trade law

Each branch of law is also populated with people having to deal with its regulations: lawmakers, officers administering the law (police, courts, lawyers and state attorneys, prison, notaries, etc) and regular people using it.

Which of all the branches, regulations, and people need psychology, and which do not?

Our answer to these questions is simple.

Every branch of law, *every* legal regulation within each branch, *every* single person making or administering the law needs psychology. No law is 'free of psychology'.

The demand of law for psychology is universal for, at least, three reasons.

(1) *Any legal regulation can direct a human action only through a chain of psychological events*
For a legal regulation to affect one's actions, this person has, first of all, to *learn* it (this involves his/her *perception*), next to *understand* it (*thinking*), then to *keep* it in his/her memory until the situation to be regulated by this law will be met (*memory*). In this situation, the person has to *recall* this law and the possible punishment. This prospect should *impress* him – to arouse his fear (*emotions*). Next, this fear must *motivate* the proper action – for example, to deter from offending (*motivation*). Perception, thinking, memory, emotions, motivation – all of them are psychological phenomena. If *any* link fails, it is up to psychology to explain why. All this is true for *every* case in *every* branch of law.

(2) *In any branch of law, any legal regulation can affect one's persona.*
The main objective of a legal regulation is to regulate, directly or indirectly, one's behavior. However, in doing so, any regulation can also affect the *rest of a person's psychology*. The point is that situations in which one deals with justice are usually highly significant, stressful, and, therefore, endangering to one's psychic well-being. The numerous ways in which an encounter with justice can affect one's psychic health are documented by extensive 'therapeutic jurisprudence' studies (see for example the extensive review by Daicoff and Wexler 2003).

The main conclusion following from theses studies is that *every* encounter with any justice may affect the person. This means that this probable effect must be considered when designing or administering every legal regulation, independently of which branch of law it belongs to.

(3)   *In any branch of law, any legal regulation has to ensure the legitimating effect of law*
Every legal regulation is supposed to evoke respect. This respect is one of the important reasons why people obey the law. People must believe that the regulation is just, rightful, and legitimate. Studies on the psychology of legitimacy demonstrated conditions in which such attitude arises. The content, shape of a law, and the way in which it is administrated should meet some psychological demands or the regulation will not be seen as legitimate (Jost and Major 2001).

Again, this is true for *every* branch and *every* legal regulation.
Some conclusions follow from all this.

1. Every legal regulation in every branch of law needs psychology to ensure its regulative effect, its proper (therapeutic) impact upon personality, and to be seen as legitimate.
2. There is a fundamental difference between psychology and other sciences in the scope and way they can be applied in the law.

Aside from psychology, many other sciences are applied in the law. Genetics, ballistics, chemistry, motor mechanics, etc – this is not the complete list. However, as opposed to psychology, these sciences can be applied only to solve some specific tasks; for example, ballistics deals with projectiles and bullet. This, of course, is important in 'shooting' cases. In other situations the law may not need any knowledge of ballistics. Genetics establishes affiliation. This can be important in some family cases, but only in such cases. Motor mechanics can provide the piece of evidence on the condition of a vehicle, but is generally only required in cases where a vehicle is involved.

Conversely, the demand of law for psychology is universal, the law always needs psychology. It is required in every branch and every case. This means that cooperation between lawyers and psychologists ought to run on an everyday, side-by-side basis in every case, in every branch of law.

This ought to be the norm, but what is it like in reality?

How much Psychology does the Law Use?

Perhaps, the most representative of the state of art are current fundamental manuals on psychology in law. Their mission is to provide students with a complete view of the subject and its applications. I have focused upon five such manuals (Ackerman 1999; Constanzo 2004; Goldstein 2003; Kapardis 1997; Melton *et al.* 1997). A review of these books shows that even though *all* branches of law need psychology, that is not the picture in given in these publications. In reality, one branch of the law dominates; criminal law. All the manuals discuss only (Kapardis 1997), or mainly, the use of psychology in this branch of law. Four manuals also pay attention to civil law (Ackerman 1999; Constanzo 2004; Goldstain 2003; Melton *et al.* 1997). In two (Goldstain 2003; and Constanzo 2004) a small chapter on Labor law can be found. And this is all.

All the other branches of law (see Table 13.1) are not represented. They are 'free of psychology'.

It is not easy to explain why just criminal law leads. It is not the largest, not the most important, not the most used, not the most modern, not the most developed, and does not having any central or special position in modern law.

We can provide only two (rather weak) explanations of its exceptional place.

Historical   Many pioneers of the application of psychology in law (for example, Hans Gross) were experts in (or just most familiar with) criminal law. For example, the pioneering Hans Gross manual 'Psychology for investigators' dealt only with crimes.

This determined further development for many decades. For example, for a long time forensic psychology had *only* been *criminal* forensic psychology. Therefore, it is still now *mainly* the psychology of criminal law. It is likely that if Hans Gross had been an expert in any other branch of law (for example, Constitutional law) then today this branch would have been leading in the application of psychology.

Psychological   Psychologists, not lawyers, are the driving force for the broader use of psychology. However, psychologists are not experts in *all* branches of law. It is just criminal and (to a lesser degree) civil law that are the most familiar to psychologists. TV and other mass-media, overwhelmed with criminal cases, play a great part in forming psychologists' ideas on law. Through watching TV and reading detective stories one can get sound ideas on criminal, and, perhaps, civil law; however, not on commercial, canonical, European and other branches of law. Therefore, only these most familiar branches attract all the attention and efforts of psychologists. It is here they channel all their energy. All other branches are still perceived by psychologists as 'alien', and, therefore, 'purely juridical', 'unsuitable' for psychology.

Both the above explanations are mere suppositions. However, two points are certain.

First, we can see that today psychology is applied only in a few of the many tens of branches of law. These represent only a small part (perhaps, 5–10%) of modern law. The rest are still 'free of psychology'.

Second, we can trace a clear trend in the long-term development of the use of psychology in law. This development started from criminal law. After several decades this branch was joined by civil law; lately, both were joined by labor law. Extrapolating this trend, we could forecast that the future development of the application of psychology to law will evolve in the same way, i.e. joining new branches of law. Today we are at the very beginning of this long development.

As mentioned above, each branch of law includes law-making, its administration and use. So far, psychology is used only in law administration. We have no information on any use of psychology in law-making, improving or designing new criminal or civil law.

The application of psychology is even more restricted by the fact that it is applied only in extreme or unusual cases. A court sees no need for psychological examination in its 'usual' cases, when a judge is satisfied with his commonsense explanation. We just do not know how often situations are presented as plain, ordinary, everyday situations when they actually go beyond 'commonsense' and need psychological examination.

This means that there is a great contrast between 'Ought' and 'Is' in the application of psychology within modern law. The real application is only a drop in the ocean of that which is needed.

During the last century, there were several rather short episodes when there were great chances for a significant expansion of psychology in law. The first was the beginning of the twentieth century. It was the peak of legal realism, represented by the great names of Karl Llewellyn, Oliver Holmes, Franz Liszt, and others. They all focused upon the chain of psychological events, mediating the effect of a law upon one's behavior. They flayed the then current legislation that took proper functioning of this chain for granted. They asserted that every single link in this chain can be poor and potentially destroy the whole chain. They insisted that here we will find many reasons for the inefficiency of the law.

There were also other episodes when the smell of a great psychological revolution in law was strong. Thirty years ago, it was the excitement caused by ideas and studies of procedural justice; 20 years ago, by legitimacy psychology; 15 years ago, by therapeutic jurisprudence.

In all these cases, the very foundations of law were criticized. Its oversimplified view of people and fundamental weaknesses in the ways in which the law works were discovered. In all these cases, extensive use of psychology was shown to be part of the solution to the most fundamental problems of the law. However, each time, it turned out to be a revolution only in psychology and not in law. The law proved to be highly resistant to any expansion of psychology. As a result, the gap has been growing between the ever-increasing potentialities of rapidly developing psychology and its restricted use in law.

Why the Law Resists Psychology?

Current Explanations

The resistance of law and lawyers against the use of psychology in law is well known. The widespread wisdom of judges states: 'The less psychology the more objectivity and justice'.

There are many well-known explanations of this resistance. The general idea of all of them is that there exists a fundamental *incompatibility* between law and psychology, because they are *absolutely different*. I will summarize several differences that are mentioned most often (see, for example, Constanzo 2004; Melton *et al*. 1997).

1. *Probabilistic vs. 'yes-no' knowledge.* Psychological knowledge is probabilistic: psychological information usually shows the probability of a trait or event. However, the law is built upon 'yes-no' information. One is either guilty or not, he offended or did not, a contract is signed or is not, etc.
2. *'Is' vs. 'ought'.* Psychology shows what *is*, law shows what *ought to be*. Psychology studies how people act in reality. The law commands what they ought to do.
3. *Objectivity vs. value.* The law is permeated with *political* and *economic* interests and the values of society and its groups. Psychology is (or, at least, tries to be) objective and impartial.
4. *Conservatism vs. innovation.* The law is rather conservative. It is termed 'The power of dead generations over living ones'. We still follow laws made hundreds years ago. On the contrary, psychology is innovative, searching to re-check old truths and to find new, improved ones.

All these differences are claimed to be liable for the incompatibility between law and psychology. These explanations are widespread and taken for granted. They have never has been criticized either by lawyers or by psychologists.

I will provide some critical review of these ideas.

1. Do these differences between the law and psychology really exist?
2. If they do, are they really the reasons for any incompatibility between the law and psychology?

My thesis is that all these differences and problems are quite normal, usually met and successfully solved for any practical application of any scientific knowledge.

Probabilistic vs. 'yes-no' knowledge

I agree that when applying psychology in law we meet the conversion problem: how to use probabilistic psychological information to take 'yes-no' legal decisions ('guilty–not-guilty', etc). However, the same problem is typically met in any practical application of theoretical knowledge. When a bridge is designed, for example, its constructors use *probabilistic* knowledge on the strength of its building material. However, they have to 'convert' this information into 'yes-no' decisions: will this material do for this bridge or not. Biology provides *probabilistic* knowledge about a living body. The major part of our biological characteristics (blood pressure, temperature, etc) is probabilistic. Medicine converts it into 'yes-no' information: whether a person is ill or not, is there a definite disease or not, will a certain course of treatment work or not, and so on. The botanist provides *probabilistic* knowledge on plants, their development and demands. Agronomy converts this knowledge into practical 'yes-no' rules and decisions about which plants to use and how they can be cultivated.

'Is' vs. 'ought'

I agree that the psychology shows what people do and the law provides rules about what they ought to do. The first produces knowledge and the second uses this knowledge to produce rules and standards. However, it is not only law and psychology that are so arranged. Any scientific knowledge is usually applied to develop rules saying where, what and how things have to be done. Medicine (an applied science) uses biological knowledge to develop rules indicating what ought to be done to cure a disease. Bridge engineering (an applied science) uses knowledge provided by physics to establish rules and standards of bridge-building.

Objectivity vs. value

It is true that any law is permeated with social and economic, political, moral values derived from the considerations of people designing it. However, the same is true for every goal-seeking activity. Any bridge is also permeated with the interests and values of people who ordered and financed its building. Depending on their intentions, demands, interests, values and tastes, the bridge can be expensive or cheap, simple or sophisticated, modest or fancy, more or less durable, destined for different tasks.

Conservatism vs. innovation

It is true that the law (in contrast to innovation-seeking psychology) is mistrustful of innovations. However, this is typical for any practical activity in which responsibility is involved. For example, designers of a bridge also are mistrustful of innovations. They resist innovations for the same reason as the law-maker. Both carry the heavy responsibility for the success of their activity. If they adopt innovation and this brings fatal consequences, they (and not the inventor) go to prison.

Thus, we can see that all these differences are not only met between law and psychology. They are usual also in many other areas of human activities. However, this does not cause any resistance similar to the one found between law and psychology.

Alternative Explanation

My explanation does not agree with the idea that the law rejects *all* psychology because of its totally different nature. I insist that the law rejects only *one* kind of psychology; scientific psychology.

The law rejects scientific psychology because it has its own independent 'basic legal psychology'. These are the psychological ideas about human nature underlying the law and its institutions. The law has its own set of psychological principles and concepts that permeate all its activities. By keeping these independent of 'basic legal psychology' its statements are protected from any criticism from scientific psychology. Therefore, the law can regard its basic psychological statements as valid even if scientific verification qualifies them as invalid.

As a first example of how the law maintains this independence, consider the basic psychological statements that underlie one of the most important aspects of the legal process – legal sanctions.

Legal sanctions (punishments provided by the law for violation of its regulations) are fundamental to law and are used in all its branches. Generally speaking, the whole of law can be seen as the legitimate way to use sanctions. Sanctions are used to achieve its most important aims; in particular, to deter people from forbidden actions and to rehabilitate offenders.

Why do legislators believe that sanctions work? We find the explanation in every law theory manual. This belief is based upon two fundamental statements on human nature.

I. Everybody has a fear of sanctions.
II. This fear holds for violation of the law.

(1) Are these statements psychological ones? The answer is 'Yes!'

The first one comments on human emotions (about the way in which fear arises). The second deals with motivation.

(2) Do these statements agree with ideas of the modern scientific psychology about human emotions and motivation? No, they do not. The picture of emotions and motivation drawn by modern psychology is infinitely more complicated. Thus, both statements are *oversimplifications*. Therefore, the belief that sanctions deter and rehabilitate is an oversimplification too. In his meta-study, Albrecht summarized results of studies on the efficiency of criminal sanctions: 'In the best case they have no effect, in the worst one they are harmful' (Albrecht 2002), see also, Martinson (1974), and Sherman (1997).

(3) Is it possible to bring the basic statements in line with modern-day scientific psychology? The answer is 'No!' This would have to mean that sanctions, fundamental for law, do not work. From this it follows that the law using them does not work. Next, this means that the very necessity of the law is controversial. This puts in question the whole legal system: court, police, and prison. Thus, an attempt to conform statements of the basic legal psychology with modern knowledge could be destructive for the law.

Another fundamental statement of law is the presumption of knowing the law. It implies that even people who never read the law know it (*Black's Law Dictionary* 1991). The psychological statement underlying this presumption is that all people are able to discover every demand of law intuitively. From the standpoint of psychological studies of intuition, this statement is, to put it mildly, oversimplified. However, to reject this statement means to allow a wrongdoer to excuse his misdeed by his supposed legal ignorance. This would be destructive of the legal system.

Contrary to therapeutic jurisprudence, the legislator simply neglects any harmful effects of a law and its institutions. And as opposed to legitimacy psychology, he simply believes that the law automatically causes legitimacy attitudes. Again, the psychological oversimplifications behind these beliefs are vital for the law.

(4) The legislator is certain that statements of basic legal psychology are valid. Therefore, hundreds of legal regulations are passed without any empirical verification of whether they will really work as they are supposed to. They are passed despite all evidence of their inefficiency.

All this means that basic legal psychology is independent of science, scientific validation, conclusions and criticism.

This is surprising. We live in the world of omnipotent science. It plays a crucial role in all areas of life. We trust it, even if its conclusions and recommendations are in sharp contrast with our everyday experience. Only the basic legal psychological statements seem to be exempt from the power of science. They are seen as valid despite the lack of their scientific validation.

This is possible only because 'basic law psychology' has its own validation methods, independent of scientific ones. These methods provide the possibility of supporting statements that are seen by scientific psychology as invalid; to 'defend' the 'basic legal psychology' against the destructive impact of the scientific one.

Many of these methods are those used by people in their everyday life to validate their common sense ideas. They are methods used by folk psychology (everyday, naïve, common-sense psychology) drawn on by lay persons (Gordon 1986).

The Mental Simulation is one such method of validation (Gordon 1986). Its essence is simple. One puts oneself in the position of another person and tries to think and feel 'for him'. Instead of knowing how another person ticks, 'we just do the ticking for him' (Goldman 1989).

Validation by Mental Stimulation 'shows' (contrary to science) that legal sanctions do work and are even highly efficient. Indeed, put yourself into the position of an imprisoned offender. Think of the years he spends in prison. Every month, day, hour, and minute, he is deprived of everything: freedom, love, normal food, friends and relatives. Therefore, every minute and second teaches him the same lesson – 'you suffer because you committed your crime'. Trying to think and to feel 'for him', we can 'clearly see' a vivid and detailed image of his thoughts, feelings, decisions. This image 'clearly shows' that in his place everybody would refuse the slightest idea of committing any new crime.

Science says that criminal sanctions *do not work*; yet commonsense Mental Stimulation depicts how they *do work*. In the same way, a regular person can 'clearly see' (despite all psychological data on intuition) that everybody can intuitively discover the demands of the law, how a threat of criminal sanction deters from an offence, and how any new law evokes public respect, etc.

Thus, this 'clear view' replaces any scientific validation and defends the basic psychological statements of law (and law itself) from scientific psychology.

Let us consider both positive and negative consequences of this situation.

Positive Consequences

1. This preserves the law, protecting it from ideas that, though scientifically valid, could be destructive for it.
2. Being defended from criticism of scientific psychology, the law is, therefore, more stable. It is protected against the often and drastic changes peculiar to scientific psychology. The stability of law is highly important, ensuring its ability to make social relations predictable. 'It is better to have a poor but stable law than a good but unstable one', advises old legal wisdom.
3. Both ordinary, lay people and basic legal psychology use the same, commonsense, validation methods. Thus, both 'see' the same reasons for which the law should work. Therefore, both believe the law. They believe that criminal punishment deters and helps to rehabilitate offenders. They 'see' that everybody can intuitively discover the demands of the law and, therefore, 'understand' why legal ignorance is no defense.
4. This is highly important in integrating the law into everyday life and encouraging people to accept the law.

Negative Consequences

1. *Inefficiency.* It is impossible to rely upon invalid, oversimplified ideas and to be efficient. Believing that 2×2 is 17, one cannot be efficient in one's calculations. In the same way, a law based upon oversimplified ideas cannot be efficient.
2. *Rigidity of law.* The law is obstructive to innovations, especially those suspected of endangering stability. The law wants 'stability for stability'. It does not distinguish 'good stability' from 'bad'. This hinders it solving its

inveterate problems. Instead of changing, the law insists. It resists innovations, increases zeal in implementing the existing state of affair. Thus, problems are intensified instead of being solved.

Collectively, the above means that the law sacrifices its efficiency for its stability. However, the price for stability is very high.

Why do we agree to pay such a price?

Imagine a car, old, inefficient, often out of use, repaired so many times that it is not safe to do any more changes to it. Of course, we are unhappy with it.

However, we *do not have any other car*. We even have no idea when we will have one. We do not even know what this new car could be like. In this situation, we would be happy when our car somehow works. We would resist any improvements and changes. We would use all possible explanations of why it should stay as it is. Even if this car does not go at all, we would believe that, perhaps, one day it will, or that it is important as tradition, prestige, moral or a precept for the young generation.

The situation of law and its interconnection with psychology is in many respects similar.

We already have no illusions about the efficiency of the sanctions. We know very well that prison is not the place where criminals can be improved. We are not so naïve as to believe that legal sanctions deter people from violating the law. However, as with our old car, we do not have any really strong alternative. Also like this car, we do not know when and how we will have an alternative and what it will be like. We cannot even picture the world without criminal punishment. Today, we cannot find any single country without prisons. They have existed for as long as human society. Therefore, the price for stability of the law is a forced one.

What to Do?

There is *no balance* between psychology and law in their efforts to expand the use of psychology. Psychology is the 'attacking side' and the law is the one defending itself. Psychology proposes, persuades and seduces. The law rather resists, objects and precludes.

What to do in this situation?

Modern psychology is a dynamic, quickly developing and highly offensive science. It actively searches for new opportunities to apply its knowledge in new areas of human life. It is the psychology that molded the modern shape of medicine, economy, engineering and even many aspects of art.

It is no wonder that modern psychology actively tries to overcome both the open and hidden resistance of the law. Several strategies in dealing with this resistance are possible.

1. Submission

To admit stability is the only efficiency criterion of the law.

Most psychological proposals are intended to improve the efficiency of the law. However, as previously seen, the law sacrifices efficiency for stability. Any efficiency proposal gets rejected for even a vague apprehension of instability which this proposal may supposedly cause.

The first possible strategy in this situation is to accept this viewpoint.

In this case, stability is regarded as the only real aim of law and, therefore, its only criterion of efficiency. Thus, only those psychological proposals are accepted that do not demand any changes in the law and legal system. As in medicine, the principle 'first of all, cause no harm' is recognized as the absolute priority.

This way of thinking is quite common among lawyers. Popular wisdom from judges like, 'The aim of judging is a just sentence' 'The aim of a penalty is the punishment' illustrate this attitude. They say that the aim of law is the law itself; this means – the law *such as it is*.

Adopting this strategy, a psychologist admits that a lawyer knows better what can be safe or unsafe for law. Therefore, he calmly waits until a lawyer asks him to do something.

Meanwhile, a psychologist does not try to widen the use of psychology. Instead, he only improves things that are permissive for law: improves methods for the examination of witness testimonies, capacities to stand trial, etc.

The positive side of this strategy is an increased mutual confidence. As usual in life, if you want nothing of another person, his confidence in you may grow. This improves mutual understanding.

This inoffensive position of psychology can be seen in many countries. Psychologists calmly work in traditional areas without much effort to widen them.

2. Restricted Expansion

The application of psychology should be widened, mainly in some selected areas that have an especially high demand for efficiency.

Generally, the law sacrifices its efficiency for stability. However, in some areas this is not so easy. In these areas, the need for efficiency is especially strong and the lack of it is especially evident.

One such area is crime detection. If you act efficiently, the offence will be detected. If not, it remains undetected. In most countries the police are responsible for crime detection. It is no wonder that here, cooperation with psychologists is the most demanded and successful. The great uptake of psychological profiling is a good example.

3. To Modify Innovations Endangering Basic Statements

Psychological proposals, which are supposed to endanger the stability of law, are modified; their non-endangering shape is promoted.

A good example of such an approach is the diversion of juvenile offenders from the full force of the law. Empirical studies discovered so-called 'spontaneous remission' of juvenile delinquents. It was demonstrated that while the great majority of juvenile offenders commit offences in their adolescence or youth (Laub and Sampson 2001), paradoxically, the probability that they will continue their criminal activities proved to be much higher if their offences were detected and prosecuted.

The most direct and logical way to react to this finding is to abolish offences of adolescents and youth.

However, such a solution endangers the basic statements that everybody has a fear of criminal sanction and this fear deters everyone. It would be a direct admission that criminal law does not work.

In this difficult situation, a skilful alternative route was found. Instead of abolishing the inefficient and harmful law, prosecutors were given discretion to cease prosecution of a juvenile at any moment. In this situation, Peter has been paid without robbing Paul. Both fundamental statements of law are left safe and the possibility of protecting juveniles from criminal prosecution, which harms them psychologically, was created. This procedural trick, first discovered in US, became highly popular and spread widely around the world (Walter 2001).

This is a good pattern for a potential and sophisticated way for expansion of psychology within the law.

4. Patience, Patience, and again Patience...Moving Ahead Very Slowly and Imperceptibly

Psychology has great experience using desensitization methods. Its main tool is slow but steady progress, weakening aversion or phobia. Following this approach the law's phobias and aversions against psychology can be cured, gradually increasing the dose of the latter, closely observing feedback, moving ahead carefully step by step.

Actually, the whole history of expansion of psychology within the law is a good illustration of such a strategy.

Think of the examination of eyewitness fallibility. Reviewing the use of witness psychology in court from Hugo Münsterberg until modern days, we can see the very slow but steady progress. Of course, this progress is much too slow. However, it is now much easier than 100 years ago to persuade the court that psychological examination of a witness statement is needed. The use of psychology has been expanding very gradually but steadily in examination of the capacity to testify, and so on.

5. The Revolutionary Strategy – Drastic Change in the Law and its Interrelations with Psychology, Placing the Responsibility of Integration on the Doorstep of Both, Refusing Oversimplifications

As seen, this may demand drastic changes in the very foundations of the law. However, perhaps, despite all this, we should think... about a new car.

Acknowledgements

The author is most grateful to Dr Mandeep Dhami and Professor Rita Zukauskiene for their highly valuable and inspiring comments and proposals on this chapter. The author would like to express deep gratitude to Professor David Canter, who read and improved the primary concept and whose comments were very important in preparing the final version of this chapter. The author also thanks all participants of the EAPL conference in Vilnius, whose comments and proposals were highly useful when writing this chapter, and to Michael Fusco who contributed so much to improving the English.

References

Ackerman, M. (1999) *Essentials of Forensic Psychological Assessment* (New York: Wiley).

Albrecht, P.-A. (2002) *Kriminologie* (Muenchen: Beck).

Black's Law Dictionary (1991) *Black's Law Dictionary* (St. Paul, Minnesota: West Publishing).

Constanzo, M. (2004) *Psychology Applied to Law* (Australia: Thomson Wadsworth).

Daicoff, S. and Wexler, D. (2003) Therapeutic jurisprudence, in A.M. Goldstein (Ed.) *Forensic Psychology*, pp. 561–580 (Hoboken, New Jersey: Wiley).

Goldman, A. (1989) Interpretation psychologized, *Mind and Language*, 4, pp. 161–185.

Goldstein, A.M. (Ed.) (2003) Forensic psychology. In I.B. Weiner (Ed.) *Handbook of Psychology*, Vol.11 (Hoboken, New Jersey: Wiley).

Gordon, R. (1986) Folk psychology as simulation, *Mind and Language*, 1, pp. 158–171.

Jost, J.T. and Major, B. (2001) *The Psychology of Legitimacy* (New York: Cambridge University Press).

Kapardis, A. (1997) *Psychology and Law. A Critical Introduction* (Cambridge University Press).

Laub, J. and Sampson, R. (2001) *Understanding Desistance from Crime. Crime and Justice (Volume 28)*, edited by M. Tonry, pp. 1–69 (Chicago: University of Chicago Press).

Martinson, R. (1974) What works – questions and answers about prison reform, *The Public Interest*, 10 (Spring), pp. 22–54.

Melton, G.B., Petrila, J., Poythress, N.G. and Slobogin, C. (1997) *Psychological Evaluations for the Court: A Handbook for Mental Health Professionals and Lawyers* (New York: Guilford Press).

Sherman, L.W. , MacKenzie, D., Eck, J., Reuter, P. and Bushway, S. (1997) Preventing crime: what works, what doesn't, what's promising. a report to the United States Congress. Prepared for the National Institute of Justice, http://www. ncjrs.gov/works/overview.htm

Walter, M. (2001) *Jugendkriminalität* (Stuttgart: Richard Boorberg Verlag).

Chapter 14

'They're an Illusion to Me Now': Forensic Ethics, Sanism and Pretextuality

Michael L. Perlin

Introduction

Each year, when I get to that part of my Criminal Law course during which the students learn about the insanity defense, I ask them, 'In what percentage of cases do you think expert witnesses agree on the question of insanity?' Generally, the answers range from zero to 10%, with an occasional brave student venturing a guess of as high as 25%. When I tell them that the answer is closer to 88%,[1] their perplexed looks are apparent. These data are utterly cognitively dissonant with everything they had come to believe – no doubt via their misplaced reliance on 'ordinary common sense' (OCS)[2] – about the criminal justice system.

I regularly attribute this error to the power of the *vividness heuristic* – the way that a single, vivid, memorable case overwhelms the mountains of abstract, colorless data on which rational choices should be made.[3] And I think that, in large part, that is true. Although the so-called 'battle of the experts' is, in most cases, a myth,[4]

---

1 See Michael L. Perlin, The Jurisprudence of the Insanity Defense 112–13 (1994), reporting on the research of Richard Rogers *et al.*, Insanity Defense: Contested or Conceded?. 141 *Am. J. Psychiatry* 885, 885 (1984); Kenneth Fukunaga *et al*, Insanity Plea: Interexaminer Agreement in Concordance of Psychiatric Opinions and Court Verdict, 5 *Law & Hum. Behav.* 325, 326 (1981).

2 See Michael L. Perlin, Psychodynamics and the Insanity Defense: 'Ordinary Common Sense and Heuristic Reasoning, 69 *Neb. L. Rev.* 3, 22–24 (1990) (discussing how 'ordinary common sense' is used as an unconscious basis for making judgments about disabled defendants in criminal cases). The concept of 'ordinary common sense' is best explained in this context in Richard Sherwin, Dialects and Dominance: A Study of Rhetorical Fields in Confessions, 136 *U. Pa. L. Rev.* 729 (1988).

3 See Michael L. Perlin, Decoding Right to Refuse Treatment Law, 16 *Int'l J.L. & Psychiatry* 151, 172.169 (1993). On the impact of heuristics on the development of mental disability law in general, see Michael L. Perlin, *The Hidden Prejudice: Mental Disability on Trial* 4–20 (2000). For an excellent analysis of all heuristic biases, see *Judgment Under Uncertainty: Heuristics and Biases* (Daniel Kahneman *et al.* (eds), 1982).

4 On myths in insanity defense jurisprudence in general, see Perlin, *supra* note 1, at 73–143.

although the vast majority of insanity cases are 'walk-throughs'[5] and although most cases involving competency to stand trial determinations never reach the contested trial stage,[6] those cases that are contested *are* vivid (not coincidentally, often because they involve high-profile crimes, victims or defendants, thus assuring saturation media coverage), and we tend to make many of our assumptions about the criminal justice system based on our knowledge about this relatively-small database.[7]

But knowing this, it is still important to consider the relatively small universe of contested cases in which there *is* a 'battle of the experts.' It is these cases that help shape our focus on an important question of forensic ethics: to what extent does a witness's pre-existing value system of political, cultural, and social beliefs shape her expert opinions (especially, though not exclusively, in criminal and quasi-criminal cases)?[8] For, if experts are allowed to testify to their opinion because the possess information 'beyond the ken' of the trier of fact,[9] it is crucial that these opinions not be contaminated by extra-judicial bias.

This is an important question and appears to be one that is addressed more frequently in the hallways of courthouses than in the academic literature. The pejorative phrase 'defendant's whore' or 'prosecutor's whore' is frequently used,[10] describing experts who would 'say anything [the side in question that has retained

---

5   See idem. at 113; see generally, Michael L. Perlin, Unpacking the Myths: The Symbolism Mythology of Insanity Defense Jurisprudence, 40 Case W. *Res. L. Rev.* 599, 652–53 (1989–90)

6   See Bruce J. Winick, Reforming Incompetency to Stand Trial and Plead Guilty: A Restated Proposal and a Response to Professor Bonnie, 5 *J. Crim. L. & Criminology* 571, 591 (1995); see generally, Bruce J. Winick, Incompetency to Stand Trial: An Assessment of the Costs and Benefits, 39 *Rutgers L. Rev.* 243 (1987).

7   On the way that the O.,J. Simpson case was seen as an example of 'typical' behavior, see for example, Christo Lassiter, The O.J. Simpson Verdict: A Lesson in Black and White, 1 *Mich. J. Race & L.* 69 (1996); see generally, Phoebe Ellsworth and Alan Reifman, Juror Comprehension and Public Policy, 6 *Psychol. Pub. Pol'y & L.* 788, 790 (2000).

8   Experts, of course, testify in a wide variety of civil and criminal cases. See for example, Michael L. Perlin, 'May He Stay Forever Young': Robert Sadoff and the History of Mental Health Law, 33 *J. Amer. Acad. Psychiatry & L.* 236 (2005) (discussing the testimony of Dr. Sadoff [the past President of the American Academy of Psychiatry and Law] in criminal cases, tort cases, civil rights cases, attorney misconduct cases, adoption cases, employment discrimination cases, jail and prison condition cases, judicial misconduct cases, and institutional rights cases (including, right to treatment and right to refuse treatment cases).

9   See for example, District of Columbia v. Arnold & Porter, 756 A.2d 427, 433 (D.C. 2000).

10   On the underlying ambivalence, see generally Douglas Mossman and Marshall Kapp, 'Courtroom Whores'? – or Why Do Attorneys Call Us? Findings from a Survey on Attorneys' Use of Mental Health Experts, 26 *J. Am. Acad. Psychiatry & L.* 27 (1998). On the potential gender connotations of this phrase, see Amy Walters, Gender and the Role of Expert Witnesses in the Federal Courts, 83 *Geo. L.J.* 635, 652 n. 26 (1994).

him] wants him to say.'[11] Yet, there has been little written about the full range of ethical issues that are raised when such an allegation is made.

Of course, there are some who do not shrink from overt identification with a particular stance on forensic matters. At one end of the spectrum is the defiant Dr. James Grigson, the so-called Dr. Death, who by one count, claimed '100 percent certainty' in 139 Texas death penalty cases that 'the defendant is a sociopath and will again be violent in the future, without having personally examined the defendant.'[12] At the other end are the principled Dr. Abraham Halpern and Dr. Alfred Freedman, who have argued eloquently that that psychiatrists should not participate in the process of determining whether a defendant facing the death penalty is competent to be executed.[13] But witnesses such as these – willing to be identified with a specific social or political position[14] – are certainly not the only ones whose personal views have an impact on their testimony. Dr. Park Dietz, for example, recently conceded:

I believe that the proper role of a forensic psychiatrist is to seek the truth, not to help any party to the case. That's my core philosophical difference with both clinical psychiatry and the defense bar. And it's one of the reasons that I appear mostly for the prosecution. One of the conditions I have for accepting a case is that I have access to all information. Prosecutors never have a problem with that because their goal is to seek truth and justice, and all the data are important in that quest.[15]

---

11 See for example, Neil Vidmar, Are Juries Competent to Decide Liability in Tort Cases Involving Scientific/Medical Issues? Some Data From Medical Malpractice, 43 *Emory L.J.* 885, 902 (1994), and see also, Chaulk *ex rel.* Murphy v. Volkswagen of America, Inc., 808 F> 2d 639, 644 (7th Cir. 1986) (Posner, J., dissenting) ('There is hardly anything, not palpably absurd on its face, that cannot now be proved by some so-called 'experts'), as discussed in Stephen Easton, Can We Talk? Removing Counterproductive Ethical Restraints Upon Ex Parte Communication Between Attorneys and Adverse Expert Witnesses, 76 *Ind. L.J.* 647, 664–65 n. 58 (2001).

12 Robert Wettstein, A Psychiatric Perspective on Washington's Sexually Violent Predators Statute, 15 *U. Puget Sound L. Rev.* 597, 625–26 n. 132 (1992). On Dr. Grigson in general, see Ron Rosenbaum, Travels with Doctor Death and Other Unusual Investigations (1991).

13 See for example, Alfred Freedman and Abraham Halpern The Erosion of Ethics and Morality in Medicine: Physician Participation in Legal Executions on the United States, 41 *N.Y.L. Sch. L. Rev.* 169 (1996); Alfred Freedman and Abraham Halpern, The Psychiatrist's Dilemma: A Conflict of Roles in Legal Executions, 33 *Australian & N.Z. J. Psychiatry* 629 (1999).

14 Compare Robert Sadoff, Practical Ethical Problems of the Forensic Psychiatrist in Dealing with Attorneys, 12 *Bull. Am. Acad. Psychiatry & L.* 243, 245 (1984) ('It is important that the forensic psychiatrist reveal his/her personal feelings about the case at the outset if there is any likelihood those feelings will influence his/her opinion or effective participation in the case').

15 Anastasia Toufexis, A Psychiatrist's-Eye View of Murder and Insanity, *N.Y. Times* (April 23, 2002), at p. F5, downloaded from www.nytimes.com/2002/04/23/health/23CONV. html (April 30, 2002). Dr. Dietz has been characterized as 'perhaps the most famous

For the purposes of this chapter, I am more interested, however in those witnesses who profess neutrality, but are not in fact neutral. Such covert biases may be 'particularly damaging' where competency evaluations and insanity defense pleas hinge on the strength of 'neutral' expert testimony.[16] Studies by Robert Homant and Daniel Kennedy, for example, tell us that an expert's opinion in insanity defense cases and civil psychic trauma trials positively correlates with the expert's underlying political ideology.[17] The authors were clear: 'Professionals' attitudes toward the insanity defense were largely a function of their personal training, experiences, and beliefs.'[18]

In a series of articles and a book,[19] I have explored the impact of what I call 'sanism' and what I call 'pretextuality' in the mental disability law system. I define 'sanism' as 'an irrational prejudice of the same quality and character of other irrational prejudices that cause (and are reflected in) prevailing social attitudes of racism, sexism, homophobia and ethnic bigotry,'[20] and I define 'pretextuality' as the means by which 'courts accept (either implicitly or explicitly) testimonial dishonesty and engage similarly in dishonest (frequently meretricious) decisionmaking, specifically where witnesses, especially *expert* witnesses, show a "high propensity to purposely distort their testimony in order to achieve desired ends."'[21] I have concluded that it is

---

prosecution psychiatrist in the country.' See Elisa Swanson, 'Killers Start Sad And Crazy': Mental Illness And the Betrayal of Kipland Kinkel, 79 *Or. L. Rev.* 1081, 1104 (2000).

16 Ellen Chun, Book Review of Denis Woychuk, Falling Between the Cracks: Attorney for the Damned: A Lawyer's Life With the Criminally Insane (1996), 17 *B.C. Third World L.J.* 395, 395 (1997), citing, in part, Charles E. Owens, Mental Health and Black Offenders 1, 1 (1980).

17 See Robert J. Homant et al., Ideology as a Determinant of View on the Insanity Defense, 14 J. *Crim. Just.* 3, 7 (1986) ; Robert J. Homant and Daniel B. Kennedy, Definitions of Mental Illness as a Factor in Expert Witnesses' Judgments of Insanity, 31 *Corrective & Soc. Psychiatry J. Behav. Tech. Methods & Therapy* 125 (1985); Robert J. Homant and Daniel B. Kennedy, Judgment of Legal Insanity as a Function of Attitude Toward the Insanity Defense, 8 *Int'l J. & Psychiatry* 67 (1986) (Homant and Kennedy, Legal Insanity); Robert J. Homant and Daniel B. Kennedy, Subjective Factors in the Judgment of Insanity, 14 *Crim. Just. & Behav.* 38 (1987).

18 Homant and Kennedy, Legal Insanity, *supra* note 17, at 68. See also, Mary Ann Deitchman et al., Self-Selection Factors in the Participation of Mental Health Professionals in Competency for Execution Evaluations, 15 *Law & Hum. Behav.* 287, 299 (1991) (forensic experts 'personal beliefs' may be 'an important predictor' of participation decisions).

19 See sources cited in Perlin, *supra* note 3, at xiii–xiv, and see *id.*

20 *Id.* at xiii–xix; see generally, Michael L. Perlin, On 'Sanism,' 46 SMU L. Rev. 373, 374–75 (1992).

21 Perlin, *supra* note 3, at xix; see generally, Michael L. Perlin, Morality and Pretextuality, Psychiatry and Law: Of 'Ordinary Common Sense,' Heuristic Reasoning, and Cognitive Dissonance, 19 *Bull. Am. Acad. Psychiatry & L.* 131, 133 (1991).

impossible to understand *any* aspect of mental disability law without an understanding of the corrosive and malignant impact of these factors.[22]

To the best of my knowledge, no one has ever yet explored the connection between sanism and pretextuality and the question of forensic ethics: to what extent does a witness's pre-existing sanism dominate and color her professional practices? I will modestly attempt a first tentative answer to this question in this chapter. In the next section, I will consider the problem of expert bias. In the section after, I will explain the roots of sanism. In the fourth section, I will make the link between sanism and expert testimony. In the fifth section, I will discuss the role and significance of social attitudes. In the sixth section, I will offer some modest conclusions.

The start of the title of this paper is adapted from Bob Dylan's brilliant anthem, *Tangled up in Blue*, from the classic *Blood on the Tracks* album.[23] *Tangled* is one of Dylan's best-known and most-frequently performed songs; it is the picaresque tale of the narrator's journey through life on both personal and political levels.[24] In the last verse, the narrator (perhaps a stand-in for Dylan himself) concludes:

> So now I'm goin' back again,
> I got to get to her somehow.
> All the people we used to know
> They're an illusion to me now.
> Some are mathematicians
> Some are carpenter's wives.
> Don't know how it all got started,
> I don't know what they're doin' with their lives.
> But me, I'm still on the road
> Headin' for another joint
> We always did feel the same, We just saw it from a different point of view,
> Tangled up in blue.[25]

Few of us will disagree that, on many levels, life is an illusion.[26] But, more to the point, so may the alleged neutrality of expert witnesses who evaluate and testify in cases involving individuals with mental disabilities also be an illusion. This chapter seeks to illuminate some of the relevant issues underlying this assertion.

---

22 Perlin, *supra* note 3, at 305–10; see generally, Michael L, Perlin, Half-Wracked Prejudice Leaped Forth: Sanism, Pretextuality, and Why and How Mental Disability Law Developed As It Did, 10 *J. Contemp. Leg. Iss.* 3, 4 (1999).

23 Bob Dylan, Lyrics, 1962–1985 (1985), at 357.

24 See for example, Robert Shelton, *No Direction Home: The Life and Music of Bob Dylan* 441 (DaCapo press ed. 1997); Michael Gray, *Song & Dance Man III: The Art of Bob Dylan* 261–62 (2000); Tim Riley, *Hard Rain: A Dylan Commentary* 232–36 (1992); *Bob Dylan, Performing Artist, 1974–86, The Middle Years* 23–30 (1994).

25 Dylan, *supra* note 23, at 359.

26 See for example, David A. Schkade and Daniel Kahneman, Does Living in California Make People Happy? A Focusing Illusion in Judgments of Life Satisfaction, 9 *Psychol. Sci.* 340, 340–341 (1998).

Expert Bias

Some expert bias is intentional and some of it is unintentional,[27] but it is still a 'real risk' even if unintended.[28] Paul Appelbaum has noted the 'frequency with which highly respected [psychiatric] experts arrive at conclusions favorable to the side for which they are working or to which they have been assigned',[29] and Eric Marcus has characterized this bias as inevitable.[30] Stephen Morse has said, flatly: 'Mental health professionals, like all other citizens, have social and political biases that extend to their views of criminal justice.'[31] Randy Otto has identified examples of both sorts of bias: intentional (financial incentives, desire to promote a particular viewpoint on a social issue, and the desire to please one's employer), and unintentional (empathy or identification with a litigant or a side; 'unwitting involvement in the adversarial process', and 'the need to defend one's position in the face of a hostile opposing attorney').[32] Bernard Diamond has argued (persuasively, to my mind) that some such bias may be inevitable.[33] I discussed this issue in this manner in 1993.

I begin with the proposition that the phrase 'neutral expert' is an oxymoron. Bernard Diamond, for one, believed that a witness's unconscious identification with a 'side' of a legal battle or his more conscious identification with a value system or ideological leanings may lead to 'innumerable subtle distortions and biases in his testimony that spring from this wish to triumph.'[34]

------

27 Jean Beckham *et al.*, Decision Making and Examiner Bias in Forensic Expert Recommendations for Not Guilty by Reason of Insanity, 13 *Law & Hum. Behav.* 79, 79 (1997).

28 Ansar Haroun and Grant Morris, Weaving a Tangled Web: The Deceptions of Psychiatrists, 10 J. *Contemp. Legal Iss.* 227, 232 (1999).

29 Paul S. Appelbaum, In the Wake of Ake: The Ethics of Expert Testimony in an Advocate's World, 15 *Bull. Am. Acad. Psychiatry & L.* 15, 21 (1987); see generally, Robert A. Prentice, The SEC and MDP: Implications of the Self-Serving Bias for Independent Auditing, 61 *Ohio St. L.J.* 1597, 1627. n. 142 (2000). On the question of 'favorable predisposition,' see Ellen Deason, Court-Appointed Expert Witnesses: Scientific Positivism, Meets Bias and Deference, 77 *Or. L. Rev.* 59, 100 (1998).

30 Eric Marcus, Unbiased Medical Testimony: Reality or Myth?, 6 *Am. J. Forensic Psychiatry* 3, 4 (1985), discussed in Prentice, *supra* note 29, at 1627 n.142.

31 Stephen Morse, Failed Expectations and Criminal Responsibility: Experts and the Unconscious, 68 *Va. L. Rev.* 971, 1057 (1982).

32 Randy Otto, Bias and Expert Testimony of Mental Health Professionals in Adversarial Proceedings: A Preliminary Investigation, 7 *Behav. Sci. & L.* 267, 268 (1989). But compare *id.* at 271 (reporting results from a laboratory study finding evidence in criminal case setting but not in civil case setting that mental health professionals' testimony often varies according to the side by which they are retained).

33 See for example, Bernard L. Diamond, The Fallacy of the Impartial Expert, 3 *Archives Crim. Psychodynamics* 221 (1959).

34 Michael L. Perlin, Pretexts and Mental Disability Law: The Case of Competency, 47 *U. Miami L. Rev.* 625, 641 (1993), quoting Diamond, *supra* note 33, at 223.

But virtually none of the published research has looked carefully at an omnipresent, yet 'below the radar' issue in the forensic evaluation/testimonial processes: the extent to which expert witnesses' testimony and evaluations reflect *sanism*. Interestingly, authors *have* considered the somewhat parallel[35] question of the impact of an expert witness's potential homophobia on testimony in gay adoption cases.[36] And, in that context, it has been asserted that *'all* child custody evaluators have some beliefs (some might call them biases) that guide their thinking.'[37] But no one has of yet considered the precise question that is at the heart of this paper.

Sanism

In earlier works, I have considered extensively the wide range of pretexts that affect forensic witnesses, both in the contexts of involuntary civil commitment and incompetency to stand trial evaluations.[38] But there has been a strange silence on the question of whether expert witnesses are inherently more or less sanist than other important participants in the judicial system:[39] judges,[40] lawyers,[41] jurors,[42]

---

35 I briefly explore the parallels between homophobia and sanism in Perlin, *supra* note 3, at 32 n. 86.

36 Susan J. Becker, Child Sexual Abuse Allegations Against a Lesbian or Gay Parent In a Custody or Visitation Dispute: Battling the Overt and Insidious Bias of Experts and Judges, 74 *Denv. U. L. Rev.* 75, 130 n. 431 (1996), quoting Diane H. Schetky, Ethical Issues in Forensic Psychiatry, in *Ethics & Child Mental Health* 265, 266 (Jocelyn Y. Hattab (ed.), 1994) ('The psychiatrist needs to consider whether her own strong personal beliefs preclude involvement in a particular case. Homophobia or bias towards mothers having custody would preclude an objective assessment of a gay father seeking custody of his child.')

37 Jonathan Gould and Phillip Stahl, The Art and Science of Child Custody Evaluations: Integrating Clinical and Forensic Mental Health Models, 38 *Fam. & Conciliation Courts Rev.* 392, 399 (2000).

38 See for example, Perlin, *supra* note 3, at 67–69; Perlin, *supra* note 34, at 641–58; Perlin, *supra* note 21, at 135–36.

39 . But see, Note, Implementing Atkins, 116 *Harv. L. Rev.* 2565, 2580–81(2003) ('expert witnesses appeared to hold a number of stereotypes about mentally retarded individuals: namely, that mental retardation is the same as mental illness, and that 'people with mental retardation have vastly lower abilities than do their age peers without mental retardation,' citing Dennis R. Olvera *et al.*, Mental Retardation and Sentences for Murder: Comparison of Two Recent Court Cases, 38 Mental Retardation 228, 232 (2000).

40 Perlin, *supra* note 3, at 50–51; Perlin, *supra* note 1, at 198–209.

41 Perlin, *supra* note 3, at 55–56.

42 See for example, Michael L. Perlin, The Sanist Lives of Jurors in Death Penalty Cases: The Puzzling Role of 'Mitigating' Mental Disability Evidence, 8 *Notre Dame J. L., Ethics & Pub. Pol.* 239 (1994); see also, Timothy Hall, Legal Fictions and Moral Reasoning: Capital Punishment and the Mentally Retarded Defendant After Penry v. Johnson, 35 *Akron L. Rev.* 327, 347 n. 165 (2002) (citing Perlin, *supra*), and LeRoy Kondo, Advocacy of the

academics,[43] legislators,[44] lay witnesses,[45] or police officers (in criminal cases involving mentally disabled criminal defendants or complainants).[46]

In writing globally about sanism, I have alleged that bias 'affects judges, lawyers, expert witnesses, therapists, hospital administrators, legislators, jurors, and the general public,'[47] but there has been virtually no prior scholarship to either support (or disprove) my assertion as to expert witnesses. This, intuitively, should be an issue of interest to researchers and other scholars: if we concede that experts may be subject to other biases (political position,[48] identification with a cause or party,[49] money,[50] desire to be liked by the judge, desire to 'promote Justice'),[51] and if we concede that sanism appears to distort the judgments of all other participants in the criminal justice system,[52] then it makes no sense to suggest that expert witnesses are somehow strangely immune to *this* one bias. Haroun and Morris have come the closest in their typology of expert witnesses:

> There is the Paternalist, who wants to help patients and who fudges findings of incompetency so that the court will order involuntary treatment. There is the Historian, who, when evaluating the patient's current mental condition, bases conclusions on the patient's past history rather than on the patient's present mental state. There is the Puritan, who cannot tolerate disability applicants, and who fudges findings in order to deny benefits to those perceived as lazy. There is the Libertarian, who fudges findings in order to preserve all

---

Establishment of Mental Health Specialty Courts in the Provision of Therapeutic Justice for Mentally Ill Offenders, 28 *Am. J. Crim. L.* 255, 276 n. 117 (2001).

43 Perlin, *supra* note 3, at 56–57.

44 Perlin, *supra* note 3, at 48–50; see also, for example, Marcia Purse, CA Mental Health Parity Bill Passes Despite GOP Lawmaker's Arguments (Oct. 28. 1999), downloaded from http://bipolar.about.com/library/weekly/aa991027.htm?terms=Purse+and+Parity (April 30, 2002) (discussing California state legislator's opposition to mental health benefits bill being based on his statements that mental illness was not a 'legitimate disease.'

45 See generally, State v. Van Horn, 528 So. 2d 529, 530 (Fla. Dist. Ct. App. 1988) (discussing probativeness of lay witnesses' 'perception of [defendant's] normalcy').

46 For example, Peter Finn and Monique Sullivan, Police Handling of the Mentally Ill: Sharing Responsibility With the Mental Health System, 17 *J. Crim. Just.* 1, 4 (1989).

47 Keri Gould and Michael L. Perlin, 'Johnny's in the Basement/Mixing Up His Medicine': Therapeutic Jurisprudence and Clinical Teaching (with Prof. Keri K. Gould), 24 *Seattle U. L. Rev.* 339, 345 n. 35 (2000); Perlin, *supra* note 3, at 266–67; see also, Michael L. Perlin, Therapeutic Jurisprudence: Understanding the Sanist and Pretextual Bases of Mental Disability Law, 20 *N. Eng. J. on Crim. & Civ. Confinement* 369, 371–72 (1994); Michael L. Perlin, A Law of Healing, 68 *U. Cin. L. Rev.* 407, 419–33 (2000).

48 Perlin, *supra* note 34, at 653–55.

49 Otto, *supra* note 32, at 268; Richard Rogers, Ethical Dilemmas in Forensic Evaluations, 5 *Behav. Sci. & L.* 149 (1987).

50 Otto, *supra* note 32, at 268; Patricia Anderten *et al*, On Being Ethical in Legal Places, 11 *Professional Psychology* 764 (1980).

51 Haroun and Morris, *supra* note 28, at 242.

52 See generally, Perlin, *supra* note 3.

the person's rights, even those who are severely mentally disordered. There is the Social Reformer, who fudges to achieve his or her personal vision of a greater society. The social reformer's attitude – whether favorable or not – toward the death penalty, to use but one example, affects the reformer's judgment in the individual case. There is the Economist, who fudges civil commitment recommendations, calculating that it is less expensive to retain a hospitalized patient involuntarily now, rather than permit release with inevitable re-hospitalization later. There is the Policeman, who fudges society's definition of dangerousness in order to lock up anyone he or she perceives as dangerous. There is the Avenger, who, when asked if an insanity acquittee has been restored to sanity will say 'no,' because the psychiatrist believes that the person was never insane and should not have succeeded with an insanity plea in the criminal trial.[53]

This classification forces us to consider the rate of biases that may affect their testimony, and leads us to consider logically whether 'The Sanist Witness' should be added to their list.

Sanism and Expert Testimony

Consider the first primal sanist myth that I have identified:

> Mentally ill individuals are 'different,' and, perhaps, less than human. They are erratic, deviant, morally weak, sexually uncontrollable, emotionally unstable, lazy, superstitious, ignorant, and demonstrate a primitive morality. They lack the capacity to show love or affection. They smell different from 'normal' individuals, and are somehow worth less.[54]

Now, consider the standard range of cases on which expert witnesses frequently consult[55] and about which they testify, and think about how sanism can distort expert opinions in each of these areas of the law.[56] I expect that there will be an easy and speedy rebuttal to this assertion: that experts are trained in psychology and psychiatry and that this training weeds out such biases. My first response is agnostic: prove it (since I know of no research on point). My second is skeptical:

---

53 *Id.* at 243–44.

54 Perlin. *supra* note 20, at 394.

55 See *supra* note 8.

56 I discuss sanism in the context of, *inter alia*, the law of involuntary civil commitment, see Perlin, *supra* note 34, at 644–52, the right to refuse treatment, see Michael L. Perlin and Deborah A. Dorfman, Is It More Than 'Dodging Lions and Wastin' Time?' Adequacy of Counsel, Questions of Competence, and the Judicial Process in Individual Right to Refuse Treatment Cases, 2 *Psychology, Pub. Pol'y & L.*114 (1996), incompetency to stand, see Perlin, *supra* note 34, at 652–58, the insanity defense, see Perlin, *supra* note 1, at 387–92, the Federal Sentencing Guidelines, see Michael L. Perlin and Keri Gould, Rashomon and the Criminal Law: Mental Disability and the Federal Sentencing Guidelines, 22 *Am. J. Crim. L.* 431 (1995), and the death penalty, see Michael L. Perlin, 'The Executioner's Face Is Always Well-Hidden': The Role of Counsel and the Courts in Determining Who Dies, 41 *N.Y.L. Sch. L. Rev.* 201 (1996).

does this rely on a fact-not-in-evidence (that issues of bias are dealt with coherently and carefully in medical school and in graduate schools of psychology or even in forensic training programs)? I do not believe that they are. My third is empirical – consider the record.

A sense of blame mirrors courts' sanist impatience with mentally disabled criminal defendants in general, attributing their problems in the legal process to weak character or poor resolve.[57] Thus, we should not be surprised to learn that a trial judge, responding to a National Center for State Courts survey, indicated his belief that incompetent-to-stand-trial defendants could have understood and communicated with their counsel and the court 'if they [had] only wanted.'[58] Is there any evidence that expert witnesses are immune from similar feelings?

When I first wrote about this in the context of 'morality' issues, I stressed:

> When courts and legislatures significantly tightened involuntary civil commitment ('ICC') criteria in the early 1970s, a large number of prominent mental health professionals responded negatively to what they saw as 'turf invasions' on the part of the courts and legislatures. Dr. Paul Chodoff counseled expert witnesses against 'succumbing to prevailing fashion' (that is, more restrictive commitment standards) if acquiescence was not in their patients' 'best interests.' Chodoff recommended exercising 'wise and benevolent paternalism,' leading to a 'moral judgment' that hospitalization is appropriate for patients 'incapable of voluntarily accepting help,' in spite of laws rejecting 'need of treatment' as a commitment standard. Even more pointedly, after considering Ontario's amended mental health law aimed at making involuntary civil commitment standards more stringent, a prominent local psychiatrist argued that the new law had little empirical weight: 'Doctors will continue to certify those whom they really believe should be certified; they will merely learn a new language.'[59]

Expert attempts at making self-referentially 'moral' decisions as to 'worth' (so as to ensure access to treatment) and either exaggerating or downplaying certain behavioral characteristics either to insure or deprive patients of treatment further accentuates the pretextual nature of the commitment system.[60]

---

57 See generally Bernard Weiner, On Sin Versus Sickness: A Theory of Perceived Responsibility and Social Motivation, 48 *Am. Psychologist* 957 (1993).

58 Perlin, *supra* note 56, at 226, citing Perlin, *supra* note 34, at 671.

59 Perlin, *supra* note 34, at 644–46, citing, *inter alia*, Paul Chodoff, The Case for Involuntary Hospitalization of the Mentally Ill, 133 *Am. J. Psychiatry* 496, 501 (1976); Paul Chodoff, Involuntary Hospitalization of the Mentally Ill as a Moral Issue, 141 *Am. J. Psychiatry* 384, 388 (1984); William McCormick, Involuntary Commitment in Ontario: Some Barriers to the Provision of Proper Care, 124 *Can. Med. Ass'n J.* 715, 717 (1981).

60 Perlin, *supra* note 34, at 649–50, citing Robert A. Menzies, Psychiatrists in Blue: Police Apprehension of Mental Disorder and Dangerousness, 25 *Criminology* 429, 446 (1987); John Petrila, The Insanity Defense and Other Mental Health Dispositions in Missouri, 5 *Int'l J.L. & Psychiatry* 81, 91 n.36 (1982); Susan C. Reed and Dan A. Lewis, The Negotiation of Voluntary Admission in Chicago's State Mental Hospitals, 18 *J. Psychiatry & L.* 137, 139 (1990).

The same sanist behavior infects experts' work in incompetency cases, in insanity cases, and in cases that involve the incompetency/insanity interplay. On the competency question, hospital evaluation staff often reveal a bias against returning defendants to trial.[61] On the insanity question, consider the case of *Francois v. Henderson*,[62] where a testifying doctor conceded that he may have 'hedged' in earlier testimony (as to whether an insanity acquittee could be released) 'because he did not want to be criticized should [the defendant] be released and then commit a criminal act.'[63] Or, consider the case of *People v. Doan*, in which the expert witness testified that the defendant was 'out in left field' and went 'bananas'.[64]

On the issue of interplay, the results are fascinating, and troubling: when Montana abolished its insanity defense, the ultimate effect was simply that courts found more defendants incompetent to stand trial who would have pled 'not guilty by reason of insanity' under the prior law, and then committed them to the same maximum security forensic facilities to which they would have been sent had they been acquitted by reason of insanity,[65] and the dispositional result was virtually the same as if the defense had not been abolished.[66]

This infects other areas of the judicial process as well. In one parental rights termination case, expert testimony that persons with disabilities 'cannot show love and affection as well as can persons of normal intelligence' was relied upon to support termination findings.[67] And, of course, we ignore at our own peril the infamous case of *Buck v. Bell*, made infamous by Justice Oliver Wendell Holmes's chilling epigram – 'three generations of imbeciles is enough.'[68] The decision in *Buck* was buttressed by expert testimony of the state mental institution's expert, the famed eugenicist Harry Laughlin: 'These people belong to the shiftless, ignorant, and worthless class of anti-social whites of the South.'[69]

---

61 Perlin, *supra* note 34, at 657.

62 850 F.2d 231 (5th Cir. 1988),

63 *Id.* at 234, discussed in Michael L. Perlin, 'There's No Success like Failure/and Failure's No Success at All': Exposing the Pretextuality of Kansas v. Hendricks, 92 *Nw. U. L. Rev.* 1247, 1257 n.59 (1998).

64 366 N.W.2d 593, 598 (Mich. App. 1985).

65 See Henry J. Steadman *et al.*, Maintenance of an Insanity Defense under Montana's 'Abolition' of the Insanity Defense, 146 *Am. J. Psychiatry* 357 (1989). See generally, Rita D Buitendorp, A Statutory Lesson from Big Sky Country on Abolishing the Insanity Defense, 30 *Val. U.L. Rev.* 965 (1996).

66 Perlin, *supra* note 34, at 658.

67 Michael L. Perlin, Hospitalized Patients and the Right to Sexual Interaction: Beyond the Last Frontier? 20 *NYU Rev. L. & Soc'l Change* 517, 538–39 (1993–94), discussing In re McDonald, 201 N.W.2d 447, 450 (Iowa 1972).

68 274 U.S. 200, 207 (1927).

69 Stephen J. Gould, Carrie Buck's Daughter, 2 *Const. Commentary* 331, 336–37 (1985); Paul A. Lombardo, Three Generations, No Imbeciles: New Light on *Buck v. Bell*, 60 *N.Y.U. L. Rev.* 30, 51 (1985); Dorothy Roberts, Crime, Race, and Reproduction, 67 *Tul. L. Rev.* 1945, 1963 (1993).

Attitudes

To a great extent, sanism is a disease of *attitudes*.[70] As I have sought to demonstrate in earlier papers, we generalize about persons with mental disabilities,[71] stereotype them,[72] typify them, and 'slot' their behavior,[73] and by focusing on alleged 'differentness,' we 'deny their basic humanity and their shared physical, emotional, and spiritual needs.'[74] When we engage in this generalization, we are doing two things:

> [W]e are distancing ourselves from mentally disabled persons – the 'them' – and we are simultaneously trying to construct an impregnable borderline between 'us' and 'them,' both to protect ourselves and to dehumanize what Sander Gilman calls 'the Other.' The label of 'sickness' reassures us that 'the Other' – seen as 'both ill and infectious, both damaged and damaging' not like us and further animates our 'keen ... desire to separate "us" and "them".'[75]

There is no longer any question that such attitudes infect judicial and juror decision-making:[76] on what grounds should we assume that they are somehow strangely absent in the reports and testimony of experts?

John LaFond and Mary Durham have perceptively noted that courts value psychiatric expertise when it contributes to the social control functions of law and disparage it when it does not, and have added:

> In the criminal justice system, psychiatrists are now viewed skeptically as accomplices of defense lawyers who get criminals 'off the hook' of responsibility. In the commitment system, however, they are more confidently seen as therapeutic helpers who get patients 'on the hook' of treatment and control.[77]

---

70 I have considered this question directly in radically different substantive contexts in Michael L. Perlin, Myths, Realities, and the Political World: The Anthropology of Insanity Defense Attitudes, 24 *Bull. Am. Acad. Psychiatry & L.* 5 (1996), and in Michael L. Perlin, The ADA and Persons with Mental Disabilities: Can Sanist Attitudes Be Undone? 8 *J. L. & Health* 15 (1993–94).

71 Perlin, supra note 20, at 377–78; Michael L. Perlin, Power Imbalances in Therapeutic and Forensic Relationships, 9 *Behav. Sci. & L.* 111, 117 (1991).

72 Perlin, *supra* note 22, at 15.

73 Michael L. Perlin, Competency, Deinstitutionalization, and Homelessness: A Story of Marginalization, 28. *Hous. L. Rev.* 63, 109–10 (1991).

74 Perlin, *supra* note 67, at 357.

75 See Michael L. Perlin, 'Where the Winds Hit Heavy on the Borderline': Mental Disability Law, Theory and Practice, 'Us' and 'Them,' 31 *Loyola L.A. L. Rev.* 775, 787 (1998), discussing Sander L. Gilman, Difference and Pathology: Stereotypes of Sexuality, Race and Madness 130 (1985).

76 See generally, Perlin, *supra* note 1,

77 John Q. La Fond and Mary L. Durham, Back to the Asylum 156 (1992).

This gives experts even more incentive to be sanist (recall that pleasing one's employer has been seen as a source of expert bias),[78] and adds yet another confounding factor to the full picture. In addition, we know that persons who are institutionalized are, by and large, *poor* people.[79] To this entire collage must be added the well-known existence of 'examiner bias' that demonstrates that doctors tend to assign more 'favorable' diagnostic labels to wealthier patients.[80] And finally, there is an additional 'fear factor' built in to this enterprise: 'while race and sex are immutable, we all can become mentally ill.... Perhaps this illuminates the level of virulence we experience here.'[81] Personal bias, in short, appears to be 'inescapable', unless and until we come to grips with its underlying causes.[82] Joel Dvoskin has perceptively noted, in this context: 'Judgments about groups of people can only lead to stigma and discrimination, while judgments about individuals if based on reason and information, can lead to better treatment outcomes and increased safety for the individuals and their communities.[83]

If experts are as sanist as all others, what impact does this have on the justice system? I believe that this impact is profound, and it is profound at all 'pressure points' at which experts interact with litigants. The initial interview, for instance, is a critical moment in the expert–litigant relationship.[84] The content of this interview will color the expert's report, and, eventually, her testimony. If the expert begins with *a priori* sanist attitudes, those attitudes will inevitably distort and bias all future aspects of the expert's work.

For example, assume that the expert is retained in an involuntary civil commitment case, and assume further that her value system has led her to believe that, in spite of a state law mandating such commitment only upon a showing of mental illness and

---

78 See *supra* note 32, and sources cited. Although the courts are often not technically the 'employer' of the expert, I believe the same incentives are present.

79 See for example, Perlin, *supra* note 3, at 37–38, and sources cited *id.* at 38 n. 137. See also, for example, L.B. Mauksch *et al.*, Mental Illness, Functional Impairment, and Patient Preferences for Collaborative Care in an Uninsured, Primary Care Population, 50 *J. Fam Pract.* 41. (2000) (people with low incomes and no insurance are nearly twice as likely as the general population to have psychiatric disorders); Kondo, *supra* note 42, at 296, quoting Carol A.B. Warren, The Court of Last Resort: Mental Illness and the Law, 12–13 (1982) (speculating that middle class or upper class mentally ill people have more financial resources rescuing them from entrance into state hospital systems and that poverty may enhance probability of mental illness).

80 See, for example, James Page, Psychopathology: The Science of Understanding Deviance 164 (1971).

81 Perlin, *supra* note 735, at 94 n.174 (discussing parallel attitudes towards mental illness and homelessness).

82 Chun, *supra* note 16, at 408, discussing Perlin, *supra* note 34, at 629.

83 Joel Dvoskin, What Are the Odds of Predicting Violent Behavior, 2 *J. Cal. Alliance For Mentally Ill* 6, 6 (1990).

84 See Michael L. Perlin, 'You Have Discussed Lepers and Crooks': Sanism in Clinical Teaching, 9 *Clinical L. Rev.* 683 (2003) (discussing this issue).

causally-related dangerousness,[85] individuals should be paternalistically committed when such commitment is 'in their best interests.'[86] Such beliefs will lead the expert in question to testify 'morally' in accordance with her own value system, in spite of the controlling state law.[87] When I first wrote about this a decade ago,[88] I denominated this allegedly 'moral' behavior as a 'pretext,' but now see that it is a pretext based on sanism[89] (for the best interests model – one that rejects autonomy values, even of a presumed-to-be-competent individual [90] – *is* sanist).

Sanist myths often lead to, and are intertwined with, pretextual decision-making. As Professor Susan Stefan has perceptively noted, courts routinely find mentally disabled women incompetent to engage in sexual intercourse (i.e., to lack sufficient competence to engage knowingly and voluntarily in such behavior), but just as routinely find such individuals competent to consent to give their children up for adoption. In one startling case, a court made both of these findings simultaneously about the same woman.[91]

Conclusion

In an article I wrote sharply criticizing the United States Supreme Court's decision upholding Kansas' 'sexually violent predator laws,' I concluded that, 'Much of what forensic mental health professionals who frequently wear the hat of expert witness say about individual cases is similarly pretextual, ostensibly for reasons of "morality."' [92] And, on many occasions, these experts defend their pretextual

---

85 See 1 Michael L. Perlin, Mental Disability Law: Civil and Criminal, chapter 2A (2d ed. 1998), at 44–191.

86 See generally, Michael L. Perlin, Therapeutic Jurisprudence: Understanding the Sanist and Pretextual Bases of Mental Disability Law, 20 *N. Eng. J. Crim. & Civ. Confinement* 369, 378 (1994), discussing Joel Haycock *et al.*, Mediating the Gap: Thinking About Alternatives to the Current Practice of Civil Commitment, 20 *New Eng. J. on Crim. & Civ. Confinement* 265 (1994).

87 See generally, Anderten, *supra* note 50.

88 See generally, Perlin, *supra* note 21.

89 I discuss this connection in Perlin, *supra* note 67, at 538

90 See Perlin, *supra* note 67, at 789, discussing Jan C. Costello, Making Kids Take Their Medicine: The Privacy and Due Process Rights of De Facto Competent Minors, 31 *Loy. L.A. L. Rev.* 907, 908–14 (1998).

91 Perlin, *supra* note 67, at 538, discussing State v. Soura, 796 P.2d 109, 113–15 (Idaho 1990) (holding that a mentally disabled woman was not competent to consent to extramarital sexual intercourse though she was married and had previously had a child) and In re Burbanks, 310 N.W.2d 138, 143–51 (Neb. 1981) (describing social service employees' testimony that parents did not have mental capability to be parents, although the employees willingly assisted the parents in processing papers to authorize the performance of an abortion on, and sterilization of, their daughter), discussed at length in Susan Stefan, Silencing the Different Voice: Feminist Theory and Competence, 47 *U. Miami L. Rev.* 763, 775 (1993).

92 Perlin, supra note 63, at 1255 (discussing Kansas v. Hendricks, 521 U.S. 346 (1997).

testimony, through teleological reasoning based on sanist social science literature and studies, disregarding or rejecting conflicting data.[93] What is now clear to me is that these pretexts are premised on sanism, and the connection between sanism and pretextuality in this context is seamless. It is an issue that, I believe, cries out for further empirical testing and evaluation.

I will end by returning to my title. In the verse of *Tangled up in Blue* that I have quoted, Dylan points out, 'Don't know how it all got started.'[94] I have speculated elsewhere as to how all of *this* 'got started':

> The roots of sanism are deep. From the beginning of recorded history, mental illness has been inextricably linked to sin, evil, God's punishment, crime, and demons. Evil spirits were commonly relied upon to explain abnormal behavior. The 'face of madness ... haunts our imagination.' People with mental illness were considered beasts; a person who lost his capacity to reason was seen as having lost his claim 'to be treated as a human being.'[95]

If I am right – and I have seen nothing in the nearly 15 years since I wrote these words to make me change my mind – then we must take seriously the questions that I raise in this paper. Perhaps then, mental disability law will be less of an 'illusion to [us] now.'

Author's note

The author wishes to thank Jeanie Bliss for her exceptional research assistance.

---

93 Michael L. Perlin, Back to the Past: Why Mental Disability Law 'Reforms' Don't Reform (Book Review of La Fond and Durham, supra note 77), 4 *Crim. L. Forum* 403, 412 (1993).

94 Dylan, *supra* note 23, at 359.

95 Perlin, *supra* note 20, at 388, citing, *inter alia*, John Biggs, *The Guilty Mind: Psychiatry & the Law of Medicine* 26 (1955); Walter Bromberg, *From Shaman to Psychotherapist: a History of the Treatment of Mental Illness* 63–64 (1975 ed.); Michael Moore, *Law and Psychiatry: Rethinking the Relationship* 64–65 (1984); Judith Neaman, *Suggestion of the Devil: the Origins of Madness* 31, 50, 144 (Anchor ed., 1975).

Index